NORMATIVE PLURALISM AND INTERNATIONAL LAW

This book addresses conflicts involving different normative orders: What happens when international law prohibits behavior, but the same behavior is nonetheless morally justified or warranted? Can the actor concerned ignore international law under appeal to morality? Can soldiers escape legal liability by pointing to honor? Can accountants do so under reference to professional standards? How, in other words, does law relate to other normative orders? The assumption behind this book is that law no longer automatically claims supremacy, but that actors can pick and choose which code to follow. The novelty resides not so much in identifying conflicts, but in exploring whether, when, and how different orders can be used intentionally. In doing so, the book covers conflicts between legal orders and conflicts involving law and honor, self-regulation, *lex mercatoria*, local social practices, bureaucracy, religion, professional standards, and morality.

Jan Klabbers has taught international law at the University of Helsinki since 1996 and has held visiting professorships in New York, Geneva, and Paris. He was director of the Centre of Excellence in Global Governance Research from 2006 to 2011 and has won a number of awards for excellence in teaching. He received his doctorate from the University of Amsterdam (with distinction), and his main publications include *The Concept of Treaty in International Law* (1996), *An Introduction to International Institutional Law* (2nd ed. 2009), *Treaty Conflict and the European Union* (2008), and, as coauthor, *The Constitutionalization of International Law* (2009).

Touko Piiparinen is a research Fellow at the Finnish Institute of International Affairs, having worked as a postdoctoral researcher at the Centre of Excellence in Global Governance Research from 2009 to 2010. He received his doctorate from the renowned Department of International Politics at the University of Wales, Aberystwyth, and is the author of *The Transformation of UN Conflict Management* (2010). He has written numerous articles on conflict management, the United Nations system, and critical realist methodology in international relations theory.

ASIL Studies in International Legal Theory

Series Editors
Elizabeth Andersen (ASIL)
Mortimer Sellers (University of Baltimore)

Editorial Board
Samantha Besson (Université de Fribourg)
Allen Buchanan (Duke University)
David Kennedy (Harvard University)
Jan Klabbers (University of Helsinki)
David Luban (Georgetown University)
Larry May (Vanderbilt University)
Mary Ellen O'Connell (University of Notre Dame)
Onuma Yasuaki (Meiji University)
Helen Stacy (Stanford University)
John Tasioulas (University College London)
Fernando Tesón (Florida State University)

The purpose of the ASIL Studies in International Legal Theory series is to clarify and improve the theoretical foundations of international law. Too often the progressive development and implementation of international law has foundered on confusion about first principles. This series raises the level of public and scholarly discussion about the structure and purposes of the world legal order and how best to achieve global justice through law.

This series grows out of the International Legal Theory project of the American Society of International Law. The ASIL Studies in International Legal Theory series deepens this conversation by publishing scholarly monographs and edited volumes of essays considering subjects in international legal theory.

Volumes in the Series:

International Criminal Law and Philosophy edited by Larry May and Zachary Hoskins (2010)
Customary International Law: A New Theory with Practical Applications by Brian D. Lepard (2010)
The New Global Law by Rafael Domingo (2010)
The Role of Ethics in International Law edited by Donald Earl Childress III (2011)
Global Justice and International Economic Law: Opportunities and Prospects edited by Chios Carmody, Frank J. Garcia, and John Linarelli (2011)
Parochialism, Cosmopolitanism, and the Foundations of International Law edited by Mortimer Sellers (2012)
Morality, Jus Post Bellum, and International Law edited by Larry May and Andrew T. Forcehimes (2012)
The Future of International Law: Global Governance by Joel P. Trachtman (2013)
Normative Pluralism and International Law: Exploring Global Governance by Jan Klabbers and Touko Piiparinen (2013)
Jus Post Bellum and Transitional Justice edited by Larry May and Elizabeth Edenberg (2013)

Normative Pluralism and International Law

Exploring Global Governance

Edited by

JAN KLABBERS
Helsinki University, Faculty of Law

TOUKO PIIPARINEN
Finnish Institute of International Affairs

CAMBRIDGE
UNIVERSITY PRESS

32 Avenue of the Americas, New York NY 10013-2473, USA

Cambridge University Press is part of the University of Cambridge.

It furthers the University's mission by disseminating knowledge in the pursuit of education, learning, and research at the highest international levels of excellence.

www.cambridge.org
Information on this title: www.cambridge.org/9781107036222

© Cambridge University Press 2013

This publication is in copyright. Subject to statutory exception and to the provisions of relevant collective licensing agreements, no reproduction of any part may take place without the written permission of Cambridge University Press.

First published 2013
Reprinted 2013

A catalog record for this publication is available from the British Library.

Library of Congress Cataloging in Publication data
Normative pluralism and international law: exploring global governance / Jan Klabbers, Touko Piiparinen.
    p. cm. – (ASIL studies in international legal theory)
Includes index.
ISBN 978-1-107-03622-2 (hardback : alk. paper)
1. International law – Moral and ethical aspects. 2. Legal polycentricity.
3. Normativity (Ethics) 4. International law – Philosophy. I. Klabbers, Jan.
II. Piiparinen, Touko.
KZ1256.N67 2013
341–dc23   2012044900

ISBN 978-1-107-03622-2 Hardback

Cambridge University Press has no responsibility for the persistence or accuracy of URLs for external or third-party Internet Web sites referred to in this publication, and does not guarantee that any content on such Web sites is, or will remain, accurate or appropriate.

Contents

Notes on Contributors   *page* vii

    Introduction to the Volume 1
    Jan Klabbers and Touko Piiparinen

PART I CONCEPTUAL AND THEORETICAL OVERVIEW

1. Normative Pluralism: An Exploration 13
   Jan Klabbers and Touko Piiparinen
2. Exploring the Methodology of Normative Pluralism in the Global Age 35
   Touko Piiparinen

PART II NORMATIVE PLURALISM IN LAW

3. Peaceful Coexistence: Normative Pluralism in International Law 67
   Jan Klabbers and Silke Trommer
4. Inside or Out: Two Types of International Legal Pluralism 94
   André Nollkaemper

PART III NORMATIVE PLURALISM AND INTERNATIONAL LAW

5. Law and Honor: Normative Pluralism in the Regulation of Military Conduct 143
   Rain Liivoja
6. Law versus Codes of Conduct: Between Convergence and Conflict 166
   Katja Creutz
7. *Lex Mercatoria* in International Arbitration 201
   Ulla Liukkunen

8. Law versus Tradition: Human Rights and Witchcraft
   in Sub-Saharan Africa............................ 229
   Timo Kallinen

9. Law versus Bureaucratic Culture: The Case of the ICC and
   the Transcendence of Instrumental Rationality 251
   Touko Piiparinen

10. Law versus Religion: State Law and Religious Norms 284
    Rubya Mehdi

11. Global Capital Markets and Financial Reporting: International
    Regulation but National Application? 301
    Pontus Troberg

12. Responsibility to Rebuild and Collective Responsibility:
    Legal and Moral Considerations 323
    Larry May

    Conclusions.................................. 340
    Touko Piiparinen and Jan Klabbers

Index   349

Notes on Contributors

Katja Creutz is a doctoral candidate in international law at the Erik Castrén Institute of International Law and Human Rights at the University of Helsinki. She received a masters of political science degree from Åbo Akademi University in 2000 and an L.L.M. from the University of Helsinki in 2004. Her research focuses on responsibility regimes in international law, which she critically explores against the background of a globalized world. Besides her current postgraduate studies, she has authored studies on international postconflict governance and privatization of security commissioned by the Finnish Ministry for Foreign Affairs.

Timo Kallinen holds a Ph.D. in social anthropology from the University of Helsinki. Kallinen's research has focused on the secularization of sacred kingship and chiefship in Ghana, West Africa. His other interests include the study of religious conversion, money and exchange systems, and commodity fetishism. He has conducted anthropological fieldwork in Ghana from 2000 to 2001 and from 2005 to 2006.

Jan Klabbers is Professor of international law at the University of Helsinki and Deputy Director of the Erik Castrén Institute of International Law and Human Rights. He was Director of the Academy of Finland Centre of Excellence in Global Governance Research from 2006 to 2011.

Rain Liivoja is a research Fellow at the Asia Pacific Centre for Military Law, Melbourne Law School, and an affiliated research Fellow of the Erik Castrén Institute of International Law and Human Rights, University of Helsinki. He has completed a doctorate in law at the University of Helsinki under the auspices of the Centre of Excellence in Global Governance Research.

Ulla Liukkunen is Professor of international private law and comparative law at the University of Helsinki.

Larry May is a political philosopher who has written on conceptual issues in collective and shared responsibility, as well as normative issues in international criminal law. He has also written on professional ethics and on the just war tradition. He is currently W. Alton Jones Professor of Philosophy, Professor of Law, and Professor of Political Science at Vanderbilt University. He has a B.S. in international affairs from Georgetown University, and a Ph.D. in philosophy from the New School for Social Research, where he was Hannah Arendt's last research assistant. He also has a J.D. in law from Washington University. He has published twenty-five books, ten of which are single-authored monographs.

Rubya Mehdi holds a Ph.D. in law from the University of Copenhagen and is a senior researcher attached to the Department of Cross-Cultural and Regional Studies, University of Copenhagen, and visiting professor at Bahauddin Zakariya University, Multan, Pakistan. She was awarded the Kafkatten Prize in 2006 for her writings. She has widely published articles and books in Islamic law, Islamization, gender and Islam, customary laws, and legal pluralism. Her publications include *Islamization of the Law in Pakistan* (London: Curzon, 1994) and *Gender and Property Law in Pakistan* (Copenhagen: DJØF Publishing, 2001).

André Nollkaemper is Professor of public international law, Vice-Dean for research at the Faculty of Law of the University of Amsterdam, and (external) advisor to the Minister of Foreign Affairs of the Netherlands. He is a member of the Board of the European Society of International Law and Chair of the International Law Association Study Group on the Principles on the Application of International Law by Domestic Courts. Since 2010 he has directed the project on Shared Responsibility in International Law (SHARES). He is also editor in chief of the *International Law in Domestic Courts* (ILDC) module of the *Oxford Reports on International Law* and author of *National Courts and the International Rule of Law* (Oxford: Oxford University Press, 2011).

Touko Piiparinen works as a research Fellow in the Global Security program at the Finnish Institute of International Affairs, Helsinki. His areas of expertise include humanitarian intervention, conflict management, postconflict peace building, critical realist methodology in international relations theory, and the United Nations system. He received his Ph.D. from the University of Wales,

Aberystwyth, in 2005, and he has previously worked in the Ministry for Foreign Affairs of Finland and at the Centre of Excellence in Global Governance Research, Helsinki.

Pontus Troberg is Professor and Head of Accounting at the Hanken School of Economics, Helsinki. His areas of expertise include international accounting, auditing, and executive education. He received his Ph.D. in 1982 at the University of Oklahoma, USA.

Silke Trommer is an affiliated researcher at the Erik Castrén Institute of International Law and Human Rights and a postdoctoral researcher at the Asia Research Centre at Murdoch University (Australia). She holds a doctorate in political science from the University of Helsinki, a B.A. in European studies from the University of Dublin Trinity College, a degree in international relations from the Institut d'Etudes Politiques in Strasbourg, and an L.L.M. in European law from the Europa-Institut Saarbrücken. Her research interests are political economy, international trade, development, and social movements.

Introduction to the Volume

Jan Klabbers and Touko Piiparinen

I. INTRODUCTION

This is a volume on normative pluralism, born within the Academy of Finland Centre of Excellence on Global Governance Research 2006–2011.[1] Having studied global governance from a variety of disciplinary perspectives and on a variety of topics, it transpired that at least one characteristic of global governance, at present, seems to be that actors can be considered to fall within the reach of norms stemming from a multitude of directions. Individuals, companies, international organizations, states, and other entities are, as before, subject to the law, whether this be the law of the state in which they reside or, more broadly, international law. But those entities also have to pay some respect to norms stemming from elsewhere. Businesses are subject not just to law, but also to professional standards and codes of self-regulation. The behavior of states can be evaluated with the help of international law but also, increasingly so it seems, by standards of morality. Individuals have long recognized that their religion may tell them to do things that may not immediately be reconcilable with legal prescriptions, and immigrants in particular may carry social norms with them wherever they settle and find that those norms exist in tension with local legislation. And that says nothing still about a possible role for that most amorphous of concepts: legitimacy, which seemingly can spring from each and every normative order without properly being part of any single one.

In short, we felt that there would be a topic here, one of relative novelty, moreover, that would warrant further study. We invited two leading scholars

---

[1] The Centre of Excellence came to an end on New Year's Eve 2011, when its funding period expired. This volume was completed with the editors affiliated with the Erik Castrén Institute of International Law and Human Rights (University of Helsinki) and the Finnish Institute of International Affairs.

working on similar issues, John Bowen and William Twining, for a brainstorming session in Helsinki, and their feedback – while not uncritical of some of our initial assumptions and intuitions – suggested that, indeed, there might be a topic here.

Subsequently, we asked several individuals, working both in practice and in academia, to shed light on how they experience normative conflict. We also had a number of structured discussion meetings within the Centre, which, being a transdisciplinary venture involving lawyers, political scientists, and anthropologists, with a sprinkling of theologians and moral philosophers, seemed the appropriate setting for a transdisciplinary exercise. The result is this volume.

In the process, a number of individuals provided comments, conceptual as well as thematic, on normative pluralism, how it relates to the governance of global affairs, and how it can possibly be studied. These include the authors of the chapters in this volume, but numerous others as well. We are heavily indebted to Mika Aaltola, John Bowen, Kirsten Fisher, Andreas Fischer-Lescano, Martti Koskenniemi, Anssi Leino, Anne-Charlotte Martineau, Jamie Morgan, James O'Connor, Heikki Patomäki, Pamela Slotte, Jukka Siikala, Teivo Teivainen, Reetta Toivanen, Kaius Tuori, William Twining, Hannele Voionmaa, Henri Vogt, and Åsa Wallendahl for sharing their insights with us; to Damarys Vigil Nolasco and Christiane Fürst for their editorial assistance; and to Betsy Andersen, John Berger, and Tim Sellers for their unwavering support.

This volume is, first and foremost, a study in global governance, written from the perspective, mostly, of academics working in the legal field but aspiring to look beyond disciplinary boundaries. A majority of the authors have been affiliated with the Centre of Excellence in Global Governance Research 2006–2011, located at the University of Helsinki, where this project was conceived. There are some exceptions to the legal background: Timo Kallinen was trained as an anthropologist, Touko Piiparinen's background is in political science, and Pontus Troberg has a background in economics and accounting. And some of authors have been trained not just in the law, but in other disciplines as well. Katja Creutz, Jan Klabbers, André Nollkaemper, and Silke Trommer all hold degrees in political science in addition to their law degrees, while Larry May was already an established and highly respected moral philosopher before he entered the field of law.

II. THE FOCUS OF THIS VOLUME

There are various ways in which people can speak about normative pluralism, but to state this is not yet saying much. What is of interest is how this pluralism plays out in a (fairly limited) number of situations. Potentially, there could be manifold conflicts to study, and manifold ways to study them. One might, for instance, think of a conflict between religion and morality: if it would be morally allowed these days to covet thy neighbor's wife, where does that leave the sixth of the Ten Commandments? Likewise, one could think of a conflict between morality (whether under the heading of business ethics or corporate social responsibility) and the internal self-regulation of companies when it comes to, say, utilizing child labor, or paying kickbacks to officials in countries of investment. These, however interesting, do not primarily concern us in this study: our concern is with normative conflicts involving law.

We are also not particularly interested, for present purposes, in how normative orders come to influence each other. Sometimes (well, quite often, perhaps), law contains traces of moral thought or religious injunctions. Leaving theocracies aside, a colorful example is that of South Korea, where, it transpires, adultery is illegal and can land one in jail. In particular, the relationship between law and morality has given rise to a vast body of scholarship and ranks as one of the main points on which lawyers identify themselves. If they feel that law and morality are essentially separate orders, they tend to think of themselves as positivists; if they feel that law should be morally acceptable (in other words: that the moral acceptability of a rule is a condition for its validity), then they tend to view themselves as working in the natural law tradition.

Those debates are fascinating in their own right but do not concern us here. Instead, our interest in this volume is with conflicts within the law, and conflicts between law and other normative orders. First, we are interested in conflicts within the law, in particular conflicts between different emanations of international law, and conflicts between international law and domestic law. While conflicts within domestic legal systems would also be of great interest, this, we felt, would be too vast a topic to study for our purposes. After all, with some two hundred states in the world, there are potentially two hundred settings to study, and even narrowing it down, as comparative lawyers typically do, to broad legal families would still result in too much ground to cover.

Second, our interest resides with conflicts between law and different normative orders: in abbreviated form, these can be presented as law versus religion, law versus chivalry or honor, law versus accountancy standards, et cetera. Our perspective is, to some extent, informed by empirical analysis of those "normative encounters" in which an individual or other agent is confronted with various normative demands: what to do when the law says one should do A, but some other normative order says one should do B. That is not to say that we rigidly stick to this question: it serves as the starting point for reflection rather than as a strict methodological device.

The latter is an important point: we think we have stumbled on a topic that has remained hitherto relatively unexplored, and for that reason, we feel that much is to be gained, at this juncture, from reflecting on basic issues, rather than insisting on a strict methodological framework in order to test hypotheses. Put differently, we hope that by allowing our authors a relatively free hand, we can start to generate and formulate hypotheses in this volume.

Nonetheless, we should explain where our focus lies. We are not all that interested (for present purposes, we hasten to add) in figuring out whether law should be morally respectable, or whether and to what extent it should be in harmony with the society it aims to regulate, or whether it can or should have any effects on that society, or even, as Aristotle thought, whether law should be such that it helps to shape individual moralities. Instead, our interest resides, first of all, with the question how to act when confronted with different commands stemming from different normative orders. On that basis, a second interest enters the picture: if it is possibly the case that different normative orders serve as justifications for different acts, is it then possible to choose? In other words (arguably more fancy words), this leads us to the politics of framing: what determines whether, say, the intervention over Kosovo is judged by moral standards or legal standards? Or what determines whether business transactions are subjected to state-ordained rules or to the *lex mercatoria*?

This is something to be clear – and frank – about. We are not trying to analyze how law is influenced by morality, chivalry, or other normative orders. Nor are we trying to discuss how those normative orders, in turn, influence the law. We are also not trying to solve normative conflicts: ours is not a mission to present possible solutions, if only because the *problematique* requires investigation before the viability of any practical suggestions can meaningfully be discussed.

Instead, our main interest resides with conducting this preliminary investigation. It resides with the possibility of normative conflict (i.e., different normative orders providing different injunctions). We stipulate the existence of various normative orders and zoom in on how conflicts may arise, and whether any ways have been developed to solve such conflicts. Additionally, we hope to signal common problems, so as to foster a future research agenda.

The plan of this book is to describe the coexistence of various normative orders in their relations with law, discuss the possible tensions, and, where possible or appropriate, suggest possible solutions. Thus, the authors inquire into relations between law and witchcraft, law and religion, law and bureaucratic standards, law and spontaneous norms. Such coexistence of normative orders has probably always given rise to conflicts: traces of it can be found in the biblical story of Abraham's being about to sacrifice his son, or the Greek drama *Antigone*.

The one area where this was most difficult is the relationship between law and morality: this can be – and has been – studied from so many angles and through so many different prisms that we felt it better to zoom in on one particular aspect rather than try to capture the entire debate in a few handfuls of pages. Moreover, as discussed in Chapter 1, morality is different in kind from other normative orders, in that it is not traceable to individual human agency in quite the same way as religion, law, or other normative orders are. Hence, we invited a highly respected lawyer and moral philosopher, Larry May, to focus on a particular emanation of the relationship between law and morality: the emerging concept of responsibility to protect. Needless to say, the structure and tone of his contribution therewith differ somewhat from those of the other contributions, but we felt this was preferable (by far) to excluding morality altogether.

III. THE SETTING OF THIS VOLUME

Normative pluralism is, in a way, hardly a novel phenomenon. Max Weber could already write, almost a century ago, that each and every individual and social group is subjected to a "plurality of contradictory systems of order" and that "it is even possible for the same individual to orient his action to contradictory systems of order," and his archetypical example was that of the duel: the gentlemen involved in a duel (we presume, for the time being, that duels mostly concerned gentlemen) would be bound to respect the appropriate code of honor, as well as applicable criminal law.[2] Yet, he did not go so far as to suggest that actors could actually choose which of these normative control systems should guide their actions: for Weber, the dueling gentleman was subject to both criminal law and the code of honor, but the dueling gentleman was not in a position to claim that one of these ought not to apply, let alone that both would not apply and ought to be replaced by, say, religion.

This element of choice then would seem to be a novel element, and it would seem that this owes much to what has become generally referred to as globalization. Globalization, many would agree, has introduced in its wake fragmentation. The leading anthropologist Thomas Hylland Eriksen submits that globalization involves both disembedding and reembedding and is better seen as a way of organizing heterogeneity than homogeneity: it involves

---

[2] See Max Weber, *The Theory of Social and Economic Organization*, Parsons ed. (New York: Free Press, 1964 [1947]), at 125.

a dialectic between global and local.³ To him, identity politics (a clear manifestation of fragmentation) is properly a "trueborn child of globalization."⁴ Anthony Giddens already observed as much more than two decades ago, noting that "radicalized modernity" (the term he used to describe what is now commonly referred to as globalization) had "a sense of fragmentation and dispersal."⁵ Not only is the world becoming a "global village," in Marshall McLuhan's felicitous phrase⁶; it is also becoming a fragmented set of global villages: globalization and fragmentation go hand in hand, sometimes in the form of an emphasis on localization (or the more ephemeral "locality"),⁷ sometimes also in other guises. The world might be subject to McDonaldization, but McDonald's is not above catering to local tastes.⁸

A most obvious form is that fragmentation entails the coexistence of cultures, and it was in this sense that the first recorded use of the adjective "global" made an appearance, in a *Harper's Magazine* article dating back to 1892 and detailing the travels of a distinctly cosmopolitan gentleman, Monsieur de Vogüé. Monsieur de Vogüé loved to travel and traveled many foreign lands in his quest to be "global."⁹ In our days, and in particular perhaps among international lawyers, "fragmentation" has become a byword for the coexistence of several fields of activity (trade, environment, security, etc.).¹⁰ This follows, to some extent, the analysis of society as having dispersed into several fragmented subsets, each with its own logic and rationality: the economy, the social, the military, et cetera.¹¹ Our intuition now is that the fragmentation also covers

---

3   See Thomas Hylland Eriksen, *Globalization: The Key Concepts* (Oxford, UK: Berg, 2007).
4   Ibid., at 146.
5   See Anthony Giddens, *The Consequences of Modernity* (Cambridge, UK: Polity, 1990), at 150.
6   See Marshall McLuhan, *The Gutenberg Galaxy* (Toronto: University of Toronto Press, 1962).
7   See Arjun Appadurai, *Modernity at Large: Cultural Dimensions of Globalization* (Minneapolis: University of Minnesota Press, 1996).
8   See George Ritzer, 'An Introduction to McDonaldization', in George Ritzer (ed.), *McDonaldization: The Reader*, 2nd ed. (Thousand Oaks, CA: Pine Forge Press, 2006), 4–25. In his entertaining study of soccer, Foer notes how globalization exacerbates local feuds and corruption: see Franklin Foer, *How Soccer Explains the World: An (Unlikely) Theory of Globalization* (New York: Harper, 2004).
9   The story is recounted with gusto in Alex MacGillivray, *A Brief History of Globalization* (London: Robinson, 2006), at 10–11.
10 See in particular Martti Koskenniemi, *Fragmentation of International Law: Difficulties Arising from the Diversification and Expansion of International Law: Report of the Study Group of the International Law Commission* (Helsinki: Erik Castrén Institute, 2007).
11 This owes much to the work of the German sociologist Niklas Luhmann. For a Luhmannian discussion of international law, see Andreas Fischer-Lescano and Gunther Teubner, *Regime-Kollisionen: Zur Fragmentierung des globalen Rechts* (Frankfurt am Main: Suhrkamp, 2006).

normativity as such: a fragmentation into morality, law, social norms, honor, witchcraft, professional standards, et cetera. And much as with the fragmentation of international law, there is no immediate response available to those who claim that one normative order should be preferred over other orders.

IV. THE CONTRIBUTIONS

For practical purposes, this book is divided into three different parts. The first part will begin with an introductory chapter, written by Jan Klabbers and Touko Piiparinen under the title "Normative Pluralism: An Exploration." The chapter posits some initial reflections on the concept of normative pluralism, the idea of what constitutes a normative order, connections between normative pluralism and global governance, and the curious role of legitimacy. While it helps to place the subsequent chapters in context (and was conceived with that purpose in mind), it can also be read independently. In the second chapter, Piiparinen suggests a methodology for the study of normative pluralism, also exploratory in nature. Piiparinen aims to create a possible way to look at normative pluralism from the perspective of critical realism. Therewith, his chapter serves as a possible prism for further study. It is important to realize, though, that neither of these two chapters aims to lay down a template for the subsequent chapters: we felt that, given the relative novelty of the topic, it would be more useful to ask our authors to apply their expertise to their understanding of normative pluralism, rather than to tell them what to do and how to do it. The price to pay for this is that the volume as a whole will, no doubt, be less unified in approach than a single-author monograph or tightly edited collection would be; on the plus side, though, asking intelligent authors freely to work on a topic is bound to result in a broader array of interesting insights.

The next part addresses intralaw conflicts and does so through two chapters. The first, written by Jan Klabbers and Silke Trommer, addresses normative conflicts within international law: conflicts between treaty provisions, or between a treaty provision and a settled rule of customary international law, or a normative conflict that in some other way involves the sources (or possible sources) of international law. They conclude that while normative conflicts are quite (and increasingly) common in international law, international law has precious little to offer such conflicts, other than the creation of tribunals or committees to decide or massage issues of normative conflict. While that may be an underwhelming conclusion, it is not unimportant to draw attention to the circumstance that international law offers no substantive solutions to this most pressing issue. Therewith, the chapter sets the tone for much of what follows. The second part also includes a chapter by André

Nollkaemper. Nollkaemper's chapter explores the relationship between international law and domestic law and distinguishes between two versions of pluralism to reach an accommodation of the distinct legal orders. In particular he suggests that national courts can influence the application and even development of international law to a considerable extent, by functioning as "gatekeepers."

The heart of the volume is Part III, consisting of eight chapters, each positing law versus a different normative order. Rain Liivoja looks at the intersection of military law and honor, and in particular at how military law incorporates honorable prescriptions. He does so by studying the punishment of disgraceful conduct (often to be found in military codes) and studying treachery. In both cases, he suggests, the law is open-ended and depends on conceptions of honorable military conduct to fill the gaps.

Katja Creutz, in her contribution on law and self-regulation, points out that the very rationale of self-regulation is its versatility: self-regulation can even take the form of law, in which case the consequence is that the character (legal or not) of the regulation becomes of great relevance, rather than its contents. Therewith, she critically hooks up to the older "soft law" discussion and draws attention to the possibility that self-regulation may be part of a broader, nonpublic, ideology.

In her chapter, Ulla Liukkunen studies what is perhaps the most well-known alternative or complement (that is an open question) to law: the *lex mercatoria*, a transnational set of rules relating to commercial transactions and often deemed to have arisen spontaneously in the marketplace. She concludes that it stands in an uneasy relationship with the more formal rules of private international law and can be used both to complement state-ordained private law and to help to develop it further. The problem in both cases, though, may well be a lack of democratic legitimacy.

Anthropologists have often occupied themselves by analyzing the relationship between state-ordained law and the customs of the nonstate actors they study. In his contribution to this volume, Timo Kallinen takes a closer look at the links between witchcraft and the law, under specific reference to Africa. Typically, the law has come down hard on witchcraft, suggesting that it stands for a lack of civilization and better be replaced by a more science-based secular law. Yet, as Kallinen concludes, such law is not free from problems either, if only because it attempts to create a new and modern society in lieu of the indigenous society. Moreover, the very attempt to do away with witchcraft has, ironically, elevated local experts (those with understanding and experience in the phenomenon to be outlawed) to positions of great power, therewith creating its own backlash.

By studying the International Criminal Court and its underlying conceptions of rationality, Touko Piiparinen introduces the reader to the conflict between law and bureaucratic culture. He advocates the promulgation of bureaucratic metanorms as one way to overcome normative conflicts and appeals to the virtue of self-limitation on the part of those confronted with problems arising from conflicts between law and bureaucratic culture.

In her chapter, Rubya Mehdi studies the interconnections between law and religion (in the particular form of Islamic law) and suggests that this relationship has been undergoing change as a consequence of patterns of migration. Her prime focus is the tension between Islamic law and the law of a secular, Western state, that is, Denmark. One source of the tension may well be the circumstance that Islamic law developed in patriarchical and hierarchical settings and therewith is based on radically different foundations than Western secular law. One way to bridge the gap, she suggests, may be to focus on religious education.

Pontus Troberg zooms in on global capital markets and the requirements related to financial reporting and suggests that while the rules relating to financial reporting are increasingly internationalized, their application remains predominantly nationally based. While some harmonization has been achieved between two of the major players (the United States and the European Union), albeit subject to local cultural differences, he concludes that the emergence of China presents a new challenge.

Larry May, in the final contribution to Part III, takes a closer look at the newly minted concept of responsibility to protect (R2P, in jargon) and unpacks some of the legal and moral ramifications associated with an aspect of the responsibility to protect concept, namely, its capacity-building aspect. To his mind, by emphasizing joint agency, states may be enabled to help prevent mass atrocities from occurring, and that, surely, is a goal that transcends any particular normative order.

Finally, the volume contains a concluding chapter by the editors, outlining the main findings of the study and suggesting some avenues for further research. In summary form, the main findings include the coexistence of ontological and epistemological conceptions on normative pluralism; they include the rejection of any grand theory on normative pluralism; and, most of all, they reject the idea that there are any easy solutions available to practical issues where normative orders collide.

PART I

CONCEPTUAL AND THEORETICAL OVERVIEW

1 Normative Pluralism: An Exploration

Jan Klabbers and Touko Piiparinen

I. INTRODUCTION

In recent years, it has become clear from the headlines that somehow, decision makers, academics, and the general public alike tend to think that several normative orders coexist and are vying for allegiance and prominence. Often one can hear colloquially that certain acts may have been illegal, but are nonetheless justifiable on moral grounds, or on religious grounds, or on the basis of some social norm or shared cultural practice. Perhaps the most well-known example in recent years is that of NATO's intervention concerning Kosovo: most observers agreed it was illegal, but nonetheless legitimate, in that NATO followed a moral injunction that allowed it to disregard international law.

The Kosovo intervention was authoritatively and thoughtfully analyzed by the leading international lawyer Bruno Simma, who seemed to speak for many. Having established as his starting point the proposition that humanitarian intervention is, as such, illegal under international law, he proceeded by stating that nonetheless

> in any instance of humanitarian intervention a careful assessment will have to be made of how heavily such illegality weights against all the circumstances of a particular concrete case, and of the efforts, if any, undertaken by the parties to get "as close to the law" as possible. Such analyses will influence not only the moral but also the legal judgment in such cases.[1]

In other words: it cannot be excluded that illegal behavior (even involving the loss of human life) is nonetheless deemed acceptable, and, what is more,

---

[1] See Bruno Simma, 'NATO, the UN and the Use of Force: Legal Aspects', (1999) 10 *European Journal of International Law*, 1–22, at 6.

the final sentence quoted can even be seen to suggest that if such action is justifiable on moral grounds, it shall not be deemed illegal.[2]

In the end, Simma, however reluctantly, conceded that there may be situations where it is opportune to break the law: "The lesson which can be drawn from this is that unfortunately there do occur 'hard cases' in which terrible dilemmas must be faced and imperative political and moral considerations may appear to leave no choice but to act outside the law."[3]

Another leading international lawyer, Antonio Cassese, went a step further. Cassese agreed with Simma that NATO's action was illegal yet, on ethical grounds, justifiable. Instead, though, of trying to limit the fallout of the argument, Cassese adhered to the classic maxim that in international law, "law breaking is an essential method of law making."[4] In other words, the violation of international law, based on ethical grounds, could lead over time to a more ethical international law.[5] This attitude points to a differently conceptualized relationship between law and morality: if morally acceptable, then a practice, however illegal, may come to embody new law. If, on the other hand, the practice is not morally acceptable, then an illegal act is simply an illegal act. The problem here then is where to draw the line between morally justifiable and morally unjustifiable behavior, a task for which lawyers are perhaps not particularly well equipped. Either way, though, what becomes clear from the Kosovo episode is that many felt there was a conflict between law and morality, with morality winning – and deservedly so.

The Kosovo episode provides a useful starting point for the broader study of "normative pluralism": the idea that behavior can be evaluated from the perspectives of a variety of normative orders or normative control systems and thus, importantly, can also be justified from a variety of such perspectives. This has, potentially, broad implications: it may come to mean (as it did in the Kosovo episode) that while behavior was deemed illegal, it was nonetheless considered justified. It may also come to mean that actors may already

---

[2] This would seem to be the most obvious reading of the final sentence, but admittedly there are other possibilities. It may also be the case that Simma wanted to exclude any legal precedential effect from illegal but morally justifiable action – this would be in line with the general tenor of his contribution.

[3] See Simma, 'NATO, the UN and the Use of Force', at 22.

[4] The words are gratefully borrowed from John G. Merrills, *Anatomy of International Law* (London: Sweet and Maxwell, 1976), at 8.

[5] See Antonio Cassese, 'Ex Iniuria Ius Oritur: Are We Moving towards International Legitimation of Forcible Humanitarian Countermeasures in the World Community?' (1999) 10 *European Journal of International Law*, 23–30. A few years later, Cassese wrote elsewhere that it was still "too early to determine whether there will emerge a customary rule legitimizing forcible intervention for humanitarian purposes" without authorization by the Security Council. See Antonio Cassese, *International Law*, 2d ed. (Oxford University Press, 2005), at 351.

anticipate that their behavior will be illegal and thus launch a campaign to have it recognized as acceptable under some other normative order – be it morality, religion, or social mores. In extremis, it may come to mean that alternative normative orders (alternative to law) will be projected as hierarchically superior to law or, at the very least, that the law is deemed insufficient because it has been unable to incorporate injunctions from other normative orders. Hence, law's authority can be contested under appeal to those other normative orders, and it would seem that the law is lacking an authoritative response.

Because the contributors to this volume are internationalists by training and vocation, it should not come as a surprise that much of what follows is written against the background of developments in global governance and international law. Indeed, it can be argued (and will be argued) that the study of normative pluralism has special relevance for the study of global governance. Nonetheless, it would seem that the phenomenon is broader than the international setting alone. We will first sketch a connection between developments in international law and the emergence of normative pluralism (section II). Subsequently, we will discuss the phenomenon more broadly and further define the concepts of "normative pluralism" and "normative order" (section III), discuss the relationship to global governance in general and to what has been called the "politics of framing" in particular (part IV), and discuss the curious role of legitimacy (section V). Section VI concludes.

II. INTERNATIONAL LAW AND ITS SURROUNDINGS

International lawyers have, over the last four decades or so, been greatly concerned about the relationship of international law to what may, for practical purposes, be called "extralegal" considerations, culminating most recently in a move to recognize the so-called constitutionalization of international law.[6] Many international lawyers have long been concerned about the apparently amoral tendencies inherent in their discipline. Those amoral tendencies are often considered to stem from the organizing concept of sovereignty, with some going so far as to proclaim sovereignty a "bad word."[7] In a world of sovereign states without overarching authority, no state can sit in judgment of another state's activities, especially not as long as the state can be said to act in accordance with international law. The world of sovereign states was based

---

[6] See generally Jan Klabbers, Anne Peters and Geir Ulfstein, *The Constitutionalization of International Law* (Oxford University Press, 2009).

[7] See Louis Henkin, 'International Law: Politics, Values and Functions', (1989/V) *Recueil des Cours*, 9–416, at 24.

for a long time, so the argument went, on rules of coexistence: such rules typically do not leave much room for other considerations. As a result, with the emergence of a law of cooperation, there emerged the sentiment that perhaps the law should aspire to do more than merely coordinate the activities of sovereign states.[8] This manifested itself in appeals to recognize that some treaties would be forbidden,[9] and later in the existence of norms binding all states, usually under Latin labels such as *jus cogens* rules, or *erga omnes* obligations. Typically, these would be norms of high moral quality or norms protecting a community interest: the prohibitions of genocide, torture, slavery, aggression, and apartheid rank among the more popular examples.

Yet, the international legal system has been rather resilient and has had problems incorporating those ideas, partly because (as was to be expected) serious political disagreement about the precise contents of the rules concerned did not dissipate by invoking Latin phrases, but partly also because the ideas of *jus cogens* norms and *erga omnes* obligations presuppose a vertical legal structure: public law–type norms presuppose the existence of a public law–type legal order, but the largely horizontal international legal order is not particularly well equipped to give effect to community concerns.[10]

This then has led to a twofold response. On the one hand, it has led to attempts to "force" a vertical system onto the horizontal legal order, and the most explicit manifestation thereof is the promulgation of the international legal order as "constitutional."[11] In this constitutionalized legal order, it is possible to give effect to values that might otherwise be left aside, precisely because the very concept of a constitution evokes associations with legitimate authority: a constitutional regime is a legitimate regime, and it is legitimate because it pays attention to, and honors, moral, religious, or social concerns.[12] The proclaimed constitutionalization of international law often involves recognition of basic human rights as baseline values, which, therewith, become binding for all; the constitutionalization of international law therewith aims

---

[8] The distinction between a law of coexistence and a law of cooperation is generally considered as paradigmatic and was coined by Wolfgang Friedmann, *The Changing Structure of International Law* (New York: Columbia University Press, 1964).

[9] The seminal piece is Alfred Verdross, 'Forbidden Treaties in International Law', (1937) 31 *American Journal of International Law*, 571–7.

[10] This was the gist of the equally seminal piece by Prosper Weil, 'Towards Relative Normativity in International Law?' (1983) 77 *American Journal of International Law*, 412–42.

[11] See, e.g., Erika de Wet, 'The International Constitutional Order', (2006) 55 *International and Comparative Law Quarterly*, 51–76.

[12] This, in turn, presupposes a substantive, liberal constitutionalism. One might also call the Westphalian order constitutional in that it is, literally, constitutive of something, but that is not the way in which current constitutionalist international lawyers use the term. See further Klabbers et al., *The Constitutionalization*.

to draw such extralegal concerns within the scope of international law and to provide them even with an elevated position.

But the second response has been to look away from international law, and to downplay its relevance, precisely by allowing the law to be replaced by injunctions stemming from other normative orders. The international lawyer who is disappointed with the circumstance that international law does not unequivocally support an intervention for humanitarian reasons can do one of two things: she can either aim to demonstrate that, appearances notwithstanding, international law actually supports humanitarian interventions; this has been the strategy behind the various proclamations of a Kantian international law[13] and informs the proclaimed constitutionalization of international law. Or she can suggest that indeed the law does not support humanitarian interventions, but that such interventions can nonetheless be justified on other grounds – those other grounds therewith come to replace the legal framework, and therewith feed normative pluralism. Thus put, from the perspective of an international lawyer, the emergence of normative pluralism owes much of its impetus to dissatisfaction among the international legal community itself with the available apparatus and vocabulary of international law.

III. NORMATIVE PLURALISM

If Kosovo may have been the most dramatic example of invoking a norm from a different normative order so as to justify possibly illegal behavior, and the example closest to the hearts and minds of international lawyers, the newspapers regularly report other examples of what can be referred to as "normative pluralism." Often, such invocations do not involve the international setting, but can also occur in domestic settings – and sometimes they transgress this distinction in that a domestic decision based on one specific normative order is challenged under appeal to another institution transcending the national scene. In some cases it may concern so-called honor killings, in which the father or brother of a girl kills the girl after she has been said to have shamed the family by dating, typically, a member of a different ethnic community. Legal systems will usually recognize this as murder or manslaughter, depending on the circumstances, yet the communities in which this takes place tend to be more forgiving: the behavior is vindicated by the existence of a (contested, to be sure) social norm holding that girls who cause their families shame can be punished – even by death.

---

[13] The most outspoken of these is, in all likelihood, Fernando Tesón, *A Philosophy of International Law* (Boulder, CO: Westview Press, 1998). A more balanced Kantian approach is formulated by John Rawls, *The Laws of Peoples* (Cambridge, MA: Harvard University Press, 1999).

Debates sometimes also flare up in the context of immigration. Typically, these days, the laws of Western states tend to be fairly unforgiving, setting strict limits as to who can be granted the right to reside permanently.[14] This sometimes results in difficult situations, with young children or the elderly threatened with expulsion. In such cases, it is not uncommon to make an appeal for leniency on humanitarian grounds. These may take the form of an argument that the law itself allows for inclusion of humanitarian considerations, but may also go further and suggest that the law be cast aside.[15]

Interesting examples also stem from the world of professional sports. On one end of the spectrum, there are cases of athletes who have done wrong on the soccer pitch and have been punished in accordance with the sports rules in force and nonetheless face separate criminal prosecution: the law does not accept the finality of sports rules, or so it seems. Conversely, sometimes athletes who have been found guilty of using illegal substances by sports tribunals look to regular courts for solace: here, it is the athletes themselves who do not accept the finality of sports rules.[16]

And other walks of life provide or may provide other examples. Thus, there may well be a tension between acting chivalrously or honorably on the battlefield and acting in conformity with the law of armed conflict, or acting in accordance with military commands. By the same token, there may be an incompatibility between what counts as good accounting practices in the accounting industry and what the law holds to be good accounting. Current and very public debates on whether or not headgear can be worn in public places, or whether Catholic crosses may hang on the walls of public schools[17] suggest a conflict between religion and law, as do reports about civil servants who refuse to perform gay marriages for religious reasons. All of these tensions may be captured under the heading of "normative pluralism."[18]

---

[14] An excellent discussion is Catherine Dauvergne, *Making People Illegal* (Cambridge University Press, 2008).

[15] For an example of such a discussion in Finland, see http://www.hs.fi/english/article/Professor+Martti+Koskenniemi+faults+politicians+for+%E2%80%9Ccowardice%E2%80%9D+over+grandmother+deportation+flap/1135257208639(accessed 17 December 2010).

[16] Indeed, sports law is a rapidly growing branch within administrative law. See Lorenzo Casini, 'The Making of a *Lex Sportiva*: The Court of Arbitration for Sport "The Provider', New York University School of Law, *Institute for International Law and Justice Working Paper* 2010/5.

[17] Arguably among the more controversial recent decisions is the *Lautsi and Others v. Italy*, decided by the European Court of Human Rights, Application no. 30814/06, judgment of 18 March 2011.

[18] Moreover, of course, earlier centuries have witnessed intense struggles for power between church and state, or religious and secular power. It would seem, however, that these battles did not solely involve normative conflicts but also, and perhaps predominantly, conflicts between institutions with their own will to power.

The very term "pluralism" (whether accompanied by the adjective "normative" or not) evokes different responses in different audiences. Political theorists tend to think of pluralism in connection with values, leading to the idea that since the almost seven billion people on planet earth are bound not to reach full agreement on all aspects of life, values may be incommensurate and may have to compete with each other. For political theorists (at least those of liberal ilk), such values cannot be meaningfully ordered or ranked, and thus we are forced to live with value pluralism.[19]

International relations scholars have their own take on pluralism and tend to think of it in broader structural terms as clashes of ideologies or even civilizations: Islam versus liberalism or, earlier, capitalism versus communism or, earlier still, civilized versus uncivilized nations.[20] Here, the leading concern will typically be that of tracking the influence of various blocs, be it the eastern bloc of the cold war, the nonaligned movement, or the influence of the Organisation of Islamic Cooperation (OIC) in today's global arena.

In circles of constitutional theorists, it has become fashionable to speak of "constitutional pluralism." In one variety, this is thought to mean that governance takes place on various levels (multilevel governance), calling for coordination and communication,[21] but sometimes the claim is more fundamental: people may be subjected to several regimes that can all legitimately claim to be constitutional, and not only is it impossible to find a hierarchy among them, it is undesirable too.[22]

Lawyers and anthropologists have been studying the relationship between state law and the norms prevailing in groups within the state (typically indigenous communities) since the late 1960s and early 1970s under the heading of legal pluralism.[23] This, in turn, has given rise to heated debates about the very

---

[19] The leading political theorist in this mold is no doubt Berlin; see, e.g., Isaiah Berlin, *Four Essays on Liberty* (Oxford University Press, 1969). See also John Gray's analysis of Berlin's work in John Gray, *Two Faces of Liberalism* (New York: New Press, 2000), and for a brief yet lucid discussion William A. Galston, *Liberal Pluralism: The Implications of Value Pluralism for Political Theory and Practice* (Cambridge University Press, 2002).

[20] The most well known of these is probably Samuel P. Huntington, *The Clash of Civilizations and the Remaking of World Order* (New York: Simon & Schuster, 1996).

[21] See, e.g., Andreas Follesdal, Ramses Wessel and Jan Wouters (eds.), *Multilevel Regulation and the EU: The Interplay between Global, European and national Normative Processes* (Leiden: Martinus Nijhoff, 2008).

[22] Representatives of this school would include James Tully, *Strange Multiplicity: Constitutionalism in an Age of Diversity* (Cambridge University Press, 1995), and Neil Walker, 'The Idea of Constitutional Pluralism', (2002) 65 *Modern Law Review*, 317–59.

[23] See, e.g., Sally Falk Moore, 'Law and Social Change: The Semi-autonomous Social Field as an Appropriate Subject of Study', (1973) *Law and Society Review*, 719–46; Simon Roberts, 'After Government? On Representing Law without the State', (2005) 68 *Modern Law Review*, 1–24.

definition of law: why would state law have to be considered law, but the same label not apply to the norms applicable within nonstate actors? At one of the more extreme ends of the spectrum, it has been posited that the label "law" is itself a monopolizing force, and there is no reason, some would say, not to treat the rules in force even within criminal organizations such as the mafia (which, reportedly, has strong codes of conduct in place) as "law."[24]

These various positions are not, to be sure, mutually exclusive; one can be a committed value pluralist yet be concerned about the conflict between Islamist and liberal ideologies, as the work of the popular political theorist Benjamin Barber makes clear.[25] In particular, constitutional pluralists are often value pluralists as well – indeed, it is on the basis of value pluralism that constitutional pluralism has been developed to begin with.

What then is so novel about normative pluralism? After all, one could claim, with considerable justification, that the history of jurisprudence is replete with debates concerning in particular the relationship between law and morality, although it seems fair to say that this has been a greater preoccupation for lawyers than for moral philosophers. For instance, the debates between Hart and Fuller,[26] Hart and Devlin,[27] and Hart and Dworkin[28] can all be seen to be debates about the precise relationship between law and morality. There is also, albeit to a lesser extent perhaps, a body of scholarship on the relations between law and social norms – in this case, those doing the work have tended to be social scientists,[29] perhaps anthropologists in particular.[30]

[24] This is, eventually, where Santos finds himself, and much the same applies to Anderson. See Boaventura de Sousa Santos, *Towards a New Legal Common Sense*, 2nd ed. (London: Butterworths, 2002), and Gavin W. Anderson, *Constitutional Rights after Globalization* (Oxford: Hart, 2005).

[25] See Benjamin R. Barber, *Jihad v MacDonald: Terrorism's Challenge to Democracy* (London: Corgi, 2003 [1995]).

[26] This debate revolved around the proper role of morality in law, with key texts being H. L. A. Hart, 'Positivism and the Separation of Law and Morals', (1958) 71 *Harvard Law Review*, 593–629, and Lon L. Fuller, 'Positivism and Fidelity to Law – a Reply to Professor Hart', (1958) 71 *Harvard Law Review*, 630–72. Their positions were more fully elaborated (and arguably had come a bit closer) in H. L. A. Hart, *The Concept of Law* (Oxford: Clarendon Press, 1961) and Lon L. Fuller, *The Morality of Law*, rev. ed. (New Haven, CT: Yale University Press, 1969).

[27] Here the main issue was to what extent law should protect individuals against themselves and thus be paternalistic, e.g., by forcing motorcyclists to wear helmets. See especially H. L. A. Hart, *Law, Liberty, and Morality* (Stanford, CA: Stanford University Press, 1963) (which also provides a good account of Devlin's position).

[28] This debate revolved around the question whether law can accommodate principles and policies, in addition to rules. See Hart, *The Concept*, and Ronald Dworkin, *Taking Rights Seriously* (Cambridge, MA: Harvard University Press, 1978).

[29] Think only of Max Weber, *Economy and Society: An Outline of Interpretive Sociology*, Roth and Wittich eds. (Berkeley: University of California Press, 1968).

[30] A fine example is Antony Allott, *The Limits of Law* (London: Butterworths, 1980).

Yet, those debates were – and are – predominantly geared to a reconciliation of distinct normative orders or, as they are sometimes called, distinct "normative control systems."[31] The debates between Hart and his contemporaries were debates on how law reflected, or should reflect, morality. Much of the anthropological or sociological work on the relations between law and social norms is about how law reflects society, or how law should reflect society.[32]

The concept of what constitutes a "normative order" requires some explanation. By way of working definition, a normative order, or normative control system (we shall refer to "normative order," for ease of reference), signifies a set of related commands, injunctions, "dos and don'ts" that stem from the same source or a multitude of similar sources. Thus, law can be seen as a distinct normative order, in all its generality: while there is some disagreement at the edges about what is and what is not law, and while law can exist within states, between groups of states (think of EU law), and among states, there is widespread agreement that law consists of rules and possibly principles and can grant powers and privileges, all stemming from a source recognized as legal authority.[33] This is not, admittedly, a very precise definition, and it collects together legal theorists often best kept at arm's length, but for present purposes it will do.

Likewise, religion can be considered as a distinct normative order, itself divided into different subordinate orders. These, however, are less interesting for present purposes: whether a law conflicts with the Bible or with the Quran, in both cases this can be construed as a law versus religion conflict. Much the same applies to orders such as professional standards, or chivalry, or social norms: these can be treated as fairly monolithic sets of norms, without (for the time being) being overly bothered by fine-grained niceties.

The biggest challenge perhaps is presented by morality as a distinct normative order. Morality as a normative order presents at least two different problems, in addition to the circumstance that it encompasses itself widely diverging traditions.[34] First, while references to morality usually

---

[31] See James M. Donovan, *Legal Anthropology: An Introduction* (Lanham, MD: AltaMira Press, 2008), at vii.

[32] Or, alternatively, about law's impact on society. But that is, on second thought, a variation on the reflection theme.

[33] This borrows from one of the classic conceptualizations: see Wesley N. Hohfeld, *Fundamental Legal Conceptions as Applied in Judicial Reasoning*, Corbin ed. (Westport, CT: Greenwood Press, 1978 [1913–17]).

[34] For a useful overview of the diverse ethical traditions as they relate to global affairs, see William M. Sullivan and Will Kymlicka (eds.), *The Globalization of Ethics* (Cambridge University Press, 2007).

sound authoritative and self-evident, it is by no means clear where morality stems from. Statements such as "what X did was illegal, but it was the morally right thing to do" clearly tap into a recognizable underlying sentiment but equally clearly remain rather opaque: the moral obligation itself is rarely spelled out; nor is it clear where the moral obligation would come from.

In fact, in Western philosophy alone there are at least three dominant traditions of ethics. Most prominent is the deontological tradition, often associated (rightly or wrongly) with Kant, which proclaims in a nutshell that behavior should be in conformity with duties: it should measure up to externally set, objectively cognizable standards. Then there is the consequentialist tradition, often associated with the likes of Bentham and Rousseau, which holds that the morally correct behavior is the behavior that brings about good consequences – however defined. And perhaps the oldest of all (although marginalized for quite a while) is the virtue ethics tradition, which goes back to Aristotle and suggests that the morally right behavior depends not on consequences or external standards, but on the actor's character: the charitable person will act charitably, the honest person honestly, et cetera. Of the non-western traditions, Confucianism is a well-known example, whereas Buddhism can probably be classified as a moral tradition as well, although it may serve as an example of the porous boundary between morality and religion. These different traditions alone may yield different answers, in concrete cases, as to what the morally right course of action will be.[35]

Second, there is a strong tendency intuitively to place morality on a pedestal: law is typically supposed to be in harmony with morality (or at least be morally neutral), rather than the other way around, and the same applies to morality's relationship to other normative orders. It somehow seems that morality has the strongest voice, with other normative orders being in subordinate positions. Statements such as "what X did was illegal, but morally right" tend to be greeted with more conviction and applause than statements such as "what X did was morally wrong, but in accordance with the law." The first reveals X as a reflective individual, who sets out to do the right thing, whereas the second statement posits X as a legalist, who acts in accordance with the law even if he should perhaps behave differently.[36]

This elevated position of morality finds its cause quite possibly in the circumstance that whereas law, religion, and other standards tend to be man-made,

---

[35] An intelligent introduction is Julia Driver, *Ethics: The Fundamentals* (London: Blackwell, 2006).

[36] The classic study of legalism is Judith Shklar, *Legalism: Law, Morals, and Political Trials* (Cambridge, MA: Harvard University Press, 1986).

morality typically is not; or rather, morality is not man-made in quite the same way.[37] Law can typically be traced back to a legislative source, however messy or confused perhaps; professional standards can typically be traced back to a few individuals who first thought of them and then went on to refine and polish them. Even religions can, more often than not, be traced back to relatively small circles of individuals: the evangelists in the case of Christianity and, in more specific religions, the likes of St. Augustine, Aquinas, and the popes in Catholicism, or Calvin or Luther in different brands of Protestantism. By the same token, Islam is traceable to the Prophet Mohammed, and Judaism owes much to Maimonides. In short, normative orders can typically be traced back to human ingenuity, which renders them, ultimately, vulnerable: if they are products of the human imagination, then it follows that in the end they can be accused of merely manifesting the preferences of the individuals imagining them and thus cannot claim universal acceptance, at least not in the face of conflicting demands. While believers may hold Aquinas's teachings, or Calvin's, in greater esteem than anything else, at the end of the day there is an intuitive sense that for all their qualities, these merely reflect "politics as usual," so to speak.

Morality, by contrast, can boast no such pedigree. While various traditions can be traced to various authors, their substance cannot. It is one thing to say that Aristotle was the founding father of virtue ethics but would be quite another (and highly inaccurate) to say that he decided on what counts as virtuous behavior. Indeed, most virtue ethicists would agree that at least some of the virtues listed by Aristotle no longer qualify: wittiness, while generally admired, will not be seen by many as particularly virtuous, and much the same may apply to righteous indignation, whereas modesty for Aristotle presumably had different connotations than what is now commonly referred to as such.[38] Likewise, some character traits have come to be recognized as virtues that Aristotle never thought of: charity might be an example.[39] But to say that the same applies to the teachings of religious leaders is to miss the fundamental point that their claims are aspiring to the status of unique

---

[37] See generally, representing many, Edmond Cahn, *The Moral Decision: Right and Wrong in the Light of American Law* (Bloomington: Indiana University Press, 1981 [1955]).
[38] See Aristotle, *Ethics*, at 104; the 1976 Penguin edition has been used, with the text translated by J. A. K. Thomson. Modesty, for Aristotle, was the mean between shyness and shamelessness and operated under the general heading of shame.
[39] Moreover, it may have lost some of its religious connotations. For Aquinas, charity was one of the three religious virtues (with faith and hope). It would seem that nowadays, charity is more widely seen as a virtue, but one demoted somewhat in standing because of the advent of rights. See, e.g., Onora O'Neill, *Towards Justice and Virtue: A Constructive Account of Practical Reasoning* (Cambridge University Press, 1996).

truth in ways that do not apply to Aristotle, or Kant, or most other moral philosophers.

It is undoubtedly the case that, in a particular way, morality is man-made: our everyday actions confirm and reestablish what counts as morality, and every time someone commits torture the moral injunction not to commit torture is weakened, in a way. By practicing torture, it may slowly, over time, come to be seen as morally acceptable – although much here may also depend on the community reaction: the process will be slower, and perhaps grind to a halt, if all acts of torture are habitually condemned. And the reverse holds true as well: every time torture is not committed where it could have been expected perhaps (every time the ticking time bomb is discovered), the moral injunction is strengthened.

But morality cannot be traced to an authoritative (quasi-legislative) source in quite the same way as other normative orders. The result is that referring to moral obligations is bound to be a viable way out of a normative quagmire, because it is well-nigh impossible to verify what exactly the moral obligation at stake was. In everyday discourse, people may simply claim to be acting "under a moral obligation," which will usually halt further discussion: no further demonstration is required as to what moral obligation is at stake. If something is "morally wrong," such a claim is usually accepted at face value: it can tap into the tremendous authority of morality, which derives, in part, from morality's being sourceless, in ways that do not apply to claims that one was acting for religious reasons. Stating the latter is to invite further questions: Which religion? Which reasons? But referring to moral obligations does not meet with quite the same response.

Indeed, there is something rather incongruous at work here, at least to the legally trained eye, which makes the case for morality as an exceptional normative order even stronger: whereas morality seems to occupy an elevated position, an otherwise identical appeal to adhere to a norm of natural law would often be frowned upon. It is perfectly acceptable, and by no means eccentric, in the company of international lawyers, to say that morality demands that humanitarian interventions be considered so as to prevent ethnic cleansing; it is far less acceptable, and quite a bit more eccentric, to say that the same is demanded on natural law grounds. This then puts a premium on how arguments are presented: the same action may be more persuasive if cast in the language of one normative order than when cast in the language of a different normative order.[40]

---

[40] For this reason, it is surely no coincidence that leading international lawyers such as Simma and Cassese referred to morality when defending the Kosovo intervention, rather than to natural law.

IV. GLOBAL GOVERNANCE

This in turn helps suggest why the topic of normative pluralism is of contemporary political significance: the way in which an issue is framed may have a large bearing on the way it will subsequently be treated, something that is sometimes referred to as the "politics of framing."[41] An example may help to clarify the point, in many ways. The HIV/Aids crisis lends itself to study from a variety of perspectives, or through a variety of different frames.[42] It can be regarded as a health issue, in which case the international response to be expected would be to call upon the World Health Organization. Given the circumstance that medication is available but not always easily accessible, the HIV/Aids crisis may also be regarded as a trade issue, thus demanding the involvement of trade lawyers, intellectual property lawyers, and the World Trade Organization. Since the availability of medication may be a matter of life and death, it can also be regarded as a human rights issue, with actors invoking the various human rights conventions and insisting on the right to life or the right to health.

And these are only the responses available within the legal arena (and even then far from exhaustive). But it is by no means self-evident that the matter is best regarded as a legal matter to begin with. Devout Christians may hold that the crisis owes much to secularization and the concomitant relaxation of religious norms: should not the HIV/Aids crisis better be seen as a religious matter? Others may hold that the HIV/Aids has something to do with public morality, either in the sense that behavior causing the disease is morally unacceptable or (more palatable, perhaps) that the continued existence of the disease, despite the availability of medication, is morally unacceptable. Some may even go so far as to suggest that the big pharmaceutical companies could – or should – take it upon themselves to do something and save human lives whenever they can: some may feel that self-regulation by the industry might be both necessary and sufficient. Hence, the way an issue is framed may affect the way it is to be handled, and since there are no "obvious" or "self-evident" ways to handle issues, the framing of issues becomes an exercise in politics.

---

[41] See, e.g., Nancy Fraser, *Scales of Justice: Reimagining Political Space in a Globalizing World* (New York: Columbia University Press, 2009). Note that Fraser largely conceptualizes framing in terms of deciding who is entitled to be treated as a subject of justice; there is no obvious reason, however, not to use the same term in a broader way.

[42] The example is borrowed from Andreas Fischer-Lescano and Gunther Teubner, *Regime-Kollisionen: Zur Fragmentierung des globalen Rechts* (Frankfurt am Main: Surhkamp, 2006).

Or rather, it would seem that there is no longer an obvious or self-evident way of handling issues. In earlier times, or so it seems, it was quite common for actors in positions of authority to hold that any issue was immediately left to the law, only for the law to figure out which body of legal rules to utilize for classification, analysis, and possibly solution – at least, this used to be the case when there was law available. In earlier days, it would not have occurred to those tasked with evaluating whether, for example, the actions of Tanzania in Uganda in 1979, or those of the United States in Grenada in 1983[43] could be evaluated in terms other than those of law. It would have been possible perhaps to justify such actions in terms of a humanitarian intervention; it would have been possible perhaps to argue that they amounted to an emanation of the traditional – if not uncontroversial – right to rescue nationals abroad; they could have been regarded as an intervention upon invitation perhaps; and it could even have been possible perhaps to view them as a blatant act of aggression, but in all cases, the available vocabulary was the vocabulary of international law. While some may have felt that the international legal vocabulary would have to be stretched to do justice to the events, few would have thought that the justifiability or otherwise would not depend on legal analysis and could be replaced by an appeal to the morality of the action. In short: actors would typically define their activities in terms of law, and those with the authority to evaluate would typically do likewise.

This automaticity has gone missing, though: the law seems to have lost its privileged position and now has to compete with other normative orders. That is not to say that legal arguments no longer matter,[44] but it is to say that they have lost the almost monopolist position they once occupied. This points to something of a paradox: it is uncontested that law has come to be ever more fine-grained and pervasive in everyday life (and this emphatically applies to international law as well), with little being left unregulated, or left to the individual sense of responsibility of actors.[45] Yet, simultaneously, other normative orders have gained in practical prominence: it seems relatively easy nowadays

---

[43] A brief but useful discussion is Antonio Cassese, 'Why States Use Force with Impunity', reproduced in Antonio Cassese, *Violence and Law in the Modern Age* (Princeton, NJ: Princeton University Press, 1988), 30–45.

[44] See, e.g., Ian Johnstone, *The Power of Deliberation: International Law, Politics and Organizations* (Oxford University Press, 2011).

[45] In a similar vein it has been observed, e.g., that the legal regulation of nuclear weapons or of genocide may involve a deactivation of individual senses of right and wrong. See Martti Koskenniemi, 'Faith, Identity and the Killing of the Innocent: International Lawyers and Nuclear Weapons', (1997) 10 *Leiden Journal of International Law*, 137–62. A broader argument to this effect is implicit in Onora O'Neill, *A Question of Trust* (Cambridge University Press, 2002).

to suggest that behavior may not quite be legal but is nonetheless justified because it is, well, the right thing to do, or to suggest that regardless of what the law says, an acceptable solution must be sought elsewhere.

It may be postulated that conflicts involving normative orders are becoming increasingly prevalent. One reason is that traditional adherence to normative orders is becoming less obvious: in the postmodern world, religion has lost some of its adherence as societies have secularized (which is not to deny an upsurge of religion in parts of the world). Law, once associated with a strong sense of obedience for the law's own sake, has lost some of its luster as well, as noted. This may have a variety of causes: increased recognition of law's indeterminacy perhaps; a lessened amount of respect for politicians as lawmakers, who are often portrayed as vaguely corrupt; and perhaps an increased sense of entitlement along with commodification of the law: if politicians evade the law claiming that the end justifies the means, then why not do the same? But none of these need concern us here.

Related, other normative orders have become increasingly prominent. The role in particular of professional standards has met with increasing recognition, which in turn is related to a general faith in expertise[46]: if the specialists say that accountants should behave in such-and-such manner in order to optimize the function of accountancy, or that builders and architects should never decide on projects without taking best practices in the construction sector into account (*lex constructionis*, as some would have it), then it becomes difficult to lodge a dissent, even if the dissent would have the color of law. Indeed, the law can only respond either by taking the experts on board and thus becoming itself a form of expert knowledge[47] or by opposing the relevance of expertise and taking on explicitly political colors. Neither course of action is probably particularly desirable: the former renders the law indistinguishable from other forms of expert knowledge, whereas the latter might result in inappropriate law, isolated from any moorings in society and not able to regulate that which requires regulation.

Either way, the net result is that a multitude of normative orders may make it possible for actors to go on a "normative-order shopping spree." In other words, if applying the norms of order A leads to a situation that a subject may

---

[46] For a general discussion involving international law, see Martti Koskenniemi, 'The Fate of International Law: Between Technique and Politics', (2007) 70 *Modern Law Review*, 1–32.

[47] Something to this effect can be seen in the use of indicators as techniques of governance. For illuminating discussion, see Kevin Davies, Benedict Kingsbury, and Sally Engle Merry, 'Indicators as a Technology of Global Governance', *New York University Institute for International Law and Justice Working Papers* 2010/2. See also Sally Engle Merry, 'Measuring the World: Indicators, Human Rights, and Global Governance', (2011) 52 *Current Anthropology* (Supplement 3), 83–95.

consider to be less than fully desirable, he or she might be inclined to look for guidance elsewhere. If the law tells me to do X, but I somehow feel that doing X may not be all that effective, or may affect some other goal negatively, or may even simply be what I do not feel like doing, then chances are that I can find a norm somewhere else that is more to my liking. The law, therewith, becomes a policy option among policy options and seems to lose some of its authority. In different terms, the law becomes instrumentalized, or even commodified: if we do not like the solution offered by the law, our response is no longer toward working to changing the law, but simply to finding a way to overrule it by invoking a different normative order and making the (often implicit) argument that this other norm should prevail.[48]

All this then should point to the relevance of normative pluralism for the study of global governance. Governance itself is often defined as government without readily identifiable governors,[49] and the study of global governance reveals that clear, transparent, and hierarchical patterns of authority are typically lacking: indeed, the relative fall from grace of law as a normative order suggests much the same.

It is possible to distinguish different kinds of authority in the global order, and some of these would seem to tap into the coexistence of a variety of normative orders. Whereas institutional authority and delegated authority will typically involve law (in that delegation will require, normally speaking, a legal instrument), principle-based authority need not involve the law, and neither does expertise-based authority or capacity-based authority.[50] Hence, the various kinds of authority identified already suggest the possibility of normative pluralism, and this is further borne out by the close connection between the "politics of framing" and the more traditionally recognized issue of agenda setting in global affairs.[51]

Normative pluralism is further related to global governance in two interconnected ways. First, normative pluralism helps the powers that be in exercising their power. Powerful military states can justify military action by appealing to morality when the law does not provide them with this option – again, the

---

[48] See Jan Klabbers, 'The Commodification of International Law', (2006) 1 *Select Proceedings of the European Society of International Law*, 341–58.
[49] See classically James N. Rosenau, 'Governance, Order, and Change in World Politics', in James N. Rosenau and Ernst-Otto Czempiel (eds.), *Governance without Government: Order and Change in World Politics* (Cambridge University Press, 1992), 1–29.
[50] These are the five kinds of authority identified as central to global governance by Deborah D. Avant, Martha Finnemore and Susan K. Sell, 'Who Governs the Globe?' in Deborah D. Avant, Martha Finnemore and Susan K. Sell (eds.), *Who Governs the Globe?* (Cambridge University Press, 2010), 1–31.
[51] Ibid.

Kosovo episode is instructive, in that NATO decided on intervention unilaterally after it became clear that Security Council approval (which would have rendered any qualms about the legality of the action obsolete)[52] was not forthcoming. Hence, the normative justification for the intervention was based primarily on moral grounds, which were viewed as overruling the UN Charter or any other possibly applicable legal rules. Likewise, powerful companies can refer to their attempts to self-regulate in those cases where legal regulation is missing or could be expected to be more demanding than self-regulation or, alternatively, point to practices that the law tolerates as being in no need of self-regulation. Those who decide on spending large amounts of money can choose whether to do so in accordance with accountancy standards (most obviously in the private sector, but also in the public sector),[53] or in accordance with legal standards. Indeed, perhaps the prevailing plethora of options is best symbolized by the so-called global compact, under which companies are called upon to adhere to certain standards in the fields of human rights, labor, and the environment but without the force of law, or even the form of law.[54]

On the other hand, normative pluralism can also offer a vocabulary of resistance and emancipation. One of the main functions, traditionally, of the separation between law and morality was to ensure the availability of a set of standards from which to criticize and help develop the law.[55] If law and morality would be identical, there would be nothing left to strive for, and no political platform for the articulation of different values. Thus put, the result would potentially be totalitarian, and therewith clearly unwanted. As a result, normative pluralism cannot be deemed undesirable in its own right. Yet, the question remains how much normative pluralism is desirable, and for whom and for what purposes.

V. LEGITIMACY

Being able to overrule the law presupposes that doing so has become acceptable, has become respectable or, as the Germans so delicately put it, *salonfähig*. The emergence of "legitimacy" as a key word in the politicolegal vocabulary

---

[52] See, e.g., with quite a bit of nuance, Vaughan Lowe, *International Law* (Oxford University Press, 2007) at 281–2.
[53] There even exist accountancy standards for the exercise of international public authority: NATO signed up for these not so long ago.
[54] A fine early study is Viljam Engström, *Realizing the Global Compact* (Helsinki: Erik Castrén Institute, 2002).
[55] See, e.g., Seyla Benhabib, *Another Cosmopolitanism* (Oxford University Press, 2006).

has done much to facilitate this. Historically, it is probably no exaggeration to state that a legal rule was presumed also to be a legitimate rule. As Weber suggested, perhaps the most common form of authority worked on the basis of the idea that norms must be respected if they form part of a broader system of norms. Hence, the fact that a legal rule existed was reason enough to presume that it was a legitimate rule, which asked for acceptance on the part of those who were subjected to it.[56]

This intimate connection between legality and legitimacy is no longer applied with the same degree of automaticity as before, and it would seem that instead of legality, legitimacy has become posited as the final arbiter for behavior: to engage in acceptable behavior is, in part, to engage in conformity with a legitimate norm, and preferably with a norm considered to be more legitimate than any of its competitors. This is problematic, for several reasons.[57] First, legitimacy is a highly fluid concept, which can relate to a variety of phenomena, all of them possibly of relevance. Thus, legitimacy can attach to states and governments,[58] in which case it often follows that the laws in force in that state or enacted by that government ought to be obeyed – with the corollary that laws in force in states considered illegitimate can be ignored, disobeyed, or rejected – hence, legitimacy (or rather, a perceived lack thereof) can constitute an excuse for civil disobedience.[59] Legitimacy can also attach to individual international institutions: it has become common, for instance, to discuss the legitimacy of the United Nations Security Council.[60] Again, then, an important corollary is that those who are less than fully convinced of the Security Council's legitimacy can easily find an excuse to ignore its injunctions.[61]

---

[56] See Weber, *Economy and Society*, 954.

[57] See Martti Koskenniemi, 'Legitimacy, Rights and Ideology: Notes towards a Critique of the New Moral Internationalism', (2003) 7 *Associations*, 349–73.

[58] See, e.g., Allen Buchanan, *Justice, Legitimacy, and Self-determination: Moral Foundations for International Law* (Oxford University Press, 2004).

[59] On the latter, see Maria José Falcon y Tella, *Civil Disobedience* (Leiden: Martinus Nijhoff, 2002).

[60] See, e.g., Ian Hurd, *After Anarchy: Legitimacy and Power in the United Nations Security Council* (Princeton, NJ: Princeton University Press, 2007). Telling is how legality and legitimacy are sometimes conflated, and sometimes juxtaposed in Kenneth Manusama, *The United Nations Security Council in the Post–Cold War Era: Applying the Principle of Legality* (Leiden: Martinus Nijhoff, 2006).

[61] The most prominent example is no doubt the decision of the CJEU in case C-402/05 P, *Kadi v. Council and Commission*, [2008] ECR I-6351. While (technically) the Court did not test the legality or legitimacy of Security Council action but limited itself to testing the legality of EU implementing legislation, it is nonetheless clear that finding fault with the implementing legislation implies finding fault with the underlying resolution. The most comprehensive defense

Legitimacy can also attach to individual rules or norms. Thus, it is often argued that a norm that has been created in accordance with correct procedure (a norm that therefore can be considered as "valid") can boast considerable legitimacy, and therewith exercise a considerable "compliance pull."[62] This would, at first sight, resurrect the connection between law and legitimacy, as law tends to be seen as the site that has given most thought to the establishment of proper procedure – indeed, to some this is the hallmark of law.[63] Still, what remains unclear in this scheme is whether a legitimate norm can emanate from an institution or government whose legitimacy is in doubt: if the Security Council is deemed illegitimate, can it nonetheless issue individual norms or decisions that can be considered legitimate if proper procedure is followed? The reverse seems more obvious: an otherwise legitimate government or institution may on occasion issue a norm that is less than fully legitimate. This may result in diminished legitimacy of the government or institution but need not be lethal.

Finally, legitimacy has even been posited in connection with the global order, or international system, at large.[64] It is here perhaps that legitimacy becomes most conspicuous: the legitimacy of the international system immediately focuses attention on issues such as global justice; the absence of global justice would suggest that the international order lacks legitimacy, to a greater or lesser extent, which in turn would justify political action to make the world a more legitimate place or, alternatively, engage in action not approved by the international order. And in such a scenario, it is but a small step to invoke the legitimacy attaching to other normative orders or their norms.

Legitimacy can derive, as the preceding analysis already suggests, from a variety of factors. It is, for instance, generally accepted that the creation of a norm, a state, a government, or an institution in accordance with the procedure prescribed for such events will normally contribute to the legitimacy of the resulting norms or institutions. A legal rule enacted by government with the approval of parliament will prima facie be a legitimate rule; a government created as the result of free and democratic elections will, likewise, be considered a legitimate government; a state created as the result of an agreed-upon

---

hereof to date in the literature is Antonios Tzanakopoulos, *Disobeying the Security Council: Countermeasures against Wrongful Sanctions* (Oxford University Press, 2011).

[62] See Thomas M. Franck, *The Power of Legitimacy among Nations* (Oxford University Press, 1990).

[63] See Fuller, *The Morality of Law*. On the utility of Fuller for international law, see Jan Klabbers, 'Constitutionalism and the Making of International Law: Fuller's Procedural Natural Law', (2008) 5 *No Foundations: Journal of Extreme Legal Positivism*, 84–112.

[64] See, e.g., Hilary Charlesworth and Jean-Marc Coicaud (eds.), *Fault Lines of International Legitimacy* (Cambridge University Press, 2010).

process of secession or devolution will be seen as a legitimate state; and an international institution created by states on the basis of a treaty freely consented to will, again prima facie, be regarded as a legitimate institution.

What complicates matters, though, is that legitimacy may also emanate from other sources. Thus, it is sometimes posited that a government, even if created legitimately, may be illegitimate when it commits gross human rights violations or engages in widespread aggression. Legal rules may come into being in accordance with right procedure yet have illegitimate contents: a rule to discriminate against minorities on the basis of race or ethnic descent will be considered illegitimate, even if adopted in accordance with the constitutionally prescribed procedure. Thus, the behavior of otherwise legitimate entities may cause these entities to lose legitimacy, and it would seem at least hypothetically possible for illegitimate entities to earn "legitimacy points" by behaving in legitimate ways. Indeed, many have suggested that the legitimacy of institutions (the term is used here in a generic sense) may depend on their output, and precisely in circumstances where democratic control may be difficult to achieve (as is often considered to be the case in international affairs), output legitimacy becomes an important factor, if only because "input legitimacy" is unlikely to materialize, or unlikely to be sufficient.[65]

Under all these meanings, whether it concerns the legitimacy of the global order, of international institutions, or of individual international legal rules, the (real, or perceived, or posited) lack of legitimacy can be invoked in order to justify behavior not in conformity with international legal prescriptions. And this can be done, importantly, in bad faith as well as good faith: legitimacy is so infinitely malleable that any judgment on its presence ultimately depends on the perspective of the decision maker. Law can claim to be an objectively cognizable yardstick (even though the legal realists and their heirs, the critical legal scholars, have demonstrated that this proposition can no longer be accepted with full force),[66] but a resort to legitimacy misses this objective, or quasi-objective, dimension. Legitimacy can be invoked as one pleases, and it is hardly an exaggeration that, free after Schmitt, it may be claimed that "whoever invokes legitimacy, wants to cheat."[67]

---

[65] See, e.g., Fritz Scharpf, *Governing in Europe: Effective and Democratic?* (Oxford University Press, 1999), at 11–13.

[66] The seminal work in international law is Martti Koskenniemi, *From Apology to Utopia: The Structure of International Legal Argument* (Helsinki: Finnish Lawyers' Publishing Company, 1989).

[67] See further Jan Klabbers, book review of Charlesworth and Coicaud (eds.), 'Fault Lines of International Legitimacy', (2011) 105 *American Journal of International Law*, 394–7. Schmitt famously wrote that 'whoever invokes humanity wants to cheat', adapting an earlier claim of

Intriguingly, moreover, legitimacy adds something new and slippery to the discussion. On the one hand, legitimacy cannot be traced back to any given normative order but potentially encompasses them all. Thus, as noted, the sources of legitimacy may include law (the concepts used to be almost coterminous), but also morality, religion, or society, or any other normative order. On the other hand, and perhaps as a result, legitimacy itself, despite its fluidity, is sometimes posited as the overarching normative order, so to speak. When Buchanan and Keohane suggest that the institutions of global governance should be legitimate, they do not mean to say that these should act in accordance with the law, or in accordance with prevailing social mores, or in accordance with moral injunctions. Instead, what they have in mind is something else, something that remains amorphous and undefined perhaps but can be recognized by cognoscenti.[68] Legitimacy therewith comes to take the place of other normative orders while tapping into those orders, and the all-important question is to inquire about the identity of those cognoscenti. That is, in itself, nothing new: political theorists from Hobbes to Schmitt have suggested that the question "who decides?" is the most pressing political question.[69] But what is new is that the question no longer hooks up, as it once did almost automatically, to law. The question is no longer "who decides on the application of law?" but rather "who decides what qualifies as legitimate?"

VI. CONCLUDING REMARKS

While the relations between law and the environments in which it operates have always given pause for reflection, it would seem that the normative pluralism identified here is of relatively recent origin and qualitatively different from what informed earlier discussions. The question is no longer solely whether law should incorporate morality, religious norms, social norms, or, indeed, any other standards. Instead, the question increasingly becomes whether law can be replaced with morality, religious norms, social norms, or indeed any other standards, whose norms may be considered, for one reason or another, more legitimate.

Proudhon's. See Carl Schmitt, *The Concept of the Political* (University of Chicago Press, 1996, Schwab trans.), at 54.
[68] See Allen Buchanan and Robert O. Keohane, 'The Legitimacy of Global Governance', (2006) 20 *Ethics and International Affairs*, 405–37.
[69] For an insightful discussion, see Anne Orford, *International Authority and the Responsibility to Protect* (Cambridge University Press, 2011).

In one sense, that is nothing to worry about. Law is, one might say, a cultural artifact and may as well be replaced by some other cultural artifact.[70] And yet, there is ground for some concern for, as has been pointed out elsewhere,[71] the advantage that law has over other normative orders is not just that it is more easily cognizable in its details, but above all that it is the result of agreement among relevant actors on some basis of equality. This applies most obviously perhaps to democratically created law[72] but also, in its own peculiar way, to international law, with its emphasis on the consent of sovereign and equal actors. By contrast, other normative orders lack this quality, typically involving top-down commands or, as with some social norms, privileging some actors over others: consumers, for example, have far less control over the contents of *lex mercatoria* than traders. With this in mind, normative pluralism entails quite a challenge to law and, ironically, to the very liberalism that helped generate it, for if the law is threatened and may be overshadowed by the type of "the ends-justify-the-means" reasoning that often accompanies resort to nonlegal standards deemed more legitimate than legal standards, then ultimately liberal democracy too is under threat.

---

[70] For a view of law as culture, see Lawrence Rosen, *Law as Culture: An Invitation* (Princeton, NJ: Princeton University Press, 2007). Rosen puts it quite nicely when claiming that law can be seen as "contributing to the formation of an entire cosmology, a way of envisioning and creating an orderly sense of the universe, one that arranges humanity, society, and ultimate beliefs into a scheme perceived as palpably real" (at 11).

[71] See Jan Klabbers, 'Law-making and Constitutionalism', in Klabbers et al., *The Constitutionalization*, 81–125.

[72] Totalitarian systems and dictatorships would form an obvious exception, but even with respect to those it has been argued that such legal orders are practically unsustainable. The argument is made with great cogency in Fuller, *The Morality of Law*.

2 Exploring the Methodology of Normative Pluralism in the Global Age

Touko Piiparinen

I. INTRODUCTION

This chapter will explore the methodology of normative pluralism, its key concepts and research puzzles. The purpose here is not to provide any cross-cutting methodological framework to be applied in the subsequent chapters, since the aim of the book is to explore the field of normative pluralism from as wide an angle as possible. Therefore, the first chapters of this book, including the present chapter, do not attempt to design any "grand theory" of normative pluralism or a prefixed methodological framework already at the outset of research, which would determine the argumentation in the rest of the book. Instead, this chapter will develop one useful, albeit not exclusive, framework of analysis of normative pluralism, which serves as a potential source of inspiration for research projects on normative pluralism.

Since the subject matter of this book concerns normative pluralism in the *globalized* world, this chapter will restrict its analysis to one specific aspect of the methodology of normative pluralism, namely, the relationship between globalization and the research of normative pluralism. In this regard, the relevant questions are not purely methodological, but also touch upon ontology and epistemology: Why is the research of normative pluralism experiencing a surge, particularly in the global age, and what implications does globalization have for such research? How does globalization increase the plurality of normative orders? Does international law continue to hold monopoly over legitimacy in the normative playing field of international relations, or will its efficacy and legitimacy be challenged by emerging new normative orders? And how should international law be studied in the global age – as a closed, hermetic system or as an open system that constantly interacts with other normative orders?

Ramesh Thakur, whose intellectual background (like the author's) lies in political science and international relations,[1] points out that the relative importance of norms (i.e., nonlegal norms) compared to law depends on the level of analysis:

> The role and efficacy of norms and laws change at different levels of social and political organization. At the local level, norms are far more important. Village society is governed principally by norms – that is what makes it a society. At the national level, in modern societies laws take over from norms.[2]

If one agrees (literally) with Marshall McLuhan's famous thesis that the world is experiencing unification into a "global village"[3] and elaborates it with Thakur's preceding argument, then one must logically infer that globalization signifies a return to the primacy of norms over law, after the exclusive focus on law in the modern age. The relationship between law and norms has developed through a pendulum swing since the premodern age (the primacy of norms), through the modern age (the primacy of law), to the present global age (the primacy of norms). Max Weber's classic text on modernity maintains that the whole modernization project of the nineteenth century rested primarily on the expansion of national law, the rational-legal authority of nation-states, and their bureaucratic form of administration to new geographical territories and societal sectors. This continuous spatial and sectoral spreading out of secular law was often endeavored at the expense of normative pluralism, as evidenced by the way in which Chancellor Otto von Bismarck – Weber's contemporary – wielded a *Kulturkampf* against the Catholic normative order in the name of secularist values.

The twenty-first century marks a new period, in which the expansion of national law is gradually reversed by the emergence of the plurality of normative orders, ranging from secular norms of *lex mercatoria* and regulatory norms of transnational corporations to religious norms, which all gain new importance around the world. Consequently, the pendulum of normativity is shifting from the exclusive focus on monolithic secular law of nation-states implicated in the modernization project back toward "neomedieval" normative pluralism. At the same time, secular international law itself is experiencing increasing pluralization – "internal pluralism," as André Nollkaemper describes in

---

[1] Ramesh Thakur is a professor of international relations and an expert on UN reform.
[2] Ramesh Thakur, *The Responsibility to Protect: Norms, Laws and the Use of Force in International Politics* (London: Routledge, 2011), at 3.
[3] Marshall McLuhan, *The Gutenberg Galaxy* (Toronto: University of Toronto Press, 1962).

his chapter.[4] In order to manage increasingly complex global problems such as climate change, international law is fragmenting into highly specialized strands and subsets, including international criminal law and humanitarian law, which are spreading around the globe.

Methods derived from legal studies might suffice to explore normative pluralism in the "global village," if it were merely a public arena where law prevails as the sole efficacious normative order, and there would not be any need for alternative methodologies – or for this book, for that matter. In reality, however, the global village is a place we cohabit permanently, not a public space like a magistrate that we enter *occasionally* to claim our rights in accordance with law. The global village is also crowded by disparate normative orders that wield real effects on us. In this way, the global village "permeates" us: we experience and feel it not merely in our public role – as law-abiding citizens – but continually and holistically, through our emotions, conscience, culture, tradition, personality, and virtue. In describing that kind of *real* global village, the usual adage to portray globalization – "everything affects everything" – is not sufficient. Instead, it is more apposite to say that the global village is a place where everything is at stake.

Thus, the first and most evident implication of globalization for the study of normative pluralism is the plurality of methodological approaches and the use of interdisciplinary analyses: we need to utilize methodologies from various disciplines of legal, human, and social science, including administrative law, philosophy, sociology, theology, political science, anthropology, and many others. The composition of the present book reflects precisely that kind of holistic methodology: it draws together savoir-faire and expertise from various disciplines, which are necessary to explore and understand fully the current normative playing field of global politics. A model of such a holistic approach to normative pluralism is presented in the Figure 2.1.[5]

There are five additional, and more substantive, methodological implications of globalization for the study of normative pluralism. This chapter will be organized in accordance with these five themes: after the conceptual overview of the term "normative pluralism" in this introductory section, each of the five subsequent sections will systematically examine one of the following recommendations for the study of normative pluralism:

1. Abstraction as a method to move beyond global complexity to normative ordering

---

[4] Chapter 4 in this volume.
[5] I am indebted to Jan Klabbers for developing this figure.

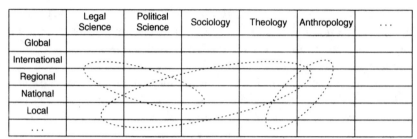

Figure 2.1. Framework of analysis on normative pluralism in the global age.

2. Normative pluralism vis-à-vis spatial and institutional pluralisms
3. Plurality of legitimating authorities underlying normative orders
4. Idea of law as an open system
5. Adoption of critical methodology

Before setting out to explore these themes in more detail, it is useful to define what a norm and a normative order actually mean. The *Oxford Dictionary of Philosophy* defines a norm as a "rule for behavior ... departure from which renders a person liable to some kind of censure."[6] Similarly, Hans Kelsen's classic text defines a legal norm as a "rule expressing the fact that somebody ought to act in a certain way."[7] Both of these descriptions suggest that all norms entail social control "programmed" in them, coupled with actual or potential censure, sanctions, or other types of ramifications, which, in turn, make norms causally efficacious. All norms and their related wholes – normative orders – are causally efficacious, at least *in potentia*.[8] They always cause something, for example, evoking compliance

---

[6] Simon Blackburn, *The Oxford Dictionary of Philosophy*, 2nd ed. (Oxford University Press, 2005), at 281.
[7] Hans Kelsen, *The General Theory of Law and State* (Cambridge, MA: Harvard University Press, 1946), at 35.
[8] "A national legal order," as Kelsen elaborates, "begins to be valid as soon as it has become, on the whole, efficacious, and ceases to be valid as soon as it loses this efficacy." Quoted in Robert H. Jackson, *Quasi-States: Sovereignty, International Relations and the Third World* (Cambridge University Press, 1990), at 34. This chapter agrees with Kelsen's position but argues that its applicability should be widened to encompass all types of normative orders, not

or imposing sanctions on deviant behavior – even though they might not be considered as "good" or legitimate from anyone's point of view. This sets norms apart from values.

The social control and causal efficaciousness of norms and normative orders may actualize in a variety of ways: not only through coercion, punishment, and the use of physical force, but also through soft power, persuasion, and voluntary compliance. The liberalist norms of global market economies wield social control over subjects through rewarding and instigating their consumerist behavior, which, in turn, sustains those economies and reproduces capitalism worldwide. The bureaucratic norms of international organizations, such as notes of guidance and directives issued by senior officials to lower levels of organizational hierarchy, control their employees in order to maximize the efficiency of these organizations. The religious norms of *shari'a* control *ummah* – a community of believers – through creating and building their intersubjective identity. The customary norms of village society control its members through disciplining those who engage in deviant behavior that violates the community's ethos. And finally, law as a distinct normative order controls the behavior of citizens.

In sum, social control and causal efficacy constitute the necessary features of norms and normative orders, but intentional behavior does not. In fact, normative orders are often produced and reproduced through unintentional action and routine behavior, as critical realist philosophers point out.[9] We do not continuously pay attention to the fact that we reproduce certain normative orders through our action. The normative order of the capitalist economy, for example, is not generated by an intentional action of individual laborers and consumers, who work and shop primarily to sustain their families and to maintain a certain standard of living, not to sustain the global system of capitalist economy; yet, that is the inexorable result of their action.

In legal and political sciences, the actual or potential social control is widely considered to constitute an intrinsic part of *legal* norms. This viewpoint is encapsulated in Thomas Hobbes's famous adage, "Where there is no common power, there is no law."[10] Hobbes's position is shared by John Austin and Hans Kelsen.

---

just legal ones: social control forms an integral part of all norms, not just national or international law, and makes them causally efficacious.

[9] As Roy Bhaskar puts it, "people do not marry to reproduce the nuclear family or work to sustain the capitalist economy. Yet it is nevertheless the unintended consequence (an inexorable result) of, as it is also a necessary condition for, their activity." Roy Bhaskar, *The Possibility of Naturalism: A Philosophical Critique of the Contemporary Human Sciences* (Brighton: Harvester Press, 1979), at 44.

[10] Quoted in Hedley Bull, *The Anarchical Society: A Study of Order in World Politics* (New York: Columbia University Press, 1977), at 129.

For Austin, law is essentially the "command of the sovereign," while Kelsen also views law as a "coercive order." According to Kelsen, what distinguishes law from other social and normative orders, for example, from religious and moral norms, is the *coercive* capacity of law.[11] Here, Kelsen reproduces the "Grotian" philosophical tradition[12] by strictly separating law from other types of norms.

The preceding examples demonstrate that the contemporary legal and political sciences have been characterized by a strict separation between legal norms and other types of norms and normative orders since Grotius's classic texts of the seventeenth century. As a result, the mainstream literature tends to overlook the fact that *all* kinds of normative orders, not just legal ones, have a degree of causal efficiency – only in different forms, as demonstrated previously. The social control wielded through national and international law may sometimes be more visible and tangible than, say, the social control of a community's customary norms in that the latter affect through habitual behavior, while the former typically manifests itself in physical coercion such as arrest warrants, detentions, criminal proceedings, penalties, and other accountability measures. Yet, also less visible forms of social control wielded through other normative orders, for example the standard setting of bureaucratic norms, can sometimes be as powerful as direct physical compulsion associated with law.

Because of the prevalence of the Grotian tradition and its fixation on the separation between law and other normative orders, the importance of normative pluralism has thus far been downplayed in legal and social sciences. The ignorance of the causal efficacy of pluralistic normative orders – and the consequent failure to appreciate the increasing importance of normative pluralism – appears rather paradoxical in light of the empirical evidence, which shows that normative orders wield substantial powers on individuals and groups in the era of globality and the strict separation between law and other normative orders is thus artificial and misguided. This, in fact, may be conceived of as one implication of globalization for normative pluralism: *all* normative orders, not just legal ones, entail some kind of social control and causal efficiency, when "social control" is understood to entail more than mere coercion and punishment, for example, legitimacy and persuasion.

II. ABSTRACTION AS A METHOD TO TRANSCEND GLOBAL COMPLEXITY TO NORMATIVE ORDERING

Although the introductory section already outlined some substantive suggestions for the research of normative pluralism, for example, the adoption of

---

[11] See Kelsen, *The General Theory*.
[12] The "Grotian tradition" will be examined in more detail later in this section.

the plurality of methodological approaches and the acknowledgment of the causal powers of pluralistic normative orders, this chapter will now begin systematically to analyze five specific methodological implications of globalization for normative pluralism. This section will present one useful, albeit not exclusive, methodological tool to study normative pluralism in the global age, namely, abstraction.

Setting aside the political implications of Karl Marx's accounts, his classic text *Grundrisse* devised the original method of abstraction that is frequently and widely applied in contemporary social science. According to Marx, abstraction leads from the chaotic conception of the whole (*Vorstellung*) such as "population" to ever more simple concepts (*Begriff*) concerning parts of that whole, such as "social classes." The second methodological move then combines these abstracted parts to form a reorganized whole: "I had finally arrived at the population again," as Marx describes the second move, "but this time not as the chaotic conception of a whole, but as a rich totality of many determinations and relations."[13]

The method of abstraction described previously remains relevant and applicable in the global age, perhaps even more so than ever before. Although the globalized world at first sight seems a highly complex and "disarrayed" normative playing field, where everything affects everything, it is possible to explore and discover normatively structured elements (e.g., normative orders) in that complexity by means of abstraction. The abstracted parts of global complexity could be normative orders, which, in turn, combine to form normative pluralism in globalization. The double move of abstraction could thus be captured in the following formula: global complexity (a whole) → normative orders (abstracted parts) → normative pluralism (a reorganized whole).

The importance of the method of abstraction described earlier is accentuated by the fact that much of the existing literature on globalization tends to be restricted to the level of global complexity, without exploring the deeper ontological level composed of orderly structured elements and mechanisms, for example, normative orders, which underlie that complexity. As a result, the overall picture of globalization remains rather chaotic and superficial. In this regard, apposite examples include John Urry's famous account *Global Complexity*[14] and the usual metaphors of "fluidity" and "mobility"[15] that are widely applied to describe globalization. These accounts are correct to point out that the global world order is constituted by disaggregated, scattered,

---

[13] Karl Marx, *Grundrisse: Foundations of the Critique of Political Economy* (rough draft) (Harmondsworth: Penguin, 1973), at 100.
[14] John Urry, *Global Complexity* (Cambridge, UK: Polity, 2003).
[15] John Urry, *Mobilities* (Malden, UK: Polity, 2008).

loosely coupled, and constantly changing centers of political power, which interact in a seemingly chaotic manner and generate unpredictable outcomes. These characteristics breed the confusing and bewildering picture of "global (dis)order" around us. However, it is necessary to go beyond the descriptive level of global complexity and explore those normative orders that underlie that seemingly anarchical and complex world, because only then is it possible to understand the real dynamics and mechanisms of globalization.

Globalization is always, to a greater or lesser degree, beyond our direct control. However, transcending the surface level of global complexity by means of abstraction allows us to realize that globality, like any other ordered thing, can be *managed*, despite the fact that it cannot necessarily be *controlled* or even *governed* by anyone. As Thomas Risse pointedly argues, "[W]e discuss 'managing globalization' rather than altering its course radically."[16] Risse's viewpoint could be elaborated here by stating that globalization can, and should, be conceived of as composed of normative orders, which can be explored and even utilized to "manage global governance," although their combined net effect in the bigger picture of globalization may at first sight appear contingent, complex, haphazard, and uncontrolled. In fact, global governance would not be possible in the first place without normative ordering of some sort.

III. EMBEDDEDNESS OF NORMATIVE PLURALISM IN THE PLURALITY OF PLURALISMS

This section will argue that normative pluralism in the global age should not be understood as a stand-alone concept, separate from developments in other sectors of global society, particularly global governance. That is because normative pluralism is "embedded" in a wider phenomenon of pluralization generated by globalization, which triggers and generates pluralisms in all fields of social life, including cultural and political ones. Pluralism characterizes virtually everything in global society – instruments and constitutive parts of global governance, as well as spaces and locations in which globalization generates effects. For the sake of conceptual clarity, the following analysis will define and examine various forms of pluralism, which all relate to normative pluralism in one way or the other.

Spatial pluralism refers to a process in which the fibers of globalization cut across national borders, bringing together diverse political, normative, and

---

[16] Thomas Risse, 'Social Constructivism Meets Globalization', in David Held and Anthony McGrew (eds.), *Globalization Theory: Approaches and Controversies* (Cambridge, UK: Polity, 2007) 126–47, at 137.

cultural orders that previously existed separated in nation-states. Amartya Sen describes this process by noting that globalization opens up the "empirical fact of pervasive human diversity."[17] Spatial pluralism creates possibilities for both cooperation and conflicts, including the potential eruption of violent clashes between disparate normative orders that were previously disconnected, isolated, and protected by geographical, normative, and political barriers. Therefore, effective regulatory mechanisms are needed to coordinate and manage the ensuing clashes between normative orders. In this context, "global governance" serves as one "regulatory mechanism" of crisis management: its primary intention is not to establish a hierarchical global government, but to provide sufficient crisis management tools, capacities, and control between clashing normative orders.

For example, the global expansion of the normative order of international criminal law, including the Rome Statute system and the International Criminal Court (ICC), has speeded up the issuance of international warrants of arrest against the perpetrators of mass atrocity crimes *across the globe*. But this development may stand in diametrical opposition to the requirements of locally efficacious normative orders. For example, the issuance of the indictment of the ICC against the Sudanese president Omar Hassan Al-Bashir in March 2009 was challenged on the grounds of *shari'a*, the Islamic law, applied in Sudan. This reflects a norm conflict between international law and local religious norms.

Normative orders as such may outdate globalization, but they existed in "solitary confinement" because of physical, political, and other barriers. Previously, nation-states functioned as "containers of pluralism,"[18] as the normative belt of state sovereignty and the sheer physical distance confined normative orders in those entities, impeding their interactions. Thus, normative pluralism was in existence, but only *in potentia*, because it was held back by the overarching metanorm of state sovereignty, as well as the absence of global technologies to create lines of communication between normative orders. Presently, the lid of the nation-state container is opened by the penetrating fibers of globalization, enabling connections between normative orders. The process of globalization thus "opens up" normative orders embedded in nation-states by unlocking their mutual interactions.

---

[17] Quoted in Andrew Hurrell, 'Power, Institutions, and the Production of Inequality', in Michael Barnett and Raymond Duvall (eds.), *Power in Global Governance* (Cambridge University Press, 2005) 33–58, at 36.
[18] This term is derived from Andrew Hurrell, *On Global Order: Power, Values, and the Constitution of International Society* (Oxford University Press, 2007), at 28.

As Anthony Giddens describes the emergence of spatial pluralism in global society, "Globalisation refers essentially to that stretching process, in so far as the modes of connection between *different social contexts or regions* become networked across the earth's surface as a whole."[19] More specifically, globalization is both an effective and enabling cause of normative pluralism. In the latter sense, globalization reveals, realizes, releases, actualizes, and triggers interactions between normative orders that had remained locked since the establishment of the Westphalian sovereignty of nation-states in 1648, as explained previously. Globalization also functions as an effective cause of pluralism, creating and generating new normative orders and their constellations.

Globalization implicates not only the multiplicity of interacting normative orders and groups located in different territories, which is encapsulated in the term "spatial pluralism" described previously, but also the multiplicity of those actors and mechanisms that aim to implement global governance. The latter aspect of pluralism could be termed *institutional pluralism*. In the existing literature on global governance, institutional pluralism alludes to "complex global governance," which emerges as a result of the shift from state-centrism to multicentrism in international relations, that is, from the system of homogeneous nation-states to a more complex and diversified constellation of transnational regimes aimed at tackling global problems."[20]

In the restrictive understanding, "institutional pluralism" indicates only an increasing number of institutions emerging in the world arena. David Held and Anthony McGrew's account, which derives the definition of global governance from the report of the Commission on Global Governance,[21] represents this restrictive viewpoint. According to their view, global governance means "a set of pluralistic arrangements by which states, international organizations, international regimes, non-governmental organizations, citizen movements and markets combine to regulate or govern aspects of global affairs."[22] This definition provides merely a descriptive "skeleton" of global governance: it describes only the quantitative aspect of institutional pluralism, without specifying or assessing any qualities thereof.

---

[19] Anthony Giddens, *The Consequences of Modernity* (Cambridge: Polity, 1990), at 64. Emphasis added by author.

[20] See, for example, Raimo Väyrynen, 'Norms, Compliance, and Enforcement in Global Governance', in Raimo Väyrynen (ed.), *Globalization and Global Governance* (Lanham, MD: Rowman & Littlefield, 1999), 25–46, at 27.

[21] Commission on Global Governance, *Our Global Neighborhood: The Report of the Commission on Global Governance* (New York: Oxford University Press, 1995).

[22] David Held and Anthony McGrew, *Globalization/Anti-Globalization: Beyond the Great Divide*, 2nd. ed. (Cambridge, UK: Polity, 2007), at 191.

Fred Halliday provides a more substantive account of institutional pluralism that provides "flesh" around the conceptual skeleton of global governance outlined by Held and McGrew. Halliday envisages not only an institutional setting of global governance but also a common objective for its various parts. Halliday defines global governance as "a set of interlocking but separate bodies which share a common purpose."[23] However, this definition is also problematic in that seemingly altruistic pleas for a "common purpose" of global governance may serve as the fig leaf of selfish political interests pursued by individual members of international society. This observation, in turn, already points to another recommendation, namely, the necessity to adopt critical methodology to explore and expose the real political interests of those actors that adopt the metanarratives of "global governance" or "global government." This chapter will later examine in more detail the use of critical methodology in the study of normative pluralism.

The term commonly used by political scientists to describe the current international system is "multipolar world." On the one hand, the term aptly connotes that the world order premised on the sole superpower, which emerged in the immediate aftermath of the cold war, is gradually shifting to one where emerging economies, notably China, Russia, India, and Brazil, are projecting increasing power in international politics along with the United States. However, the description "multipolar world" also appears insufficient in terms of the overall ontology of world politics: in addition to states there are other kinds of actors that wield growing influence, over and beyond great powers. These actors include nongovernmental, international, and regional organizations, as well as multiple global networks promoting global initiatives. Thus, the term "multipolar world" is no longer consistent with the realities of world politics, in which globalization is increasingly replacing the nation-state, the centerpiece of the old international relations (IR) theory, with new bases of authority and power.

Some IR theorists, including Andrew Hurrell, who represents the English school, attempt to reconcile the traditional focus on nation-states with the changing realities of global politics. With that aim, Hurrell develops the model of the "triple anchorage of states," which argues that state policies are determined not only by governments but also by transnational civil society, the international political system, and the global capitalist economy.[24] Other IR theorists devise completely new conceptualizations and theories

---

[23] Fred Halliday, 'Global Governance: Prospects and Problems', in David Held and Anthony McGrew (eds.), *The Global Transformations Reader: An Introduction to the Globalization Debate*, 2nd. ed. (Cambridge, UK: Polity, 2003) 489–99, at 489.

[24] See Hurrell, 'Production of Inequality', at 33.

of world politics. Andrew Jones calls the emerging system of global politics "polyarchic,"[25] implying that the international system is a much more diversified and fragmented one than the "multipolar world."

Similarly, James N. Rosenau terms the globalized world a "bifurcated system," which differs from the whole Westphalian world order in that the key interacting units of international relations are no longer nation-states. The bifurcated system consists of "two worlds of world politics ... one an interstate system of states and their national governments that has long dominated the course of events, and the other a multicentric system of diverse types of other collectivities that has lately emerged as a rival source of authority."[26] Rosenau proceeds to argue that the bifurcated system of world politics is not static, but made up of "proliferating centres of authority,"[27] including official and unofficial ones.

The preceding theories are mainly restricted to describing the material side of world politics. However, Rosenau's theory also entails a normative account of the bifurcated world order, which appears particularly interesting for the subject matter of this book. Rosenau claims that global politics is based on a "vast multiplicity of SOAs [spheres of authority] that collectively constitute a new global order."[28] SOAs may derive their power not only from legal prerogatives, commands, and other types of direct control wielded by official actors, such as governments, but also from their legitimacy, credibility, and ability to evoke the *compliance* of people.[29] This means that SOAs can mobilize people to political action by mere persuasion, rather than compulsion.

For this book, Rosenau's preceding insights imply that normative orders, like SOAs, can derive their powers from legitimacy, the allegiance of people, and power of persuasion, not from material power alone. With the help of these reflections on spatial and institutional pluralism, it is possible to elaborate the meaning of "normative pluralism" applied here: *normative pluralism* could be understood as the plurality of normative orders that have the potential to mobilize individuals or groups not only through compulsion but also by evoking their compliance. One apposite example of the way in which normative orders can exercise power is *fatwa*, a religious directive issued by Islamic clerics.

---

[25] See Andrew Jones, *Dictionary of Globalization* (Cambridge, uk: Polity, 2006), at 102.
[26] James N. Rosenau, 'Governance in a New Global Order', in Held and McGrew (eds.), *The Global Transformations Reader*, 223–34, at 225.
[27] Ibid.
[28] Ibid., at 227.
[29] Ibid. In the existing literature, compliance is typically associated with legitimacy. Thomas M. Franck, for example, defines legitimacy as a "property of a rule or rule-making institution which itself exerts a pull towards compliance on those addressed normatively." Thomas M. Franck, *The Power of Legitimacy among Nations* (Oxford University Press, 1990), at 16.

Fatwa has the potential to mobilize subjects to global action anywhere in the world through persuasion, rather than direct force or control. It also emerges from a clearly delineated normative order composed of religious norms that can be used for various purposes, including political manipulation.

According to Giddens, globalization has the potential to disembed norms and social relations from local contexts and to transform and reconstruct them at the global level. As Giddens argues, "Expert systems are disembedding mechanisms because, in common with symbolic tokens, they remove social relations from the immediacies of context."[30] Global technologies, such as the Internet, can function as such disembedding mechanisms that remove social relations and norms from local contexts and make them applicable to wider distances of space and time. For example, the Internet has the potential to establish a virtual community of believers and to transform *fatwa* (a religious directive) from a locally valid norm to a global norm. In the process, also the meaning and purpose of *fatwa* are crucially changed.

In this way, *fatwa*, like any other normative artifact, can be disembedded from local contexts and reconstructed in new settings through global technologies. Globalization has facilitated the emergence of what Olivier Roy terms the "internet virtual *ummah*,"[31] that is, a community of believers connected through the Internet. The emergence of the virtual *ummah* also entails drawbacks. Through the virtual *ummah* rootless minority Muslims living in Europe, excluded by the majority populations, can imagine the globe as a whole and anchor their identities in the perceived global cause of Islamism against unbelievers. In this way, old concepts and norms like *fatwa* incepted in local communities not only become applicable to subjects in a wider geographical area but may also attain a wholly new meaning at the global level.

At the level of local communities, *fatwa* typically serves the purposes of indigenous dispute settlement or mediation mechanisms. But when *fatwa* is disembedded from the local context and elevated to the global level – to form part of the virtual *ummah* described by Roy – it may serve a completely different function, such as global jihad. *Fatwa* no longer serves a communal function, but a global one, and provides an instrument through which Muslims can be mobilized – and manipulated – to direct action. In short, globalization has the potential to *transform* norms through disembedding processes. *Fatwa* also provides a perfect example of the way in which new centers of authority

---

[30] See Giddens, *The Consequences of Modernity*, at 28.
[31] Olivier Roy, *Globalised Islam: The Search for a New Ummah* (London: Hurst & Company, 2004), at 183.

emerge in the age of globalization, ranging from nongovernmental organizations to religious and charismatic authorities. The next section will in more detail explain this "pluralization" of legitimate authorities in globalization.

IV. THE PLURALITY OF LEGITIMATING AUTHORITIES

This section will argue that any research project on normative pluralism should address, or at least acknowledge, the plurality of legitimating authorities and power bases from which normative orders emerge. While globalization "opens up" the plurality of normative orders, as described in the previous section, it simultaneously increases the plurality of their underlying power bases and legitimating authorities. In this way, Weber's theory of pluralistic authorities incidentally gains new importance in the global age.

Weber's classic text, which was originally developed to describe and explain social relations in modernity, identifies three basic legitimations of domination: traditional, charismatic, and legal. The first of these justifications appeals to ancient beliefs and habitual orientation, and it was typically applied by patrimonial princes and patriarchs. Charismatic authority, in turn, is based on the popularity of a leader stemming from his/her personal gift and from the widespread confidence of the people in his/her heroism, revelation, or other unique personal qualities. Finally, Weber defines the third base of legitimation, namely, legality, which denotes the "belief in the validity of legal statute and functional 'competence' based on rationally created *rules*. In this case ... obedience is expected in discharging statutory obligations."[32]

In the global age, Weber's theory seems more pertinent than ever. Even his argument on the charismatic authority seems relevant in today's world politics. Interestingly, Weber put both a prophet and a political demagogue in the same category (charismatic leaders), in terms of the main basis of their authority. This classification still appears relevant in the age of globality, although today the charismatic authority of politicians is associated more with their disguised rationality than with religious revelation. Political leaders tend to portray themselves as rational actors whose authority is mainly derived from legality, that is, from their capacity and propensity to act in accordance with the statutory obligations of national and international law. But in reality that *appearance* of rule-abiding behavior may constitute a façade that hides other intentions of their political decisions.

---

[32] Max Weber, 'Bureaucracy', in H. H. Gerth and C. Wright Mills (eds.), *From Max Weber: Essays in Sociology* (London: Routledge, 1948), at 79.

Western constituencies may, for example, have faith in the argument made by their political leaders that humanitarian interventions aimed at protecting civilians from genocidal regimes in faraway countries are committed as "humanely" as possible, without collateral victims and human suffering. Such a confidence is founded on the (occasionally unfounded) belief that the political leaders act as rational technocrats, who can put global technologies, such as precision-guided munitions and satellite imagery, into effective use and thus prevent the collateral casualties of military interventions. According to this technocratic belief, the humanitarian outcomes generated by military interventions, including the protection of civilians from tyrannical governments, by far outweigh the risks involved in such operations. But during the actual conduct of these operations such a belief often turns out completely misguided, as the operations experience mounting casualties. David Rieff aptly summarizes this overconfidence in global technology by pointing out that our self-image as global managers and architects of the human future has actually itself been a major cause of human suffering.[33]

The need to acknowledge the plurality of legitimating authorities behind normative orders and to examine them critically concerns not only Western societies but also non-Western ones. In the present book, Timo Kallinen, for example,[34] demonstrates that African witchcraft norms arise not only from charismatic authorities invoking enchantment and magic but also from traditional rules. In the case in point here, the acknowledgment and differentiation between relevant legitimating authorities – charismatic and traditional – enable one to realize that witchcraft norms actually serve an important societal function in local communities, namely, the building of "social fabric," that is, unity, between individual members of those communities. This realization, in turn, will challenge the stereotypical Western viewpoint, in which African witchcraft norms are typically understood as quite irrational, useless, and objectionable.

Inspired by Weber, IR theorists have already set out to develop detailed analyses of pluralistic legitimating authorities and their powers in global politics. Raimo Väyrynen points out that political power in the globalized world is inherently diffused and diversified: "In the multicentric world power not only is dispersed, but it also assumes more forms than the traditional power analysis suggests."[35] One of the most influential models to illustrate the diffusion of power in global politics is provided by Michael Barnett and Raymond

---

[33] David Rieff, *A Bed for the Night: Humanitarianism in Crisis* (London: Vintage, 2002).
[34] See Chapter 8.
[35] See Väyrynen, 'Norms, Compliance, and Enforcement', at 27.

Duvall. They identify four main bases of authority in global politics: compulsory, institutional, structural, and productive. The first, compulsory, form of power outlined by Barnett and Duvall reflects the traditional political realist position, according to which power emanates from "relations of interaction that allow one actor to have direct control over another."[36] Productive power, in turn, refers to the capacity to generate intersubjective meanings, that is, the "socially diffuse production of subjectivity in systems of meaning and signification."[37]

The influence of national and international law is mainly derived from compulsory and institutional powers outlined earlier, which enable state authorities, national and international bureaucracies, to wield direct control over individuals, for example, through the issuance of indictments, warrants of arrest, sentences, and penalties. However, normative pluralism encompasses not only law but also other normative orders, which can emerge from the compulsory, institutional, structural, and productive power bases. Therefore, the ontological horizon of research on normative pluralism should be extended to cover all the four sources of power identified by Barnett and Duvall.

The empirical evidence shows that globalization empowers particularly those actors that can *produce "intersubjective meanings,"* convey those meanings intelligibly to other actors, organize them around a norm, and, eventually, mobilize their support for a global cause enshrined in that norm. In short, globalization brings to the fore productive power and increases its relative importance compared to that of the two other forms of power. Even if a norm was not backed up by sanctions mechanisms like legal norms typically are (compulsory power), it can be highly effective though its capacity to provide meaningful global causes to subjects (productive power). Such global causes that have recently emerged on the normative playing field of international relations range from the responsibility to protect principle, aimed at the protection of civilians from genocidal regimes, to *fatwa* regulating global jihad.

Hence, productive power is the key to explaining and understanding the causal powers and effectiveness of normative orders in current global politics, although the outcomes of productive powers may be more implicit and intersubjective, and less tangible and visible, than the material powers of compulsory legal norms of international and national law. In this regard, *fatwa* again provides an illustrative example: religious authorities can effectively mobilize individuals and groups around the world to global action by producing (and

---

[36] Michael Barnett and Raymond Duvall, 'Power in Global Governance', in Barnett and Duvall (eds.), *Power in Global Governance*, 1–32, at 3.
[37] Ibid.

manipulating) meanings and people's identities, without direct compulsion, coercion, or sanctions mechanisms. Through the productive power of globalization, these new centers of power and authorities can be influential, only in a different form than nation-states with their armies and law with its enforcement mechanisms. Even if normative orders did not possess the material clout of compulsory and institutional mechanisms to wield direct control over subjects, which national and international law usually has, they can be influential by exerting productive power – by generating new meanings, identities, and modes of action.

V. THE IDEA OF LAW AS AN OPEN SYSTEM

The first sections of this chapter explained the way in which the age of globalization signals a return to a medievalist, and seemingly chaotic, normative playing field, in which individuals and groups no longer organize around one prevailing and homogeneous set of rules, namely, national law, but are subjected to a plurality of various normative orders and can choose which of these they want to pursue. This section will elaborate that pluralization in more detail, arguing that one major implication of globalization for normative pluralism relates to the (re)conceptualization of law as an open system.

Methodologically, the aforementioned "neomedievalist" moment of globalization implicates a departure from the long-held tradition of legal positivism premised on the exclusive focus on law as the centerpiece of legal and social science. For centuries, the prevailing legal positivist approach has emphasized that law holds the primacy over other normative orders. The positivist worldview has also portrayed law as a closed system, which should be insulated from other normative orders. These positivist tenets date back to the seventeenth century, notably to Hugo Grotius's classic *De Jure Belli ac Pacis Libri Tres* (1625).

Setting aside the huge historical importance and merits of Grotius's account, what appears striking in his theory is the focus on a singular normative order, namely, *secular* international law, which is viewed as a closed system. That hermetic system is isolated from its normative surrounding, impeding its interactions with other normative orders, including religious ones. Robert H. Jackson, a famous theorist of political pluralism of the English school, assesses Grotius's classic texts:

> His primary aim ... was to establish rules of war and peace that were immune to theological and political controversy and depended only on the faculty of reason – like mathematics – and could therefore secure acceptance from

all statesmen. Natural law was the only certain foundation for such rules: it was the voice of human reason and would exist even if God did not (*etiamsi daremus non esse Deum*).[38]

Grotius's account has left a deep (or lasting) footprint on both legal and political science and on contemporary practice of international law. Yet, Grotius's heritage has also been complicit in producing and reproducing the conception of international law as an "autopoietic," that is, self-referential, system, to use Niklas Luhmann's terminology here. Since Grotius's time, international law has been widely understood to constitute a hermetic system. To apply Jackson's earlier description here, law has been viewed as "immune to" other normative orders, including religious and political ones.

In the present global age, the Grotian tradition is challenged by globalization, which inevitably opens up the closed system of law, leading to its intertwinement with the plurality of other normative orders. Globalization generates interactions and networks of interdependence not only between individuals, groups, and organizations but also between diverse normative orders in which people – "global citizens" – are embedded. The material tools and vehicles of these increased interactions between normative orders are global trade, telecommunications, and other types of global technologies that transcend state borders. As a result, law (both international and national law), like any other normative order, is subjected to interaction and "enmeshment" with normative orders.

Thus, international and national law can no longer – conceptually or causally – be isolated from normative pluralism as in Grotius's times. This also means that law is forced to *communicate* with other normative orders, which constantly challenge and transform the rationality of law. Law is currently confronted on several fronts by different normative orders, including religious and customary ones. These orders may entail requirements that stand in direct opposition to those enshrined in secular legal norms. Just as globalization has (in the political sphere) opened up the hermetic container of sovereign nation-state through intrastate networks of interdependence and global trade, challenging its rationality – raison d'état – which previously called for unquestioned loyalty to the pursuit of national interest, so too globalization has (in the normative sphere) opened up the hermetic container of secular international law and subjected it to the plurality of normative orders, which constantly put its rationality into test, and sometimes into question.

---

[38] See Jackson, *Quasi-States*, at 57.

The transformation of law from a closed system to the open one described earlier breeds *self-contradictions* of law. On the one hand, law by definition works on the basis of binary codes such as legal/illegal and permitted/prohibited, the logic of which is impervious, unresponsive, and "blind" to the rationality of other normative orders, even to moral considerations. In fact, such autopoiesis is a necessary precondition for law to be able to produce and reproduce itself – that is, to exist. On the other hand, the entanglement of law in thickening cobwebs of normative orders also exposes its substance and rationality to critique emanating from the rationalities of different other normative orders and morality. Law is expected to be responsive to other normative orders and to act responsibly in relation to "global citizens." Yet at the same time it cannot survive without a degree of autopoiesis and isolation: the complete openness of law would undermine its consistency and ultimately transform it into just another, ordinary normative order. These mutually contradicting goals of law – openness and autopoiesis – occasionally make its operations and adjudications paradoxical in the global age.

An illustrative example of the self-contradictions of law is provided by the so-called cartoon crises that erupted during the first decade of the twenty-first century. The publishing of twelve caricatures of Prophet Mohammad in a Danish newspaper on 30 September 2005, their reprinting in other European tabloids, and their distribution through global media by January 2006 became a Muslim concern worldwide. They instigated violent demonstrations and clashes, raids against European embassies, desecration of flags, the issuing of religious death sentences in the form of *fatwas*, and, eventually, casualties.[39] The first reaction of Western politicians and legislators was defensive, aiming to protect the freedom of expression enshrined in national and international law. But at the same time they were forced to *respond* to the demands of Islamic actors to incorporate the "blasphemy norms" – norms aimed at promoting the respect for religious customs – in national and international law. Theoretically, then, the cartoon crises involved a norm clash, or tension, between religious and legal norms, which generated a strong political pressure against Western actors to *transform* national and international law.

---

[39] The cartoon crisis reemerged two years later on 19 August 2007 when a regional newspaper, *Nerikes Allahanda*, based in Örebro, Sweden, published a drawing of Prophet Muhammad depicted with the body of a dog, drawn by a Swedish artist, Lars Vilks. However, the Swedish cartoon controversy, unlike the Danish one, did not escalate into a conflict of global proportions. See, for example, Göran Larsson and Lasse Lindekilde, 'Muslim Claims-Making in Context: Comparing the Danish and the Swedish Muhammad Cartoons Controversies', (2009) 9 *Ethnicities* 361–82, at 362.

For example, in the immediate aftermath of the cartoon crises the Organization of the Islamic Conference (OIC, today termed the "Organisation of Islamic Cooperation") initiated a diplomatic campaign at the UN aimed at incorporating the concept of "defamation of religions" in the terminology of international law, as well as in the parlance of multilateral diplomacy and human rights discourse. The first reaction of Western decision makers to that initiative, as to the cartoon crises in general, was to challenge it on account of the legal principle of freedom of expression enshrined in national and international law. In fact, the Western actors viewed that the fundamental moral principle underlying the whole normative order of secular international law, namely, individualism, was at stake.[40]

Consequently, Western politicians and legislators found themselves in a paradoxical decision-making situation, in which they were forced to play a double role: on the one hand, their action was primarily premised on their self-image as guardians of the secular international law and the sanctity of its underlying principles, but they also simultaneously needed to act responsively and responsibly in relation to their Islamic counterparts, for they could not simply ignore the concerns raised by the Islamic communities, including those situated in their own constituencies. At the UN, this communication, and the consequent "compromise," between the two normative orders – the requirements of Islamic law and those of secular international law – led to the emergence of new soft law on the defamation of religions, such as General Assembly resolutions,[41] but not to new binding international conventions or to the alteration of existing ones. Hence, international law was only partially, or superficially, transformed.

---

[40] For example, the EU Presidency Explanation of Vote from 20 November 2007 states, "The European Union does not see the concept of 'defamation of religions' as a valid one in a human rights discourse.... International human rights law protects primarily individuals in the exercise of their freedom of religion or belief, rather than the religions as such." *EU Presidency Explanation of Vote – United Nations 3rd Committee: Combating Defamation of Religions.* Summary: 20 November 2007, New York – Explanation of Vote by Ms. Sara Martins, Counsellor, Permanent Mission of Portugal to the United Nations on behalf of the European Union, United Nations 62nd Session of the General Assembly, 3rd Committee, 'Combating Defamation of Religions – L.35 Explanation of vote'. http://www.eu-un.europa.eu/articles/en/article_7543_en.htm (accessed 10 April 2009).

[41] More specifically, it led to the adoption of the resolution 'Combating Defamation of Religions' by the General Assembly. The tenth operational paragraph of the resolution "emphasizes that everyone has the right to hold opinions without interference and the right to freedom of expression, and that the exercise of these rights carries with it special duties and responsibilities and may therefore be subject to limitations as are provided for by law" (UN Doc. A/RES/62/154, 6 March 2008, p. 3).

VI. ADOPTION OF CRITICAL METHODOLOGY

The Oxford Dictionary of Philosophy defines "pluralism" as the "general tolerance of different kinds of thing," which also occasionally involves "general suspicion of a notion of 'the truth.'"[42] The first, descriptive, part of the definition appears quite self-evident, while the latter part is more evaluative and revealing: it implies that "normative pluralism" is not merely an analytical concept but a critical and practice-oriented *approach*. It demonstrates that normative pluralism calls for a *critical*[43] or suspicious, stance on norms and "truth" in general. In this way, normative pluralism logically opposes value monism as well as hegemonic and suppressive discourses that (mis)use the notion of truth as a pretext to dominate and subjugate alternative worldviews regarded as "less truthful."

In the field of international law, legal scholars have already adopted critical methodologies to reveal drawbacks of legal pluralism in the global age. These disadvantages include accountability deficit caused by the increasing application of soft law, regulatory norms, and other nonbinding rule making in globality, which do not necessarily arise from representative legislatures but from more informal settings and from unofficial organizations.[44] Critical approaches to globalization have also been applied in the field of social science. Piiparinen (2011), for example, argues that globalization raises renewed interest in critical theory derived from the Frankfurt school, which emphasizes that knowledge in policy making is produced and reproduced to reinforce power structures and to serve hidden political interests. This type of critical methodology should also be applied on global governance, including its seemingly benevolent and harmless discourses and techniques of global governance and "objective" information produced by the practitioners and experts of global governance.[45]

---

[42] See Simon Blackburn (ed.), *The Oxford Dictionary of Philosophy*, 2nd ed. (Oxford University Press, 2005), at 281.

[43] The term "critical" applied here is derived from the Frankfurt school, which posits that critical methodologies do not apply to the "Other" (a research object) alone, but they also encompass reflection on the normative and moral premises of one's own social behavior. One of the most prominent theorists of the Frankfurt school, Theodor W. Adorno, has famously termed such a methodological approach as "reflection of the mind on its own failure." Quoted in Rolf Tiedemann, 'Introduction: "Not the First Philosophy, but a Last One": Notes on Adorno's Thought', in Rolf Tiedemann (ed.), *Can One Live after Auschwitz? A Philosophical Reader* (Stanford, CA: Stanford University Press, 2003), xi–xxvii, at xv.

[44] See, for example, Nico Krisch, 'The Pluralism of Global Administrative Law', (2006) 17 *European Journal of International Law*, 247–78.

[45] Touko Piiparinen, 'Empirical Closure in the Democratic Peace Theory', (2011) 2 *Helsinki Review of Global Governance*, 20–4.

However, the mainstream literature on globalization is characterised by "globoptimism." Francis Fukuyama's influential theory posits that globalization generates prosperity, peaceful convergence, and accommodation among its interacting units, actors, and normative orders. These points per se are unlikely to prompt any counterarguments. However, his theory is underlain by ontological shallowness and uncritical acceptance of "global goods" offered by the liberalist world order to humanity. Fukuyama's famous hypothesis of the "end of history"[46] takes for granted the ideal of Kantian perpetual peace and the deterministic expansion of democracy and liberal democratic values worldwide.

There is widespread agreement among political scientists on the *substance* of Fukuyama's arguments regarding the global trend toward liberal democracy. Moreover, there is agreement on the liberal peace thesis, which points to the decreased likelihood of democratic societies to resort to war compared to authoritarian regimes. However, critics point out that the *process* of democratization projected by Fukuyama is far too deterministic and mechanistic.

First, Fukuyama declares, somewhat prematurely, an "unabashed victory of economic and political liberalism."[47] Robert O. Keohane criticizes Fukuyama's idea of the inevitable and unproblematic expansion of liberal democracy by arguing that "it seems unlikely not only that democracy will sweep the world but also that all states will be governed by stable institutions, even authoritarian ones. Hence, a global security community is unlikely soon to come into existence."[48] Second, Fukuyama's method leads to a somewhat simplistic and uncritical presumption of peaceful convergence among normative orders generated by globalization. As Andrew Hurrell notes, the liberalist theory endorses "too cosy a view of institutions and of global governance."[49]

Perhaps the most influential critique of Fukuyama's hypothesis is outlined in Robert Kagan's *The Return of History and the End of Dreams*.[50] Although the neoconservative overtone (particularly in the latter part of Kagan's book) has been widely criticized by reviewers,[51] Kagan perfectly captures the antithesis of the liberalist theory of globalization: "The great fallacy of our era has been the belief that a liberal international order rests on the triumph of ideas

[46] Francis Fukuyama, *The End of History and the Last Man* (London: Penguin, 1992).
[47] Francis Fukuyama, 'The End of History?', (1989) 16 *National Interest* 3–18, at 3.
[48] Robert O. Keohane, 'Sovereignty in International Society', in Held and McGrew (eds.), *The Global Transformations Reader*, 147–61, at 157.
[49] See Hurrell, 'Production of Inequality', at 33.
[50] Robert Kagan, *The Return of History and the End of Dreams* (New York: Alfred A. Knopf, 2008).
[51] See, for example, Edward Luce, 'The Neo-cons' Black and White World', *Financial Times*, 2 June 2008.

and on the natural unfolding of human progress."⁵² On the one hand, Kagan's own account is no less restrictive than Fukuyama's theory in that it reproduces the old political realist worldview of international relations, which reduces most of global politics to strategic and material interactions among states, ignoring developments taking place at other levels of analysis such as civil society actors – or indeed normative orders.

On the other hand, Kagan persuasively analyzes the weaknesses and shortcomings of the Fukuyamian idea of normative and political monism in current world affairs. Kagan pointedly notes that *political pluralism* has remained as the key feature of international relations. It has, in fact, been amplified since the unipolar world order of the 1990s. Alongside the United States, the economic powerhouses of Russia, China, Europe, Japan, India, and Iran wield greater influence in international politics,⁵³ and South Africa and Brazil could also be added in the list. Kagan continues to argue that the main driving forces of the liberalist world order, namely, the integration of nation-states, interactions of cultures, free commerce, and global communications, have not radically changed the world in terms of *material* power, realpolitik.⁵⁴

Kagan's theory is partly supported by empirical evidence. The emerging new political, economic, and normative centers such as Russia, China, and the OIC (Organisation of Islamic Cooperation) have recently formed a powerful "axis of sovereignty"⁵⁵ at the UN, particularly at the Human Rights Council and at the Third Committee of the General Assembly. Their aim is to reinvigorate the principles of sovereignty, noninterference, and nonintervention in world politics. This newly emerged group of "sovereigntists" increasingly challenges Western great powers that used to portray themselves as "norm-entrepreneurs"⁵⁶ of human rights norms and humanitarian intervention in the 1990s. From the Fukuyamian liberalist viewpoint, this development

---

[52] Kagan, *The Return of History and the End of Dreams*, at 102.
[53] Ibid. at 4.
[54] However, it is argued here contra Kagan that the interconnecting fibers of globalization *have* changed the world in terms of *normative pluralism* by increasing interactions and conflicts among diverse normative orders.
[55] Quoted in Richard Gowan and Franziska Brantner, *A Global Force for Human Rights? An Audit of European Power at the UN* (London: European Council on Foreign Relations, 2008), at 3.
[56] The term "norm-entrepreneur" is used by researchers of international relations theory to describe those states that developed and implemented the idea of humanitarian intervention in the 1990s, particularly the United States and Western European powers. See, for example, Nicholas J. Wheeler, 'The Humanitarian Responsibilities of Sovereignty: Explaining the Development of a New Norm of Military Intervention for Humanitarian Purposes in International Society', in Jennifer M. Welsh (ed.), *Humanitarian Intervention and International Relations* (Oxford University Press, 2004) 29–51, at 48.

is somewhat surprising: the growing political pressure and critique wielded by the "axis of sovereignty" against the global expansion of Western-centric values of liberal democracy and human rights do not fit with Fukuyama's hypothesis that the export of Western liberalist values to the global South would be imminent and unproblematic.

Although Kagan's arguments mainly concern political pluralism, they also have important implications for normative pluralism: along with the plurality of political power centers there is the plurality of normative orders that these great powers represent and promote. On the one side, liberal theorists promote the ideal of *normative monism* based on the Western values of liberal democracy and the ultimate harmony (or, in Fukuyama's terms, the "end of history") derived from that monism as the teleological end state of globalization. Critical theorists, on the other side, argue for the continuing relevance of *normative pluralism* in global politics (at least in the short term and midterm) and the need to engage in discussion with the nonliberal "Other," over the boundaries of normative orders in global governance.

This chapter argues for a middle position – an empirically informed methodology that could acknowledge both benefits and drawbacks of globalization that exist *in potentia*, and that could allow a given case study to show their *actual* "balance" in any particular situation. Globalization has the potential to generate not only positive effects, such as increasing interconnectedness, but also negative ones, including conflicts. To demonstrate the Janus-faced nature of globalization here, it is useful to present one illustrative empirical example of the globalization process, namely, the case of the Kingdom of Saudi Arabia.[57] Two of the perhaps most important milestones of the globalization process in Saudi Arabia to date have been the accession of the kingdom to the World Trade Organization (WTO) in 2003 and its connection to the Internet in 1999. In many ways, these two developments initiated, or at least crucially intensified, the globalization process by enabling the encroachment of secular normative orders into the territory of the kingdom, including the regulatory norms of international trade law, which went into effect as Saudi Arabia joined the WTO.

On the positive side, globalization has allowed Saudis to access high-tech entertainment and luxury retails, which are readily available in multinational enterprises operating in the kingdom. "The beauty of globalization," as Philippe Legrain aptly describes, "is that it can free people from the tyranny

---

[57] The case study is chosen here on account of the fact that the Saudi kingdom has been viewed as one of the most closed societies in the world, which therefore provides an interesting case study from the viewpoint of the enmeshment of normative orders through globalization.

Exploring the Methodology of Normative Pluralism 59

of geography."[58] For inhabitants of Riyadh one of the greatest benefits of globalization has been the availability of the same industrial products and luxury goods that consumers in affluent Western economies can get their hands on, ranging from Carrefour's dairy products to Chevrolet Suburban vans.

On the other hand, globalization has simultaneously opened the floodgates of Western lifestyle and values, including consumerism and secularism, to the global South and to the Arab world. As a result, two macrolevel normative orders are set in a collision course in Saudi Arabia: the liberalist lifestyle involving free markets, competitiveness, commodification, and the Western secular worldview, on the one side, and the indigenous normative system premised on the Wahhabi interpretation of *shari'a*, on the other.[59] In sum, globalization works on two fronts: it creates new possibilities for material prosperity and certainly releases us from the tyranny of geography, as Legrain points out. But it simultaneously opens the door to another kind of tyranny, namely, the secular normative order. The latter may implicate clashes between indigenous and inborn normative orders, including religious customs, and the secular normative order, at least in the beginning of the globalization process.

VII. CONCLUSIONS: THERE ARE ALWAYS TWO STORIES TO TELL ABOUT GLOBALIZATION – AND A THIRD IN THE MAKING

The present literature on globalization entails two "metatheories" to explain and understand globalization. One group of authors, which could be termed "global utopians," emphasizes that globalization enables radically new forms of cooperation and may soon lead to the Kantian liberalist peace, as envisaged by Fukuyama.[60] The other group, "global apologists," considers that globalization does not mark an "epochal change" but actually constitutes a continuum to those social, economic, and political developments that began already in the modern age, such as bureaucratization. For example, Paul Hirst

---

[58] Quoted in Jones, *Dictionary of Globalization*, at 155.

[59] Wahhabism alludes to a worldview that promotes the strict interpretation of Islam. It constitutes the cornerstone of the religious, legal, cultural, and political orders of the Saudi kingdom.

[60] Martin Albrow, for example, maintains that globalization displaces modernity by radically decentring the state, economy, and culture and thus constitutes an "epochal change" in world politics. Albrow identifies five ways in which globalization crucially differs from modernity: the global environmental consequences of aggregate human activities, the loss of security where weapons of mass destruction have potential or actual global destructiveness, the globality of communication systems, the rise of a global economy, and the reflexivity of globalism, where people and groups of all kinds refer to the globe as the frame for their beliefs. Martin Albrow, *The Global Age: State and Society beyond Modernity* (Cambridge, UK: Polity, 1996), at 2.

and Kevin Robins argue – contra Martin Albrow – that globalization deepens economic interdependence but is not historically unprecedented, since it neither supersedes nor displaces the sociohistorical conditions that preceded it.[61] Global apologists thus typically envision a more realistic teleological cause of globalization.

The aforementioned two "metatheories," or "metastories," of globalization are actually derived from the classic literature on globalization. The global utopian worldview is captured in McLuhan's famous, and optimistic, image of the "global village" (1962), which predicts both the shrinking and unification of the world in the wake of new technological advances, for example, those relating to the global media. The global apologist viewpoint, in turn, is associated with a much gloomier metaphor outlined by Karl Jaspers. He noted in 1955 that the term "globalization" intrinsically dates back to the dropping of the atomic bomb in 1945, which also implicates the globe as a whole, only in a different – more destructive – way. It alludes to the possibility of the extinction of the human race by means of nuclear weapons. While atomic bombs and nuclear arsenals implicate the globe as a whole *in potentia*, the Second World War illustrates the actual – imminent – unity of the world in a similarly ominous way.[62] Globalization has the potential to generate a "butterfly effect," in which an event happening in one part of the world can lead to another event far away through a chain reaction, but it also entails a similar possibility, in which nuclear races and conventional wars are triggered through the domino effects of military alliances.

According to the *global utopian* viewpoint, globalization signals not only a radically new period, or epoch, in human history, but also a promising one: it enables new avenues of cooperation and possibilities of human emancipation. Anne-Marie Slaughter, for example, envisages that globalization opens up direct communication channels, information sharing, and cooperation among subunits of states, for example, between sectoral ministries. In this way, it enables effective decision making on global problems such as climate change, as officials of sectoral ministries can engage in direct decision making and bypass arduous political wrangling at the intergovernment level. In Slaughter's vision, the international politics of unitary sovereign states is increasingly replaced with global politics of disaggregated states, in which the component parts and institutions of states interact principally with

---

[61] See Jones, *Dictionary of Globalization*, at 6–7; Kevin Robins, 'Encountering Globalization', in Held and McGrew (eds.), *The Global Transformations Reader*, at 241.

[62] "It was the Second World War," as Jaspers elaborates, "which first accorded full weight to the contribution from everywhere, to the globe as a whole. The war in the Far East was just as serious as that in Europe." Quoted in Albrow, *The Global Age*, at 75.

Exploring the Methodology of Normative Pluralism 61

their foreign counterparts across national borders.[63] Whenever a global problem emerges, experts embedded in sectoral ministries around the world can directly communicate with each other in order to tackle that problem, bypassing the usual realpolitik at the interstate level, where the first and foremost concern of sovereign states is to pursue their national interests, not to solve a functional global problem at hand.

Slaughter admits that "the disaggregated state sounds vaguely Frankenstinian, a shambling, headless bureaucratic monster."[64] However, she immediately reverses that line of argument by saying, "In fact, it is nothing so sinister. It is simply the rising need for and capacity of different domestic government institutions to engage in activities beyond their borders, often with their foreign counterparts"[65] This hypothesis leads Slaughter to paint an optimistic picture of global politics, in which the new world order arises from the horizontal and vertical networks of global governance:

> "World order" ... describes a system of global governance that institutionalizes cooperation and sufficiently contains conflict such that all nations and their peoples may achieve greater peace and prosperity, improve their stewardship of the earth, and reach minimum standards of human dignity.[66]

Slaughter unveils the "Frankensteinian" side of globalization but never fully develops it – in fact, it is dropped from her argumentation altogether. Nevertheless, that picture haunts a reader and invokes the *global apologist* viewpoint, which portrays a world order where asymmetrical relations among unequal partners and functionally differentiated systems prevail. Slaughter is correct to point out that individuals working in the sectoral ministries of disaggregated states tend to accept one another as equal partners for cooperation. But normative orders, which are ignored in Slaughter's theory,[67] do not necessarily operate under the same terms of reference and may not even communicate with each other at all. Worse still, individuals and groups embedded in those normative orders may be unequal and silenced by their contemporaries.

To apply Niklas Luhmann's system theory, normative orders are, in the worst scenario, self-referential (i.e., autopoietic) systems, organized along structural

---

[63] Anne-Marie Slaughter, *A New World Order* (Princeton, NJ: Princeton University Press, 2004).
[64] Ibid., at 12.
[65] Ibid.
[66] Ibid., at 15.
[67] Normative orders exist over and beyond relations between governments and sectoral ministries, which are the centerpiece of Slaughter's theory.

and functional lines.[68] In other words, they are self-referential, self-producing, self-legitimating, and self-contained systems. These systems usually establish their terms of reference and communication channels internally (between the constitutive parts of each system), but not externally (between the systems). Therefore, normative orders, like any other type of autopoietic systems, are essentially "blind and deaf" to each other, and their representatives are silenced across the boundaries of those systems.

From the viewpoint of Luhmann's theory, the possibility of the Frankensteinian headless bureaucratic monster cannot be excluded at the outset of any particular research project on globalization and normative pluralism. As opposed to Slaughter's utopian vision of sectoral ministries tackling functional problems in the global age, the global order is, at least potentially, an unruly constellation of self-contained and autopoietic functional regimes and normative orders. Agents embedded in autopoietic normative orders, unlike those working for sectoral ministries, often treat their counterparts in other normative orders strategically – as instruments for the pursuit of their own global causes, or as targets of those global causes that need to be silenced. From the viewpoint of the autopoietic system of the virtual *ummah*, for example, the objects of global interventions are infidels, not equal members of global society who are entitled to enjoy the same respect and integrity as any other global citizen.

The "blindness" of autopoietic systems is also illustrated by the way in which legal interventions initiated by the Rome Statute system (an autopoietic system) overlook the detrimental side effects of these global interventions on its external realm. These side-effects include the potential disruptions or collapse of international assistance to vulnerable groups who are in need of lifesaving assistance in fragile states. These may result from the issuance of criminal indictments against political leaders and elites of those states, who may (mis)use the humanitarian lifeline to their citizens in conflict zones as a bargaining chip to avoid facing trial.

In the case in point here, the inequality and unfairness pertaining to the functional differentiation of global politics lie in the fact that the side-effects of the application of international criminal law hit hardest the *most vulnerable* groups and individuals in weak, fragile, and failed states, who lack means to resist the tyranny of their political leaders or to stop external legal interventions, the combination of which may seal their fate. In the case of Sudan, for example, the primary target of the ICC indictment – President Omar Al-Bashir – remains at large, while the most affected groups of the issuance of

---

[68] Niklas Luhmann, *Social Systems* (Stanford, CA: Stanford University Press, 1995).

that indictment were actually the poorest parts of the population in Darfur, whose humanitarian relief was temporarily suspended as a result of the indictment. This predicament will be examined in more detail in Chapter 9 concerning the side effects of the working of the ICC and possible avenues to avert them.

This chapter has argued for a *via media* approach to globalization – an empirically informed critical methodology that could navigate between the utopian and apologist positions. The critical approach acknowledges the potential Frankensteinian scenario of global politics but nevertheless rejects the wholesale apologist viewpoint and instead aims to seek ways of human emancipation in any particular case. A researcher of normative pluralism should recognize the failure of normative orders, which combine to constitute the global order, to establish sufficient lines of communication with one another. Yet, this acknowledgment does not mean that we should succumb to the Frankensteinian reality of functional (in)difference. On the contrary, we should explore solutions to solve dysfunctional interactions between normative orders and to elaborate concrete visions of human emancipation that are applicable in local contexts.

PART II

NORMATIVE PLURALISM IN LAW

3 Peaceful Coexistence: Normative Pluralism in International Law

Jan Klabbers and Silke Trommer

I. INTRODUCTION

It is almost inevitable, in a globalizing world where time and space compress, that states (and other international actors) end up being confronted with different obligations under international law, stemming from different treaties or, more broadly still, from different sources of the law. Examples are not hard to find and sometimes come to dominate the headlines. A celebrated instance in the early 1990s was the *Soering* case, which revolved around a conflict between the United Kingdom's obligation (under a bilateral extradition treaty) to extradite a fugitive to the United States, and its simultaneous obligation under the European Convention on Human Rights not wittingly to expose the individual concerned to inhuman or degrading treatment: his punishment in the United States could have been the death penalty, which would have resulted in many years on "death row."[1] More recently, the EU was confronted with the situation that under environmental agreements, it would have to apply the precautionary principle, whereas under trade law, applying the precautionary principle could have resulted in an unlawful import ban of biotech products.[2] The twenty-seven member states of the EU are, since 2008, extremely puzzled about how to give effect to UN-ordained sanctions: they are obliged under the UN Charter to give effect to sanctions, yet these sanctions are imposed with some disregard for human rights, which renders them impossible to reconcile with the human rights standards prevailing in the European Union (EU).[3]

---

[1] See *Soering v. United Kingdom*, judgment of the European Court of Human Rights, application no. 14038/88, 7 July 1989, reproduced in 98 *International Law Reports* 270.
[2] See *European Communities – Measures Affecting the Approval and Marketing of Biotech Products*, WT/DS291.292.293, 29 September 2006.
[3] As the CJEU held in case C-402/05 P, *Kadi v. Council and Commission* [2008] ECR I-6351.

In short: normative conflicts are a pervasive phenomenon in international law, and given the fact that treaties and other legal instruments are concluded in increasing numbers, and given the circumstance that customary international law is often fairly quickly said to exist (far more quickly than, say, half a century ago),[4] it stands to reason to expect that normative conflicts will only increase. That is not to say the topic is novel: it has captured the attention of international lawyers, however intermittently, for a century or so.[5] Still, if the literature is anything to go by, normative conflict is experiencing a boom: over the last two decades, quite a few relevant studies have been published.[6]

This chapter will discuss how international law aims to solve (or dissolve) conflicts between competing obligations. Before doing so, however, a number of conceptual issues need to be addressed. Thereafter, we will systematically discuss treaty conflicts, conflicts between treaty provisions and rules of customary international law, and conflicts between hard rules and so-called soft law. The general argument will be that international law has little or no means at its disposal to resolve serious normative conflicts, but that the reasons for this vary depending on whether the conflict involves two treaties, a treaty rule and a customary rule, or a "hard" rule and a "soft" rule. This implies that international law has learned to live with "internal" normative pluralism (i.e., normative pluralism within the normative control system of international law itself).[7] Moreover, the absence of workable conflict norms is not necessarily a bad thing: it opens up space for pragmatic and diplomatic solutions.

[4] See Robert Y. Jennings, 'What Is International Law and How Do We Tell It When We See It?' (1981) 37 *Schweizerisches Jahrbuch für Internationales Recht*, 59–88.
[5] Classic contributions include Quincy Wrights, 'Conflicts between International Law and Treaties', (1917) 11 *American Journal of International Law*, 566–79; Charles Rousseau, 'De la compatibilité des normes juridiques contradictoires dans l'ordre international', (1932) 39 *Revue Générale de Droit International Public*, 133–92; Hans Aufricht, 'Supersession of Treaties in International Law', (1951–2) 37 *Cornell Law Quarterly*, 655–700, and C. Wilfred Jenks, 'The Conflict of Law-making Treaties', (1953) 30 *British Yearbook of International Law*, 401–53.
[6] See, in addition to the works mentioned elsewhere in this text, Guyora Binder, *Treaty Conflict and Political Contradiction: The Dialectic of Duplicity* (New York: Praeger, 1988); Joost Pauwelijn, *Conflict of Norms in International Law: How WTO Law Relates to Other Rules of International Law* (Cambridge University Press, 2003); W. Czaplinski and G. Danilenko, 'Conflict of Norms in International Law', (1991) 22 *Netherlands Yearbook of International Law*, 3–42; Seyed Ali Sadat-Akhavi, *Methods of Resolving Conflicts between Treaties* (Leiden: Martinus Nijhoff, n.y.), Wilhelm Heinrich Wilting, *Vertragskonkurrenz im Völkerrecht* (Cologne: Carl Heymans Verlag, 1996); Jan Mus, *Verdragsconflicten voor de Nederlandse rechter* (Zwolle: Tjeenk Willink, 1996), and Martti Koskenniemi, *Fragmentation of International Law: Difficulties Arising from the Diversification and Expansion of International Law: Report of the Study Group of the International Law Commission* (Helsinki: Erik Castren Institute, 2007).
[7] On the concept of normative order, or normative control system, see Jan Klabbers and Touko Piiparinen, 'Normative Pluralism: An Exploration', Chapter 1 in this volume.

II. CONCEPTUAL ISSUES

Before being able to discuss the way international law aims to solve conflicts among various rules of international law, some clarity needs to be created as to what exactly such rules are and what they entail. A first useful question to ask is whether a rule invoked is actually a legal rule or whether it is something else. This can come about in (at least) two ways. On the one hand, international law recognizes some norms – the word is used here in the most generic sense possible – as foundational, but do they also qualify as legal rules? An example might be the norm of "sovereign equality": this is one of the cornerstones of the United Nations, but is it a legal rule of the sort that can be violated? In everyday language such is often suggested, but somehow it would be awkward to approach a court claiming that one's sovereign equality has been violated. Perhaps the better view is that such a norm functions as shorthand for a bundle of more concrete rules or principles (think of nondiscrimination, e.g., or nonintervention). Hence, in what follows, we will by and large avoid discussing such foundational norms.

On the other hand, the question of what qualifies as law also presents itself when "soft law" instruments may be at stake or agreements that are deliberately kept away from the realm of law (sometimes referred to as "politically" or "morally" binding).[8] Examples are abundant and range from Memoranda of Understanding on technical cooperation to such politically significant documents as the 1975 Helsinki Final Act or, possibly, the 1941 Atlantic Charter. This is not the place to develop a stand on the issue[9]; suffice it to say, for the moment, that there may be merit in not excluding a priori conflicts involving such documents. Whether they are deemed to constitute hard or soft law, they have in common that they aim to regulate the behavior of actors and, where appropriate, demand from actors that they change the way they act.[10]

A second question to ask is whether the legal rules invoked actually are rules of international law or whether one or both of them form part of some other body of legal rules. It is, for instance, by no means implausible to suggest that

---

[8] On the sources of international generally, see, e.g., G. J. H. van Hoof, *Rethinking the Sources of International Law* (Deventer: Kluwer, 1983); G. M. Danilenko, *Law-making in the International Community* (Dordrecht: Martinus Nijhoff, 1993); Alan Boyle and Christine Chinkin, *The Making of International Law* (Oxford University Press, 2007); Jean d'Aspremont, *Formalism and the Sources of International Law* (Oxford University Press, 2011).

[9] One of us has done so elsewhere and reached the conclusion that speaking of agreements that are binding not in law but still somehow binding is not terribly plausible. See Jan Klabbers, *The Concept of Treaty in International Law* (The Hague: Kluwer, 1996).

[10] See, e.g., Anthony Aust, *Modern Treaty Law and Practice*, 2nd ed. (Cambridge University Press, 2007).

the principles on the basis of which states can claim jurisdiction are mostly rules (or concepts) of domestic law, falling within a broad range of possible approaches that are all deemed acceptable according to international law. One might thus construe this as follows: international law leaves it to states to decide whether to prosecute individuals for crimes committed abroad and, if so, on what basis. All international law does is create this facility; it does not itself prescribe that prosecution should take place but does not prohibit it either.[11] In jurisprudence, this is sometimes referred to as the distinction between rights and powers: is the possibility to prosecute a foreigner the result of a right or rather the result of a power? If the latter, is it still part of international law if international law leaves states free to decide or not? And what, to make matters even more complicated, would Hohfeld say, given his classic division of law into rights, powers, obligations, immunities, and liabilities?[12]

The third question is related: how far do legal rules actually go? It is clear that the prohibition of torture forbids the commission of torture; it is less clear whether incitement to torture or facilitating torture is also covered. This may come to play a role precisely in normative conflicts: a state confronted with an extradition request from a state where torture is practiced may not, when extraditing, itself commit torture, but it may facilitate torture or become complicit in acts of torture, as the *Soering* example mentioned previously suggests.[13] On a strict definition (torture is only the act itself), such a state may have no conflicting obligations; on a broader construction, however, it has.

Fourth, there is the complicated issue of how to treat EU law. On the one hand, the EU is a creation of international law; on the other, its legal rules are deemed to be part of the domestic law of its twenty-seven member states. Hence, for those twenty-seven, a conflict between their obligations under EU law, on the one hand, and those under some other international legal rule, on the other, can be classified as either a treaty conflict or a conflict between international and domestic law.[14]

---

[11] There is a nuance here, of course: some treaties lay down the rule 'aut dedere, aut judicare'; such a rule creates an obligation to prosecute in certain circumstances, and it is at least arguable that the Genocide Convention creates an obligation of this kind as well.

[12] See Wesley N. Hohfeld, *Fundamental Legal Conceptions as Applied in Judicial Reasoning* (New Haven, CT: Yale University Press, 1964 [1913–17]).

[13] Strictly speaking, the death row phenomenon in the United States that was at issue in *Soering* was deemed to constitute 'inhuman or degrading treatment', not quite amounting to torture but regulated in the same article of the ECHR that also prohibits torture. Usually, torture and inhuman and degrading treatment are seen as involving a sliding scale of unacceptable behavior. See Clare Ovey and Robin C. A. White, *Jacobs and White European Convention on Human Rights*, 3rd ed. (Oxford University Press, 2002), 58–66.

[14] On this, see Jan Klabbers, *Treaty Conflict and the European Union* (Cambridge University Press, 2008).

This points to a fifth consideration: much conflict can be recharacterized as involving a wrongful act. In a sense, this often assumes what requires proof: the statement that the Security Council, for example, can be held accountable for a human rights violation presupposes that the states concerned are no longer confronted with a conflict, but that the conflict has been solved and the council has been held in the wrong.[15]

Sixth, it is useful to realize what norms can potentially enter into conflict with one another. Easily imaginable is the possibility of treaty conflict, where a state has obligations to another state or group of states that it cannot reconcile with its commitments to yet another state. The same is highly unlikely to happen with respect to customary international law, though: a state cannot be considered to have a customary obligation to A that is irreconcilable with – or even just different from – its customary obligations toward B. Such is by definition excluded, as a state cannot engage in two different practices on the same topic at the same time – let alone in two contradictory practices. A state cannot consistently seize foreign fishing vessels in times of war, and simultaneously refrain from seizing foreign fishing vessels in times of war, to use the matter at the heart of one of the more celebrated cases.[16] If it nonetheless does so, either there is no fixed customary rule or the state involved consistently breaches the customary rule. Obviously, while doing so may over time result in a new rule,[17] the coexistence of contradictory rules of customary international law is a logical impossibility, save perhaps upon the loosest definition of custom. What could happen is that several regional customs exist side by side, but even then, this cannot result in a single state's being subject to two conflicting rules of customary international law: participating in one regime by definition means that the state concerned must be regarded as a "persistent objector" to the second regime.

By the same token, mutatis mutandis, conflicts involving general principles of law are unlikely to happen.[18] Partly the reason is the same: a state cannot blow hot and cold. It cannot both act in good faith and act in bad faith at the same time or, to refer to a more concrete principle, it cannot simultaneously be a judge in its own cause and not be a judge in its own cause. This then makes it well-nigh impossible for a state to be under two

---

[15] See, e.g., Antonios Tzanakopoulos, *Disobeying the Security Council: Countermeasures against Wrongful Sanctions* (Oxford University Press, 2011).

[16] See *The Paquete Habana*, 175 US 677 (1900).

[17] In Merrills's memorable phrase, "Law breaking is an essential method of law making." See John G. Merrills, *Anatomy of International Law* (London: Sweet and Maxwell, 1968), at 8.

[18] The seminal work is still Bin Cheng, *General Principles of Law as Applied by International Courts and Tribunals* (Cambridge University Press, 1987 [1953]).

conflicting obligations derived from general principles. What is more, though, principles tend to be open-ended at any rate and tend to have, as legal philosophers suggest,[19] a relative weight, which renders them, if and when they do conflict (in the sense that different principles can demand different activities and therewith lead to potential conflicts), eminently suitable for "balancing" or for an analysis in terms of proportionality.[20] Either way, conflicts involving general principles of law are not likely to occur in ways that interest us at present – at least not as reflecting underlying fundamental value struggles.

Other conflicts may be likely to occur as a hypothetical proposition, but not very likely to occur in practice. Presuming, for example, that unilateral declarations[21] can be seen as sources of international obligations (a position the World Court has endorsed on several occasions), it would follow that such declarations can be irreconcilable with a state's commitments either under a treaty or under customary international law. While it may not always be obvious which state can claim a right under a declaration issued by another state,[22] nonetheless normative conflicts are a distinct possibility.

Finally, some attention needs also to be paid to the distinction between the status of norms and their contents. To give an example: *jus cogens* norms are generally considered to be nonderogable, and of higher status or rank than ordinary treaty provisions. There are, however, also norms that are nonderogable but, quite possibly, not *jus cogens*. In such a case, there is a treaty providing that the parties may not derogate; it is doubtful, however, whether the same also applies to nonparties. Surely, it would be awkward to apply the European Convention's nonderogability regime to, say, Bolivia, although it is by no means implausible to state that Bolivia would be bound by *jus cogens* provisions. Sometimes (quite often, perhaps) the categories overlap, but not invariably so. In the light of Security Council sanctions regimes, for example, it might not be all that easy to argue that the rule "no punishment

---

[19] See in particular Ronald Dworkin, *Taking Rights Seriously* (Cambridge, MA: Harvard University Press, 1978), and Robert Alexy, *Theorie der Grundrechte* (Frankfurt am Main: Suhrkamp, 1994 [1985]).

[20] For a general (and somewhat rosy) study of the latter, see David Beatty, *The Ultimate Rule of Law* (Oxford University Press, 2004).

[21] See generally Eric Suy, *Les Actes Juridiques Unilatéraux en Droit International Public* (Paris: LGDJ, 1962).

[22] In *Nuclear Tests*, the ICJ seemed to suggest that statements are valid *erga omnes*, but it remains doubtful whether, say, Iceland could have insisted that France stop its testing on the basis of the French declarations in the absence of any link to the conflict. And if that is so, then the *erga omnes* nature of the statements would not create *erga omnes* obligations. See *Nuclear Tests Case* (Australia v. France), [1974] ICJ Reports 253.

without law"[23] forms part of *jus cogens*, yet under the ECHR it is held to be nonderogable.[24]

III. TREATY CONFLICTS (AND HOW TO SOLVE OR DISSOLVE THEM)

A. *The Law (Such as It Is)*

One of the more obvious examples of normative conflict in international law is the occurrence of conflicting treaty obligations. Yet, obvious as it may sound, it is by no means self-evident what constitutes a treaty conflict, and while international law has developed some rules to apply to them, it is by no means evident which rules must be applied and in which situations. Problems arise when a new treaty contains obligations that cannot be reconciled with those under an existing treaty. While the relevant (or the most relevant, perhaps) provision of the Vienna Convention seems to limit its regime to treaties dealing with the same subject matter, this must not be taken too literally[25]: the most salient conflicts are those between provisions dealing with the same subject matter but laid down in treaties on sometimes radically diverging topics such as trade versus environment or security versus human rights. It seems highly unlikely that the International Law Commission, drafting the Vienna Convention, intended to exclude the most salient conflicts from the convention's reach, and indeed there is no evidence in the drafting of the convention to back up such a proposition. Hence, the better view is not to focus on treaties dealing with the same topics, but rather on whether actors can simultaneously give effect to provisions laid down in different treaties.[26]

In the easiest situation two states, having concluded an earlier bilateral treaty, conclude a new one. In such a situation, article 30 of the Vienna Convention specifies, without too many problems, that the new one shall prevail,[27] and

---

[23] See article 7 ECHR.
[24] The leading study of those sanctions regimes is Jeremy Matam Farrall, *United Nations Sanctions and the Rule of Law* (Cambridge University Press, 2007).
[25] This is article 30 of the Vienna Convention, which is titled 'Application of Successive Treaties Relating to the Same Subject-Matter'.
[26] So also E. W Vierdag, 'The Time of the Conclusion of a Multilateral Treaty: Art. 30 of the Vienna Convention on the Law of Treaties and Related Provisions', (1988) 59 *British Yearbook of International Law*, 92–111. For the narrow view, see Christopher J. Borgen, 'Resolving Treaty Conflicts', (2005) 37 *George Washington International Law Review*, 573–648.
[27] It is by no means clear, however, how to determine which is the new treaty and which the older, especially when it comes to marking the commencement of obligations under multilateral treaties. See generally Vierdag, 'The Time of the Conclusion'.

doing so makes some political sense. After all, the new treaty embodies the most current form of political concord between those two states; it embodies the most recent political power configuration and is thus bound to command some respect. Hence, the net result is that everyone is happy with applying the later treaty: the parties are happy, because the later treaty is a more accurate and up-to-date reflection of their wishes, and the international system as a whole may happily expect that the treaty will be respected – therewith, the community interest in seeing the *pacta sunt servanda* norm upheld can also be deemed satisfied.

This then is the easy scenario, and with a little slippage it can be applied to all treaties comprising the same parties, since these all follow, by and large, the same model and the same logic.[28] There is, however, a catch. Suppose that a group of fifteen like-minded states decides, in 2011, to conclude a treaty on a compulsory minimum salary, revolving around the provision that all workers in public employment are to be guaranteed a minimal salary. To this end, an international institution is set up, as well as a complicated system to ensure that states where salaries are higher do not suffer from a comparative disadvantage.

Suppose now that the same group of states decides, ten years later, to conclude a new treaty, which leaves the core idea intact but under which teachers and nurses will be excluded: they may earn less than the earlier agreed minimum salary. Under the Vienna Convention, this later treaty will replace the earlier regime, yet it is also clear that something of value is lost. It is precisely this circumstance that prompted Judges Van Eysinga and Schücking to hold, in their separate opinion to the 1934 *Oscar Chinn* case, that a treaty that can be said to create a constitutional regime cannot be replaced by a later one. To them, the *lex prior* warranted protection in such circumstances.[29]

This problem becomes more pronounced when the treaties concerned do not comprise identical parties. In such a case, even with bilateral treaties problems arise: if A has a treaty with B and concludes a later one with C containing an incompatible obligation, it is no good simply to apply the later in time. After all, doing so would disadvantage B for no good reason: B has a treaty with A and should not suffer from A's fickleness or carelessness. That said, C is in rather the same position: it too should not suffer from A's behavior.

---

[28] Under article 59 of the Vienna Convention, moreover, the parties to a treaty can conclude a new treaty to abrogate an older one, providing all of them are involved in doing so.

[29] See the *Oscar Chinn* case, [1934] Publications PCIJ, Series A/B, no. 63. Ironically, the constitutional treaty they sought to uphold was the Berlin Act of 1885, dividing Africa among the European powers. Many nowadays would suggest that such a treaty would itself be incompatible with *jus cogens*.

The Vienna Convention is of not much help here: it specifies that the later in time should be applied except in case of conflict [sic] or, between parties to the same treaty, that their treaty governs their relations. Needless to say, this does little to solve any conflict, resulting effectively in the position that if the conflicting obligations cannot be reconciled, state A has to choose which one to uphold and compensate the losing side. With a fine sense of irony, this has become known as the "principle of political decision."[30]

The Vienna Convention therewith offers little direct solace for those cases where conflicts involve different obligations to different parties, and as a result, several other solutions have been proposed. One is to make more use of the classic principle of the *lex specialis*: special law may derogate from general law.[31] This suffers from a number of drawbacks, however.[32] First, it is not always clear how to determine which treaty is the special one, and which is the general one. One can make such a decision by looking at the subject matter of the treaties or by looking at the circle of parties, but in both cases, the normative consequences may be undesirable. Surely, applying the *lex specialis* rule in case of a conflict involving the obligation to extradite under a bilateral treaty and the obligation not to expose an individual to inhuman treatment under a human rights convention would result in the unpleasant situation that the extradition treaty would prevail. Testing *lex specialis* by looking at the circle of parties would posit the extradition treaty as the special treaty, deserving of priority, and the same result would be reached by looking at the subject matter: an extradition treaty is bound to be more "special" than a general human rights convention and is bound to have fewer parties.

The one way out, then, would be to claim that certain treaties may embody community values and thus should be granted priority in case of conflict, but doing so would invite difficult political discussions on which treaties it concerns and which community values deserve protection. Indeed, ironically perhaps, the Vienna Convention's drafters did their utmost to prevent having to enter into any discussions on substantive values by focusing on treaties not as obligations, but as instruments.[33] The only exception in the Vienna Convention is

---

[30] See Manfred Zuleeg, 'Vertragskonkurrenz im Völkerrecht. Teil I: Verträge zwischen souveränen Staaten', (1977) 20 *German Yearbook of International Law*, 246–76.

[31] For a useful discussion, see Anja Lindroos, 'Addressing Norm Conflicts in a Fragmented Legal System: The Doctrine of *Lex Specialis*', (2005) 74 *Nordic Journal of International Law*, 27–66.

[32] See also Jan Klabbers, 'Beyond the Vienna Convention: Conflicting Treaty Provisions', in Enzo Cannizzaro (ed.), *The Law of Treaties beyond the Vienna Convention* (Oxford University Press, 2011), 192–205.

[33] Partly this found its cause in the circumstance that some formal issues needed codification: think of signature and ratification. More importantly, though, a conception of the treaty as

the reference to *jus cogens*, perhaps accompanied by the repeated references to the object and purpose of treaties – these too can be seen as references to a treaty's substance.[34] In such an intellectual framework, with a focus on the treaty as instrument rather than obligation, a choice to concentrate on community values would have great difficulties fitting in – and that presupposes that any decisions on community values could be reached to begin with.[35]

B. Diversion Techniques

Since the law does not have all that much to say on treaty conflicts and most definitely refrains from providing a one-size-fits-all answer, it should not come as a surprise that courts and policy makers have been looking for alternative ways to settle their disputes about treaty conflicts or at least mitigate the worst consequences thereof. Perhaps the easiest way of coming to terms with treaty conflict is to pretend that none exists. States and their courts, as well as international courts, have become adept at finding all sorts of arguments suggesting that no conflicts exist or, alternatively, to fend off their own legal orders from any outside interference. By now the leading example of such an approach is the decision of the CJEU in *Kadi*, where it held that the implementation of a Security Council resolution by the EU should be done in conformity with EU standards; consequently, since an EU regulation was found wanting on this score, it was (partly) annulled. The circumstance that in doing so the CJEU sponsored the disobedience of its member states when it comes to Security Council resolutions seems to have been of little concern to the Court: the conflict between EU law and UN law, central to the case, was "defined away" by simply ignoring the UN context.[36]

The CJEU has quite a track record by now in doing so. Under the slogan that the task of the Court is to ensure the application of EU law, and nothing else, the Court has opted for a limited array of law to be applied and, most famously, has steadfastly held that it cannot apply WTO law in any direct fashion. While this attitude has political motivations far beyond the scope

---

obligation would have rendered it unavoidable to deal with the consequences of breach, and this was considered too difficult, too vast, and overlapping with the project on codifying the rules on state responsibility (which, as it happened, would come to occupy the International Law Commission for half a century).

[34] And as is well known, the Vienna Convention refrained from providing a list of *jus cogens* norms – precisely because no agreement on such a list could be expected.

[35] It is no doubt for this reason that the Vienna Convention does not even refer to the *lex specialis* maxim: *lex specialis* refers more directly to the substance of treaties than *lex prior* or *lex posterior*, and this is incompatible with the convention's intellectual setup.

[36] See *Kadi*.

of the present chapter,[37] a pleasant side effect of the CJEU's refusal to apply WTO law is that it also does not have to come to terms with possible conflicts between obligations of its members under either EU law or WTO law. And by the same token, but from the other end, the CJEU castigated one of the EU's member states for trying to submit a dispute involving some elements of EU law elsewhere, even if it could be argued that the dispute only marginally involved EU law.[38]

The EU is, however, by no means the only entity operating in such a way as to build fences around its own legal order. Indeed, the hallmark of the so-called fragmentation of international law is precisely that functional regimes apply the law relating to themselves at the expense of competing legal rules. WTO panels are under strict instruction only to apply WTO law and have, thus far, taken this very seriously. While it has been held that WTO law cannot be "read in clinical isolation" from public international law,[39] effectively this is rather what happens: WTO law is applied, and competing rules (stemming from competing regimes) are often effectively ignored.[40] Again then, on this reasoning, there is no identifiable conflict, because the competing part of the equation never enters the judicial decision-making process.[41]

The tendency to do this is universal. Environmental lawyers tend to look no further than environmental law; trade lawyers look no further than trade law, and human rights lawyers tend to put a premium on human rights law. The tendency is also understandable. The various functional regimes form their own epistemic communities[42] and will predominantly have to account

---

[37] See generally Jan Klabbers, *The European Union in International Law* (Paris: Pédone, 2012).

[38] See case C-459/03, *Commission v Ireland (MOX Plant)*, [2006] ECR I-4635. Perhaps as a result, the arbitrators in the *Iron Rhine* arbitration did their utmost to downplay the applicability of EU law to the case before them. See Permanent Court of Arbitration, *Arbitration Regarding the Iron Rhine ('Ijzeren Rijn') Railway* (Belgium/The Netherlands), award of 24 May 2005.

[39] As held by the Appellate Body in *US – Standards for Reformulated and Conventional Gasoline*, WT/DS2/R, 16. The precise scope of the injunction is opaque, moreover, and it could be argued (although not very plausibly perhaps) that 'reading' WTO law and 'applying' it are still two different things. It would go too far to enter into that debate, however.

[40] Note, however, that recently a panel agreed that standards developed outside the WTO context, in fisheries, could be relied on before it (although in the end it also held that the respondent state was justified in departing from those standards). See the panel report in *United States – Measures Concerning the Importation, Marketing and Sale of Tuna and Tuna Products*, WT/DS381/R, 15 September 2011.

[41] Koskenniemi has suggested that one way to mitigate the effects of fragmentation is to sensitize lawyers to the existence of various competing regimes. See Martti Koskenniemi, 'The Case for Comparative International Law', (2009) 20 *Finnish Yearbook of International Law*, 1–8.

[42] The concept of epistemic communities was coined by Peter M. Haas, 'Epistemic Communities and International Policy Coordination', (1992) 46 *International Organization*, 1–35. For a fine application of the role of so-called interpretive communities – a related concept – in

to fellow members of the same epistemic community. The trade lawyer who decides that a trade rule should give way to environmental protection may come in for criticism by his or her own community, whereas the possible appreciation by environmentalists is likely to be less noticeable. Indeed, a clear example is the critical response of the human rights community to the decision of the European Court of Human Rights in *Behrami and Saramati*.[43] In these cases, involving human rights protection against UN mandated governance in Kosovo, the Court argued, in preliminary proceedings, that since the behavior complained of was attributable to the UN, and the UN is not a party to the European Convention, the Court could not decide the case. The human rights community reacted furiously, claiming that this was an affront to human rights and would allow violations to occur with impunity. On the other hand, the decision does leave intact the relevant role of the UN in maintaining peace and security in Kosovo.

In some circumstances, conflict can be defined away by means of harmonious interpretation.[44] This applies especially when treaties do not provide absolute obligations, but obligations within a range, such as an obligation under which a value added tax must be somewhere between 12 and 20 percent of the retail price. In such circumstances, a later treaty listing 17 percent as obligatory falls within the bandwidth and is thus not in any conflict. This may apply to fields such as taxation law, but also private international law. Indeed, in principle it may also be possible to structure agreements on environmental protection and even disarmament in this way: imposing a bandwidth, allowing for quite a bit of discretion on the part of later treaty makers.

If the bandwidth is the invention of treaty drafters, another invention, pioneered by the EU, is that of the so-called disconnection clause.[45] Under this clause, the parties to multilateral agreements agree that some of them may apply different rules in their relations *inter se*. Typically, the EU often insists on such a clause while negotiating agreements to be concluded under auspices of the Council of Europe: the EU thus allows itself (with the consent of its partners) to be disconnected from the multilateral agreement at issue. The practice is not without its critics, and it must be acknowledged

---

international law, see Ian Johnstone, *The Power of Deliberation: International Law, Politics and Organizations* (Oxford University Press, 2011).

[43] See Joined cases *Behrami and Behrami v. France* and *Saramati v. France and others*, decision of 2 May 2007, reproduced in 133 *International Law Reports* 1.

[44] See in particular Pauwelijn, 'Conflict of Norms'.

[45] See generally Constantin P. Economidès and Alexandros G. Kolliopoulos, 'La clause de déconnexion en faveur du droit communautaire: une pratique critiquable', (2006) 110 *Revue Générale de Droit International Public*, 273–302.

that it is mainly possible in those settings where the participation of the EU is required and the EU has the clout to insist on carving out a privileged position.[46]

In addition to treaty makers, courts too have found ways of downplaying the impact of normative conflicts. In particular in the field of human rights, techniques such as "balancing" are well known and generate less discussion than might have been expected. Balancing works, within the human rights fields, by trying to find a workable median between two conflicting rights. On the presumption that rights are not absolute, it might be possible to reconcile my right to practice the trumpet twenty-four hours a day with your right to read Sanskrit poetry in peace and quiet, and one practical way of doing so is imposing a window for my trumpet practices. This renders my right relative (I cannot practice at 2:00 a.m.), and yours too (you might have difficulties concentrating while I'm practicing), but both of us are still reasonably well off: this leave ample opportunity for my trumpet playing as well as your poetry reading.[47]

C. Claiming or Granting Priority

There is one treaty demanding priority, and that is the UN Charter. The UN Charter, in article 103, holds that in case of conflicting obligations, obligations arising under the UN Charter shall prevail, a position confirmed in Vienna Convention article 30. The rationale is obvious: if the UN is to organize collective security and impose sanctions on states, then it would be no good if those sanctions could be undermined by states claiming to have a preexisting commitment to the sanctioned state. Hence, in order for collective sanctions to work, they demand priority, and it is no coincidence that the UN's predecessor, the League of Nations, entertained a similar provision.[48]

By its very nature, though, there cannot be many treaties demanding priority – otherwise, the need would arise to have a rule settling conflicts between priority-demanding treaties, therewith merely shifting the problem. More common, therefore (although not quite common, perhaps), is it to insert a clause granting priority. The leading example here, at least nominally, is article 351 TFEU, which aims to protect the rights of third states under treaties concluded by member states of the EU before they joined the EU.

---

[46] For further discussion, see Klabbers, *Treaty Conflict*, 219–23.
[47] See Dworkin, *Taking Rights Seriously*, and Alexy, *Theorie der Grundrechte*.
[48] An insightful discussion is Rain Liivoja, 'The Scope of the Supremacy Clause of the United Nations Charter', (2008) 57 *International and Comparative Law Quarterly*, 583–612.

The extensive case law of the CJEU suggests that article 351 TFEU may be more about achieving a balance between the European Union interest and the interests of third states than about respect for international law,[49] but nonetheless, the article does entail that the EU cannot simply ride roughshod over preexisting international law commitments of its member states.

It is no accident that provisions to grant or demand priority are fairly uncommon. Treaty conflict is not (yet) a topic that has been internalized by negotiators; most of these know to pay some attention to topics such as (possible) reservations and amendments but have yet to come to think of the relationship between "their" treaty and other treaties in the same terms. More importantly though, the open-ended provisions of the Vienna Convention suggest that there is no easy way out: treaties are, in legal terms, *res inter alios acta*: they are matters between the parties, having a life that only affects their parties. In such circumstances, a treaty among A, B, and C on protecting the environment has, in law, no relationship to a treaty among A, B, and F on trade in hazardous products, or a treaty among B, C, and X on river navigation and management. To demand priority, as noted, is unhelpful unless the treaty concerned (like the UN Charter) aspires to become something of a global constitutional instrument, and even then, there is no room for many treaties demanding priority. And while technically it may be easier to grant priority (as in article 351 TFEU), it takes a strange mind-set to do so: to grant priority means to deemphasize one's own efforts, at least for the time being. It amounts to saying that however important "our" treaty may be, it is not quite as important as other treaties – and that is a mind-set not lightly to be expected among negotiators. Indeed, even the TFEU looks more rosy than it actually is: under paragraph 2 of article 351, member states must do their utmost to eliminate any incompatibilities with earlier agreements, and the Court has maintained a strict line here.[50]

As a result, perhaps the most popular attempt to come to terms with possible treaty conflicts resides in the establishment of conciliation committees or similar institutional devices. In particular in the field of international environmental protection, many treaties envisage the creation of some kind of panel or forum to iron out possible conflicts.[51] In other words: conflicts are channeled back to the world of politics. This is only fitting, of course, as a treaty conflict, in most cases, will derive from a political difference of

[49] See generally Klabbers, *Treaty Conflict*. See also Panos Koutrakos, *EU International Relations Law* (Oxford: Hart, 2006).
[50] See Klabbers, *Treaty Conflict*.
[51] An impressive overview is Rudiger Wolfrum and Nele Matz, *Conflicts in International Environmental Law* (Heidelberg: Springer, 2003).

opinion. Where treaty conflicts arise from clerical errors or unfortunate drafting, a solution can usually quickly be found, but it is precisely where political values clash that conflicts become unsolvable by legal means alone, and in such cases, resort to political organs is nothing less than appropriate.

IV. TREATIES AND CUSTOMARY INTERNATIONAL LAW

A. *What Conflicts?*

Conflicts involving obligations under a treaty and different obligations under a rule of customary international law raise different issues than treaty conflicts per se, but even so, conflict resolution is rarely self-evident. One point to remember is that even against the background of existing customary rules, states generally retain their contractual freedom (barring *jus cogens* considerations). Hence, a treaty departing from a customary rule does not represent a conflict so much but rather manifests a modification between states bound by a customary obligation *inter se*. Put differently, here, the situation is premised on the *lex specialis* rule.

The reverse situation is different, though: it is perfectly possible for a customary practice to grow on the basis of a multilateral treaty. This may not always lead to conflicts (and, indeed, usually does not). The new custom, more likely, is an elaboration of the treaty, often starting out as "subsequent practice" and then solidifying.[52] Such a custom can remain limited to the parties to the treaty but can also spread beyond the circle of parties. Either way, this situation is both quite rare and quite common: it is common for treaties to develop and be regarded as "living instruments"; it is less common to treat this as the formation of customary law.[53]

Matters are most problematic perhaps where the claim is made that a multilateral treaty exists alongside a different customary practice, and that both continue to exist while pulling in opposite directions, or at least do not point in the same direction. The most well-known example of such a claim is heard in connection with the right to use force: the UN Charter allows, narrowly, only for self-defense once an armed attack has taken place, while (so the argument goes) customary international law allows for anticipatory and perhaps

---

[52] See generally Wolfram Karl, *Vertrag und spätere Praxis im Völkerrecht* (Heidelberg: Springer, 1983); Nancy Kontou, *The Termination and Revision of Treaties in the Light of New Customary International Law* (Oxford University Press, 1995).

[53] Just for the record, the situation here differs from that where practice is based on a treaty provision and follows the provision quite closely.

even preemptive self-defense, either by virtue of the *Caroline* doctrine[54] or by virtue of being silent, and therewith permissive.[55]

A general rule concerning conflicts between treaties and customary international law, however, does not exist, neither as a matter of treaty law (and how could it? it would have to meet with the assent of all states) nor as a matter of customary international law. It is generally accepted that treaties can replace custom, and that custom can come to replace treaties, and even that, hypothetically at any rate, treaties and custom can continue to exist side by side. As with treaty conflict, the absence of a general rule suggests that much conflict is resolved by sheer pragmatism.

B. (Dis)solving Conflicts

Along with treaties and general principles, customary rules are formal sources of international law.[56] The normative pluralism inherent in the treaty-custom relationship is of two orders. First, treaties and customary law can create directly contradictory rights or obligations. Where this happens, conflicts need to be solved on a case-by-case basis. The core question is whether the normative force of customary law is such that states cannot contract out of the norm. Obvious examples are the general prohibitions of genocide or torture. Where no *jus cogens* or general rule is breached, the treaty would normally apply as a clear expression of the will of the states to be bound by the rule that the treaty establishes. As certain treaties gain adhesion from more and more states, they may in this way alter the customary law on a given issue over time. Hence, such conflicts pose few specific problems.

Still, the treaty-custom relationship exposes a second kind of normative pluralism in international law. In fact, conceptual differences about how social change comes about mark the international community.[57] This stems from two considerations. First, while constituting formal sources of international law in their own right, treaties are also evidence for state practice and can thus

---

[54] See Abraham D. Sofaer, 'On the Necessity of Pre-emption', (2003) 14 *European Journal of International Law*, 209–26. This refers to a famous incident in 1838, which led to correspondence between the United Kingdom and the United States on the requirements for self-defense and, on one reading, can be interpreted as broader than 1 UN Charter article 5 in that it allows for self-defense against imminent attacks.

[55] See Michael J. Glennon, 'Why the Security Council Failed', (2003) 82 *Foreign Affairs*, 16–35.

[56] Bederman makes a forceful case that custom is an inherent element of legal systems generally. See David J. Bederman, *Custom as a Source of Law* (Cambridge University Press, 2010).

[57] See Oscar Schachter, 'Entangled Treaty and Custom', in Yoram Dinstein and Mala Tabory (eds.), *International Law at a Time of Perplexity* (Dordrecht: Martinus Nijhoff, 1989), at 717–38.

be constitutive of customary law; second, under customary law, unlike under treaties,[58] a violation can over time lead to a new rule.

To grasp the delicate and disputed relationship between treaty and custom, it is necessary to recall quickly the legal nature of customary rules. In essence, customary rules emerge when state practice is accompanied by *opinio juris* in international life. The difficulty arises with establishing general state practice and its so-called psychological element, namely, the conviction of the state to be acting according to an international legal obligation when exercising a specific practice.

In order for a customary rule to exist, there must be a generalized state practice. Although the practice does not have to be universal, states that are particularly affected by the rule should adopt the practice and the practice should be consistent over time. In principle, treaties, decisions of national and international courts, national legislation, diplomatic correspondence, the practice of international organizations, and scholarly writings can all serve as evidence of state practice, and something similar may come to apply to private regulatory practice.

The *opinio juris* element requires that states consider their practice to be an expression of an international legal rule. Where there are declarations from the international community or individual states to this effect, *opinio juris* can be presumed to be strong. However, like most of us, states often act without explicitly declaring that they are following a legal obligation. While article 38 of the ICJ Statute requires that general state practice must be shown to have been accepted as law, the ICJ stated in *Nicaragua* that practice is required to confirm *opinio juris*, thus inversing the relationship.[59] From a purely logical perspective, establishing *opinio juris* is thus not without a circular quality.

With the *opinio juris* element, any rationalistic approach to international law breaks down. In practice, the state's general behavior should be taken into consideration to test whether the presumption that it was acting within the conviction to be bound by international law can be rebutted. Where customary rules convey a duty, rather than a right, or where a state does not participate in a state practice, the international lawyer must look at the circumstances

---

[58] This statement requires the qualification that subsequent practice can subtly modify the provisions of a treaty. The most well-known example perhaps is how the meaning of the 'concurring' in article 27, paragraph 3 UN Charter underwent change following the modifying practice of the Security Council. The change received the imprimatur of the ICJ. See *Legal Consequences for States of the Continued Presence of South Africa in Namibia (South West Africa) Notwithstanding Security Council Resolution 276 (1970)*, advisory opinion, [1971] ICJ Reports 16.

[59] See *Military and Paramilitary Activities in and against Nicaragua* (Nicaragua v. United States of America), [1986] ICJ Reports 14, para. 188.

surrounding the alleged rule in order to determine whether the situation warrants the consideration that *opinio juris* on the customary rule exists. It is clear that customary law must be distinguished from behavior that is simply general *usus* in international life. In general, patterns of behavior have to reside within the domain of international law in order to count toward state practice. At the same time, both elements go together. Strong *opinio juris* can lessen the need to show general state practice.⁶⁰

The first type of normative pluralism arises when treaty and customs collide. In this instance, international law relies on the principle of equivalence of sources. The answer to the question of which source should prevail in any given case is thus a confident and affirmative "It depends." The answer is not as unsatisfactory as it may seem at first sight. International law solves (or dissolves) conflicts between the two sources through its general principles and philosophical foundations. On the one hand, treaties often spell out details to a general rule, regulate its application to a specific case, or quite simply fill a gap in international law.⁶¹ It is moreover common for legal scholars to think about customary law as the law that would apply in the absence of a treaty regulating a specific matter. Thus, the idea that a treaty spells out a specific, rather than general, right or obligation principally informs international law. Where there is no prohibitive or customary rule opposing its execution, there is no reason not to give effect to the will of the parties as expressed in the treaty.

On the other hand, it may well be that certain customary rules prevail over treaties that attempt to contract out of them. Although the scope and contents of the body of *jus cogens* are disputed, fundamental rules that are of an existential quality for international law, such as *pacta sunt servanda*,⁶² or that capture norms of a high moral order, such as the prohibition of genocide, are often considered to form part of this set of rules. These rules provide an example where strong *opinio juris* can weigh more than inconsistent state practice.

The second type of normative pluralism is specific to the treaty-custom relationship and potentially far-reaching. While both are formal sources of international law, and are thus in principle equal, treaties are at the same

---

⁶⁰ See generally Schachter, 'Entangled Treaty and Custom'.
⁶¹ See Richard R. Baxter, 'Treaties and Custom', (1979) 129 *Recueil des Cours*, 25–106.
⁶² This is sometimes mentioned as an example of a *jus cogens* rule, but this may not be the most plausible qualification: a treaty circumventing *pacta sunt servanda* is not so much invalid as it can hardly be considered a treaty to begin with. Perhaps the better qualification is to treat such rules as logically indispensible, as the legal order cannot function in their absence. For such a notion, see Gerald Fitzmaurice, 'Some Problems Regarding the Formal Sources of International Law', in F. M. van Asbeck et al. (eds.), *Symbolae Verzijl* (The Hague: Martinus Nijhoff, 1958), 153–76.

time evidence of state practice and are hence one constitutive element, although not the only one, of customary international law. The normative pluralism has two consequences. Arguably, international law in this way maintains the flexibility and adaptability that characterize – and need to characterize – every legal system. Ultimately, conflict resolution necessitates case-by-case considerations in every legal tradition, because rendering justice is not a technocratic, rationalistic activity. It always needs to take into account various elements such as specific circumstances of the case, the intention of the lawmakers, the greater social good, et cetera. The existence of a plurality of sources allows the international lawyer to craft international law into such a vivid legal system through interpretive techniques, including virtuous interpretation.[63]

Second, and connected to this point: all legal systems are "living" in the sense that they can and do change with altering social realities, on which they attempt to impact at the same time. Thus, the crux in the treaty-custom relationship resides not so much in instances of direct confrontation where a treaty and a custom envisage actions that point in directly opposite directions. In such cases, an examination of the nature of the specific treaty and customary rule in question normally allows for the identification of the source that should prevail. Rather, the normative pluralism becomes intriguing as treaties and customary law mutually influence each other in international law's evolution through time and space.[64]

This may include directly conflicting treaty-based and customary provisions but may also occur as law emerges in areas that were previously not regulated. As we have seen, rules of customary law evolve through changing practices and convictions. Similarly, treaties are amended and replaced as the realities and preoccupations of international life alter. The question thus is to what extent and under which conditions the interplay between treaties and customary rules shapes the creation and transformation of international law. Put more simply, how do treaties influence customary law? How does customary law influence treaties?

---

[63] For the concept of virtuous interpretation see Jan Klabbers, 'Virtuous Interpretation', in Malgosia Fitzmaurice, Olufemi Elias and Panos Merkouris (eds.), *Treaty Interpretation and the Vienna Convention on the Law of Treaties: 30 Years On* (Leiden: Martinus Nijhoff, 2010), 17–37.

[64] A fine example resides in the scope of the doctrine of command responsibility, which, according to some, is determined by a customary practice on the basis of the Second Additional Protocol to the Geneva Conventions and has been applied in the case law of the ICTY, yet the 1998 Statute of the International Criminal Court departs from this recognized custom. The argument is made in Bing Bing Jia, 'The Relations between Treaties and Custom', (2010) 9 *Chinese Journal of International Law*, 81–109, esp. at 104–5.

International law starts from the hypothesis of state sovereignty in the conduct of international relations. Thus, international law is primarily consensual in nature. Under both treaty-based and customary law, the will of the state(s) and convictions of what counts as an international legal rule are important elements of establishing what international law prescribes. It therefore requires a diligent screening of international life (and, it would seem, a formal validity rule)[65] to determine, on the basis of state behavior, which rule states value as legally binding. For this reason, there is no universal answer to the questions raised earlier. The impacts of treaties and custom on one another have to be assessed on a case-by-case basis. Nonetheless, case law and the literature provide some guidance.

In essence, the way in which treaties or treaty provisions enter into customary law follows the same determination procedure as the normal procedure for the creation of customary rules. In the *North Sea Continental Shelf* cases in 1969, the ICJ declared that in order to form a customary rule, a treaty-based provision must be "norm-creating," that is to say that it "at all events potentially, be of a fundamentally norm-creating character such as could be regarded as forming the basis of a general rule of law."[66] Furthermore, the ICJ established three conditions under which a treaty rule may be considered customary international law. Thus, a treaty – or treaty provision, more likely – may be declaratory of preexisting customary law, or it may crystallize into customary law, or it may generate new customary law subsequent to its adoption.[67]

On the face of it, the first mechanism, where a treaty codifies existing customary law, seems to pose few problems. In practice, it is, however, rare for treaties "only" to provide a snapshot of customary law as it stands. Codification treaties most of the time go beyond simple reflection of the customary rule and elaborate, extend, or develop existing rules, even if ever so slightly. In fact, codification treaties generally are often considered to incorporate some sort of progressive development of the law. For this reason and because customary law can evolve after the snapshot has been taken, the problems that arise with the other two mechanisms haunt codification treaties also.

Their simultaneous identity as sources of international law makes the treaty-custom relationship subject to wide debate. One important question is

---

[65] On this, see Jan Klabbers, 'Law-making and Constitutionalism', in Jan Klabbers, Anne Peters and Geir Ulfstein, *The Constitutionalization of International Law* (Oxford University Press, 2009), 81–125.

[66] See *North Sea Continental Shelf Cases (Germany v. Denmark; Germany v. the Netherlands)*, [1969] ICJ Reports 3, para. 41.

[67] See generally Mark E. Villiger, *Customary International Law and Treaties* (Dordrecht: Martinus Nijhoff, 1985).

to what extent the application of a treaty modifies what is considered as existing state practice. We can imagine a scenario where a large number of states develop state practice under a given treaty. There is no "magic number" of parties at which state behavior under a treaty can be considered to qualify as state practice for the purpose of establishing customary law. "What counts," Baxter explains, "are the number and diversity of States that have accepted the rule by becoming parties or by adhering to the rule of the treaty."[68] In particular, the behavior of nonparties and of those states particularly affected by the treaty is crucial in determining whether a treaty is evidence of general state practice.

The *opinio juris* element gains centrality in the impact that treaties have on customary law, especially in view of multilateral treaties, which by their nature bind a large number of states. Where a tribunal finds concordant *opinio juris* as to the binding nature of the new practice, a treaty can modify the general customary rule and thus, perhaps surprisingly, deploy a legal effect on nonparties. Although the point is disputed in the literature, ratification of a multilateral treaty probably would not suffice for the treaty to pass into custom. While the treaty may well present evidence of state practice, *opinio juris* would need to be found also outside the treaty and could not be deduced from simple ratification alone. As with state practice, the view of nonparties is crucial in this respect. Where nonparties to a treaty are found to apply its rules and there is evidence of *opinio juris*, it is safe to say that the treaty has passed into custom and starts deploying legal effect on third parties.

Once treaty provisions have passed into customary law, this can affect reservations that states had made to the treaty. In the *Nicaragua* case before the ICJ, the Court could in principle not rule on the United States' compliance with the UN Charter because the United States had taken a reservation when accepting the jurisdiction of the ICJ. According to the carve out, the Court could not express itself on the United States' compliance with a multilateral treaty unless all parties affected by the decision were parties to the case. Since El Salvador, with which the United States claimed it had acted in collective self-defense, was not a party in the *Nicaragua* case, jurisdiction of the ICJ over the United States' compliance with the UN Charter was thus in principle not possible. The Court nonetheless found that the rules at dispute – notably on nonintervention and the use of force – enjoyed a parallel existence in customary international law independently of the charter. It stated: "The Charter gave expression in this field to principles already established in customary international law and that law has in the subsequent four decades developed

---

[68] See Baxter, 'Treaties and Custom', at 63.

under the influence of the Charter to such an extent that a number of rules have acquired a status independent of it."[69] In the view of the Court, the UN Charter was declaratory of principles already established in general public international law when it entered into force and it generated new customary law throughout its existence.

Nonetheless, the circumstances in which treaties have such far-reaching effects are probably rare or, rather, limited to obligations of high moral standard, such as certain basic human rights provisions, or very specific rules that affect the functioning of international law itself. The Vienna Convention on the Law of Treaties is an often-quoted example of such a treaty, since many of its provisions have been deemed to have entered into customary international law. This presumably does not apply to all its provisions, though: despite the awkward Freudian slip according to which the Vienna Convention is sometimes referred to as the Vienna Convention on the Interpretation of Treaties,[70] it is doubtful whether a general, let alone customary rule on treaty interpretation existed prior to the Vienna Convention or that rules of interpretation – being methodological instructions – could ever be of customary character.[71]

Another important result of the *Nicaragua* ruling is the assertion that treaty and custom retain a separate legal existence, even if the norms appear identical in content.[72] Hence, they do not subsume or supplant each other. It is, of course, an open question to what extent it is possible to differentiate lawful conduct of parties to a treaty from conduct following an identical customary rule. However, the separate existence is of relevance in instances where a number of states are party to a specific treaty while other states recognize the right or obligation in question as customary international law. In such cases, invalidity, denunciation, or termination of a treaty does not necessarily affect states' obligation to respect the customary rule. At the same time, if enough states denounce a treaty and show nonconforming conduct to the identical customary rule to the point where they create new state practice coupled with *opinio juris*, this can affect the state of customary law and the very nature of the rule.[73]

In *Nicaragua*, the ICJ further addressed the question of inconsistent state practice. In order to establish state practice, the Court held, it is sufficient that

---

[69] See *Nicaragua*, para. 181.
[70] See Lori Wallach and Patrick Woodall, *Whose Trade Organization? A Comprehensive Guide to the WTO* (New York: New Press, 2004), at 235.
[71] See Klabbers, 'Virtuous Interpretation'.
[72] See *Nicaragua*, para. 178.
[73] See Schachter, 'Entangled Treaty and Custom'.

the conduct of states is in general consistent with an alleged customary rule and that inconsistent practices are generally treated as breaches of the rule, and not as recognition of a new rule. As in the formation of customary law, the question of how to assess inconsistent practice is therefore also important in the treaty-custom relationship. A treaty may, for example, incorporate a rule that is an exception to a general customary rule. As we have seen, inconsistent practice as such does not warrant the conclusion that the customary rule is undermined. Instead, international lawyers have to bear in mind the state of customary and treaty law on a given subject matter, including the existence of other inconsistencies in agreements or state practice, to assess the legal significance of inconsistent behavior.[74]

The question of inconsistent practice points to the fundamental difference between treaty and custom as formal sources of international law. In the same vein as Merrills, Schachter calls this the "element of irony in customary law – namely, that violations create new law."[75] Whereas under a treaty, inconsistent behavior is usually simply unlawful (if not defined away as a difference in interpretation), under customs, "enough inconsistent behaviour," so to speak, can form a new rule. As pointed out previously, customary law changes over time through variations in state practice and *opinio juris*. For this reason, an emerging customary rule can potentially cast existing treaty law aside. Just as much as the conduct of nonparties can help treaties to pass into customary law, it can equally move a treaty out of the sphere of custom.[76]

Preferences for international lawmaking through treaties or through customs differ. In the legal profession, there is perhaps a tendency to ask which process is less "political." It can be argued that custom gives more leeway to the law of the strongest, since certain states may be in a geopolitical position in which their behavior is deemed as more important or attracts imitation more readily. A treaty can be thought to be more democratic in the sense that all parties are in principle sovereign entities and negotiate treaty obligations in a reciprocal manner. However, as one of us has argued elsewhere, small economies can, for example, have severe difficulties to impact on negotiations in the field of economic policy.[77] Another complication arises from the fact that both private organizations and civil society organizations increasingly participate in regulatory activity that affects international relations. Although the law is a good tool for attenuating existing power asymmetries

---

[74] See Baxter, 'Treaties and Custom'.
[75] See Schachter, 'Entangled Treaty and Custom', at 733.
[76] See Baxter, 'Treaties and Custom'.
[77] See Alisa DiCaprio and Silke Trommer, 'Bilateral Graduation: The Impacts of EPAs on LDC Trade Space', (2010) 46 *Journal of Development Studies*, 1607–27.

in the international order, the view that these can be entirely neutralized remains wrong.[78]

In this sense, a sociological perspective can help to shed light on the difference between both sources and their complex interrelation. Law (legislation, treaties) is typically made with the intention, and effect, of altering society's normative convictions and functioning. Customary law, by contrast, is formed "from below" – that is to say from the practices and convictions among the members of the relevant political community on the way in which they behave and feel they should behave toward one another. In international law, the variety of sources is arguably one means through which power can be tamed. The fact that international law continues to evolve, inter alia, through the interplay among its different sources, indicates that even where power is at play, relations of interdependence can be a lot more complex than they appear at first sight.

V. TREATIES VERSUS INFORMAL INSTRUMENTS

A topic of growing concern, and no recorded solutions, is what to do when an obligation contained in a treaty collides with one contained in an instrument that is ostensibly not legally binding. Such documents are said to be often concluded, and while not binding in law, they are nonetheless expected to yield some results: something is supposed to happen when a non–legal binding agreement "takes effect" or becomes activated.[79]

The easiest solution would be to hold that the nonlegal obligation can never trump the legal obligation, but such a solution would be question begging. There are, to be sure, settings in which this is a possible construction: thus, within the EU, the CJEU has on occasion held that a nonbinding recommendation may need to be applied to the fullest extent in conformity with existing law.[80] This then can be understood as an affirmation that the legal instrument prevails over the nonlegal instrument. Much depends, however, on the institutional setting: this may work within a tight framework such as the EU but would not necessarily apply elsewhere. Something similar applies to other instruments that are recognized as having no binding force, such as General Assembly resolutions: there is general agreement that such resolutions will have to bow to legally binding instruments colliding with them.

---

[78] For a fine general discussion, see Boyle and Chinkin, *The Making of International Law.*
[79] So already Vierdag, 'Spanningen tussen recht en pratijk in het verdragenrecht', (1989) *Preadvies Nederlandse Vereniging voor Internationaal Recht,* 3–87.
[80] See case C-322/88, *Salvatore Grimaldi v. Fonds des maladies professionnelles* [1989] ECR I-4407.

As a matter of principle, moreover, it remains unclear why law should trump nonlaw. While good arguments to this effect can be found,[81] at the very least it is not a foregone conclusion. If states (or other actors) intentionally withdraw their obligations from the legal realm, then allowing the law to reenter through the backdoor by claiming supremacy would require an explanation. This can mean two things. First, and highly plausible, it may mean that the theory concerning non–legally binding agreements is incoherent: if law can be deactivated at the moment of the conclusion of agreements (in that many claim that legal force is intentionally withheld when a non–legally binding agreement is concluded), then it would stand to reason also to expect that it can be deactivated later in the existence of such agreements, for instance, when they are in conflict with law. This may not solve the conflict, but a coherent theory of non–legally binding agreements would have to posit that these agreements exist next to law, rather than coming to form part of the legal edifice after all.[82] If the intention of parties to stay extralegal is to be given pride of place, then it is too easy, and incoherent, to claim that in case of conflict, law prevails, despite the intentions of the drafters of non–legally binding agreements.

This then would have to mean, second, that some kind of framework needs to be devised for addressing normative conflict. In other words: the existence of a viable category of non–legally binding agreements presupposes the existence of an overarching normative order comprising both these agreements and the more regular kind known as treaties, for it is only in such an overarching order that normative conflicts can plausibly be settled. Otherwise, one would have to draw the conclusion that both law and "nonlaw" (or soft law, or informal law) are separate and self-referential categories. The closest international law has come to such a set of rules involving conflicts between hard and soft obligations is to define them away: it has been suggested, for example, that soft law often serves to complement or replace hard law,[83] an idea that suggests harmony rather than conflict. Still, in particular replacement of hard law by soft law is difficult to grasp legally if the soft law nature of the replacing instrument is taken seriously: if states agree by instrument B to set aside hard

---

[81] See, e.g., Klabbers, 'Law-Making'.
[82] Virally realized as much in his reports to the Institut de Droit International. See Michel Virally, 'La distinction entre texts internationaux de portée juridique et textes internationaux dépourvus de portée juridique (à l'exception des texts émanant des organisations internationales', (1983) 60 *Annuaire de l'Institut de Droit International*, 166–257.
[83] See, e.g., Alan Boyle, 'Reflections on the Treaty as a Law-making Instrument', in Alexander Orakhelashvili and Sarah Williams (eds.), *40 Years of the Vienna Convention on the Law of Treaties* (London: British Institute of International and Comparative Law, 2010) 1–28.

instrument A, it would stand to reason to presume that B is a legal, hard instrument: how else could A be legally terminated?[84]

VI. CONCLUDING REMARKS

If there is one conclusion to draw from the preceding analysis, it is the Janus-faced conclusion that international law has a hard time devising principled mechanisms to solve normative conflicts but that, in practice, such conflicts nonetheless turn out to be reasonably manageable. Partly this finds its cause, perhaps, in the great flexibility offered by international law: form-free as international law generally is (except, arguably, when it comes to participation: states jealously guard their privileged status),[85] what matters most is the reality of political agreement. If a treaty more accurately reflects political agreement than a customary rule, then the treaty usually prevails; if an informal agreement more accurately reflects political agreement than a treaty, then it too may prevail.[86] And should a customary rule be more realistically reflecting power configurations, then no doubt the customary rule can be seen to prevail – even if, by the very nature of custom, this is unlikely to happen. Hence, while system builders may be disappointed by the lack of appreciation for considerations of legal principle, normative conflicts rarely give rise to protracted disputes or worse.

Instead, the absence of a one-size-fits-all solution, while it may disappoint the legal mind, is probably beneficial, in that it allows for normative conflicts to be dealt with in the arena of politics, which is, ultimately, where they belong. For, typically, the type of conflict that is serious enough to escape easy solutions will be a conflict involving deeply held political values: security or human rights? Trade or environment? These, almost by definition, cannot be gratifyingly solved on the basis of a single legal rule without doing some amount of injustice: in a pluralist world, pragmatic choices involving compromise may have to be made, and the paucity of rules concerning what to do in case of normative conflict in international law would seem to be the ultimate recognition thereof. The obvious trap to avoid then is to have politics be a matter of the powerful telling others how to behave or just doing as they please while disregarding the rights of the powerless, but here too the paucity of rules

---

[84] Unless, of course, instrument A has its own termination clause that either is activated by the passage of time or specifies that conclusion of instrument B, even in nonlegal form, will bring instrument A to an end.

[85] We owe this particular insight to Duncan Hollis.

[86] This too is an excellent reason for downplaying the relevance of the distinction between legally binding and legally nonbinding arrangements.

can be deemed beneficial: at least, the law does not assist the powerful in trampling over the powerless by means of a forceful yet biased conflict rule. In this sense, the normative conflict scenario only underlines that international law is still a matter of sovereign states operating on the basis of equality: free after Vattel, the international law (such as it is) on normative conflict protects the dwarf as much as the giant.[87]

---

[87] See Emer de Vattel, *The Law of Nations* (Indianapolis, IN: Liberty Fund, 2008 [1758]), preliminaries, § 18, on equality of states: "A dwarf is as much a man as a giant; a small republic is no less a sovereign state than the most powerful kingdom."

4 Inside or Out: Two Types of International Legal Pluralism

André Nollkaemper

I. INTRODUCTION

In this chapter I explore the distinction and relationship between two types of international legal pluralism. Both types recognize a pluralistic relationship between autonomous international and national legal orders in which the final legal authority is contested.[1] However, they differ fundamentally in scope and nature.[2]

---

[1] Compare the concept of legal pluralism in D. Halberstam, 'Constitutional Heterarchy: The Centrality of Conflict in the European Union and the United States', in J. L. Dunoff and J. P. Trachtman (eds.), *Ruling the World? Constitutionalism, International Law, and Global Governance* (Cambridge University Press, 2009), 326–55, at 12; P. S. Berman, 'Global Legal Pluralism', (2007) 80 *Southern California Law Review*, 1155 ("we live in world of hybrid legal spaces *where a single act or actor is potentially regulated by multiple legal or quasi-legal regimes*"); B. Tamanaha, 'Understanding Legal Pluralism: Past to Present, Local to Global', (2008) 30 *Sidney Law Review*, 375 ("What makes this pluralism noteworthy is not merely the fact that there are multiple uncoordinated, coexisting or overlapping bodies of law, but that there is diversity amongst them. They may make competing claims of authority; they may impose conflicting demands or norms; they may have different styles and orientations").

[2] The scope of the article is narrow in that it is limited to forms of pluralism that relate directly to the relationship between international and national law. I use the term "international legal pluralism" to refer to this relationship. The complexity is far greater than this, as additional layers of normativity, each creating its own pluralist dynamics, take place outside the legal orders of international and national law, even though they may well impinge on these legal orders; see for a concise discussion L. Catá Backer, 'Inter-Systemic Harmonisation and Its Challenges for the Legal State', in S. Muller et al. (eds.), *The Law of the Future and the Future of Law* (Oslo: Torkel Opsahl Academic Epublisher, 2011), 427. See also G. Teubner, '"Global Bukowina": Legal Pluralism in the World Society', in G. Teubner (ed.), *Global Law without a State* (Hants: Dartmouth Publishing Group, 1997), 3.

I thank Jean d'Aspremont, Aristotelis Constantinides, Yvonne Donders, Machiko Kanetake, Hege Kjos, Antonios Tzanakopoulos, and Ingo Venzke for comments on an earlier version; Tom de Boer and Natasa Nedeski for research assistance; and Belinda Macmahon for editorial assistance.

I use the term "types" of legal pluralism to refer to two distinct understandings and constructions of the pluralistic relationship between the international and national legal orders. The term "type" functions as an equivalent of the term "paradigms." The two types of pluralism do not so much represent factual descriptions of such relationships between legal orders, though both are supported by empirical data and conform to particular factual constellations. Rather, they represent ways to perceive, understand, and think about them. They represent alternative ways for making sense of a complex reality that – and this can be stipulated at the outset – cannot be captured fully by either of them.[3]

I refer to the first type of pluralism as "internal" as it construes a pluralism that is internal to the international legal order. This type recognizes the divide between the international and national legal orders and the diversity between autonomous national legal orders. It reflects the political and social reality that any workable system of international law needs to allow for a wide diversity, exceptions, and even contradictions in the interpretation and application of norms among different actors. Yet, it postulates that in the final analysis this type of pluralism remains normatively confined by rules of international law. It has some similarity with what a number of authors refer to as "pluralism under international law"[4] or "constitutional pluralism" – a pluralism that is accommodated by a common standard (though the term "constitutional" in this particular international law context has connotations that go beyond the supremacy claim and that for purposes of this chapter can be left aside).[5] It may be contended that this "pluralism within international law" is not pluralism proper, as conflicts are ultimately settled by international law. However, this chapter takes the position that there can be many forms and facets of pluralism, and that much of modern literature may fail to appreciate the inherently pluralistic nature of the international legal order.[6]

---

[3] See for a useful and concise discussion of the term "paradigm" in legal scholarship R. Michaels, 'Two Paradigms of Jurisdiction', (2005–6) 27 *Michigan Journal of International Law*, 1022, citing M. Van Hoecke and M. Warrington, 'Legal Cultures, Legal Paradigms and Legal Doctrine: Towards a New Model for Comparative Law', (1998) 47 *International & Comparative Law Quarterly*, 495.

[4] See N. MacCormick, 'Risking Constitutional Collision in Europe?', (1998) 18 *Oxford Journal of Legal Studies*, 517.

[5] See for the concept N. Walker, 'The Idea of Constitutional Pluralism', (2002) 65 *Modern Law Review*, 317–59. It might be critiqued that this type is not really pluralist since it does accept a claim to hierarchy. However, as will be argued later (text accompanying notes 85–6), the diversity within international law is such that the use of the term "pluralism" in this context is not improper. See also A. Peters, 'Rechtsordnungen und Konstitutionalisierung: Zur Neubestimmung der Verhältnisse' (2010) 65 *Zeitschrift für öffentliches Recht* 3–63.

[6] See further *infra* Section III.B.

The second type of pluralism construes a pluralism that is external to the international legal order. Empirically, it is based on the fact that much of the diversity between legal systems is not actually limited by rules of international law. As a matter of fact, many legal systems contest international obligations and prioritize nationally defined values and rights over incompatible rules of international law. In its normative dimension, this position is based on the belief that subjecting pluralism to international law would not do justice to legitimate political and social differences among states and communities within states and moreover would fail to address concerns over the quality and (il)legitimacy of international law. This pluralism is thus not contained by international law but is positioned outside, and is to some extent opposed to, international law. This external pluralism is hugely popular in recent legal scholarship and has found an eloquent formulation in Nico Krisch's *Beyond Constitutionalism*.[7]

The distinction between internal and external pluralism is not sharp. The judgment of the Court of Justice of the European Union (CJEU) in *Kadi*[8] is often seen as an example of the external type of pluralism.[9] Had the CJEU used somewhat different wording and relied more on international human rights law binding on the United Nations, it could just as easily be seen as an example of internal pluralism. The thin line between the categories may make the use of particular cases as support for either type of pluralism, depending on rhetorical motives, reflecting different opinions on which conceptualization has more normative appeal, as well as the different political agendas of those who qualify a particular practice in terms that can be construed either inside or outside the international legal system.

Yet, in several respects the distinction between internal and external pluralism is a fundamental one. The two paradigms are each based on a different level of analysis.[10] They reflect a different reading of and appreciation for the

---

[7] See N. Krisch, *Beyond Constitutionalism* (Oxford University Press, 2011). See also P. Schiff Berman, 'A Pluralist Approach to International Law', (2007) 32 *Yale Journal of International Law* 301; M. Kumm, 'The Jurisprudence of Constitutional Conflict: Constitutional Supremacy in Europe before and after the Constitutional Treaty', (2005) 11 *European Law Journal* 362; M. Rosenfeld, *The Identity of the Constitutional Subject, Selfhood, Citizenship, Culture, and Community* (Routledge, 2009); M. Rosenfeld, 'The Challenges of Constitutional Ordering in a Multilevel Legally Pluralistic and Ideologically Divided Globalised Polity', in S. Muller, S. Zouridis, M. Frishman and L. Kistemaker (ed.), *The Law of the Future and the Future of Law* (Oslo: Torkel Opsahl Academic Epublisher, 2011), 109.

[8] Joined cases C-492/05 P and C-402/05, *Kadi and Al Barakaat International Foundation v. Council and Commission* [2008] ECR I-06351; [2008] 3 CMLR 41.

[9] And indeed treated as such by Krisch, *Beyond Constitutionalism*, chapter 5.

[10] The internal pluralistic model may be seen as first-order pluralism, whereas the external pluralism is a second-order pluralism; see N. Walker 'Rosenfeld's Plural Constitutionalism', (2010) 8 *International Journal of Constitutional Law*, 677.

position of national systems vis-à-vis the international legal system, particularly of the forms and degrees in which legal systems accept or contest the normative claims of international law. They also reflect a difference in the level of faith in the scope, power, and legitimacy of international law. And perhaps, above all, they reflect a different understanding of the relationship between law and politics. While the internal pluralist paradigm assumes that conflicts among legal orders can be solved by international legal principles, in the external paradigm the relationship is shaped by politics rather than by law.[11] That is, it is recognized that the question of which order prevails is a political, not a legal question. The internal paradigm thus postulates a modest and restricted form of pluralism, in contrast with the more "radical" external pluralism that subjects legal claims to political dynamics.[12]

This chapter critically explores the foundations, ambitions, and weaknesses of the two types of international legal pluralism and their interactions. I will argue that while internal pluralism has merit, in that it emphasizes the interests of stability in interstate affairs, it may fail to recognize the interests of states, but notably also those of communities within states, that may seek change and may resist subjection to what they perceive as illegitimate or undemocratic laws. External pluralism articulates precisely the interests of such states and communities. But at the same time its normative project seems difficult to reconcile with the interests of legal certainty and stability of the international legal system, thereby endangering the protection of the rights and interests of the same states and communities in whose name the supporters of the external paradigm appear to speak.

My central argument is that the two types of pluralism, in a somewhat paradoxical way, depend on each other. While the international legal order needs its hierarchical claim to supremacy in order to provide the stability and legal certainty to serve the essential interests of states, communities, and individuals, the legitimacy of its claim to supremacy relies on the inspiration, legitimacy, and politics that are articulated in the paradigm of external pluralism. In turn, the paradigm of external pluralism seems difficult to reconcile with the interests of stability of the international legal system, and yet it relies at least in part on that system since its primarily political project cannot provide

[11] See Krisch, *Beyond Constitutionalism*, at 305–6. See, on the connection between the law/politics and the international/national distinction, A. Huneeus, 'Rejecting the Inter-American Court: Judicialization, National Courts, and Regional Human Rights', in J. Couso, A. Huneeus, R. Sieder (eds.), *Cultures of Legality: Judicialization and Political Activism in Latin America* (Cambridge University Press, 2010), at 136.
[12] See L. Zucca, 'Monism and Fundamental Rights in Europe and Beyond' (4 January 2011). Available at SSRN: http://ssrn.com/abstract=1734602 (discussing constitutional and radical pluralism).

stability at the international level. In this sense the international and national legal orders both threaten and depend on each other.

I will first explore the dynamics that underlie international legal pluralism (section II) and then examine the foundations, manifestations, and limitations of the internal and external pluralistic paradigms (sections III and IV). Next, I will analyze the interactions and feedback loops between them (section V). Section VI contains conclusions.

II. DYNAMICS OF PLURALISM

I distinguish the dynamics that underlie international legal pluralism by using two categories: the dynamics of conventional pluralism that have always been part of international law (section II.A) and the pluralism that is driven by new forms of international lawmaking (section II.B). The distinction is obviously a fluid one, as old dynamics continue to exercise their power and new dynamics are not really as new as is often contended, but it serves to identify distinct factors that underlie both the internal and external pluralistic paradigms.

A. *Conventional Pluralism*

International legal pluralism is as old as the international legal order itself. It reflects the failure of the monistic project to unite the international and national legal orders. The unrelenting normative appeal of that project in terms of protection of individual rights has failed to persuade the states, which have resisted a full subjection of national legal orders to international law. Many states determine that in the case of a conflict between international law and domestic law, national law (constitutional or statutory law) by definition prevails, or, alternatively, that the latest expression of the will of parliament prevails – also if that is national law.[13] The formal relationship between the international and national legal orders could only reflect these political and legal realities and, thus, is essentially dualistic.

Inevitably reflecting uncoordinated but substantively largely identical political choices, international law allows for and indeed is, in its fundamental dimensions, determined by a duality between international and national spheres. That duality necessarily implies pluralism, both in a vertical sense (international law and national law can contest the ultimate claim to authority)

---

[13] See A. Peters, 'The Globalization of State Constitutions' in J. Nijman and A. Nollkaemper (eds.), *New Perspectives on the Divide between International and National Law* (Oxford University Press, 2007), 251; J. Nijman and A. Nollkaemper, 'Beyond the Divide', in ibid, 341. See also the overview in D. Carreau, *Droit International* (Paris: Pédone, 2004), 58–68.

and horizontally, between legal systems. Indeed, in view of the diversity of national constitutional approaches to the reception of international law, many authors have preferred the term "pluralism" to dualism to designate the relationship between international and national legal orders.[14] Tamanaha notes that "if one envisions matters from the standpoint of a global or transnational legal system, that legal system is immediately pluralistic because it contains and interacts with a multitude of coexisting, competing, and overlapping legal systems at many levels and in many contexts."[15]

The political choices of virtually all states to preserve a duality with international law, thus dictating a pluralistic relationship between legal systems, have been propelled by intertwined considerations of control and legitimacy. Control is relevant, in that states that were subjected to the power of "the west" generally have not shown an interest in recognizing the hierarchical claims of a normative system that they did not control. This explains much of the dualism maintained in most, though not all, Asian states.[16] It also explains the weak position of customary law in most, if not all, states. Even though many states accord some legal effect to custom, they rarely allow it to trump domestic law, as the process of development of customary law remains too obscure to allow it a priori, without consideration of its substantive merits, to overrule national law.

Conversely, many (mostly European) states may be said to control the process of international lawmaking, at least through treaties (always with the availability of a safety valve, in the form of withholding consent, as an exit strategy), and feel relatively comfortable with allowing international law not only to be part of national law, but even to trump national law.[17]

---

[14] See, e.g., G. Gaja, 'Dualism – a Review', in Nijman and Nollkaemper (eds.), *New Perspectives*, at 52, 53.

[15] See Tamanaha, 'Understanding Legal Pluralism', at 389.

[16] See M. Sornarajah, 'The Asian Perspective to International Law in the Age of Globalization', (2001) 5 *Singapore Journal of International and Comparative Law*, 284 (referring to the Asian position toward international law as "the result of a shared experience of colonialism of the Asian people"); K. G. Lee, 'A Critical Perspective on the (Lack of) Interfaces between International Human Rights Law and National Constitutions in East Asia', (2010) 5 *National Taiwan University Law Review* 155 (discussing the "instrumental (ab)use of modern international law" by Western states). There are exceptions to this pattern; see for an overview Lin Chun Hung, 'Asean Charter: Deeper Regional Integration under International Law?', (2010) 9 *Chinese Journal of International Law*, 821.

[17] See, e.g., Constitution of the Czech Republic, 1992, article 10; Constitution of the Kingdom of the Netherlands, 1983, article 94; Bulgaria, Supreme Administrative Court, *Al-Nashif v. National Police Directorate at the Ministry of the Interior*, Administrative Case no. 11004/2002; ILDC 608 (BG 2003) [H11] (holding that "the provision of Article 6(1) of the ECHR proclaiming the right to a fair trial was a directly applicable norm and took priority over the provision of Article 46(2) of the Law for Foreigners, which contradicted it").

Lack of control may be complemented by a lack of legitimacy, and these factors may strengthen each other – a point well made by the "Third World Approaches to International Law" (TWAIL) critique on international law – and this both explains and justifies a deep and continuing divide by a largely suspect body of international law and national legal orders.[18]

But (lack of) legitimacy also functions as a freestanding factor. Even states that do exercise some control over the process of international lawmaking may refrain from accepting it as part of a monistic system, as a result of deficits in the democratic legitimacy of international law. That holds in particular for states where parliaments are not engaged in the process of ratification of treaties, such as the United Kingdom. Considerations of democratic legitimacy then induce a formal separation of legal orders that protects the process of democratic decision making over the governing laws. On the same ground, states that in principle recognize supremacy of international law at the national level mostly preserve the ultimate priority of national constitutional law, so as to allow for domestically induced contestation and change, even when that would override international law.[19] Conversely, states or communities have on a variety of grounds expressed a belief and hope in an international legal system (that they apparently take to be legitimate, and probably more legitimate than the domestic legal order) that should provide protection against state law and could even outbalance the absence of any meaningful control over the making of law.[20]

These political and normative foundations of the pluralistic relationship with international law also underlie the doctrinally constructed separation between international and national spheres in terms of sources, subjects, and substance. From the traditional perspective, at least, international law derived from different sources and was concerned with different actors and different subject matters – thereby removing any basis for a hierarchical nesting of national legal orders within a supreme international legal

---

[18] See R. Buchanan, 'Writing Resistance Into International Law', (2008) 10 *International Community Law Review*, 1–10.

[19] See T. Ginsburg, S. Chernykh and Z. Elkins, 'Commitment and Diffusion: How and Why National Constitutions Incorporate International Law', (2008) *University of Illinois Law Review*, 201 at 237 ("International policies are dynamic, and the policies protected at the time the constitution was adopted may change over time, particularly with regard to customary international law").

[20] See V. S. Vereshchetin, 'Some Reflections on the Relationship between International Law and National Law in the Light of New Constitutions' in R. Müllerson, M. Fitzmaurice, and M. Andenas (eds.), *Constitutional Reform and International Law in Central and Eastern Europe* (The Hague: Kluwer Law International, 1998); Ginsburg, Chernykh and Elkins, 'Commitment and Diffusion' (discussing the functions of accepting international law at domestic level for new democracies).

order.[21] That doctrinal separation could only be conceptually useful in light of the underlying dynamics of control and legitimacy.

The practical manifestation of all of this is that while international law proclaims supremacy over national law at the international level[22] and requires effective performance of international obligations, it cannot proclaim, let alone enforce, its precedence at the national level. Making use of the liberty left by international law, states and their courts have chosen radically different solutions – resulting, inevitably, in pluralism.[23]

In the twenty-first century, this depiction of the differences between international and national legal orders has largely become something of a straw man. If ever it was true that international law does not concern itself with the same actors and subject matter as domestic law, that is no longer the case. Much of international law is now regulatory in nature and governs domestic matters, including legal rights and obligations of private persons.[24] While the fundamental distinction in terms of sources has remained (even though the traditional sources doctrine has been transformed in a much more complex system of validation), in principle, substance and subjects have come to overlap with domestic legal systems. This might open the door for at least a limited acceptance of a less dualistic relationship between international and national law.

In some of the world, this is indeed what has happened. In parts of Europe, Latin America, and, to a lesser extent, North America and Africa, we have seen some osmosis between the international and national spheres, reflecting the parallel in substance and subjects of these two spheres.[25] States in these

---

[21] See G. Fitzmaurice, 'The General Principles of International Law Considered from the Standpoint of the Rule of Law', (1957) 92 *Recueil des Cours*, 68.

[22] Gerald Fitzmaurice wrote that the principle of supremacy is "one of the great principles of international law, informing the whole system and applying to every branch of it"; ibid., at 85. See for an application by the ICJ *Applicability of the Obligation to Arbitrate under Section 21 of the United Nations Headquarters Agreement of 26 June 1947*, Advisory Opinion, [1988] ICJ Reports 12, at 34.

[23] See for a good overview of such differences also D. Shelton, *International Law and Domestic Legal Systems. Incorporation, Transformation, and Persuasion* (Oxford University Press, 2011).

[24] See generally J. Weiler, 'The Geology of International Law: Governance, Democracy and Legitimacy', (2004) 64 *Zeitschrift für Ausländisches öffentliches Recht und Völkerrecht*, 547; M. Kumm, 'The Legitimacy of International Law: A Constitutionalist Framework of Analysis', (2004) 15 *European Journal of International Law*, 907; V. C. Jackson, *Constitutional Engagement in a Transnational Era* (Oxford University Press, 2010), 261; J. K. Cogan 'The Regulatory Turn in International Law', (2011) 52 *Harvard International Law Journal*, 322; A. Tzanakopoulos, 'Domestic Courts as the "Natural Judge" of International Law: A Change in Physiognomy', (2010) 3 *Select Proceedings of the European Society of International Law*, 155.

[25] See the review of practice in A. Nollkaemper, *National Courts and the International Rule of Law* (Oxford University Press, 2011).

regions do not generally accept domestic effects of the hierarchical claim of international law on the basis of the abstract normative claim of the supremacy of international law. Rather, they base such effects on a substantive choice that reflects and conforms to domestic fundamental values and, moreover, that is by definition based on domestic law.[26] Moreover, a resort to international law also may legitimize policies dictated by (more or less legitimate rules of) international law that are unpopular among local constituencies (e.g., liberalization of trade, austerity measures, rights of aliens).

In some states, however, the hierarchical claim of international law was justified not only as the result of a national (constitutional) political choice, but also as a consequence of international law's supremacy itself. Courts in Belgium[27] and Latvia[28] expressly referred to article 27 of the Vienna Convention on the Law of Treaties (VCLT).[29]

While we thus see a not insignificant body of practice in which international law infiltrates domestic legal orders,[30] viewed from a worldwide perspective the practice is very uneven. The inroads of the "new," internally and individually focused international law on traditional pluralism have been uneven. Most states (also in Europe) that have accepted some legal effect of such international law have maintained the ultimate control of constitutional law. Many other states, notably in Asia, similarly have not accepted a hierarchically higher status of international law at all – neither in general, nor for human rights in particular. They may have acquired more power and control, and in that respect one of the conditions for some form of osmosis may be satisfied, but they have used such power to maintain the traditional principles

---

[26] See T. Cottier and D. Wüger, 'Auswirkungen der Globalisierung aus das Verfassungsrecht: Eine Diskussionsgrundlage' in B. Sitter-Liver, *Herausgeforderte Verfassung: Die Schweiz im globalen Konzert* (Freiburg, Schweiz: Universitäts Verlag, 1999), cited in Peters, 'The Globalization', at 267.

[27] See *ING België v. B.I.*, Appeal Judgment, no. C.05.0154.N; ILDC 1025 (BE2007), 2 March 2007.

[28] See *Linija v. Latvia*, Judgment of the Constitutional Court, no. 2004-01-06; ILDC 189 (LV 2004), 7 July 2004. The court had to consider whether the Latvian Code of Administrative Penalties was compatible with the International Convention on Facilitation of International Maritime Traffic, which provides that states shall not impose any penalty on shipowners if their passengers possess inadequate control documents. The Court derived from the obligations of Latvia under the Vienna Convention on the Law of Treaties (VCLT), in particular the obligation to perform treaties in good faith that in a case of contradiction between rules of international law and national legislation, the provisions of international law must be applied. Hence, the court set aside the domestic law.

[29] See Vienna Convention on the Law of Treaties, Vienna, 23 May 1969, in force 27 January 1980, 1155 UNTS 331.

[30] See the review of practice in Nollkaemper, *National Courts*.

of international law, such as sovereignty and its corollary separation between the international and the national. The doctrinal construction of international law as a body of interstate law being separated from national law has become a reality of its own and has become rather insensitive to any change in control and legitimacy.

A major explanation of the only very partial effect that the overlap in substance/subjects of international and national legal orders has had on the formal legal relationship between international and national law is the essentially localized nature of the meaning and application of much of the "new" international law. While human rights law is the paradigmatic driving force of international law's claim to monism and unrivaled in its success for securing, across the world, a modest degree of osmosis between international and national law (in that international human rights are accepted as part of national law), the content of the law itself is intrinsically localized and will differ among states.[31] There is an inherent tension between the universal aspirations of international (human rights) law, on the one hand, and the local context in which rights and obligations have to be realized, on the other. While international law to some extent accommodates diversity,[32] the extent to which it does so is ambiguous, and states and international institutions with the agenda and power to seek to "enforce" such laws may not always respect the interpretations adopted by target states. International institutions and states using human rights as a basis for normative critique of other political systems have more often than not sought to lessen room for localized differentiation and pursue particular political interpretations.[33] In that situation, resistance in parts of the world (notably Asia) to a full domestic legal status of international human rights law is understandable. The substance/subject parallel between international and domestic law appears to be imperfect, after all, and is unable to transform fundamentally the prevailing dualistic and pluralistic constellation.

---

[31] See D. Kinley, 'Bendable Rules: The Development Implications of Human Rights Pluralism (October 21, 2010)', in C. Sage, B. Tamanaha and M. Woolcock (eds.), *Legal Pluralism and Development Policy*, Sydney Law School Research Paper no. 10/104. Available at http://ssrn.com/abstract=1695304, 13 (referring to the need to provide "space and opportunity for the particular to influence the general"); S. Benhabib, 'Claiming Rights across Borders: International Human Rights and Democratic Sovereignty' (2009) 103 *American Political Science Review*, 691.

[32] See section III later.

[33] See also J. Tully, On Global Citizenship and Imperialism Today: Two Ways of Thinking about Global Citizenship, Presented at the Political Theory Workshop, Yale University, New Haven, CT, naming 'the "Trojan horse" of a neoimperial order extending around the world'. Cited in Benhabib, 'Claiming Rights across Borders', at 694.

B. Modern Pluralism

The sustained duality between international and national law has been strengthened by a new, no less powerful set of dynamics that helps to support the political opposition against any such claims to a more open relationship between the legal systems. The now well-documented deficits of new processes of international lawmaking would make any major steps at the national level to remove the protections against international law rather irresponsible to domestic constituencies, as they would both release control and complicate legitimacy. The overlap in substance and subjects, captured by the "regulatory turn" in international law,[34] may force some form of osmosis between the international and national domains, but it may also enhance the demands on the qualities of international rule making. Retaining the power to give supremacy to national rather than international law may serve useful societal purposes in an internationalized society where patterns of authority and control are sometimes difficult to grasp. The already weak legitimizing power of consent[35] is often sidelined by the emergence of new forms of lawmaking – notably by international institutions and indeed by the wider phenomenon of rule making beyond the state – that, even if they do not match the traditional sources doctrine, have indisputable normative effects.[36] Even where consent might formally be available, its role is reduced by the fact that it appears late in the process and for many states, nonparticipation in international regimes is not an option.

While, theoretically, the weak legitimating role of consent might be compensated by other features of the international lawmaking process (such as transparency, protection of fundamental rights, or accountability),[37] that potential remains largely unrealized. The problems of lack of rule of law

---

[34] See Cogan, 'The Regulatory Turn'.
[35] See A. Buchanan, 'The Legitimacy of International Law', in S. Besson and J. Tasioulas (eds.), *The Philosophy of International Law* (Oxford University Press, 2010), 90.
[36] See, e.g., V. Heyvaert, 'Leveling Up, and Governing Across: Three Responses to Hybridization in International Law', (2009) 20 *European Journal of International Law*, 647–74; S. F. Hallabi, 'The World Health Organization's Framework Convention on Tobacco Control: An Analysis of Guidelines Adopted by the Conference of the Parties', (2011) 39 *Georgia Journal of International and Comparative Law*, 1; N. Hachez and J. Wouters, 'A Glimpse at the Democratic Legitimacy of Private Standards: Assessing the Public Accountability of Global G.A.P.', (2011) 14 *Journal of International Economic Law*, 677–710; J. K. Levit, 'A Bottom-up Approach to International Lawmaking: The Tale of Three Trade Finance Instruments', (2005) 30 *Yale Journal of International Law*, 125.
[37] The role of such factors as legitimacy enhancing qualities is examined in many of the studies on global administrative law; see, e.g., the special issue on global administrative law in (2009) 6 *International Organizations Law Review*, no. 2.

quality and democratic legitimacy of international law are real and pressing.[38] It is a plausible hypothesis, supported by anecdotal empirical data, that states with a strong practice of democratic and rule of law-based governance will be reluctant to allow full domestic effect of international obligations that seek to control matters within the national jurisdiction when those obligations result from processes that do not conform to the standards of democratic legitimacy, protection of the rule of law, and in particular protection of fundamental rights that apply at the domestic level. It is a compelling normative argument that they should do so.[39]

This may apply to treaty obligations that, though duly ratified by a state, may collide with fundamental rights at the domestic level. An example is the agreement between the European Union (EU) and the United States on the processing and transfer of passenger name records, which may conflict with the right to privacy.[40] It may also apply to the regulatory chill that is created by bilateral investment treaties.[41] The problem is most pervasive in respect of decisions of international organizations. Such decisions may go beyond the initial consent granted by the underlying treaty,[42] will generally not be subjected to domestic political debate before they acquire binding effect, and will not be embedded in institutional structures that can make up for this. States will accept the performance of international obligations as long as it is ensured that the preexisting fundamental rights are secured – whether at the international or the domestic level. If that standard cannot be met, backlashes at the domestic level are likely to emerge and indeed have emerged.

---

[38] See J. L. Cohen, 'Sovereignty in the Context of Globalization: A Constitutional Pluralist Perspective', in Besson and Tasioulas (eds.), *The Philosophy*, 261, at 276–7.

[39] See J. Crawford, 'International Law and the Rule of Law', (2004) 24 *Adelaide Law Review*, 3–12. Compare D. Bodanksy, 'The Legitimacy of International Governance: A Coming Challenge for International Environmental Law?', (1999) 92 *American Journal of International Law* 596, at 606 (noting that the more international law resembles domestic law, the more it should be subject to the same standards of legitimacy).

[40] Agreement between the European Union and the United States of America on the processing and transfer of Passenger Name Record (PNR) data by air carriers to the United States Department of Homeland Security (DHS), OJ L 204/18, 4 August 2007.

[41] See, e.g., D. Schneiderman, *Constitutionalizing Economic Globalization* (Cambridge University Press, 2008); S. E. Spears, 'The Quest for Policy Space in New-Generation International Investment Agreements', (2010) 13 *Journal of International Economic Law*, 1037 at 1039.

[42] See, e.g., T. Gehring, 'Treaty-Making and Treaty Evolution', in D. Bodansky et al. (eds.), *The Oxford Handbook of International Environmental Law* (Oxford University Press, 2007), 466. See for an example of domestic resistance to the domestic legal force of decisions of international institutions after the expression of the initial consent: *Natural Resources Defense Council v. Environmental Protection Agency*, 373 US 223 (2006) (holding that decisions by the parties to the 1987 Montreal Protocol were not judicially enforceable in the United States).

Increasing adjudication, which brings about more and more international judicial lawmaking, adds to these dynamics.[43] Whatever good may have been conferred by the proliferation of international courts and tribunals, their practice raises fundamental questions about procedural and substantive fits with the prevailing normative conceptions in a particular society. This holds for the International Court of Justice (ICJ),[44] the European Court of Human Rights (ECtHR),[45] the Inter-American Court on Human Rights,[46] and the World Trade Organization Dispute Settlement Understanding (WTO DSU).[47]

There may be a temptation to overstate the risk on this point. There are not so many instances where acts of international institutions have the power to adopt binding rules. And while the risk that international rules – whether binding or not – will have preemptive effects on national policy making is a real one, its scope has hardly been properly researched, giving the debate a somewhat speculative character.

Yet, the preceding trend makes it understandable why domestic institutions (and likewise the CJEU at the European level) may have reservations about the wisdom and desirability of accepting, domestically, precedence of international law over conflicting fundamental rules of domestic law. *Kadi* fits this pattern, as the Court of Justice declined to give effect to a resolution of the Security Council that would be incompatible with the fundamental values of

---

[43] See the individual contributions in A. von Bogdandy and I. Venzke (eds.), Beyond Dispute: International Judicial Institutions as Lawmakers (2011) 12 *German Law Journal*, available at http://www.germanlawjournal.com/index.php?pageID=2&vol=12&no=5 (accessed 27 September 2011); P Schiff Berman, 'A Pluralist Approach', at 314.

[44] See the opinion of the U.S. Supreme Court in *Medellín v. Texas*, 552 US 491 (2008).

[45] See, e.g., A. Follesdael, 'The Legitimacy of International Human Rights Review: The Case of the European Court of Human Rights', (2009) 40 *Journal of Social Philosophy*, 595–607; T. Barkhuysen and M. Van Emmerik, 'Legitimacy of European Court of Human Rights Judgments: Procedural Aspects', in N. J. H. Huls et al. (eds.), *The Legitimacy of Highest Courts Rulings* (The Hague: TMC Asser Press, 2009), 37.

[46] See A. Huneeus, 'Rejecting the Inter-American Court' (discussing cases of rejection in Chili, Argentina, and Venezuela).

[47] See I. Venzke, 'Making General Exceptions: The Spell of Precedents in Developing Article XX GATT into Standards for Domestic Regulatory Policy', (2011) 12 *German Law Journal* 1111, available at http://www.germanlawjournal.com/index.php?pageID=11&artID=1355; R. Rajesh Babu, 'Interpretation of the WTO Agreements, Democratic Legitimacy and Developing Nations', (2010) 50 *Indian Journal of International Law*, 45–90 (noting that the discretionary power has been used to read into the WTO rules new obligations that were not foreseen or negotiated during the Uruguay Round of negotiations, and that the panels and the Appellate Body have consistently made improper use of the techniques of interpretation and often made policy choices resented by and to the detriment of a large majority of the WTO membership).

the European Union itself.[48] Several claims have been brought before domestic courts challenging the implementation of Security Council decisions (or, rather, national legislation that incorporated such decisions), based on an alleged conflict with fundamental rights.[49]

States thus justifiably continue to insist on control at the national level – necessarily implying some form of pluralism due to differing interpretations and patterns of application. Even the Netherlands, often heralded as a monist state that grants supremacy to international law over the Constitution, has initiated discussions on the need to protect constitutional values against the effect of international decisions that would fall short of rule of law standards.[50]

These dynamics allow us to appreciate Asian practices that preserve supremacy of national law not so much as an old-fashioned anti-internationalist policy, but as a process with acute relevance that recognizes the frailties and shortcomings of the international legal order. These practices also allow us to appreciate national decisions in other parts of the world that seek to keep international law out of national legal orders not so much as decisions that frustrate the morally impeachable goals of international law, but rather as decisions that function as necessary checks and balances on the institutions of the international legal order.

Given the fact that a relatively large part of international law seeks to regulate domestic matters (and it is precisely that part that is problematic in terms of legitimacy), we may see a sustained or even widening gap between the international level – where the principle of supremacy continues to reject any reliance on domestic law to justify nonperformance of an international obligation – and the domestic level – where defects in the procedure and substance of international law may enhance the resistance of the state to the application of international law in the domestic order – leading to a sustained pluralism that preserves legitimate space for political decision making at the national level.

---

[48] See *Kadi*.
[49] An overview of claims is contained in the UNSC Eleventh Report of the Analytical Support and Sanctions Implementation Monitoring Team established pursuant to Security Council resolution 1526 (2004) and extended by resolution 1904 (2009) concerning Al-Qaida and the Taliban and associated individuals and entities (13 April 2011), UN Doc S/2011/245, 28. See also A. Tzanakopoulos, 'Domestic Court Reactions to UN Security Council Sanctions', in A. Reinisch (ed.), *Challenging Acts of International Organizations before National Courts* (Oxford University Press, 2010), at 54.
[50] See the Report of the State Commission on the revision of the Dutch Constitution (Rapport Staatscommissie Grondwet), 15–11–2010, Tweede Kamer (House of Representatives of the Netherlands), session 2010–11, attachment to Kamerstuk (Parliamentary Paper) 31570 no. 17. Available at www.staatscommissie.nl.

III. INTERNAL PLURALISM

While the internal pluralistic paradigm cannot but reflect the preceding dynamics and the resulting separation between the international and domestic legal systems, it nonetheless construes a hierarchy that constrains such differences. It is essentially based on a combination of formal supremacy (section III.A) and deference to the national level (section III.B). However, the question is whether this combination is sufficient to address the challenges arising out of the separation between legal orders (section III.C).

A. *The Premise of Formal Supremacy*

The paradigm of internal pluralism is based on the fundamental premise of the supremacy of international law, which prioritizes international law over national law. Gerald Fitzmaurice wrote that the principle of supremacy is "one of the great principles of international law, informing the whole system and applying to every branch of it."[51] In general terms, the principle of supremacy of international law seeks to subordinate the power of states to international law.[52] One of its manifestations is that international law is supreme over national law and in the international legal order takes precedence over it.[53] In the event of a conflict between international law and domestic law, international law will have to prevail in the international legal order, with domestic law considered a fact from the standpoint of international law.[54] This aspect is at the heart of the law of treaties[55] and the law of international responsibility.[56] The principle of supremacy of international law is central to

---

[51] See Fitzmaurice, 'The General Principles', at 85.
[52] Ibid., at 6.
[53] See for a comprehensive treatment of this aspect of the principle of supremacy, Carreau, *Droit International*, at 43; G. Fitzmaurice, 'The General Principles', at 68. See also C. Santuli, *Le Statut International de L'Ordre Juridique Étatique* (Paris: Pédone, 2001), at 427.
[54] *Certain German Interests in Polish Upper Silesia* (*Germany v. Poland*) (Merits), PCIJ Rep Series A, no. 7; See also J. d'Aspremont, 'The Permanent Court of International Justice and Domestic Courts: A Variation in Roles' in M. Fitzmaurice, C. J. Tams, P. Merkouris (eds.), *The Lasting Legacy of the Permanent Court of International Justice* (Leiden: Martinus Nijhoff, forthcoming).
[55] Art. 27 and 46 of the Vienna Convention on the Law of Treaties.
[56] Articles 3 and 32 of the Articles on the Responsibility of States for Internationally Wrongful Acts (hereafter Articles on State Responsibility): see UN Doc A/Res/56/83 (2002) and J. Crawford, *The International Law Commission's Articles on State Responsibility: Introduction, Text and Commentaries* (Cambridge University Press, 2002). A comparable principle is contained in Art. 35 of the Draft Articles of the ILC on the Responsibility of International Organizations, UN Doc A/CN.4/L.270 (2007). The Draft Articles of the ILC on the Responsibility of International Organizations do not contain an article comparable to Art. 3 of the State Responsibility

the international rule of law, which, if anything, requires that states exercise their powers in accordance with international law, not domestic law.[57] There cannot be an international rule of law without the precedence of rules stemming from recognized sources over rules stemming from sources outside the system.[58] Any other organizational principle would allow states to escape compliance with their obligations on the basis of domestically defined priorities and would undermine the rule of international law.

B. Accommodating Pluralism

The combination of its universalist ambitions and its claim to supremacy have made international law an easy victim of caricature. More than a few authors have described international law as a straw man, a depiction totally insensitive to both the empirical realities underlying pluralism as well as its normative appeal. Thus, Berman writes that "a universalist vision tends to respond to normative conflict by seeking to erase normative difference altogether. Indeed, international legal theory has long yearned for an overarching set of commitments that would establish a more peaceful and harmonious global community."[59] One is hard pressed to find support for such a universalist vision that would seek to "erase normative difference altogether." Such arguments overstate the universal and hierarchical claims that international law, or even a significant number of international legal scholars, would make.

As international law is largely the product of political choices made by states, one cannot expect anything other than an international legal system that allows for, and indeed facilitates, the diversity of national political and legal systems. Indeed, states have recognized international law's claim to supremacy only because it allows for legitimate differences. International law is based on, and necessarily reflects, a coexistence of competing national legal orders. The same actors that make international law seek to preserve pluralistic ordering.

Articles; see International Law Commission, Report on the Work of Its 55th Session (2003) UN Doc A/58/10, 48.

[57] See I. Brownlie, *The Rule of Law in International Affairs, International Law at the Fiftieth Anniversary of the United Nations* (Leiden: Brill, 1998), at 213. See also G. Fitzmaurice, *The Law and Procedure of the International Court of Justice*, vol. II (Cambridge: Grotius Publications, 1986), 587 (noting that the principle is generally accepted as 'a *sine qua non* of the efficacy and reality of international obligation').

[58] See Fitzmaurice, 'The General Principles', at 69 (equating the principle that the sovereignty of states is subordinated to the supremacy of international law with the rule of law in the international field). See also (more critically) A. Watts, 'The International Rule of Law', (1993) *German Yearbook of International Law*, at 15, 22.

[59] See Berman, 'Global Legal Pluralism', at 1189.

Apart from the obvious options to preclude the binding effect of international norms that may conflict with national law altogether, for instance, through withholding consent, whether or not through constitutional review preceding ratification,[60] a variety of principles and processes allow states to ensure that (fundamental) national norms are immune to the effect of international obligations. These are not necessarily means to escape compliance but instead preserve legitimate policy space and are essential to further cooperation between states that seek to protect such policy space while pursuing common interests.[61]

The structure of international obligations in many areas of international law, often critiqued by those pursuing a human rights, environmental, or free trade agenda for being unduly open or textured and overly protective of sovereignty, is reflective of the need to protect policy space. The lack of direct effect of much of international law is not only a matter of constitutional law, but precisely an attribute of international obligations that reflects the intention of states to preserve policy space.[62]

Policy space is further protected by the very heterogeneity of international rights and obligations that may come into conflict with each other. This allows and indeed requires states to curtail particular rights in order to protect others. This will inevitably lead to a divergence of interpretation and application, which can be qualified in terms of pluralism.[63] The phenomenon of regime complexity, which allows states choice in which regimes to follow and which institutions to use, points in the same direction.[64]

Limitation clauses in human rights law and international trade law allow states more room to accommodate local context. They are essentially a

---

[60] See, e.g., for the power of the Constitutional Court of Slovenia in this regard, *Case Concerning the Constitutionality of the Agreement between the Republic of Slovenia and the Republic of Croatia on Border Traffic and Cooperation*, Constitutional Court, no. 43/2001; ILDC 402 (SI 2001), 19 April 2001.

[61] See generally L. R. Helfer, 'Flexibility in International Agreements', in J. Dunoff and M. A. Pollack (eds.), *International Law and International Relations: Taking Stock* (Cambridge University Press, 2012), available at http://ssrn.com/abstract=1930379.

[62] See on the international aspects of self-executing treaties (thus also explaining how international law can preclude or at least not require direct effect) T. Buergenthal, 'Self-Executing and Non-Self-Executing Treaties in National and International Law', (1992) 235 *Recueil des Cours*, 303. See on the political function of direct effect Jan Klabbers, 'International Law in Community Law: The Law and Politics of Direct Effect', (2002) 21 *Yearbook of European Law*, 263.

[63] See, e.g., N. Petersen, 'International Law, Cultural Diversity, and Democratic Rule: Beyond the Divide between Universalism and Relativism', (2011) 1 *Asian Journal of International Law*, 149 at 153.

[64] See K. J. Alter and S. Meunier, 'The Politics of International Regime Complexity', (2009) 7 *Perspectives on Politics*, 13–24.

"vehicle for protecting pluralistic sensibilities."[65] International human rights law does not impose solely (nor, perhaps, even primarily) one set of standards for universal application, but also provides for a common standard that can be given meaning in different political, cultural, and legal contexts and cultures in a legitimate variety of ways.[66] Limitation clauses thus do not so much restrict rights, or provide exceptions to rights, but instead provide a basis for "engagement and inclusion by which states can interpret and apply rights in ways that reflect their inescapably varied histories, cultural mores, political circumstances and legal traditions."[67]

References to domestic law essentially fulfill the same function.[68] The Vienna Convention on Consular Relations allows states to exercise the individual right to consular assistance in conformity with the laws and regulations of the receiving state.[69] In principle, a state that applies a domestic law in the performance of obligations to protect the individual right will not be in conflict with the international obligation, and no issue of supremacy arises. In *Avena*, the ICJ went to great lengths, though from the perspective of the United States perhaps not far enough, to accommodate concerns over the ability of the United States to rely on domestic law in moderating the domestic impact of the convention and the Court's earlier judgment in *LaGrand*.[70] The room for such differentiation is dictated by the content and structure of the obligations in question. The reliance of the Court of Justice in *Kadi* on a *renvoi* to domestic law to justify its course was less persuasive, since the resolutions in question left less space.[71]

Reservations provide yet another level of accommodation that allows states to safeguard provisions of domestic law and thus prevent conflict at the

---

[65] See Kinley, 'Bendable Rules', at 3.
[66] This even holds for the European Convention on Human Rights; see A. Stone Sweet, 'A Cosmopolitan Legal Order: Constitutional Pluralism and Rights Adjudication in Europe' (*Journal of Global Constitutionalism*, 2012), The Selected Works of Alec Stone Sweet available at http://works.bepress.com/alec_stone_sweet/41 (arguing that the European Court has transcended rights minimalism while maintaining a meaningful commitment to principles of national diversity and regime subsidiarity; Kinley, 'Bendable Rules' at 3, citing M. Glendon, '*A World Made New: Eleanor Roosevelt and the Universal Declaration of Human Rights*' (New York: Random House 2001), xviii–xix.
[67] See Kinley, 'Bendable Rules', at 3–4.
[68] See generally also G. Fitzmaurice, *The Law and Procedure*, at 591.
[69] Vienna Convention on Consular Relations, Vienna, 24 April 1963, in force 19 March 1967, 596 UNTS 261, TIAS 6820, 21 UST 77.
[70] *Avena and Other Mexican Nationals (Mexico v. United States of America)*, Judgment, [2004] ICJ Reports 12, at para. 113; *Sanchez-Llamas v. Oregon and Bustillo v. Johnson*, 548 US 331 (2006).
[71] See *Kadi*, par. 298 (it noted that the UN Charter requires that Security Council resolutions are given effect "in accordance with the procedure applicable in that respect in the domestic legal order of each of the Member States of the United Nations").

international level. The compromise in the Vienna Convention on the Law of Treaties, which does not produce the automatic nullity of reservations even if they contravene the object and purpose of a treaty, and in any case does not affect the legality of reservations to which other states may object, is not so much an unintelligible arrangement that fails to provide legal certainty but a successful attempt to maintain legitimate diversity within treaty regimes.[72]

On this point, a further distinction that shapes pluralism in the international legal order needs to be introduced. In a sovereignty-based conception, which construes the international legal order in a private law model, space for reservations and, indeed, pluralism is maximized. In contrast, in a public law model, the room for reservations is limited by the object and purpose of treaties.[73] The more the latter perspective is emphasized, as is commonly done with respect to human rights treaties, the more the room for diversity within a treaty regime is minimized.[74] The European Court of Human Rights (ECtHR) has declared such reservations illegal and considered states bound without the benefit of incompatible reservations.[75] This trend, based on good grounds from the perspective of the substantive values underlying treaties, has uncertain implications for international legal pluralism. It cannot be excluded that once the safety valve of particular reservations is removed, this will either affect the acceptance of international obligations in the first place or fuel rejectionist approaches at the national level.

Generally, though (and thus apart from the practice of human rights institutions that challenge the power to make reservations), international institutions

---

[72] Such diversity of course cannot be unlimited. See rule 3.1.5.5. of the Guide to Practice on Reservations to Treaties, UN Doc. A/66/10/Add.1 (A reservation by which a State or an international organization purports to exclude or to modify the legal effect of certain provisions of a treaty or of the treaty as a whole in order to preserve the integrity of specific rules of the internal law of that State or of specific rules of that organization in force at the time of the formulation of the reservation may be formulated only insofar as it does not affect an essential element of the treaty nor its general tenor).

[73] See *Reservations to the Convention on Genocide*, Advisory Opinion, [1951] ICJ Rep 15.

[74] International Law Commission, Report on the Work of Its 59th session (7 May to 5 June and 9 July to 10 August 2007), General Assembly, Official Records Sixty-second Session Supplement no. 10; UN Doc. A/62/10 (2007), 84–7.

[75] *Belilos v. Switzerland*, 29 April 1988, Series A no. 132, par. 55; *Loizidou v. Turkey* (preliminary objections), 23 March 1995, Series A no. 310, par. 95. See also HRC, General comment no. 24: Issues relating to reservations made upon ratification or accession to the Covenant or the Optional Protocols thereto, or in relation to declarations under article 41 of the Covenant: 04-11-1994. CCPR/C/21/Rev.1/Add.6, General Comment no. 24. (General Comments), in particular paras. 17 and 18. See also the HRC's view in *Rawle Kennedy v. Trinidad and Tobago*, Communication no. 845, UN Doc CCPR/C/67/D/845/1999 (31 December 1999), para. 24 ("it is for the Committee, as the treaty body to the International Covenant on Civil and Political Rights and its Optional Protocols, to interpret and determine the validity of reservations made to these treaties").

recognize and sustain the room for diversity. The margin of appreciation that the ECtHR allows in its review of domestic law and practice is the most discussed example of this.[76] The supervisory practice of human rights treaty bodies also bolsters the pluralistic ordering of legal systems[77]: the procedures that are often critiqued for their lack of bite are in fact construed to allow for and indeed promote "assimilation of the human rights cause, rather than conversion to it."[78]

More generally and fundamentally, it can be argued that the combination of the principle and practice of auto-interpretation[79] with weak enforcement powers within the international legal order is a precondition for states' willingness to recognize supremacy in the first place. While enforcement powers as such do not affect the status of an obligation as law – though that argument has been made – they should be considered as an essential aspect that explains the normative ambitions and effect of international obligations.[80]

The combined effect of all of this is a contained form of pluralism. International law necessarily allows much deference toward, and to a large extent accommodates, the divergence of interpretations among different legal systems.[81]

---

[76] See E. Benvenisti, 'Margin of Appreciation, Consensus, and Universal Standards', (1999) 31 *New York University Journal of International Law and Politics*, 843; Y. Shany, 'Toward a General Margin of Appreciation Doctrine in International Law?', (2005) *European Journal of International Law* 907, at 912; compare M. Kumm, 'The Legitimacy', at 927.

[77] See Kinley, 'Bendable Rules', at 6 ("Pluralistic strains are perhaps most evident in the political and diplomatic interactions between states and the international human rights bodies. Such relations are often characterized as engaging rather than didactic, and suggestive rather than admonitory").

[78] Ibid.

[79] See L. Gross, 'States as Organs of International Law and the Problem of Autointerpretation', in G. A. Lipsky (ed.), *Law and Politics in the World Community* (Berkeley: University of California Press, 1953) 59, 76–7; P. Weil, 'Le droit international en quête de son identité: cours général de droit international public', (1992) 237 *Recueil des Cours* 9, 220; G. Abi-Saab, '"Interprétation" et "auto-interprétation" – quelques réflexions sur leur role dans la formation et la résolution du différend international', in U. Beyerlin (ed.), *Recht zwischen Umbruch und Bewährung. Festschrift für Rudolf Bernhardt* (Berlin: Springer, 1995), 11.

[80] See K. W. Abbott et al., 'The Concept of Legalisation', (2000) 54 *International Organization*, 17–35; M. Reisman, 'A Hard Look at Soft Law' (1988) *Proceedings of the 82nd Annual Meeting of the American Society of International Law*, at 373, available at http://digitalcommons.law.yale.edu/fss_papers/750; J. E. Alvarez, *International Organisations as Law-makers* (Oxford University Press, 2006).

[81] Compare Halberstam, 'Constitutional Heterarchy', at 3 (referring to systems as 'constitutional heterarchical', meaning that although the exact hierarchy is unsettled, constitutional claims are nevertheless mutually accommodated). Also Berman, 'Global Legal Pluralism', at 1192 (a pluralist framework recognizes that normative conflict is unavoidable and so, instead of trying to erase conflict, seeks to manage it through procedural mechanisms, institutions, and practices that might at least draw the participants to the conflict into a shared social space).

It implies a fragmentation that may endanger the very stability that the principle of supremacy seeks to protect.[82]

However, while all of this allows for a pluralistic variation across legal systems, in the final analysis such pluralism is limited by international law. The situation with respect to the Vienna Convention on Consular Relations is illustrative: while it preserves the right to perform obligations in conformity with national law, article 36(2) provides that the deference to domestic law is "subject to the proviso, however, that the said laws and regulations must enable full effect to be given to the purposes for which the rights accorded under this Article are intended."[83] The general point is that it is international law that determines what matters are governed by domestic law and the extent to which they are so governed.[84] The sensitivity of international law to fundamental rules of domestic law, through any of the preceding devices, thus does not result in a general exception to the principle of supremacy in the international legal order.

One might argue that in view of the ultimate claim to authority of international law, the differentiation within the international legal order is not really pluralistic, because in the end it is subject to a hierarchical system. However, that argument would understate the necessary connection between the premise of supremacy and the diversity of national legal systems that makes it possible, as well as the weakness of enforcement powers that allow the diversity to

[82] Most authors use the term "fragmentation" to refer to horizontal fragmentation between institutions and functional regimes within the international legal order (see, e.g., the conclusions of the work of the Study Group on the Fragmentation of International Law, International Law Commission Report on the Work of Its 58th Session (2006) UN Doc A/61/10, 407; M. Koskenniemi and P. Leino, 'Fragmentation of International Law? Postmodern Anxieties', (2002) 15 *Leiden Journal of International Law*, 553; A. L. Paulus, 'Subsidiarity, Fragmentation and Democracy: Towards the Demise of General International Law?' in T. Broude and Y. Shany (eds.), *The Shifting Allocation of Authority in International Law: Considering Sovereignty, Supremacy and Subsidiarity: Essays in Honour of Professor Ruth Lapidoth* (Oxford: Hart, 2008), 99; J. Pauwelyn, 'Bridging Fragmentation and Unity: International Law as a Universe of Inter-Connected Islands', (2004) 25 *Michigan Journal of International Law*, 903. However, the term is as relevant at the interface of domestic and international orders. The connection between the role of national courts and fragmentation is noted by A. Kunzelmann, 'Australian International Law: The Impact of Australian Courts on the Fragmentation of International Law', (2008) 27 *Australian Yearbook of International Law* 225, at 248. See also M. McDougal, 'The Impact of International Law upon National Law: A Policy-oriented Perspective', reprinted in McDougal and Associates, *Studies in World Public Order* (New Haven, CT: Yale University Press, 1960) 225.
[83] The Court concluded in *LaGrand* that the application of the procedural default rule by the United States had the effect of preventing such 'full effect' and concluded on that basis that the United States was in breach of its international obligation; *LaGrand (Germany v. United States of America)*, Judgment, [2001] ICJ Reports 466, at paras. 90–1.
[84] See also Fitzmaurice, *The Law and Procedure*, at 592.

sustain itself. Indeed, the very fact that the international legal order recognizes and reconstitutes sovereignty as the basis of statehood implies that we have to acknowledge that normative claims of international law coexist alongside those of states and their legal orders.[85] It is thus perfectly possible to speak of a "pluralism under international law."[86] It is noteworthy that even the EU legal system, which proclaims a supremacy that is even more forceful than the claim of supremacy of international law, is often sketched in pluralistic terms. Halberstam notes that the unsettled nature of authority in the United States and the EU

> is not a defect, but an essential feature of the system. And in both, the lack of settlement does not result in anarchy within the system or destruction of the system, but in productive conflict. Constitutional heterarchy is therefore not a principle of disorder, but a principle of organization.[87]

If this holds for relatively strong hierarchical and (quasi-) federal systems such as those of the United States and the EU, it certainly holds for the much looser and far more heterogeneous international legal order.

C. Unresolved Challenges

The internal pluralistic perspective on the international legal order has, from both a descriptive and a normative perspective, a number of limitations. Despite its inherent flexibility, the internal paradigm cannot properly capture the diversity of legal systems and underlying political constellations. Two aspects should be distinguished.

First, there is much lawmaking and legally relevant rule making beyond the state that is not subjected to international law and thus cannot be subjected to its hierarchical claims. Lawmaking outside the state (or, extending to the international legal system, outside the state-centric system of sources) is even

---

[85] See Cohen, 'Sovereignty', at 274.
[86] See MacCormick, 'Risking Constitutional Collision', at 527. See also A. Stone Sweet, 'Constitutionalism, Legal Pluralism, and International Regimes', (2009) 16 *Indiana Journal of Global Legal Studies*, 632; W. Burke-White, 'International Legal Pluralism', (2004) 25 *Michigan Journal of International Law*, 977 (referring to a pluralist system that accepts a range of different and equally legitimate policy choices by national governments and international institutions but does so "within the context of a universal system"); B Kingsbury, 'Confronting Difference: The Puzzling Durability of Gentili's Combination of Pragmatic Pluralism and Normative Judgement', (1998) 92 *American Journal of International Law*, 713; D. Held, 'Law of States, Law of Peoples: Three Models of Sovereignty', (2002) 8 *Legal Theory*, 38; Peters, 'Rechtsordnungen'.
[87] See Halberstam, 'Constitutional Heterarchy', at 32.

a defining feature of legal pluralism.[88] The supremacy of international law is powerless in regard to many national laws that aim at transnational regulation, to rules adopted by international standard-setting institutions, or to self-regulation by multinational corporations.[89] Such bodies of rules may make claims to the actors that they address that compete with normative claims made by international law, resulting in a situation of pluralism that cannot be accommodated or resolved by international law itself, simply because these systems are outside the purview of international law. Significantly, they will thus also neither profit from nor be controlled by the mechanism of domestic law that recognizes the legal effect of, and sometimes the partial supremacy of, international law, even though it is undeniable that they have significant effects on domestic law or policy.[90]

This proposition does not as such undermine the internal pluralistic paradigm – whose combination of supremacy and sensitivity by definition only extends to those areas actually covered by international law. International law is a limited system in terms of what it does and does not regulate, and it cannot possibly claim to accommodate all forms of pluralism constituted by normative systems and therefore cannot be critiqued on that basis. International law only represents part of the normative spectrum and is necessarily part of a larger pluralistic system.[91]

Various attempts have been made to extend the scope of international law or to redefine its basic premises – resulting necessarily in a deformalization of international law – with a view to new forms of normativity within international law.[92] Such attempts aim to accommodate different forms of normativity within the system of international law. That holds both for older attempts to subject so-called soft law to the system of international law[93] and to newer arguments that informal rule making by international institutions should be

---

[88] See B. Z. Tamanaha, 'The Folly of the Social Scientific Concept of Legal Pluralism', (1993) 20 *Journal of Law & Society*, 193.

[89] See Berman, 'A Pluralist Approach', at 312.

[90] E.g., the Greek Conseil d'Etat held on 21 June 2011 that the memorandum signed with IMF, EU, and the ECB was not a treaty (on file with author). Similarly, the Supreme Court of the Philippines held in 2008 that a peace agreement that was in conflict with the Constitution was neither a treaty nor a unilateral act binding under international law in *The Province of North Cotabato v. The Government of the Republic of the Philippines et al.*, G.R. nos. 183591, 183572, 183893, and 183591 [2008] PHSC 1111, 14 October 2008.

[91] See Tamanaha, 'Understanding Legal Pluralism'.

[92] See for a critical review of deformalization of international law, Jean d'Aspremont, 'The Politics of Deformalization in International Law', (2011) 3 *Goetingen Journal of International Law*, 503.

[93] See Jan Klabbers, 'The Redundancy of Soft Law' (1996) 65 *Nordic Journal of International Law*, 167.

considered from the standpoint of a reconceptualized international law. Such constructions may have their merits, to the extent that in several respects the line between international law and soft law or informal law is a thin one, and that from both an empirical and a normative aspect such bodies of normativity should be considered together.[94] Nonetheless, lumping them together may sacrifice the distinct nature of international law and,[95] with that, relinquish the foundational role of the principle of supremacy as a principle that can accommodate pluralism within the international legal system.

The second and, in certain respects, more serious challenge to the internal pluralist paradigm is that even in those areas that it does cover and where its claim to supremacy does extend, international law's accommodating principles and its sensitivity to diversity are ineffective in that it arguably cannot curtail competing normative claims by states. MacCormick argued that pluralism under international law provided a safe alternative to radical pluralism. Conflicts between legal systems would not occur in a legal vacuum, but in a space "to which international law is not only relevant but indeed decisively so," given the continuing normative significance of *pacta sunt servanda*.[96] However, his argument seems to rest on a formal construction of international law that does not take into account the possibility that the substance and procedure of international law itself may become problematic in the manner discussed in Section II.B previously.

Empirically, the weakness of the internal pluralist paradigm is that it cannot account for the many cases where states, or their courts, decline to give effect to international obligations because doing so would conflict with fundamental rights defined under national law. The very exceptional nature of the few cases that expressly base their conflict rules on the supremacy of international law[97] makes clear that otherwise states and courts in their day-to-day practice reject such supremacy claims. The standard rejoinder to the gap between paradigm and reality is that all these cases in which states do not accept the supremacy of international law are simply cases of noncompliance, both with the obligations to conduct themselves in a given way and with the secondary obligation to terminate nonperformance of international obligations and secure a return to legality. However, the number of cases where states principally and unconditionally accept the supremacy claim over conflicting national (constitutional) law is so limited that its premise itself must be called into question. It is thus forced to retreat to the narrow claim that its supremacy

[94] See Heyvaert, 'Leveling Up'.
[95] Compare Tamanaha, 'The Folly', at 193.
[96] See MacCormick, 'Risking Constitutional Collision', at 527.
[97] See notes 27 and 28.

is only to guide action in the international legal order itself, without any effect for national legal orders.

Normatively, the weakness of the internal paradigm is its relative blindness to shortcomings in terms of substance and procedure. It is a compelling argument that international law should not be allowed to control matters within the national jurisdiction when international obligations result from processes that do not conform to the standards of democratic legitimacy, protection of the rule of law, and, in particular, the protection of fundamental rights that apply at the domestic level.[98] It should also be recalled that blind obedience to the supremacy of international law is not the same thing as the rule of law.[99] The drawbacks of the internal paradigm are thus clear: states would have to comply even if a decision of an international institution were of doubtful quality in terms of deliberative democracy, rule of law, or protection of human rights, unless such defects could be framed in terms of international law itself. Moreover, it would freeze the law precisely in an area where emerging practice at the national level can lead to, or change, hierarchies at the international level, notably in the area of human rights.[100]

At this point it should be noted that some of the recent work that has advanced this empirical and/or normative challenge to the internal paradigm may underestimate the ability of international law to accommodate competing claims. After all, there is a significant overlap between fundamental rights under domestic law and international human rights. Decisions to refrain from giving effect to international obligations that are formally based on a conflict with a domestic law may in fact conform to or give effect to a(nother) rule of international law. When a state denies the domestic effect of an international obligation because doing so would violate the right to a fair trial, the right to property, or another human right, this may be consistent with internationally recognized human rights. Domestic constitutional, legislative, and judicial challenges to the full application of international law need not be regarded as nationalistic reflexes that seek to undermine the performance of international obligations – and that sustain an external pluralistic ordering – but may be seen as legitimate responses that are demanded of international law itself,

---

[98] See text accompanying note 39.
[99] See Watts, 'Rule of Law', at 22. See also G. Palombella, 'The Rule of Law beyond the State: Failures, Promises and Theory', (2009) 7 *International Journal of Constitutional Law*, 442.
[100] See also Peters, 'Rechtsordnungen', at 52 ("Jeder Konfliktfall ist ein Stimulus für Entwicklung neuer Ideen, für die Suche nach der bestmöglichen Reaktion. Damit wird die Problemlösung optimiert"). Of course, change in practice of relevant actors can lead to a change in customary law, even where this practice involves a breach of existing law; see *Military and Paramilitary Activities in and against Nicaragua (Nicaragua v. United States)*, Merits, [1986] ICJ Reports 14, par. 186.

on the basis of a substantive overlap between international law and domestic law and a commonality of constitutional values at the international and the domestic level.[101]

One example of a case that may be explained and justified from this perspective is the *Görgülü* decision. The German Bundesverfassungsgericht held that, while it normally should give effect to a judgment of the European Court, this would not be so when that would restrict or reduce the protection of the individual's fundamental rights under the Constitution.[102] The Court noted that the commitment to international law takes effect only within the democratic and constitutional system of the basic law. Significantly, it referred in this context to a joint European development of fundamental rights.[103] As to the effects on third parties, it stated that it is the task of the domestic courts to integrate a decision of the ECtHR into the relevant partial legal area of the national legal system by balancing conflicting rights, and that the ECtHR could not aim to achieve such solutions itself.[104]

Likewise, challenges in domestic courts of decisions of the Security Council Sanctions Committee that impose restrictions on individual human rights, which would score low on most indicators of the international rule of law, may be seen as justifiable attempts to preserve individual rights and, indeed, the rule of law.[105] In some respects this also holds for the *Kadi* judgment. The Court protected fundamental rules of Union law that in substance overlapped and indeed were informed by international (European Convention of Human Rights (ECHR)) standards.[106] It may be noted in this context that the Court of Justice in *Kadi* understated its case, and perhaps limited its acceptability at the international level, by not putting more emphasis on the commonality between the European standards it sought to protect, on the one hand,

---

[101] See further discussion in Nijman and Nollkaemper, 'Beyond the Divide', at 341–60; A. Tzanakopoulos, 'Domestic Courts in International Law: The International Judicial Function of National Courts', (2011) 34 *Loyola of Los Angeles International and Comparative Law Review*, 153.

[102] *Görgülü Case*, Individual constitutional complaint, BVerfG, 2 BvR 1481/04; ILDC 65 (2004), 14 October 2004, par. 32; see also par. 62.

[103] Ibid. par. 62.

[104] Ibid. par. 58.

[105] See E. De Wet and A. Nollkaemper, 'Review of Security Council Decisions by National Courts', (2002) 45 *German Yearbook of International Law*, 166.

[106] See *Kadi*. In par. 283 the Court recalled that "according to settled case-law, fundamental rights form an integral part of the general principles of law whose observance the Court ensures. For that purpose, the Court draws inspiration from the constitutional traditions common to the Member States and from the guidelines supplied by international instruments for the protection of human rights on which the Member States have collaborated or to which they are signatories. In that regard, the ECHR has special significance."

and the human rights standards under the UN conventions and customary law that were relevant to the exercise of powers by the Security Council, on the other.[107]

The conflict that emerges in such cases is of a different nature from a conflict between international law and domestic law. The fact that a state seeks to justify noncompliance with an international obligation by reference to another international obligation, rather than to a rule of domestic law, changes the parameters of the conflict. Rather than being analyzed in a black and white manner (where either domestic law or international law has to trump the competing obligation), the conflict is now subjected to rules of international law pertaining to conflicts between two or more international norms.[108]

However, the scope of this argument, according to which challenges to international obligations can be resolved within the international legal order and thus can be compatible with the internal pluralistic paradigm is relatively limited. Many conflicts between international and national law cannot be translated or transformed into international law terms. While *Medellín* may in some readings of the case still be seen as a conflict between two norms of international law and as such can be subject to accommodating principles of international law, that is already much harder for challenges to international obligations based on the Sharia.[109]

Moreover, even if a conflict between domestic law and international law can be translated into a conflict between two international norms, the institutions tasked with balancing such norms may well produce different results, depending on whether they are part of the international or of a particular national legal order. The weighing of interests and obligations between human rights treaties and extradition treaties, applied, for instance, in Dutch and Czech extradition cases,[110] does not easily conform to international principles for the reconciliation of competing obligations and may well have led to a different result from that at which a hypothetical international court would have

---

[107] Article 24(2) of the UN Charter; see further discussion in De Wet and Nollkaemper, 'Review of Security Council Decisions'; Tzanakopoulos, 'Domestic Courts'.

[108] See A. Tzanakopoulos, 'Collective Security and Human Rights', in E. de Wet and J. Vidmar (eds.), *Hierarchy in International Law: The Place of Human Rights* (Oxford University Press, 2012), 42.

[109] Though obviously not all such challenges would necessarily violate international law, see discussion by J. Rehman, 'The Sharia, Islamic Family Laws and International Human Rights Law: Examining the Theory and Practice of Polygamy and Talaq', (2007) 21 *International Journal of Law, Policy and the Family*, 108.

[110] See, respectively, *C.D.S. v. The Netherlands*, Supreme Court of the Netherlands, 30 March 1990, (1991) NYIL 432 and *Recognition of a Sentence Imposed by a Thai Court*, Constitutional Complaint, I ÚS 601/04; ILDC 990 (CZ 2007), 21 February 2007.

arrived.[111] Domestic courts may establish a hierarchy of norms (with fundamental rights on top) or arrive at a balance of interests that international courts may reject, depending on their particular jurisdictional context. An international court is likely to reject the attempt of a state to justify nonperformance by reference to a fundamental obligation that is not recognized as hierarchically superior.[112]

The substantive aspects of pluralism are thus sustained and, indeed, strengthened by the institutional context, in particular by the availability (or lack thereof) of international courts with jurisdiction in regard to the claims decided by national courts. International law can only partly accommodate the dynamics in, and differences between, national political choices. Theoretically, the capacity to accommodate differences might be increased by a widening of the principle contained in article 27 of the VCLT, to allow a party to rely on provisions of its internal law as justification for its failure to live up to the provisions of a treaty, perhaps limited by the qualification that it should concern a rule of its internal law of fundamental importance. However, doing so would collapse the international legal order as such and thus also the internal pluralistic paradigm.

IV. EXTERNAL PLURALISM

The paradigm of external international legal pluralism builds on the weaknesses of the paradigm of internal pluralism. It is precisely the inability of the internal paradigm to accommodate practices that contest international legal prescriptions and, more importantly, to provide normative justifications for such practices, that has fueled an articulation of a perspective that finds such justifications outside the international legal order.

A. *The Resistance against Supremacy of International Law*

Empirically, the case for external pluralism is a compelling one. Cases such as *Ahmed and Others* (where the UK Supreme Court declined to give effect to international obligations and urged the parliament to decide on the implementation of the counterterrorism resolution – a retreat to national democracy)[113] and *Kadi* (defended by a reference to the autonomous European

---

[111] See the various principles governing the conflict of norms discussed in the Report of the Study Group of the ILC on Fragmentation of International Law: Difficulties Arising from the Diversification and Expansion of International Law, UN Doc. A/CN.4/L.682 (2006).

[112] This is indeed suggested by the Judgment of the ECtHR in *Al-Adsani v. the United Kingdom* [GC], no. 35763/97, ECHR 2001-XI.

[113] See *Her Majesty's Treasury v. Mohammed Jabar Ahmed and others* [2010] UKSC 2.

legal order)[114] are but the more well-known examples of a much wider phenomenon. According to Krisch, the practice of national courts reviewing decisions of international organizations proves that legal pluralism is taking root.[115]

The claim of external pluralism rests in particular on three related premises. First, "plural, divided identities, loyalties, and allegiances that characterize postnational society are better reflected in a multiplicity of orders than in an overarching framework that implies ultimate authority."[116] It thus reflects the reality of states (in their dual manifestation as international and national legal persons), communities, and individuals who operate in separate legal orders and who are bound to be subject to competing loyalties, commitments, and obligations stemming from these respective legal orders.[117]

Second, it is premised on the legitimacy concerns that largely outstrip the legitimating power of formal legality and that may justify noncompliance with international obligations where international law cannot accommodate such concerns.[118]

Third, the external pluralist paradigm allows for change. Where the hierarchy-based internal paradigm fixes values, rights, and obligations, thus confirming the underlying power constellations, external pluralism provides for change, development, and contestation.[119] The necessarily conservative nature of international law means that it fails to keep up with changing policies and priorities. Whether change is assessed positively or negatively depends, of course, on the eye of the beholder, but it would seem that change is a value in itself that needs to be facilitated by legal systems. It may well be that some of the external pluralistic literature understates the capacity of international law, and international institutions in particular, for change without depending

---

[114] See joined cases C-492/05 P and C-402/05, *Kadi and Al Barakaat International Foundation v. Council and Commission* [2008] ECR I-06351; [2008] 3 CMLR 41.

[115] See Krisch, *Beyond Constitutionalism*, part 2. See, for instance, his chapter on the decisions regarding the UN Security Council Resolutions, at 153–88.

[116] See ibid., at 103.

[117] Compare A. von Bogdandy, 'Pluralism, Direct Effect, and the Ultimate Say: On the Relationship between International and Domestic Constitutional Law', (2008) 6 *International Journal of Constitutional Law*, 397, at 398; A. Mills and T. Stephens, 'Challenging the Role of Judges in Slaughter's Liberal Theory of International Law', (2005) 18 *Leiden Journal of International Law*, 20 (noting that a role of the judiciary "as servants of transnational norms contradicts their role as servants of the domestic rule of law").

[118] See M. Kumm, 'Democratic Constitutionalism Encounters International Law: Terms of Engagement', in S. Choudhry (ed.), *Migration of Constitutional Ideas* (Cambridge University Press, 2007), 263.

[119] See Krisch, *Beyond Constitutionalism*, at 79, 81; Berman, 'Global Legal Pluralism', at 1155 ("we need to realize that normative conflict among multiple, overlapping legal systems is unavoidable and might even sometimes be desirable, both as a source of alternative ideas and as a site for discourse among multiple community affiliations").

on cumbersome processes of negotiation and ratification – as evidenced especially in human rights areas such as the death penalty and rights of homosexuals. But on the whole, international law is rather static, particularly in areas where powerful institutions are lacking.[120] And, of course, the question is whether change propelled by international institutions is the change that is sought by domestic constituencies.

National constitutional arrangements that oppose international law's claim to supremacy should be seen not so much as a threat to legal certainty and stability, but as providing checks and balances that are lacking at the international level[121] and thus promoting legitimate change and adjustment. Control and even rejection at national level can be seen as an ex post facto form of an accountability mechanism that is missing at international level.[122] Indeed, such external pluralism should not be seen in terms of conflicts between competing claims, but in terms of accommodation and adjustment.[123]

It may especially be said in this latter respect that the external pluralist paradigm may overstate its case in view of the long tradition of national challenges to supremacy of the rule of law. Indeed, there is something odd in the statement that pluralism is taking root, in view of the fact that resistance and rejection are as old as the international legal order itself. For centuries, national courts have decided conflicts between international and national law in favor of national law and indeed had no other option under domestic law. It might even be said that any refusal of a state (or court) to decline to give effect to an international obligation based on domestic priorities implicitly makes a claim that international law should allow that particular exception, and to that extent seeks accommodation.

What may be new in the recent string of cases, then, is that these may be construed as part of a dynamic pattern of adjustment and accommodation at the interface between international law and national law. It is thus not so much the pluralism that is new, but the articulation of principles and processes that justify rejection and that rise beyond the particular national context.[124] This opens up possible dialogue between states/courts on their justification for contestation,[125] as well as exchanges between states/courts,

---

[120] See Krisch, *Beyond Constitutionalism*, at 240.
[121] Ibid., at 78–89.
[122] See for a discussion of the modes of ex post facto accountability Hachez and Wouters, 'A Glimpse'.
[123] See Krisch, *Beyond Constitutionalism*, at 100.
[124] Ibid., at 240.
[125] See A. Tzanakopoulos, 'Judicial Dialogue in Multi-level Governance: The Impact of the Solange Argument', in O. K. Fauchald and A. Nollkaemper (eds.), *The Practice of International and National Courts and the (De-) Fragmentation of International Law* (Oxford: Hart, 2012).

on the one hand, and international institutions, on the other.[126] Indeed, key to the external pluralist paradigm as defined in this chapter is that it is not internal to the national legal order in a way that the internal pluralist paradigm is internal to the international legal order, but that by definition it pertains to the interface between legal systems. I will return to this aspect in Section V.

Thus the external paradigm can better normatively justify a wide range of practices that have to be deemed problematic from the perspective of the internal pluralistic paradigm. Appreciating the pluralist structure of law in the postnational constellation will provide better mechanisms for accommodating and stabilizing competing claims than any overarching blueprint.[127] While according to both the internal and the external paradigm there is no fixed rule of priority, the internal perspective would still take the position that general principles, namely, those of international law, can accommodate the competing positions by ultimately requiring conformity with international law. The external paradigm releases that single point of normative control – inevitably meaning that states and courts deal only with those conflicts by engaging in politics.[128]

B. Accommodation of International Rules

The proposition that international and national legal orders contest normative claims without a common point of reference, of course, does not mean that international law will lack effect in national legal orders. Both in the EU and in the United Kingdom, whose judicial decisions have often been cited as an example of modern external pluralism, there is ample evidence that international norms are generally accepted as guiding and constraining the exercise of public power.

This practice does not rebut the external pluralists' perspective as such, since the recognition of any legal effect is ultimately still based on national law. However, surely there is a difference between the fairly limited normative appeal of domestic law in the international legal order – except the influence on general principles[129] and the not unproblematic possibility of domestic

---

[126] Section V later.
[127] See Krisch, *Beyond Constitutionalism*, at 299.
[128] See N. Krisch, 'The Open Architecture of European Human Rights Law', (2008) 71 *Modern Law Review*, at 183. See also A. Torres Perez, *Conflicts of Rights in the European Union* (Oxford University Press, 2009).
[129] See B. Cheng, *General Principles of Law as Applied by International Courts and Tribunals* (Cambridge University Press, 2006).

analogies[130] – on the one hand, and the normative appeal that international law has in most, if not all, states, even if its formal recognition remains based on national law, on the other. Even states that retain a rigid formal duality with the international legal order in several respects recognize and allow for domestic effects of international law that mitigate and to some extent control pluralism. Indeed, the dynamics that fuel and sustain both conventional and modern pluralism are complemented by a countervailing normative appeal that pushes the legal orders toward each other, and without which the phenomenon of pluralism, and the respective merits of the paradigms of internal and external pluralism, cannot be properly understood.

In part, these contrasting dynamics reflect the unity of substance and subjects that, as noted earlier, has resulted in a significant, be it partial, osmosis between the international and the internal national levels, particularly in Europe but also in Latin America. For another part, this also reflects acceptance of a value-based hierarchy – resulting in a domestic recognition of supremacy of international law for international human rights. In this respect it is significant that many states allow for but also restrict the precedence of international law in the domestic legal order to international human rights treaties.[131] Contrasting dynamics also result from more pragmatic and interest-serving considerations – the interests of states in having a regime in the first place will generally extend to making that regime function.[132]

Even though particularly the first two sets of factors may be a largely Western European construction, courts in non-European states have also engaged in the practice of maintaining an interpretative connection between domestic law and international obligations.[133] While Asian states generally resist accepting a legal effect of international law that would overcome pluralism, the fact is that many Asian states now have a constitutional or statutory human rights practice that in substance is intimately connected to international law, even though the role of such norms is thus quite different.[134] Moreover, courts across such dualistic states engage in interpretative practice that accords legal weight to international law. For instance, in Bangladesh, in *Ershad v. Bangladesh and ors*, it was observed that Bangladesh's national courts should

---

[130] See, e.g., H. Lauterpacht, *Private Law Sources and Analogies of International Law* (London: Longmans, Green, 1927), see also L. R. Helfer, 'Constitutional Analogies in the International Legal System' (2004) 37 *Loyola of Los Angeles Law Review*, 193.

[131] See Peters, 'The Globalization'.

[132] See A. T. Guzman, *How International Law Works: A Rational Choice Theory* (Oxford University Press, 2008).

[133] See the review of practice in Nollkaemper, 'National Courts'.

[134] See X. Hanqin and J. Qian, 'International Treaties in the Chinese Domestic Legal System', (2009) 8 *Chinese Journal of International Law*, 299; see also Lee, 'A Critical Perspective'.

not immediately ignore the international obligations undertaken by the state. If domestic laws were not clear enough or there were nothing therein, the national courts should draw upon the principles incorporated in the international instruments.[135]

All of this leads to processes of interpretation, communication, and dialogue between international and national spheres that in part offset the formal duality between the international and the national legal spheres, even though in the final analysis the latter maintains its essential trumping power. To maintain its distinct identity, the external pluralist claim needs to be that despite all this infiltration of international norms, states do and should maintain the normative space to define their own political priorities that may contest international legal obligations.

C. Unresolved Challenges

The main problems faced by the external pluralist paradigm are where to draw the line and how to reconcile it with the interests of a stable international legal order. While in the internal paradigm fragmentation is still constrained by a common, even though open-textured, point of reference, that is given up in the external perspective. Once we accept that a claim based on domestic values or principles can override a claim for performance of international obligations, the question is whether there are any limits to the values or principles that can be invoked.

Is there a distinction to be made between, say, *Kadi* and *Medellín* or, even if there is not, between a rejection based on *Kadi* and *Medellín*, on the one hand, and a rejection based on the Sharia, on the other? For instance, the Egyptian Administrative Court had to review a claim by a person who was organically Muslim and had converted to Christianity in 1973. In 2009, his request to change the personal information on his identification card in accordance with his changed religion was denied. While Egypt is a party to the International Covenant on Civil and Political Rights (ICCPR), and by virtue of article 56 of the Constitution of Egypt, treaties, once ratified by that country, become part of the law of the land, the Administrative Court refused to apply article 18 of the ICCPR on the basis that it contradicts Islamic Sharia law. The Court held that according to article 2 of the Constitution, Islamic Sharia (Law) is reputed

---

[135] See *Ershad v. Bangladesh and ors*, Appeal Judgment (2001) 21BLD (AD) 69 ILDC 476 (BD 2000), 16 August 2000. See also *Chaudhury and Kendra v. Bangladesh and ors*, written petition, no. 7977 of 2008, 29 BLD (HCD) 2009; ILDC 1515 (BD 2009), 19 January 2009 (human rights treaties could be used as an aid to the interpretation of the provisions on fundamental rights guaranteed in the Constitution).

to be the supreme law of the land, and as such that preempts the implementation of article 18 of the convention.[136] Should such a case be considered on the same footing as the *Kadi* decision?

Rosenfeld notes that

> what is required ... is some combination of formal and material points of convergence. The formal would reflect an acceptance of the function of the prevailing constitutional and legal order as a means to settle issues over which no material agreement among the plurality of competing views within the polity seems possible. The material points of convergence, on the other hand, would result from a normative commonality or overlap that spreads across a vast majority of competing normative outlooks within the polity.[137]

The key question is how far one shifts from the formal to the material, and how much convergence is needed in order to justify embarking on a disconnection from the formal convergence. Without limitation, we end up simply with a set of competing requirements – leaving it unclear how individuals, or states, should act, and what law will be applied and enforced.[138]

Some of the literature that advances the external pluralist paradigm is based on a substantive position that human rights justify national decisions that contravene international obligations.[139] A core, and a relatively safe common ground, of international human rights would seem to exist. Indeed, many cases cited in support of the external pluralist position revolve around human rights. But this position is question begging. On the one hand, as argued previously, part of such claims can be based on international law itself, which recognizes room for differing interpretations and is built on contradictions.[140] We may not need the external perspective for this. On the other hand, beyond the core of internationally recognized rights, convergence will be quickly lost. This will not be helped greatly by limiting this power to an undefined category of "fundamental constitutional norms." While some agreement can be expected, that is precisely in areas covered by international law, and thus will not further the cause of the external paradigm. Beyond this, what is fundamental will differ from one state to another. This may be different in the EU context, where the proposition that supremacy of EU law should not be understood as

---

[136] See *El Gohary v. the President of the Arab Republic of Egypt*, Egyptian Administrative Court, Case no. 53717, 13 June 2009. Note that on accession to the ICCPR, Egypt submitted the following declaration: "Taking into consideration the provisions of the Islamic Sharia and the fact that they do not conflict with the text annexed to the instrument, we accept, support and ratify it."
[137] See M. Rosenfeld, *The Identity of the Constitutional Subject*, at 113–14.
[138] See MacCormick, 'Risking Constitutional Collision', at 530.
[139] See e.g., Kumm, 'The Legitimacy'.
[140] See Section III.B.

blind precedence over fundamental constitutional rules of the Member States is compelling.[141] The relative homogeneity would arguably make it possible to accept an exception to the principle of supremacy.[142] At the international level, such an exception would be much more difficult to accept, as its risks for instability in treaty performance would be much greater.

Various authors have pointed to principles that would provide delineation. However, more often than not these are not neutral principles, nor principles that are universally accepted – they reflect particular choices that may be common to particular states or regions. Rosenfeld refers to the values of "liberty, equality or dignity" that would induce convergence.[143] However, such indeterminate concepts do not seem to be capable of solving the problem. As they would need to be interpreted by actors on different levels of governance, who are likely to disagree, they seem inherently incapable of leading to any convergence. As noted by Walker, "even such a seemingly modest specification of its ethical core may take pluralism in a dangerously perfectionist direction, reinstating constitutionalism as the promoter of morally acceptable conceptions of the good life rather than as the ringmaster between any and all such conceptions whose contemplation is not entirely incompatible with the existence of a plurality of other such conceptions."[144]

Likewise, Halberstam suggests that the fundamental judgment on authority is not decided by a *Grundnorm*, but on the basis of three fundamental values: voice, expertise, and rights.[145] No doubt, as a matter of political philosophy, good reasons can be given for one over the other, but is there any indication that these can and do function as norms reflecting some consensus at the international level? As Halberstam admits, these values are of a modern liberal color and might not find universal appreciation.[146]

Using the label of legitimacy to capture these normative choices does not lead to a neutral standard.[147] As noted by Koskenniemi, the term "legitimacy"

---

[141] See, e.g., C. Joerges, 'Rethinking European Law's Supremacy', (2005) *EUI Working Paper LAW no. 2005/12*.

[142] See L. F. M. Besselink, *A Composite European Constitution* (Groningen: Europa Law Publishing, 2007), at 10 (arguing on the basis of article 5 of the Treaty on the European Union that "European acts which do not respect ... fundamental values do not take precedence over national rules and acts which express that national identify and the common values of the democratic rule of law.").

[143] See Rosenfeld, 'The Identity of the Constitutional Subject', at 277.

[144] See N. Walker, 'Rosenfeld's Plural Constitutionalism', at 682.

[145] See D. Halberstam, 'Local, Global and Plural Constitutionalism: Europe Meets the World' in G. de Burca and J. Weiler (eds.), *The World of European Constitutionalism* (Cambridge University Press, 2012), at 16.

[146] Ibid.

[147] See Kumm, 'Democratic Constitutionalism', at 263.

Inside or Out

is only rhetorically successful when it is not tied to any particular formal or moral set of principles – but that is precisely what is not done by those who, under the external pluralist model, contest the legitimacy of claims based on international obligations. The diversity of normative, value-based agendas of both actors as well as (external) pluralist scholars reflects a struggle to gain control over international law to further a particular political value-based agenda.

In the external pluralist paradigm this is not problematic: indeed, this is its asset. Krisch recognizes that the core of his pluralist understanding is precisely when actors on different levels of governance do *not* share a common, overarching point of reference.[148] The external perspective would thus legitimize contestation precisely on the basis of norms that might not be as "universal" as human rights, such as national interest or religious norms.[149] External pluralism is a normative (and political) project that, as such, is invulnerable to a critique based on its effects on another legal system from which it necessarily has to be autonomous.

Yet, the questions of what the implications of the external pluralistic position are for the supremacy of international law and the interests that that principle serves cannot be circumvented.[150] A fundamental consideration in this respect is that supremacy of international law (as it is key to the internal pluralist paradigm) cannot really be sustained if international law is not supported at the domestic level. This is a fundamental and perhaps controversial position, for it may be argued that the stability of the international legal order can be sustained *without* implementation at the domestic level. To some extent that indeed may be the case. However, the better argument is that it is precisely the internal focus of much of modern international law[151] that makes international law, the performance of its obligations, and the stability that it seeks necessarily contingent on a proper connection with and acceptance at the national level. If so, a pluralistic position that makes such acceptance at the national level

---

[148] See Krisch, *Beyond Constitutionalism*, at 81.

[149] Take, for instance, the reservations made by Islamic countries to many human rights treaties. These reservations are in a way comparable to the *Solange* approach taken by the German Bundesverfassungsgericht in the European context, regarded by Krisch as representing a pluralist tendency. Both form an *ex ante* restraint on the basis of values. Legal pluralism favored by Krisch would open the possibility of *ex post* reviewing on the basis of the same values; examples of protection of national interests are the British *Horncastle* case (R v. *Horncastle and others* [2009] UKSC 14) and the *Medellín* decision of the U.S. Supreme Court (*Medellín v. Texas*, 552 US 491 [2008]).

[150] See Krisch, *Beyond Constitutionalism*, who recognizes the problem of stability at 234–5; see also at 240.

[151] See Weiler, 'The Geology'; Cogan, 'The Regulatory Turn'.

subject to a normative critique and contestation cannot but undermine the power of the claim to supremacy. Of course, one could on normative grounds debate and critique the decision of the Egyptian Administrative Court that prioritized Sharia law over article 18 of the ICCPR.[152] But that contestation would not be based on hierarchy but on substantive arguments, and at the end of the day, one would have to respect the different political judgments in different societies.

The effects would go far beyond incidental cases of nonperformance of international obligations. An organizational principle that supports a state's contestation of international obligations based on domestically defined priorities would undermine the rule of international law. It would obliterate boundaries of legality and "might reinforce perceptions of international law as non-law (or quasi-law) – i.e., a loose system of non-enforceable principles, containing little, if any real constraints on state power."[153] The external pluralist perspective could thus open up a Pandora's box.

Of course, saying that this external pluralism undermines article 27 of the VCLT is trite, since the countervailing arguments do not accept the normative power of article 27 beyond the international legal order in the first place. However, it would also seem that given the dependence of much modern international law on national law, one cannot have the cake and eat it too. Even though coherence might not be achievable politically, it seems difficult to maintain at the same time that the international legal order should, as a normative requirement, demand particular conduct, whereas a particular state should be allowed to pursue different conduct. Coherence then would demand that the customary principle, as contained in article 27 of the VCLT, would be read as saying that a party may invoke the provisions of its internal law as justification for its failure to perform a treaty, perhaps limited by the qualification that this should concern a rule of its internal law of fundamental importance. It is quite obvious that this would undermine the legal certainty and, indeed, the rule of international law.

V. CONFRONTING THE IN- AND THE OUTSIDE

Notwithstanding the fact that in many cases relevant actors can reconcile requirements stemming from the international and the national legal orders,

---

[152] See *El Gohary*.
[153] See Shany, 'Margin of Appreciation', at 912; Peters, 'Rechtsordnungen', at 53 ("Das zweite Fundamentalproblem ist, dass der Pluralismus, konsequent zu Ende gedacht in dem Sinne, dass wirklich alle Auffassungen zu jedem Zeitpunkt gleichberechtigt sind, die Rechtsfolge der völkerrechtlichen Haftung eines vertragsbrüchigen Staates im Aussenverhältnis leugnen müsste").

in the final analysis the competing claims from the international and the national or local levels, relying, respectively, on the supremacy claims of the international or the national and the local, are largely irreconcilable. This is certainly a hallmark of a situation of pluralism.[154]

The internal and external paradigms take different approaches to that complexity, but the way in which they do so seems incompatible in itself. While they both have an empirical basis, and as such can be used to describe and explain certain practices of relevant actors, totally different empirical material supports the paradigms. Also, their normative grounds seem largely contradictory, as one focuses on the interests of cooperation and stability that can serve the substantive interests, and the other on particularity and locality. Perhaps most fundamentally, the differing pluralist conceptions part ways in their answer to the question of what is "law" in the first place.[155] Rules recognized as law in the internal paradigm need not be recognized as law in the external paradigm, and vice versa.

Yet to some extent the weaknesses of either type are the strengths of the other. The internal paradigm, without concern for external dynamics, is on empirical and normative grounds a poor measure for describing the development and application of international law. The European ideal of hierarchy is a tempting model for lessening complexity, but it does not provide a basis for judging and incorporating countervailing practices. It cannot capture the normative complexity and the loss of legal stability and legitimacy that have emerged as a by-product of new processes of international rule making. Relying on hierarchy to trump conflicting rules may have the virtue of resolving conflicts within the system of law, but it does not resolve the problem that the trumping rules themselves fall short on normative grounds and cannot resolve the complexity of rules stemming from outside the system.

Conversely, an apologetic embrace of diversity and locality – as that is part of the external pluralistic model – falls short on descriptive and normative grounds, because the practices that support it undermine the key interests of stability and predictability, without which much of the international cooperation aimed at the protection of transnational interests breaks down.

However, the differences may easily slip into stereotypes. Each paradigm may provide what the other considers to be its distinctive appeal. The need for change and dynamics, rightly noted by authors writing from the external pluralist perspective, often arises precisely from international institutions

---

[154] See Halberstam, 'Constitutional Heterarchy', at 2.
[155] Compare W. Twining, 'Normative and Legal Pluralism: A Global Perspective', (2010) 20 *Duke Journal Comparative & International Law*, at 476 (noting that the question of what counts as legal is one of the main puzzles in the debate about pluralism); Tamanaha, 'Understanding Legal Pluralism', at 376.

whose decisions are countered at the domestic level. Compare, for example, the 1982 decision of the Supreme Court of Cyprus refusing to follow the ECtHR *Dungeon* decision[156] on decriminalizing homosexuality by invoking the perception of public morals in Cyprus,[157] with later change triggered by the case law of the ECtHR.[158] Such examples illustrate that international (human rights) law is more prone to change than external pluralists contend. Conversely, history provides all too many examples in which local and particular interests, highlighted by the external pluralist paradigm, have proved immune to change and have furthermore resisted the protection of communities that international law – now with modest success – protects.

The nature of strengths and weaknesses allows us to identify and conceptualize a complementary connection between the two paradigms.[159] While the international legal order needs its hierarchical claim to supremacy in order to provide the stability and legal certainty to serve the essential interests of states, communities, and individuals who need the protection of international law, the legitimacy of the claim to supremacy relies on the dynamics that underlie the paradigm of external pluralism that provide the necessary inspiration and politics, without which international law will be static and arid.[160] International law not only needs external acceptance for effectiveness, but also requires contestation for its legitimacy.[161]

The external paradigm thus provides the political context for the international legal order. It is a trite observation that the development, interpretation, application, and change of international law depend on politics.[162] Political processes are not limited to negotiations of treaties or the framework of international institutions – the processes of acceptance and rejection of international obligations provide a necessary political context for the international legal order that otherwise lacks organized political structures. For instance,

---

[156] See *Dudgeon v. the United Kingdom*, 22 October 1981, Series A no. 45.
[157] See *Yiannakis Panayiotou Costa v. The Republic of Cyprus*, Supreme Court of Cyprus, 8 June 1982.
[158] See *Modinos v. Cyprus*, 22 April 1993, Series A no. 259.
[159] See Von Bogdandy, 'The Ultimate Say', at 397. See for the notion of complementarity between international and national legal orders A. Nollkaemper, 'Multilevel Accountability in International Law: A Case Study of the Aftermath of Srebrenica', in T. Broude and Y. Shany, *The Shifting Allocation of Authority in International Law: Considering Sovereignty, Supremacy and Subsidiarity* (Oxford: Hart, 2008), 345.
[160] See on the connection between supremacy and legitimacy Cohen, 'Sovereignty', at 978 (noting that "the pluralist conception of the international legal system recognizes – and possibly thrives on – the diversity of the system").
[161] See Berman, 'A Pluralist Approach', at 323.
[162] See M. Koskenniemi, 'The Politics of International Law', (1990) 1 *European Journal of International Law*, 4.

the lack of a proper political context of the European Court of Human Rights (given the rather limited role of the Committee of Ministers) is necessarily supplemented and corrected by the partly legal, but more often than not political, decisions of national organs (whether courts, legislatures, or executive branches) that may respond to earlier decisions of the court, whether by outright rejection or by more constructive means of engagement.[163]

This political context allows for checks and balances, and change, in a legal environment that prefers uncontrolled hierarchies and stability.[164] Acceptance, but also rejection that leads to change, is a necessary element of legitimacy of the international legal order. Rather than seeing domestic filters as an unwarranted barrier to the full effect of international law, such filters may be complementary to the ambitions of international law itself as a dynamic body of law that can cater to competing and diverse social interests. Rather than being faithful but blind enforcers of international law, domestic courts may have to fulfill a role as a safety valve, or "gatekeeper."[165] In that way they also can put pressure on international decision makers to get it right, much in the same manner as the *Solange* case law in Germany put pressure on decision makers in the EC to recognize and protect fundamental rights. Similarly, the *Kadi* decision may put pressure on the Security Council to adjust the procedures, as the council could not but be concerned about the effects of its resolutions in the European Union and that the defects in terms of rule setting cannot be resolved at the European level.

From this perspective, the external pluralist paradigm does not add much that is new to the discussion – it is just a different label, albeit a particularly articulate one – for the inevitable and necessary political context of international

---

[163] See, e.g., in reaction to the 2004 judgment by the European Court of Human Rights, upheld in 2005 by the Grand Chamber (*Hirst v. the United Kingdom* (no. 2) [GC], no. 74025/01, ECHR 2005-IX), where the Court ruled that the United Kingdom was in breach of the ECHR by not granting prisoners the right to vote, the Cabinet Office in December 2010 confirmed proposals which will grant certain categories of prisoners the right to vote but will prevent the most serious offenders from voting. See 'Government Approach to Prisoner Voting Rights' (17 December 2010), at: http://www.cabinetoffice.gov.uk/news/government-approach-prisoner-voting-rights (accessed 29 September 2011).

[164] See Krisch, *Beyond Constitutionalism*, at 85–9; see also E. Benvenisti, 'Reclaiming Democracy: The Strategic Uses of Foreign and International Law by National Courts', (2008) 102 *American Journal of International Law*, 241 (arguing that the practice of national courts has potential of both providing an effective check on executive power at the national and international levels alike and promoting the ideals of the rule of law in the global sphere).

[165] See F. V. Kratochwil, 'The Role of Domestic Courts as Agencies of the International Legal Order', in R. A. Falk, F. V. Kratochwil, S. H. Mendlovitz (eds.), *International Law, a Contemporary Perspective* (Boulder, CO: Westview Press, 1985), 236, 237; Peters, 'The Globalization', at 267. See also P. Capps, 'The Court as Gatekeeper: Customary International Law in British Courts', (2007) 70 *Modern Law Review*, 458.

law. The claim to conceptual and theoretical innovation of modern (external) pluralism seems instead to lie elsewhere. It lies in its ambition to shape and justify the interfaces between the international and the national legal orders. External pluralism is not only about rejection, but also about defining the relationship – rejection is a means to an end that lies beyond the protection of national values and interests.[166]

Conversely, the external paradigm highlights the virtues of processes of contestation that address the shortcomings of international law yet in itself does not provide a plausible alternative for producing the stability that is needed for deep international cooperation. The dynamics of external pluralism, however, while allowing precisely for legitimacy and politics, may be difficult to reconcile with the interests of a stable international legal order and, in particular, the interests of effective performance of international obligations.

To be sure, there is one essential difference between the internal and external paradigms that limits the degree to which they depend on each other. While the internal paradigm needs to recognize the "outside" processes of contestation in order to compensate for its own shortcomings, the external type of pluralism, in principle, can stand on its own as a coherent descriptive and normative model. The need for a complementary role of international law is thus not intrinsic to the external pluralist paradigm in the way that the need for contestation is intrinsic to a viable internal pluralist paradigm.

Rather, the complementary role of the internal paradigm kicks in once the interests of stability of transnational cooperation and regulation are recognized. Those interests may not necessarily be accepted by supporters of the external paradigm. But it should be recalled that international law also protects the rights and interests of the very communities and individuals that the external paradigm seeks to empower. In the absence of an alternative principle that can organize stability and prevent the international legal order from slipping into chaos, there seems to be no alternative but to rely on the normative pull of international law's supremacy. In short, for any stable system of international governance, there will be a need for convergence after all. This will have to be located outside the international legal order, but because of the vulnerability of common ground, it cannot discard supremacy altogether. In this sense, the internal and external paradigms do not necessarily cancel each other out but support each other and are essentially interlocking.

The partly complementary roles of the internal and external paradigms naturally draw attention to the norms at the interface of the legal orders.

---

[166] Compare on this point the concept of the 'jurisgenerative power of cosmopolitan norms' in Benhabib, 'Claiming Rights', at 696.

Seen from the international legal order, these provide common ground that can eventually justify noncompliance and induce change. From the external perspective, they provide common ground that prevents a radical loss of stability. It is there that we can place, for instance, Kumm's reliance on principles of subsidiarity, participation/accountability, and reasonable outcomes.[167] These are certainly not principles that on any reading of positive international law would justify nonperformance of international obligations, yet they are also not merely interests serving the politics of individual states. They instead rest on constitutional principles that are not entirely alien to domestic (constitutional) law (at least in states with a tradition of democratic constitutionalism) or to international law – even though they may not have risen to the level of binding international law. They can be said to be part of a normative space in between, which mediates between these two spheres.[168]

Democracy and the rule of law are other possible candidates for this category. International law could not possibly accept as exculpatory reasons a prioritization of domestic law based on the argument that international decisions suffer democracy deficits.[169] The same may hold for the rule of law.[170] Although the General Assembly has repeatedly reaffirmed the value of the rule of law at both international and national levels,[171] the concept is too ill defined to function as a workable limitation on the operation of the principle of supremacy. But both democracy and the rule of law have found their fair share of application across legal systems and have come to function, though not without problems, as a perspective for governance at national and international levels.

The standard for identifying such "in between norms"[172] is thus a different one from the traditional sources doctrine. We are looking at a set of norms

---

[167] See Kumm, 'Democratic Constitutionalism', at 260–1.
[168] Ibid., at 293.
[169] See Cottier and Wüger, 'Auswirkungen'.
[170] In this regard it is perhaps significant that the Court of Justice in *Kadi* said in par. 281 that "it is to be borne in mind that the Community is based on the rule of law, inasmuch as neither its Member States nor its institutions can avoid review of the conformity of their acts with the basic constitutional charter, the EC Treaty, which established a complete system of legal remedies and procedures designed to enable the Court of Justice to review the legality of acts of the institutions." The rule of law thus provided part of the review that led to eventual denial of effect of a Security Council.
[171] See, e.g., UNGA Resolution 62/70 of 8 January 2008, UN Doc A/RES/62/70.
[172] A similar concept ('interstitial norms') is used by V. Lowe, 'The Politics of Law-Making: Are the Method and Character of Norm Creation Changing?' in M. Byers (ed.), *The Role of Law in International Politics* (Oxford University Press, 2000). See also Krisch, *Beyond Constitutionalism*, at 294 (discussing 'interface rules').

that are widely shared across national legal systems and that have found some recognition at the international level, without rising to the level of a binding obligation. Thus there is truth in the observation that while outside the sphere of international law, there may not be full agreement in terms of traditional sources, the more two states share the same fundamental values, the more unlikely it becomes that "a truly disruptive actual conflict will occur."[173] Indeed, the practice of fundamental rights displays a considerable degree of harmony and convergence that cuts across these paradigms.[174]

However, the content and role of this "in between" category remain uncertain. Take Kumm's argument that the presumption of compliance with international law can be overridden by reason of the weight of the criteria of subsidiarity, procedure, and outcomes.[175] These principles may well be considered as normative principles that shape political contestation of international obligations. But inevitably, and certainly at a global level, interpretations of these criteria will differ. And as to outcomes, can states be trusted to second-guess outcomes of international decision-making procedures without relatively clear methods of determining which standards can be accepted, and which not? If international law were to allow such challenges, the end of international law as an effective and stable set of norms, and indeed of the international rule of law, would be near.[176] Likewise, Krisch's argument that collectives and polities should find recognition and consideration by others only if they have a sufficient basis in the public autonomy of citizens – both in terms of links to citizens within the respective polity and of inclusiveness toward affected outsiders'[177] – cannot hold us back from a slippery slope. Does this mean that we must decide whether an international obligation finds recognition by the collective it represents, and if it does not, would that be a basis for rejection of the norm?

In view of the open and disputed nature of principles in the interface between legal orders, a key role at the interface is played by procedure rather than substance, based on willingness to avoid conflict by anticipating conflict and trying to resolve it.[178] The core of accommodation then lies in exchange

---

[173] See Rosenfeld, 'The Identity of the Constitutional Subject', at 113–14.
[174] See Krisch, *Beyond Constitutionalism*.
[175] See Kumm, 'The Legitimacy', at 920; Kumm, 'Democratic Constitutionalism', at 260–1
[176] See M. Rosenfeld, 'The Identity of the Constitutional Subject', at 113 ("Without a centripetal movement to counter the strong centrifugal tendencies associated with globalisation and particularisation, the world may be headed for a war among legal regimes that could culminate in an erosion of the rule of law itself").
[177] See Krisch, *Beyond Constitutionalism*, at 275, 295–6.
[178] See Cohen, 'Sovereignty', at 275. See also J. Habermas, 'Paradigms of Law', (1995–6) 17 *Cardozo Law Review*, 771.

and communication.[179] Exemplary in this respect is the statement of Lord Phillips in the *Horncastle* case:

> The requirement to "take into account" the Strasbourg jurisprudence will normally result in this Court applying principles that are clearly established by the Strasbourg Court. There will, however, be rare occasions where this court has concerns as to whether a decision of the Strasbourg Court sufficiently appreciates or accommodates particular aspects of our domestic process. In such circumstances it is open to this court to decline to follow the Strasbourg decision, giving reasons for adopting this course. This is likely to give the Strasbourg Court the opportunity to reconsider the particular aspect of the decision that is in issue, so that there takes place what may prove to be a valuable dialogue between this court and the Strasbourg Court. This is such a case.[180]

The fact that in such cases international and national courts may arrive at different conclusions reflects the normative ambiguity of international law and uncertainty as to its desired development, and not a black and white resistance between international and domestic law.

It is to be recognized that the interpretative choices as to the meaning of obligations and their desired development necessarily reflect political choices. The term "political" here is not used in opposition to the term "law," but rather as an inherent and necessary element of law's interpretation, application, and development. It also is true, though, that the question of which interpretation eventually prevails also is a political one, and it in that respect that the construction and exploitation of ambiguity and the backing out of international obligations under the guise of the merits of the external pluralist paradigm may sit uneasily with the rule of law quality of the international legal order.[181]

VI. CONCLUSION

The central propositions of this chapter can be summarized as follows. First, the internal pluralist paradigm is, despite its accommodation of diversity, based

---

[179] See also Krisch, *Beyond Constitutionalism*, at 104 ("polities and institutions gain respect from others only if ... they are grounded in social practices with deliberative pedigree and can make a claim to bring inclusiveness and attention to particularity into a plausible balance").

[180] See *R v. Horncastle and others* [2009] UKSC 14, at 11.

[181] Cf. Eyal Benvenisti and George W. Downs, 'The Empire's New Clothes: Political Economy and the Fragmentation of International Law', (2007) 60 *Stanford Law Review*, 595 (arguing that fragmentation represents an ongoing effort on the part of powerful states to preserve their dominance in an era in which hierarchy is increasingly viewed as illegitimate, and to reduce their accountability both domestically and internationally). See also Peters, 'Rechtsordnungen', at 53 ("die pluralistische Deutung der Verhältnisse zwischen den Rechtsordnungen überlässt alle damit zusammenhängenden Fragen der Politik").

on the recognition of international law's hierarchical claim to supremacy in order to provide the stability and legal certainty to serve the essential interests of states, groups, and individuals who need the protection of international law. In this respect it continues to rest on powerful normative grounds. Despite the emergence of other modes of regulation and normativity, international law remains central to the coordination of state interests and to the achievement of common aims. Downplaying the claim to supremacy would entitle states to prioritize national law over conflicting international obligations and would be the end of the aspiration.

Second, international law remains weak for its lack of a political context around international institutions and the thin legitimizing role of consent. As international law more directly impinges on the interests of non-state actors, and as the processes of lawmaking more often bypass whatever legitimization may have been provided by consent, processes of acceptance, contestation, and rejection become key to the legitimacy of international obligations as well as the claim to supremacy of the system. A deferential approach, recognizing different hierarchies and the possible formation of new hierarchies, is essential.[182]

While international law has difficulty in combining its aspirations of binding force and supremacy with deference, one should not underestimate the ability of the international legal order to cope with inconsistencies – accept legal order, but keep open an option to exit – through the intentionally less than powerful means to enforce. The weak enforcement power of international law is built into the entire system and sustains liberty and reduces the full normative claim of supremacy.[183]

Third, this ability to accomodate and in particular to change remains limited, and the legitimacy of the claim of international law to supremacy, and thereby the descriptive and normative viability of the internal paradigm, relies on the destabilizing dynamics that underlie the paradigm of external pluralism for necessary inspiration, legitimacy, and politics. The external paradigm highlights exactly what the internal paradigm lacks in terms of room for contestation and the possibility of processes of conversion from the national to the international level.

Fourth, pluralism as it is central to the external paradigm may lead to the end of international law and to unwanted instability between legal orders. Scholarship has not succeeded in identifying compelling alternative principles

---

[182] See text accompanying notes 117–20.
[183] Compare Brad R. Roth, 'Sovereign Equality and Bounded Pluralism in the International Legal Order', (2005) 99 *Proceedings of the American Society of International Law*, 394.

or processes that can produce the necessary stability of expectations. It would not be inconsistent with an external paradigm to relinquish that ambition altogether. But if we postulate the need for such stability of expectations as a given, there seems to be no alternative for reliance on the larger system of international law that rests on the principle of supremacy, even if it is contested when it conflicts with external norms.

Fifth, principles and processes at the interface of legal orders (that can either be substantive, notably circling around human rights, or procedural) can mitigate the tension between the paradigms and allow for communication accommodation. The contestations and exchanges between legal orders will primarily be political and ought to be political, but they are not completely devoid of a common framework of reference.

PART III

NORMATIVE PLURALISM AND INTERNATIONAL LAW

5   Law and Honor: Normative Pluralism in the Regulation
    of Military Conduct

Rain Liivoja

I. INTRODUCTION

In early 1991, two days after the Security Council-imposed deadline for Iraq to withdraw its forces from Kuwait had passed,[1] a U.S.-led coalition began a massive air campaign against Saddam Hussein's forces. The campaign had unprecedented intensity and its effects were devastating: *Newsweek* recounted that six weeks of precision bombing "reduced the Iraqi Army to a brainless, stumbling hulk."[2] The coalition followed up with a land campaign, which in less than seventy-two hours forced Iraqi troops to begin to withdraw from Kuwait City. During this retreat, coalition forces continued to inflict such heavy casualties on the Iraqi army that two northbound roads out of Kuwait attracted the collective nickname "Highway of Death." According to William Polk, a notable American foreign policy expert, "nothing on that scale of massacre had occurred in the Middle East wars since Hulagu Khan took Baghdad [in 1258]."[3]

In a meeting at the White House on 27 February, having briefed President George H. W. Bush on the results of the military action, General Colin Powell, the chairman of the Joint Chiefs of Staff, argued against pressing the attack further. The president took the advice and declared a cease-fire.

It is interesting to consider General Powell's motives for giving this advice. On the one hand, he and rest of the U.S. military leadership were mindful of

---

[1] See SC Res. 678 (29 November 1990), operative ¶ 2.
[2] See Douglas Waller and John Barry, 'The Day We Stopped the War', *Newsweek*, 20 January 1992, 16–25.
[3] See William R. Polk, *Understanding Iraq* (New York: Harper Perennial, 2005), at 152. According to contemporary estimates, the Mongol armies killed some eight hundred thousand townspeople. Ibid., at 57.

I am grateful to Touko Piiparinen and Gerry Simpson for helpful comments on an earlier draft. The responsibility for the final text, however, is mine alone.

the limited mandate that had been given to the coalition. As General Norman Schwarzkopf, the commander of Operation Desert Storm, expressed it:

> We could have invaded Iraq easily.... [But] that's not what we were asked to do. That was not our military mission. Our military mission was to kick Iraq out of Kuwait, and that's exactly what we did.[4]

On the other hand, according to several sources, General Powell was repulsed by the images of the Highway of Death, where Iraqis were killed by the thousand.[5] He did not wish the American public to see U.S. soldiers engaged in a turkey shoot: according to Powell's own recollection, he told the president, "We don't want to be seen as killing for the sake of killing."[6]

There are slightly conflicting accounts of how General Powell put the matter to the president. According to *Newsweek*, Powell had said that to engage the retreating Iraqis further would have been "un-American and unchivalrous."[7] A biographer writes that Powell considered killing that had little to do with the outcome of a war that had already been won as "ungallant."[8] In his autobiography, Powell does not recount the conversation in exactly those terms, but he does note that "as a professional soldier, [he] honored the warrior's code" by advising the president to end the hostilities.[9]

II. HONOR AND LAW

This example – and there are no doubt many others – illustrates that professional soldiers perceive normative limits to their conduct beyond law and political expediency. The law of armed conflict, which is the usual normative framework for evaluating the use of force in war, makes no special provision for the withdrawing enemy. While enemy troops who have surrendered are immune from attack,[10] enemy combatants in retreat are, from a legal viewpoint, fair game. Yet, as the end of the Gulf War suggests, there is something in the ethos of a professional soldier that can render such an attack distasteful.

---

[4] Cited in Howard Means, *Colin Powell: Soldier/Statesman – Statesman/Soldier* (New York: Donald I. Fine, 1992), at 306.

[5] Ibid., at 307 (citing David Hackworth, a retired highly decorated U.S. officer and military commentator); Karen DeYoung, *Soldier: The Life of Colin Powell* (New York: Knopf, 2006), at 207 (citing Joseph E. Persico, coauthor of Powell's autobiography).

[6] See Colin L. Powell, *My American Journey* (New York: Random House, 1995), at 521.

[7] See Waller and Barry, 'The Day We Stopped the War'.

[8] See DeYoung, *Soldier*, at 207.

[9] See Powell, *My American Journey*, at 521.

[10] See Protocol Additional to the Geneva Conventions of 12 August 1949, and Relating to the Protection of Victims of International Armed Conflicts, signed at Geneva, 8 June 1977, in force 12 July 1978, 1125 U.N.T.S. 3 (AP I), art. 41(2)(b).

Law and Honor 145

According to one account, General Powell referred to the dictates of "chivalry." That would not be altogether surprising, as even contemporary military publications make occasional use of the term.[11] However, chivalry is a somewhat problematic notion: it is intimately linked to the Middle Ages, when European battlefields were dominated by knights. Hence, the concept has particular geocultural overtones and may sound anachronistic to the modern observer. To complicate matters further, chivalry has certain connotations of religiosity, especially as medieval knights were crusaders.[12] And finally, chivalry entails an aspect of (benevolent) sexism,[13] which is illustrated by the countless troubadouresque stories of faithful knights and fair ladies.

But military codes of conduct are a universal and timeless phenomenon. Michael Ignatieff notes that "while such codes vary from culture to culture, they seem to exist in all cultures, and their common features are among the oldest artifacts of human morality."[14] This view enjoys considerable support in the military community and is, for example, approvingly quoted in the leadership and ethics handbook of the Royal Australian Navy.[15] In addition to the code of chivalry, Ignatieff refers to *Bushidō* ("the Way of the Warrior"), the ethical code of conduct of the samurai.[16] The common feature of both of these historical examples of martial codes is that "as ethical systems, they were primarily concerned with establishing the rules of combat and defining the system of moral etiquette by which warriors judged themselves to be worthy of mutual respect."[17] Unsurprisingly, then, some commentators prefer to speak of a "code of the warrior,"[18] with the word "warrior" having the connotation of a combatant with an elevated moral standing.

---

[11] See notes 80–85 and accompanying text.
[12] See G. I. A. D. Draper, 'The Interaction of Christianity and Chivalry in the Historical Development of the Law of War' (1965) 5 *International Review of the Red Cross* 3–23.
[13] See Gerhard Kümmel, 'Chivalry in the Military', in Gerhard Kümmel and Helena Carreiras (eds), *Women in the Military and in Armed Conflict* (Wiesbaden: VS Verlag für Sozialwissenschaften, 2008) 183–99, especially at 189–92; René Moelker and Gerhard Kümmel, 'Chivalry and Codes of Conduct: Can the Virtue of Chivalry Epitomize Guidelines for Interpersonal Conduct?' (2007) 6 *Journal of Military Ethics* 292–302, at 298–9.
[14] See Michael Ignatieff, *The Warrior's Honor: Ethnic War and the Modern Conscience* (London: Chatto & Windus, 1998), at 116–17; see also Shannon E. French, *The Code of the Warrior: Exploring Warrior Values Past and Present* (Lanham, MD: Rowman & Littlefield, 2003), at 3: "Warrior cultures throughout history and from diverse regions around the globe have constructed codes of behaviour based on their own image of the ideal warrior."
[15] See Royal Australian Navy, *The Royal Australian Navy Leadership Ethic* (June 2010), at ¶ 2.15.
[16] See Ignatieff, *Warrior's Honor*, at 117.
[17] Ibid., at 117.
[18] See French, *Code of the Warrior*.

A more technical designation for a military code of conduct would be "professional ethics." After all, many established professions – most obviously perhaps doctors and lawyers – subscribe to some sort of an ethical code. In the military context it therefore makes sense to speak of military ethics. But for the armed forces ethics appears to have a special significance: in a sense, it defines the profession. On an individual level, the subscription to certain professional moral precepts distinguishes soldiers from murderers.[19] In fact, as Shannon French, a scholar of military ethics, argues, "the code is a kind of moral and psychological armor that protects the warrior from becoming a monster in his or her own eyes."[20] And, as Ignatieff points out, on the level of warfare as a collective activity, a code of military conduct separates warfare from slaughter.[21]

In many instances, professional codes of conduct can be reduced to a small number of fundamental principles or core ideas. At the risk of gross oversimplification, one of the central tenets of medical ethics can perhaps be captured by the injunction "Strive to help, but above all, do no harm."[22] (In the contemporary discourse this exhortation sadly loses some of its poignancy when it is referred to as the "principles of beneficence and nonmaleficence.") For lawyers, one of the keywords appears to be "integrity" – both the personal integrity of the individual legal professional and procedural integrity of the judicial process.[23]

When it comes to the professional virtues of military personnel, no notion appears to make a more frequent and pervasive appearance than "honor."[24] Soldiers must conduct themselves honorably in order to earn the respect of their fellow professionals, and indeed that of the public at large. Thus, honor is a complex notion. It is individual and private in that it relates to one's

---

[19] See ibid., at 1–3.
[20] Ibid., at 10. The same has been said about the law of armed conflict. See Mark J. Osiel, *The End of Reciprocity: Terror, Torture, and the Law of War* (Cambridge University Press, 2009), at 331: "It is humanitarian law that draws the line between murder and legitimate killing in war, and for this reason professional soldiers have rarely been dismissive of it. Such norms help constitute their very identity as law abiding, even for officers otherwise sceptical or airy claims on them by 'the international community.'"
[21] See Ignatieff, *Warrior's Honor*, at 117: "Such codes [of warrior's honor] may have been honored as often in the breach as in the observance, but without them war is not war – it is no more than slaughter."
[22] For a discussion of the latter part of this maxim, see Cedric M. Smith, 'Origin and Uses of *Primum Non Nocere* – Above All, Do No Harm!' (2005) 45 *Journal of Clinical Pharmacology* 371–7.
[23] See, e.g., Principles of Professionalism for Delaware Lawyers (1 November 2003), ¶ A(1): "Personal integrity is the most important quality in a lawyer." See also Tim Dare, 'Philosophical Legal Ethics and Personal Integrity' (2010) 60 *University of Toronto Law Journal* 1021–30.
[24] See Paul Robinson, *Military Honour and the Conduct of War: From Ancient Greece to Iraq* (London: Routledge, 2006).

professional judgment and personal merit.[25] But it is public as it is premised on a collective sense of right and wrong[26] or a community's ideals of conduct and is supported by public recognition for living up to that code.[27] Despite – or perhaps because of – this complexity the code of ethics of a military professional appears to be almost synonymous with a "code of honor."

As is the case with other systems of ethics, the code of honor has a complicated relationship with law. Ideally, the legal and ethical regulations should mirror each other, and, fortunately, that is often the case. There is broad agreement that the modern law of armed conflict is in large parts a codification of moral principles emanating from within the military profession, in particular the medieval code of chivalry.[28] Accordingly, there exists a substantive element of mutual reinforcement between the two normative systems.

But in some instances that may not be the case. The preceding example of General Powell's preferring not to attack enemy troops that he was perfectly entitled to attack under the law of armed conflict demonstrates, as pointed out by Mark Osiel, that "in many situations, the internal morality of soldiering prove[s] more restrictive and humanitarian than international law."[29] The ongoing "global war on terror" has forced some military professionals to face this potential problem squarely. For example, Rear Admiral Michael Lohr, the Judge Advocate General of the U.S. Navy, expressed his opposition to coercive interrogation techniques approved of by the Bush administration

---

[25] See Richard Adams, 'Honour' (Royal Australian Navy, undated), 117.55.225.121/Honour: "Honour is ... a complex idea, which embraces notions of professional judgment and personal merit in addition to [a] collective sense of right and wrong."
[26] ibid.
[27] See Osiel, *End of Reciprocity*, at 331, citing Sharon Krause, *Liberalism with Honor* (Harvard University Press, 2002), at 2: "Honor is public in that it entails external recognition. Its requirements for conduct are reflected in codes of honor, enshrining a community's ideals of conduct for all members. Finally, honor is a quality of character. The last of these characteristics relates to the preceding two in that it entails 'the ambitious desire to live up to one's code and to be publicly recognized for doing so.'"
[28] See, e.g., Edwin R. Micewski, 'Military Morals and Societal Values: Military Virtue versus Bureaucratic Reality', in Edwin R. Micewski (ed.), *Civil-Military Aspects of Military Ethics* (Vienna: Austrian National Defense Academy, 2003), vol. i, 22–8, at 24: "a large part of the modern laws of war has developed simply as a codification and universalization of the customs and conventions of vocational and professional soldiery"; Hubert M. Mader, '"Ritterlichkeit": Eine Basis des humanitären Völkerrechts und ein Weg zu seiner Durchsetzung' (2002) *Truppendienst* 122–6, at 122: "Es gibt wohl einige durchaus starke Anhaltspunkte dafür, den Ehrenkodex des mittelalterlichen Rittertums zu den geistigen Wurzeln des heutigen humanitären Völkerrechtes zu zählen ...."
[29] See Mark J. Osiel, *Obeying Orders: Atrocity, Military Discipline and the Law of War* (Piscataway, NJ: Transaction, 2002), at 25.

by noting that "while technically legal, [they] are inconsistent with our most fundamental values."[30]

Conversely, law and honor may conflict directly in that they may require different and mutually incompatible conduct.[31] The best example – albeit a historical one – is that of dueling. Between the sixteenth and nineteenth centuries, dueling was a frequent means of settling disputes – which, one might add, often related to obscure points of honor.[32] Duels began to fall into disfavor in the early seventeenth century, but the practice was not completely eradicated until the beginning of the twentieth century. From the eighteenth century onward, duels were explicitly prohibited, first by military laws and then by civilian laws, but this prohibition proved exceedingly difficult to enforce.[33] The reason was that dueling formed a part of the code of honor of military officers, and a refusal to accept a challenge to duel automatically meant dishonor.

There are a number of ways in which law, having made inroads into areas previously only covered by codes of honor, can try to reconcile itself with these codes. One way, as already noted, has been for the law to replicate the relevant rules of honorable military conduct. But a particularly interesting phenomenon is that the law in some instances appears to refer to the code of honor, without elucidating the content of that code. In what follows, I will briefly consider this type of relationship between law and honor in the context of both the (international) law of armed conflict and (national) military disciplinary law.

This approach may at first sight seem awkward. After all, this volume is devoted to the relationships that *international law* has with other normative orders. But the law of armed conflict as a distinct branch of international law has its roots in the development of national military discipline. Many of the international law rules on the conduct of warfare made their first appearance in a form recognizable to us in national military codes. For example, the Articles of War decreed by King Gustavus Adolphus of Sweden in 1621[34] and General Orders No. 100 drawn up by Professor Francis Lieber and promulgated by

---

[30] See Michael F. Lohr, *Working Group Recommendations Relating to Interrogation of Detainees*, Memorandum to the General Counsel of the Air Force (6 February 2003), at ¶ 3.

[31] See Arthur N. Gilbert, 'Law and Honour among Eighteenth-Century British Army Officers' 19 (1976) *Historical Journal* 75–87, at 76: "the honour code was often at odds with the law.... Indeed, just as there was often no simple and honourable road to follow, military officers sometimes had to choose between the code and the law."

[32] See, e.g., ibid., at 79ff.

[33] See, e.g., C. A. Harwell Wells, 'The End of the Affair? Anti-Dueling Laws and Social Norms in Antebellum America' (2001) *Vanderbilt Law Review* 1805–1847, at 1817.

[34] Articles and Military Lawes to Be Observed in the Warres 1621 (Sweden) (Articles of Gustavus Adolphus).

President Abraham Lincoln in 1863[35] both undoubtedly had a national character. Yet these documents are routinely cited as forerunners of the law of armed conflict. Thus, even as the law of armed conflict has developed into a subsystem of international law, it shares its roots and, ultimately, a part of its ideology, with military disciplinary law more generally. Accordingly, I think that it is quite appropriate to have a look at both legal regimes.

III. HONOR AND MILITARY DISCIPLINARY LAW

Military disciplinary law refers to the body of national law that proscribes certain conduct in the armed forces with the threat of penalties. In some states one can distinguish between military criminal law (involving the most serious offenses), and military disciplinary law in the narrow sense (encompassing offenses and punishments falling below what would be deemed criminal). However, in other states the line between the criminal and strictly disciplinary side of military disciplinary law is unclear.

In any event, military law defines a number of offenses that have no civilian equivalent whatsoever. A good example is "absence without leave,"[36] colloquially known as "being AWOL." In a nonmilitary setting, not showing up for work would be a violation of a contract and, at most, subject to an administrative reprimand. However, in a military context such an act would directly injure the legal interest of military effectiveness and thereby rise to the level of an offense. Other military offenses have a civilian counterpart but gain a particular significance in the military context. An example would be violence against a superior officer.[37] Such an act certainly offends against the legal interest of bodily integrity, just like the civilian offense of assault. However, the offense also entails an element of insubordination, which is detrimental to the discipline of the armed forces.

A. *Prejudicial and Discrediting Conduct*

On top of the specific military offenses just mentioned, military law of many countries contains one or more catch-all clauses that render punishable acts harming military effectiveness in some unspecified way. A provision of this sort

---

[35] General Orders no. 100 – Instructions for the Government of Armies of the United States in the Field, 24 April 1863 (U.S.).
[36] See, e.g., Armed Forces Act 2006 (UK), c. 52 (AFA), s. 9; Uniform Code of Military Justice, 5 May 1950 (U.S.), 64 Stat. 109, codified at 10 U.S.C. §§ 801–946 (UCMJ), art. 86; Defence Force Discipline Act 1982 (Australia) (DFDA), s. 24.
[37] See, e.g., AFA, s. 11; UCMJ, art. 90; DFDA, s. 25.

is often called the "general article" or "the devil's article" and deals with conduct "prejudicial to military discipline" or something along the same lines.

This type of an offense, like many other elements of contemporary systems of military justice, can be traced back to Roman military law, which provided that "every disorder to the prejudice of general discipline is a military offence, such as, for instance, the offense of laziness, or insolence, or idleness."[38] The previously mentioned 1621 Articles of War of Gustavus Adolphus listed a number of different military offenses and finally made punishable conduct not specifically mentioned but "repugnant to Military Discipline."[39] A similar provision was subsequently incorporated into the military law of many states, including the eighteenth-century British and American Articles of War,[40] through which they entered the military law tradition of the English-speaking world.

The current British formulation of the general article can be found in section 19 of the Armed Forces Act 2006: "A person subject to service law commits an offence if he does an act that is prejudicial to good order and service discipline."[41] In Canada, the National Defence Act 1985 contains very similar language.[42] A number of other states prefer a somewhat broader definition. For example, the general article in the U.S. Uniform Code of Military Justice makes punishable not only "all disorders and neglects to the prejudice of good order and discipline in the armed forces" but also "all conduct of a nature to bring discredit upon the armed forces" when committed by service members.[43]

---

[38] Justinian, *Digest*, bk. XLIX, pt. 16, at ¶ 6, cited in James K. Gaynor, 'Prejudicial and Discreditable Military Conduct: A Critical Appraisal of the General Article' (1971) 22 *Hastings Law Journal* 259–89, at 260.

[39] Articles of Gustavus Adolphus, art. 116: "Whatsoever is not contained in these Articles, and is repugnant to Military Discipline, or whereby the miserable and innocent country may against all right and reason be burdened withall, whatsoever offence finally shall be committed against these orders, that shall severall Commanders make good, or see severally punished unlesse themselves will stand bound to give further satisfaction for it."

[40] Cited in William Winthrop, *Military Law and Precedents*, 2nd ed. (Washington, DC: Government Printing Office, 1920), at 946, 957.

[41] AFA, s. 19(1). An omission is likewise punishable: s. 19(2). The punishment for the offense cannot exceed imprisonment for two years: s. 19(3). This is rather similar to the earlier Army Act 1955 (UK), c. 18, s. 69: "Any person subject to military law who is guilty, whether by any act or omission or otherwise, of conduct to the prejudice of good order and military discipline shall, on conviction by court-martial, be liable to imprisonment for a term not exceeding two years or any less punishment provided by this Act."

[42] National Defence Act 1985 (Canada), c. N-5, s. 129(1): "Any act, conduct, disorder or neglect to the prejudice of good order and discipline is an offence and every person convicted thereof is liable to dismissal with disgrace from Her Majesty's service or to less punishment."

[43] UCMJ, art. 134. I have omitted here the third limb of the provision – "crimes and offenses not capital" – which has the effect of incorporating civilian offenses into military law and making them triable by court-martial.

A general article in the Australian Defence Force Discipline Act 1982 similarly provides that "[a] defence member is guilty of an offence if the member does an act that is likely to prejudice the discipline of, or bring discredit on, the Defence Force."[44]

These provisions are, of course, open ended, and necessarily so. In the Federal Court of Australia, Justice Lockhart once noted that "it is impossible, indeed unwise, to attempt any exhaustive definition of the words employed" in the general article.[45] Indeed, one cannot comprehensively enumerate the kinds of conduct that prejudice good order and discipline. That said, the Australian Defence Force Discipline Appeals Tribunal (DFDAT) has clarified that while a reference to "prejudicial conduct" is "concerned with the internal organisation of the military forces and the maintenance of discipline therein," the "bringing discredit" clause "looks to the protection of the reputation" of the armed forces.[46]

As regards the intersection of unlawful and dishonorable conduct, it is particularly the latter clause that is interesting. It appears to invoke the public dimension of honor – the public perception of an individual service member, and by extension the entire armed force. Thus, the DFDAT has held that for a conduct "to be likely to bring discredit," the conduct must (i) have a degree of publicity outside the Australian Defence Force (ADF) and (ii) have a good or real chance of lowering the esteem of the ADF in the eyes of an ordinary citizen or a hypothetical person.[47]

The case where these observations were made also well illustrates how these requirements play out in practice. *In casu*, the DFDAT had before it a thirty-seven-year-old male army sergeant who had stored pornographic material depicting "ordinary sexual activity" in a password-protected section of an ADF computer accessible only by him and four system administrators. The tribunal was not convinced that either of the two conditions of bringing discredit on the ADF was met. As regards the first condition, the DFDAT observed that there must be "a good chance, not a remote possibility, that some person(s) other than a member of the force will become aware of the impugned conduct."[48] The tribunal thought that to hold in the present case that this condition was met beyond reasonable doubt would "be drawing a long bow."[49] But,

---

[44] DFDA, s. 60(1). An omission with the same effect is similarly punishable. Ibid., s. 60(2). In both instances the maximum punishment is 3 years imprisonment. Cf. Armed Forces Discipline Act 1971 (New Zealand), no. 53, s. 73(1).
[45] *Chief of the General Staff v. Stuart* (1995) 58 FCR 299, at 323.
[46] *Mocicka v. Chief of Army* [2003] ADFDAT 1, at ¶ 13.
[47] Ibid., at ¶ 14.
[48] Ibid., at ¶ 14.
[49] Ibid., at ¶ 17.

in any event, in the eyes of the DFDAT, the second condition proved fatal to the prosecution's case: the tribunal believed that, on being told of the sergeant's conduct, "the ordinary citizen would not raise an eyebrow."[50]

Thus, what kind of conduct would raise to the level of an offense would depend on how the acts reflected, in the eyes of the general public, on the reputation of the armed forces. Whether or not some act amounts to prejudicial or discrediting conduct depends on the circumstances prevailing at the time, societal expectations, and, significantly, the culture of the armed forces. As one commentator has rightly noted, the general article "has been a basic weapon in punishing conduct contrary to the *prevailing service ethic*."[51] While the wording of these provisions has not changed much over the years, the open-endedness of the terms employed has allowed for flexibility in light of the changes in the professional ethics of the armed forces.

B. Conduct Unbecoming an Officer and a Gentleman

Even though the general article already illustrates the open-endedness of military law, some military law systems also recognize a quintessentially honor-related offense that is related to the customary higher standards of conduct for officers.

These standards initially were derived from the medieval code of chivalry and made their way to written military codes.[52] The first appearance of a provision criminalizing "conduct unbecoming an officer" appears to have been in British Articles of War sometime in the eighteenth century. Certainly the 1765 British Articles of War already provided that "whatsoever Commissioned Officer shall be convicted before a General Court-martial, of behaving in a scandalous Infamous Manner, such as is unbecoming the Character of an Officer and a Gentleman, shall be discharged from Our Service."[53] The provision appeared in fairly similar language in the eighteenth-century U.S. Articles of War.[54]

---

[50] Ibid., at ¶ 17.
[51] See D. B. Nichols, 'The Devil's Article' (1963) 22 *Military Law Review* 111–37, at 111 (emphasis added).
[52] See James Snedeker, *Military Justice under the Uniform Code* (Boston: Little, Brown, 1953), at 887: "Military custom establishing a higher standard of conduct required of an officer has been traced back to the Norman Conquest and William the Conqueror."
[53] Rules and Articles for the Better Government of Our Horse and Foot Guards, and All Other Our Forces in the Kingdoms of Great Britain and Ireland, Dominions beyond the Seas and Foreign Parts (Articles of War) 1765 (UK), s. XV, art. 23.
[54] Articles of War, 30 June 1775 (U.S.), 2 Journals of the Continental Congress 111, art. 47. "Whatsoever commissioned officer shall be convicted before a general court-martial, of behaving in a scandalous, infamous manner, such as is unbecoming the character of an officer and a gentleman, shall be discharged from the service." Articles of War, 20 September 1776 (U.S.), 5 Journals of the Continental Congress 778, s. XIV, art. 21: "Whatsoever commissioned officer

The provision has gone through notable changes in different states, in some of them being abolished altogether, ostensibly having been considered anachronistic. Notably, by 1881, British law had dropped the requirement that the conduct be "infamous" – simply "scandalous" would do.[55] The *Manual of Military Law* then explained:

> Scandalous conduct may be either of a military or social character. But a charge of a social character is not to be preferred under this section, unless it is of so grave a nature as to render the officer unfit to remain in the service, and therefore is scandalous in respect of his military character.[56]

In 1971, the reference to a "gentleman" was dropped as well.[57] The debates in the House of Commons relating to the amendment are quite instructive. The minister of defence noted:

> I think that [the] phrase ["unbecoming the character of an officer and a gentleman"] is redolent of soldiering in the Punjab, of brandy glasses, card tables. I suppose this is a bit anachronistic. I imagine lawyers would find it very difficult to define what gentlemanly and ungentlemanly conduct is.[58]

One honorable member, expressing support for the disappearance of the reference to ungentlemanly conduct, went further and questioned the need for a special provision dealing with the conduct of officers.[59] The government responded by explaining:

> This offence has been a feature of Service disciplinary Acts for a long time. We considered it again very carefully when reviewing the systems, and we

---

shall be convicted, before a general court-martial, of behaving in a scandalous, infamous manner, such as is unbecoming the character of an officer and a gentleman, shall be discharged from the service." Articles of War, 31 May 1786 (U.S.), art. 20. "Whatever commissioned officer shall be convicted before a general court-martial, of behaving in a scandalous and infamous manner, such as is unbecoming an officer and a gentleman, shall be dismissed the service."

[55] Army Act 1881 (UK), 44 & 45 Vict., c. 58, s. 16: "Every officer who, being subject to military law, commits the following offence; that is to say, behaves in a scandalous manner, unbecoming the character of an officer and a gentleman, shall on conviction by court-martial be cashiered."; Army Act 1955 (UK), s. 64: "Every officer subject to military law who behaves in a scandalous manner unbecoming the character of an officer shall, on conviction by court-martial, be liable to dismissal from Her Majesty's service with or without disgrace."

[56] UK War Office, *Manual of Military Law*, 5th ed. (London: HM Stationery Office, 1907), at 283.

[57] Armed Forces Act 1971 (UK), c. 33, s. 29(1).

[58] UK House of Commons Debates, 13 January 1971, vol. 809, c. 99 (The Minister of State for Defence (Lord Balniel)).

[59] Ibid. c. 106 (Member for Dundee, East (Mr George Thomson)): "In our egalitarian age, I wonder why 'scandalous conduct', even in this amended Bill, should be an offence committed by officers but not, apparently, by any other Servicemen. Why do officers have a monopoly of this sin?"

have concluded that it is essential if the standards required of an officer are to be maintained. Every profession has its own system of ethical standards – examples are medicine and the law – which has to be accepted by members and which goes beyond the requirements of the ordinary law.... This provision enables the Service to deal with the case of an officer who has not necessarily committed a criminal offence and may not even have conducted himself in a way "to the prejudice" [of military discipline], but who nevertheless is unsuitable for further service in the Armed Forces. We believe that this provision is right.[60]

The provision was completely removed from British law with the entry into force of the Armed Forces Act 2006. Yet a provision of this sort remains, for example, in Irish law,[61] as well as the legislation of several Commonwealth states.

U.S. law has developed somewhat differently. The 1806 Articles of War dropped the references to both "infamous" and "scandalous."[62] According to Colonel William Winthrop, a preeminent authority on military law, the purpose of this change was to "extend materially the scope of the Article, and thus indeed to establish a higher standard of character and conduct for officers of the army."[63] Subsequent Articles of War[64] and the Uniform Code enacted in 1950 provide a broader definition of the offense. Thus, the current text reads, "Any commissioned officer, cadet, or midshipman who is convicted of conduct unbecoming an officer and a gentleman shall be punished as a court-martial may direct."[65]

An interesting point about this offense is that, until fairly recently, the only available punishment was dismissal from the service. The idea was that when an officer engages in unbecoming conduct it "exhibits him as morally

[60] Ibid., c. 150 (Under-Secretary of State for Defence (Mr Peter Kirk)).
[61] Defence Act 1954 (Ireland), s. 139: "scandalous manner."
[62] An Act for Establishing Rules and Articles for the Government of the Armies of the United States, 10 April 1806 (U.S.), c. 20, 2 Stat. 359, art. 83: "Any commissioned officer convicted before a general court-martial of conduct unbecoming an officer and a gentleman, shall be dismissed the service."
[63] Winthrop, *Military Law*, at 710–11. However, a contemporary study suggests that the amendment related to the difficulty of interpreting the word "infamous" as used in common law. Snedeker, *Military Justice*, at 888.
[64] Articles of War, 22 June 1874 (U.S.), ch. 5, 18 Stat. 228, art. 61: "Any officer who is convicted of conduct unbecoming an officer and a gentleman shall be dismissed from the service." Subsequently, cadets were added to the reach of the provision. Articles of War, contained in An Act Making Appropriations for the Support of the Army for the Fiscal Year ending June 30, 1917, and for Other Purposes, 29 August 1916 (U.S.), Pub. L. no. 64–242, ch. 418, 39 Stat. 619, at 650, art. 95: "Any officer or cadet who is convicted of conduct unbecoming an officer and a gentleman shall be dismissed from the service."
[65] UCMJ, art. 133.

unworthy to remain an officer of the honorable profession of arms."⁶⁶ The argument has been made that those who proposed (and succeeded in) the removal of mandatory dismissal misunderstood the offense.⁶⁷ This change made the provision applicable to minor infractions, effectively turning it into a general article for officers.⁶⁸

In any event, as with prejudicial and disgraceful conduct, it is futile to look for the meaning of unbecoming conduct in the black letter law. Recourse must be had to authoritative commentaries and judicial practice. Colonel Winthrop explained in his important textbook that to constitute conduct unbecoming an officer and a gentleman, the act that forms the basis of the charge must have a double significance and effect. Though it need not amount to a crime, it must offend so seriously against law, justice, morality, or decorum as to expose the offender to disgrace, socially or as a man, and at the same time must be of such a nature or committed under such circumstances as to bring dishonor or disrepute upon the military profession that he represents.⁶⁹

These views were expressed more than a century ago. But the explication of the offense in the current Manual of Courts-Martial remains strikingly similar:

> Conduct violative of this article is action or behavior in an official capacity which, in dishonoring or disgracing the person as an officer, seriously compromises the officer's character as a gentleman, or action or behavior in an unofficial or private capacity which, in dishonoring or disgracing the officer personally, seriously compromises the person's standing as an officer. There are certain moral attributes common to the ideal officer and the perfect gentleman, a lack of which is indicated by acts of dishonesty, unfair dealing, indecency, indecorum, lawlessness, injustice, or cruelty. Not everyone is or can be expected to meet unrealistically high moral standards, but there is a limit of tolerance based on customs of the service and military necessity below which the personal standards of an officer, cadet, or midshipman cannot fall without seriously compromising the person's standing as an officer, cadet, or midshipman or the person's character as a gentleman. This article prohibits conduct by a commissioned officer, cadet, or midshipman which, taking all the circumstances into consideration, is thus compromising.⁷⁰

---

[66] *Manual for Courts-Martial, United States* (1949), at ¶ 182, cited in Keithe E. Nelson, 'Conduct Expected of an Officer and a Gentleman: Ambiguity' (1970) 12 *U.S. Air Force JAG Law Review* 124–41, at 129.
[67] See ibid., at 129.
[68] See along these lines ibid., at 138.
[69] Winthrop, *Military Law*, at 711–12. Approvingly cited in *U.S. v. Howe*, 37 C.M.R. 429 (U.S. Court of Military Appeals, 1967), at 441–2, and *Parker v. Levy*, 417 U.S. 733 (1974), at 753–4.
[70] *Manual for Courts-Martial, United States* (2012), pt. iv, at ¶ 59.

The Navy–Marine Corps Court of Military Review has had the occasion to explain further that unbecoming conduct patently goes beyond the unsuitable, the inappropriate, the poor taste, the impropitious, or the inconsonant with usage. It encompasses the morally unbefitting and unworthy, characteristics with deleterious effects on officer status in particular and good order and discipline in general.[71]

Even though these tests leave room for interpretation as to what conduct could be deemed unbecoming, it is clear that conduct need not reach the level of "general criminality."[72] Courts have gone out of their way in explaining that they are applying to officers a higher standard than what would be applicable in the civil society. Thus, in 1891, the U.S. Court of Claims noted that "in military life there is a higher code termed honor, which holds its society to stricter accountability; and it is not desirable that the standard of the Army shall come down to the requirements of a criminal code."[73] This view – or at least the part referring to a higher standard of honor – has been paraphrased by the Navy Board of Review[74] and cited with approval by justices on appellate military courts[75] and the Supreme Court.[76]

In conclusion, it is pertinent to cite a historian who points out that "conduct unbecoming an officer and a gentleman was not defined in the Articles of War. By keeping it vague and indefinite, the charge remained flexible enough to change as ideas of honour changed."[77] The same doubtless holds true for more contemporary proscription of the offense.

IV. HONOR AND THE LAW OF ARMED CONFLICT

I turn now more specifically to international law and the rules governing the use of violence in armed conflict. Here I have in mind the branch of

---

[71] *U.S. v. van Steenwyk*, 21 M.J. 795 (Navy–Marine Corps Court of Military Review, 1985), at 803.

[72] Interestingly, the charge of conduct unbecoming has been used to "protect [officers] from being charged with more serious offences such as embezzlement, fraud or even rape." Gilbert, 'Law and Honour', at 78–9.

[73] *Fletcher v. U.S.*, 26 Ct. Cl. 541 (U.S. Court of Claims, 1891), at 563 (Nott C.J.).

[74] *U.S. v. Free*, 14 C.M.R. 466 (U.S. Navy Board of Review, 1953), at 471: "We refuse to subscribe to the proposition that the Code of Military Justice operates to lower the standards of honor and conduct in the military service to that of a civilian criminal code."

[75] See, e.g., *U.S. v. Tedder*, 24 M.J. 176 (U.S. Court of Military Appeals, 1987), at 182; *U.S. v. Moore*, 38 M.J. 490 (U.S. Court of Military Appeals, 1994), at 493; *U.S. v. Guaglione*, 27 M.J. 268 (U.S. Court of Military Appeals, 1988), at 271; *U.S. v. Wales*, 31 M.J. 301 (U.S. Court of Military Appeals, 1990), at 311 (Cox J., dissenting in part and concurring in result); *U.S. v. Harvey*, 67 M.J. 758 (U.S. Air Force Court of Criminal Appeals, 2009), at 762.

[76] *Parker v. Levy*, at 765 (Blackmun J.).

[77] Gilbert, 'Law and Honour', at 76.

international law that, according to a popular conception, aims at limiting violence in conflict to what is necessary for obtaining legitimate military aims and specially protecting persons not taking part in hostilities.[78]

In order to make sense of the relationship between law and honor in this context, it is particularly instructive to glance at military manuals on the law of armed conflict. These are publications produced by national governments for use in the armed forces, consolidating and summarizing the law applicable to the forces of that particular state.[79] Such manuals often contain not only statements of what is regarded to be black letter law, but also policy guidance and commentary, allowing a look at the underpinnings of the law of armed conflict, which sometimes remain hidden behind the sanitized and legalistic language of multilateral treaties.

A. *The Principle of Chivalry*

Tellingly, military manuals continue to invoke the ideal of chivalry or honor in explaining the function of the law of armed conflict. For example, the currently effective U.S. Field Manual on the Law of Land Warfare states:

> The law of war places limits on the exercise of a belligerent's power ... and requires that belligerents refrain from employing any kind or degree of violence which is not actually necessary for military purposes and that they conduct hostilities with regard for the principles of humanity and chivalry.[80]

Thus, chivalry is regarded as one of the three pillars on which the entire phenomenon of the law of war stands – the other two being military necessity and humanity. Military necessity relates to the idea that the purpose of armed hostilities is to bend the enemy to one's will, and nothing more than that. The principle of humanity requires respect, protection, and humane treatment of persons not taking part in hostilities. These principles roughly correspond to the dual objective of the law of armed conflict mentioned earlier. On top of these requirements, chivalry, as the 1958 British military manual explains,

---

[78] See, e.g., Marco Sassòli and Antoine A. Bouvier, *How Does Law Protect in War?* 3rd ed. (Geneva: ICRC, 2011), vol. i, ch. 1 (footnotes omitted): "International Humanitarian Law (IHL) can be defined as the branch of international law limiting the use of violence in armed conflicts by: a) sparing those who do not or no longer directly participate in hostilities; b) restricting it to the amount necessary to achieve the aim of the conflict, which – independently of the causes fought for – can only be to weaken the military potential of the enemy."
[79] See generally Nobuo Hayashi (ed.), *National Military Manuals on the Law of Armed Conflict*, 2nd ed. (Oslo: Torkel Opsahl, 2010).
[80] U.S. Department of the Army, FM 27–10 – *Law of Land Warfare* (1956), at ¶ 3.

"demands a certain amount of fairness in offence and defence, and a certain mutual respect between the opposing forces."[81]

The impact of chivalry on the modern law of armed conflict is manifold.[82] It has clearly inspired some rules, for example, those relating to the protection of prisoners of war (which were essential in knightly warfare), those dealing with the legal status of *parlamentaires* (the functional descendant of medieval heralds), and those prohibiting particular means of warfare (notably poison). Certainly, the principle of chivalry has lost ground to the principle of humanity in underpinning the specific rules of armed conflict, but the development of many of these rules cannot be explained away by reference to considerations of humanity alone.[83]

But there is one set of rules in the law of armed conflict whose honorable overtones are well recognized by military manuals. For example, a Joint Doctrine Manual of the U.S. armed forces, published in 2001, notes as follows:

> The concept of chivalry is difficult to define. It refers to the conduct of armed conflict in accordance with certain recognized formalities and courtesies. An armed conflict is rarely a polite contest. Nevertheless, the concept of chivalry is reflected in specific prohibitions such as those against dishonorable or treacherous conduct and against misuse of enemy flags or flags of truce. The concept of chivalry makes armed conflict slightly less savage and more civilized for the individual combatant.[84]

This equation of treacherous and dishonorable conduct, and its link to chivalry, is echoed widely in other military manuals and legal scholarship.[85] I will now turn more specifically to the prohibition of treacherous conduct.

---

[81] UK War Office, *The Law of War on Land (being Part III of the Manual of Military Law)* (London: HM Stationery Office, 1958), ¶ 3. Cf. Lassa Oppenheim, *International Law: A Treatise*, 7th ed. (London: Longmans, 1952), vol. ii, at 227 (¶ 67) taking the view that the principle of chivalry "arose in the Middle Ages, and introduced a certain amount of fairness in offence and defence, and a certain mutual respect."

[82] See generally Rain Liivoja, 'Chivalry without a Horse: Military Honour and the Modern Law of Armed Conflict', in Rain Liivoja and Andres Saumets (eds.), *The Law of Armed Conflict: Historical and Contemporary Perspectives* (Tartu: Tartu University Press, 2012) 75–100.

[83] Ibid.

[84] Office of the Judge Advocate General, *Law of Armed Conflict on the Operational and Tactical Levels: Joint Doctrine Manual* (Washington, DC: Government Printing Office, 2001), at ¶ 202(7).

[85] Royal Australian Air Force, AAP 1003 – *Operations Law for RAAF Commanders* (2004), at ¶ 6.14; U.S. Department of the Navy, NWP 1–14M – *The Commander's Handbook on the Law of Naval Operations* (1995), at ¶ 5.2: "Dishonorable (treacherous) means, dishonorable expedients, and dishonorable conduct during armed conflict are forbidden." Keith E. Puls (ed.), *Law of War Handbook* (Charlottesville, VA: Judge Advocate General's Legal Center and School,

B. Treachery and Perfidy

It is convenient to begin this discussion by referring to the 1899 and 1907 Hague Regulations. These key instruments on the conduct of hostilities undoubtedly reflect customary international law[86] and to a significant extent remain relevant today. Article 23(b) of the Regulations states that "it is especially forbidden ... to kill or wound treacherously individuals belonging to the hostile nation or army." This rule has been picked up almost verbatim by the Rome Statute of the International Criminal Court, which regards "killing or wounding treacherously individuals belonging to the hostile nation or army" a war crime in international armed conflicts.[87] The Statute also considers the equivalent conduct to be a war crime in noninternational armed conflicts.[88] However, neither the Hague Regulations nor the Rome Statute specifies what "treacherously" means. Admittedly, the ICC Elements of Crimes do provide a definition of sorts but one that does not entirely accurately reflect the concept under the Hague Regulations.[89]

In this situation, it is useful to start from what is generally agreed upon. Clearly, treachery is a kind of deception. Yet not all deception in war is, or has been, prohibited. Quite the contrary, trying to mislead the enemy by what are known as "ruses of war" has always formed a crucial part of military tactics. Only a certain kind of deception has been outlawed as treachery. The problem at hand is, then, how to distinguish treachery from legitimate ruses of war.

Article 8(b) of the Oxford Manual on the Laws of War on Land attempts to explain the meaning of treachery by giving two examples, namely, "keeping assassins in pay" and "feigning to surrender." A lengthier list can be found in academic writings. For instance, in the 8th edition of *Oppenheim's*

2005), at 190: "Condemnation of perfidy is an ancient precept of the LOW, derived from principle of chivalry." Thomas C. Wingfield, 'Chivalry in the Use of Force' (2001) 32 *University of Toledo Law Review* 111–36, at 113: "As strongly as the law of chivalry is woven into the fabric of the modern law of war, it remains most intact in the distinction between lawful ruses and treacherous perfidy." Stefan Oeter, 'Methods and Means of Combat', in Dieter Fleck (ed.), *The Handbook of International Humanitarian Law*, 2nd ed. (Oxford University Press, 2008) 119–235, at 228 (footnotes omitted): "Elementary rules of international law, the observance of which should be a matter of honour (and a product of a genuine sense of justice) are grossly abused by perfidy. Accordingly, the old notion of breach of honour is still present in the notion of perfidy: the (dishonourable) violation of the rules of 'chivalry', which in medieval customs constituted the core of perfidy."

[86] See *U.S. et al. v. Göring et al.*, 1 Trial of the Major War Criminals before the International Military Tribunal 171 (International Military Tribunal at Nuremberg, 1946), at 253–4.
[87] Rome Statute of the International Criminal Court, Rome, 17 July 1998, in force 1 July 2000, 2187 U.N.T.S. 90, art. 8(2)(b)(xi).
[88] Ibid., art. 8(2)(e)(ix) ('Killing or wounding treacherously a combatant adversary').
[89] See note 113 and accompanying text.

International Law, the editor, Hersch Lauterpacht, regarded the prohibition of treachery as demanding that

> no assassin must be hired, and no assassination of combatants be committed; a price may not be put on the head of an enemy individual; proscription and outlawing are prohibited; no treacherous request for quarter must be made; no treacherous simulation of sickness or wounds is permitted.[90]

These examples can be broadly classified into two groups: on the one hand, assassination, outlawry, and the like, and, on the other hand, the simulation of wounds, sickness, or surrender.

As regards the first form of treachery, further sources provide clarification of the range of acts contemplated. Thus, the Lieber Code states:

> The law of war does not allow proclaiming either an individual belonging to the hostile army, or a citizen, or a subject of the hostile government an outlaw, who may be slain without trial by any captor, any more than the modern law of peace allows such international outlawry; on the contrary, it abhors such outrage.[91]

The consecutive editions of the U.S. Field Manual explain that article 23(b) of the Hague Regulations should be "construed as prohibiting assassination, proscription, or outlawry of an enemy, or putting a price upon an enemy's head, as well as offering a reward for an enemy 'dead or alive.'"[92] Similarly, but in some more detail, the 1958 UK manual states in conjunction with article 23(b) that

> Assassination, the killing or wounding of a selected individual behind the lines of battle by enemy agents or partisans, and the killing or wounding by treachery individuals belonging to the opposing nation or army, are not lawful acts of war.... In view of the prohibition of assassination, the proscription or outlawing or the putting of a price on the head of an enemy individual or any offer for an enemy "dead or alive" is forbidden.[93]

Turning now to the second form of treachery – malicious simulation of surrender or incapacitation – it is also well recognized in military manuals. Thus, in giving further examples of treachery, the U.S. Field Manual states that "it is improper to feign surrender so as to secure an advantage over the opposing belligerent thereby."[94]

---

[90] See Oppenheim, *International Law*, vol. ii, at 341 (¶ 110).
[91] General Orders no. 100, art. 148.
[92] U.S. Department of the Army, *Law of Land Warfare* (1956), at ¶ 31. See also Michael N. Schmitt, 'State-Sponsored Assassination in International and Domestic Law' (1992) 17 *Yale Journal of International Law* 609–85, at 630.
[93] UK War Office, *Law of War on Land*, at ¶ 115.
[94] U.S. Department of the Army, *Law of Land Warfare* (1956), at ¶ 50.

The scope of this limb of the prohibition was modified by the 1977 Additional Protocol I to the Geneva Conventions (AP I). Article 37(1) of AP I stipulates that "it is prohibited to kill, injure or capture an adversary by resort to perfidy."[95] Leaving aside the slight terminological change[96] and adding the capture of an enemy combatant to the list of modalities, the crucial development was the definition of perfidy in the abstract. Article 37(1) defines perfidy as "acts inviting the confidence of an adversary to lead him to believe that he is entitled to, or is obliged to accord, protection under the rules of international law applicable in armed conflict, with intent to betray that confidence."[97]

The critical part of this definition is the characterization of the deception as an attempt to invoke a "legal entitlement ... to immunity from attack."[98] For example, since a combatant incapacitated by wounds or sickness is protected under the law of armed conflict from attack,[99] feigning such incapacitation so as to kill, injure, or capture an adversary would amount to perfidy.[100] In brief, "perfidy is the deliberate claim to legal protection for hostile purposes."[101]

Conversely, "[a] betrayal of confidence not related to this form of legal protection does not amount to perfidy" within the meaning of AP I.[102] In this respect article 23(b) of the Hague Regulations is wider than article 37(1) of AP I: perfidy under the latter is shorthand for hostile acts that constitute the abuse of the protective veil of the law of armed conflict, whereas treachery under the former includes perfidious acts but also covers at least assassinations and outlawry.

Of course, assassinations and outlawry are only examples of treachery. This raises the question whether treachery can be defined in some more principled way. The various U.S. manuals' attempt to explain the distinction between permissible ruses of war and treachery/perfidy is helpful in this respect.[103]

---

[95] AP I, art. 37(1).
[96] For the rationale, see Jean de Preux, 'Article 37 – Prohibition of Perfidy', in Yves Sandoz et al. (eds), *Commentary on the Additional Protocols to the Geneva Conventions* (Geneva: ICRC & Martinus Nijhoff, 1987) 429–44, at ¶ 1488.
[97] AP I, art. 37(1).
[98] See Yoram Dinstein, *The Conduct of Hostilities under the Law of Armed Conflict* (Cambridge University Press, 2004), at 201.
[99] AP I, art. 41(1) and (2)(c).
[100] Ibid., art. 37(1)(b).
[101] de Preux, 'Article 37', at ¶ 1500.
[102] See Frits Kalshoven and Liesbeth Zegveld, *Constraints on the Waging of War: An Introduction to International Humanitarian Law*, 3rd ed. (Geneva: ICRC, 2001), at 93.
[103] U.S. War Department, *Rules of Land Warfare (Part Two of Basic Field Manual, Volume VII, Military Law)* (Washington, DC: Government Printing Office, 1934), at ¶ 39; U.S. War Department, FM 27–10 – *Rules of Land Warfare* (Washington, DC: Government Printing Office, 1940), at ¶ 39; U.S. Department of the Army, *Law of Land Warfare* (1956), at ¶ 50: "ruses of war are legitimate so long as they do not involve treachery or perfidy on the part of the

According to the current Field Manual, the fundamental principle is that "it would be an improper practice to secure an advantage of the enemy by deliberate lying or misleading conduct which involves a breach of faith, or when there is a moral obligation to speak the truth."[104] This is not very far from an explanation given by James Spaight:

> It is the essence of treachery that the offender assumes a false character by which he deceives his enemy and thereby is able to effect a hostile act which, had he come under his true colours, he could not have done. He takes advantage of his enemy's reliance on his honour.[105]

Morris Greenspan states in roughly similar terms that "among unlawful ruses are those that involve killing and wounding by treachery. Lying to the enemy in order to secure a military advantage is wrong, when there is a legal or moral obligation to be truthful."[106]

I would argue, on the basis of these observations, that breaching a defined legal obligation to be truthful while harming the enemy amounts to perfidy, whereas breaching a moral obligation or an obligation as a matter of honor to be truthful breaches the prohibition of treachery.

So conceived, treachery boils down to the betrayal of faith, a failure in moral obligations and dishonor. It relies on extralegal concepts on what is proper and honorable in warfare at a particular point in time. For example, as concerns the prohibition of assassinations, the U.S. and British military manuals published in the 1950s contain a rather narrow reading of the rule. The 1956 edition of the U.S. manual explicitly states that the prohibition of assassinations, as deriving from the general rule against treachery, "does not ... preclude attacks on individual soldiers or officers of the enemy whether in the zone of hostilities, occupied territory, or elsewhere."[107] The 1958 British manual

---

belligerent resorting to them. They are, however, forbidden if they contravene any generally accepted rule."

[104] U.S. Department of the Army, *Law of Land Warfare* (1956), at ¶ 50. See also Schmitt, 'State-Sponsored Assassination', at 617: "Treachery exists ... if the victim possessed an affirmative reason to trust the assailant."

[105] See J. M. Spaight, *War Rights on Land* (London: Macmillan, 1911), at 87; approvingly cited in Schmitt, 'State-Sponsored Assassination', at 633.

[106] See Morris Greenspan, *The Modern Law of Land Warfare* (Berkeley: University of California Press, 1959), at 320. "For instance, it would be improper to gain a respite from enemy action by claiming that an armistice had been concluded when no such agreement had been made. Such a statement involves the good faith of the party making it. On the other hand, it is legitimate to make false assertions to the enemy where there is no legal or moral duty to tell the truth. It would, therefore be proper to persuade an enemy force that it was surrounded when such was not the case, or to threaten a bombardment when there were no guns to back up the threat. It is the duty of the enemy to be on guard against such ruses." Ibid.

[107] U.S. Department of the Army, *Law of Land Warfare* (1956), at ¶ 31.

similarly mentions that "it is not forbidden to send a detachment or individual members of the armed forces to kill, by sudden attack, members or a member of the enemy armed forces."[108]

The question has gained prominence more recently in connection to the Israeli practice of targeted killings of certain "terrorists." In assessing the legality of the practice, the Israeli Supreme Court took the position that if a person is a legitimate target – either a combatant or a civilian "taking a direct part in hostilities" – targeting him or her would be permissible under international law (and hence, by implication, not prohibited as assassination), as long as less injurious means are not available.[109] It is difficult to argue against this position, especially as the once valid distinction between attacks on the enemy on the battlefield and behind enemy lines is exceedingly difficult to maintain in modern conflicts. Thus, it may well be that the contemporary prohibition of assassinations is basically covered by other rules of humanitarian law, such as the prohibition of perfidy as contained in AP I (ruling out an attack disguised as a civilian)[110] or by the prohibition of disproportionate attacks or attacks by weapons causing unnecessary suffering.[111]

However, the prohibition of putting a price on the enemy's head, even if he or she is a legitimate target, is more difficult to deal with under other rules of the law. It may be regarded as inciting civilians to commit acts of violence, thereby to take part in hostilities, and commit perfidy. However, it is hard to see how turning the enemy soldiers against their own commanders with monetary inducements could violate any specific rule of international law.[112] Yet, the act would be "unfair" and thus prohibited as treachery.

Returning briefly to the war crime of treacherous killing or wounding under the Rome Statute, it is worth noting that the Elements of Crimes require that "the perpetrator invited the confidence or belief of one or more persons [or, as the case may be, combatant adversaries] that they were entitled to, or were

---

[108] UK War Office, *Law of War on Land*, commentary to art. 115.
[109] HCJ 769/02 *Public Committee against Torture in Israel et al. v. Government of Israel et al.* [2006] 2 IsrLR 459 (Supreme Court, Israel).
[110] A textbook example from the pre–AP I era is the assassination of SS-Obergruppenführer Reinhard Heydrich by Czech soldiers in civilian clothing in 1942. Presuming that the U.S. and British position on assassination was valid law already then, the legal problem would not have been singling out Heidrich for attack or attacking him behind enemy lines – he was, beyond doubt, a legitimate military objective – but the fact that his attackers masqueraded as civilians.
[111] AP I, arts. 51(5)(b) and 35(2).
[112] See Waldemar A. Solf, 'Article 37 – Prohibition of Perfidy', in Michael Bothe et al. (eds), *New Rules for Victims of Armed Conflicts: Commentary on the Two 1977 Protocols Additional to the Geneva Conventions of 1949* (The Hague: Martinus Nijhoff, 1982) 201–7, at 204; Dinstein, *Conduct of Hostilities*, at 202.

obliged to accord, protection under rules of international law applicable in armed conflict."[113] Thus, the statute takes a conservative approach and avoids entering the debate as to what acts that do not strictly speaking qualify as perfidy might still amount to treachery. In other words, for the purposes of the Rome Statute, only perfidious acts are regarded as treacherous acts.

V. BY WAY OF CONCLUSION

As the preceding discussion shows, in circumstances where legal regulation and notions of honor overlap, the law makes use of phrases like "discrediting conduct," "conduct unbecoming an officer," and "treacherous conduct." In my view, the open-endedness of the general articles in national military law and the vagueness of the prohibition of treachery in international law demonstrate that in some instances the law relies on the essentially nonlegal idea of honor.

The reason for doing so seems to be twofold. On the one hand, reliance on notions like honor and military ethos allows the law to take into account changes occurring within the military profession. Rather than having to revise the legal regime regularly, those in a position to apply the law are permitted to consider ethical and cultural factors in a particular temporal context. On the other hand, this indeterminacy of black letter law is an indication of a deeper problem in attempting to enact specific rules. The problem is that ideas such as honor cannot be easily verbalized in the abstract and reduced to legal prescriptions.[114] Thus, Australian Navy doctrine acknowledges that "as a Navy value, honour guides our actions in a way explicit rules cannot; it shapes our conscience and determines our notions of pride, self-respect and shame."[115]

The symbiosis of law and honor described in this chapter highlights a broader issue in legal philosophy that should be of some interest when dealing with normative pluralism. This is the general question of the law's occasional references to what appear to be extralegal standards. These kinds of standards are particularly common in constitutional law, which may prohibit "cruel and unusual punishment" without any explanation as to what "cruel" means or, in other contexts, invoke broad notions of fairness.

"Hard" legal positivists like Joseph Raz suggest that in such cases there are gaps in the law. Those gaps can be filled by the courts' exercising

---

[113] Elements of Crimes, Doc. no. ICC-PIDS-LT-03–002/11_Eng, art. 8(2)(e)(ix), element 1, and art. 8(2)(b)(xi), element 1.
[114] See Osiel, *End of Reciprocity*, at 334.
[115] See Royal Australian Navy, *Leadership Ethic*, at ¶ 2.19. See also Royal Australian Navy, *Navy Values: Serving Australia with Pride* (September 2009) and Adams, 'Honour'.

discretion – Raz argues that "the Constitution, by deploying many moral categories, gives discretion to the courts and directs them to use it in light of the true, or the best, moral understanding of what is cruel, etc."[116]

Without reproducing here the criticisms made by other legal philosophers of this theory,[117] I merely note that this approach becomes difficult to maintain in the context of criminal law. A situation where a judge (or a court martial panel) can freely determine whether certain conduct is or is not criminal is intolerable. Yet this would precisely be the case where the definition of the offense of "conduct unbecoming an officer" would be regarded a "gap" in the law to be filled by judicial discretion.

The argument has been advanced before U.S. courts that the general articles of military law are impermissibly vague and therefore unconstitutional. However, the U.S. Supreme Court has rejected this argument.[118] The Navy–Marine Corps Court of Military Review has taken the position that "practice, usage and custom guide the determination of what misconduct is reasonably governed by the statute and under what circumstances a contemplated act may violate the statute."[119] In this light, the better view, acceptable perhaps to the "soft" legal positivists, might be to think of codes of honor as being incorporated into the law by reference, and given legal effect within the confines of notions such as discrediting conduct and treachery.

---

[116] See Joseph Raz, 'Dworkin: A New Link in the Chain' (1986) 74 *California Law Review* 1102–19, at 1110.

[117] See, e.g., Timothy A. O. Endicott, 'Raz on Gaps: The Surprising Part', in Lukas H. Meyer et al. (eds.), *Rights, Culture and the Law: Themes from the Legal and Political Philosophy of Joseph Raz* (Oxford University Press, 2003) 99–115.

[118] *Parker v. Levy*. For an overview of earlier case law, see Frederick Bernays Wiener, 'Are the General Military Articles Unconstitutionally Vague?' (1967) 54 *American Bar Association Journal* 357–64.

[119] *U.S. v. van Steenwyk*, at 802.

6 Law versus Codes of Conduct: Between Convergence and Conflict

Katja Creutz*

I. INTRODUCTION

Normative pluralism can embrace two – albeit related – approaches: either the coexistence of several normative orders is in focus, or alternatively one purports to look at concrete situations in which two (or more) specific norms from different normative orders prescribe conflicting behavior. In the former situation the focus should be on the relationship between the relevant normative orders – are they separate or do they overlap? Does one affect the other, and if so, how? In the latter case of normative pluralism one is more concerned with how to solve a situation that is instructed by different or even contradictory prescriptions; as Jan Klabbers and Touko Piiparinen in their opening remarks recalled about the Yugoslavia bombings in 1999, it was to be considered unlawful under international law but morally necessary.[1] Another case illuminating normative pluralism in everyday life concerned the Egyptian grandmother Eveline Fadayel, who was denied a residence permit under Finnish law and was eventually to be extradited from Finland in 2010 but was offered a safe haven by the Orthodox Church in Finland. The decision to help Fadayel was, according to Archbishop Leo, the morally right thing to do.[2]

In this chapter the focus will be on two normative orders that perhaps at first glance do not collide very often, namely, law and the (more or less) internally formulated rules of companies. With these internal company rules I here understand a range of different initiatives that go under a variety of names, mostly codes of conduct. I shall hereafter refer to these as codes of conduct.

---

* The author wishes to thank Ms. Ida Repo and Ms. Maria José for research assistance.
[1] See Jan Klabbers and Touko Piiparinen, 'Normative Pluralism: An Exploration', Chapter 1 in this volume.
[2] See Janne Laitinen, 'Arkkipiispa Leo piilotti Eveline Fadayelin Lintulan luostariin', 16.1.2011, *Savon Sanomat*, available at www.savonsanomat.fi/uutiset/kotimaa/arkkipiispa-leo-piilotti-evel ine-fadayelin-lintulan-luostariin/637032 (accessed 11 April 2011).

Whereas they share with law the aim of instructing how to behave, they are nevertheless limited to regulating the conduct of private companies. Moreover, two main features separate codes of conduct from law. First, these codes have a self-regulatory background; they are the product of companies regulating themselves. The difference with law thus lies in the fact that codes of conduct do not emanate from recognized lawmaking powers, but from self-regulation, whose purpose and effectiveness have generally been contested. Second, codes of conduct are considered voluntary commitments that stand out from "the strictly binding normative system called law."[3] The very rationale of these codes of conduct is indeed that they are different from legal rules.

The aim of this chapter is to analyze the conjunction of self-regulatory codes of conduct and law from the perspective of normative pluralism. What happens when one is confronted with legal norms as opposed to corporate codes of conduct? Do their prescriptions generally conflict or do they instead overlap? Even though the main focus of this book lies with *conflicts* between law and various other normative orders rather than the *relationship* between normative orders, both aspects will be an integral part of this study. In this chapter the argument from the outset will be that self-regulation and law have a close relationship. It will be set forth that self-regulation is actually a paradox: it never is truly "self"-created; instead, it is dependent on law in many ways. In fact, it may even constitute an alternative to law, which is, after all, imperfect in many cases. Thus, the contents of the rules mostly overlap and the difference between the two normative orders rather lies in their different characters. It will be argued that self-regulation is an instrument whose very rationale is versatility; it can be portrayed as nonlaw, as soft law, and even as law. Thus, the character of regulation becomes decisive, not the content of the rules.

In this chapter I will examine the effect of globalization upon the normative setting surrounding transnational corporations in Section II. The third section examines corporate codes of conduct as a tool of self-regulation. In addition to a general look into different kinds of codes of conduct and the character of the rules embodied in them, the study will proceed to show in the fourth section that norms embodied in codes of conduct and law actually converge rather than conflict. The fifth and main section of the chapter will focus on an analysis of the discourse on self-regulation and law. The analysis is divided into three parts: self-regulation as nonlaw, self-regulation as soft law, and, finally,

---

[3] See Claes Lundblad, 'Some Legal Dimensions of Corporate Codes of Conduct' in Ramon Mullerat (ed.), *Corporate Social Responsibility: The Corporate Governance of the 21st Century* (The Hague: Kluwer Law International, 2005), 385–99 at 386.

self-regulation as law. In the sixth and final part I will sum up my findings and turn to aspects of self-regulation and law that contribute to a more general discussion on normative pluralism in a globalized world.

II. TRANSNATIONAL CORPORATIONS, NORMATIVE PLURALISM, AND GOVERNANCE GAPS

Normative pluralism may paradoxically generate from situations in which a normative void exists – either as a matter of principle or as a matter of fact. In other words, law exists but it might not apply to the entity in question or it might be inadequate.[4] One fitting example is the regulation of transnational corporations (TNCs), which is under study in this chapter. To begin with, international law does not directly regulate TNCs. The extent to which national laws regulate TNCs varies; although national laws regulate the activities of companies in a specific state, some states may be too weak to enforce their regulation or regulation is undeveloped, characteristics that may attract companies in the first place.[5] Jonathan I. Charney has claimed that their "nonstatus immunizes them from direct accountability from international legal norms and permits them to use sympathetic national governments to parry outside efforts to mold their behavior."[6] Neither is there any general universal moral code that guides their behavior nor any other normative order that clearly regulates TNCs. Further, the question of corporations as moral actors is debated; many scholars consider it impossible for corporations to be subjected to morality and thus claim that companies cannot act morally or immorally to begin with.[7] What is interesting with regard to transnational corporations and their

---

[4] See Armin von Bogdandy, 'Codes of Conduct and the Legitimacy of International Law', in Rüdiger Wolfrum and Volker Röben (eds.), *Legitimacy in International Law* (Heidelberg: Springer, 2008), 299–307 at 299.

[5] See, e.g., César A. Rodríguez-Garavito, 'Global Governance and Labor Rights: Codes of Conduct and Anti-Sweatshop Struggles in Global Apparel Factories in Mexico and Guatemala', (2005) 33 *Politics & Society* 203–33 at esp. 212.

[6] See Jonathan I. Charney, 'Transnational Corporations and Developing International Law', (1983) *Duke Law Journal* 748–88 at 767.

[7] For instance, Manuel G. Velasquez has argued that "it makes little sense to say that corporations are morally responsible for their wrongful acts." See Manuel G. Velasquez, 'Why Corporations Are Not Morally Responsible for Anything They Do', in Larry May and Stacey Hoffman (eds.), *Collective Responsibility: Five Decades of Debate in Theoretical and Applied Ethics* (Lanham, MD: Rowman & Littlefield, 1991), 111–31 at 123. Methodological individualism also lies at the heart of H. D. Lewis and J. W. N. Watkins's rejections of collective forms of responsibility in general. In the words of Lewis: "Responsibility belongs essentially to the individual." See H. D. Lewis, 'Collective Responsibility' in May and Hoffman (eds.), *Collective Responsibility*, 17–33 at 17, and similarly Watkins has explicated that social phenomena can be explained only in terms of the individual. See J. W. N. Watkins, 'Methodological Individualism: A Reply',

governance is the fact that there seems to be disagreement about whether there is a gap in the governance of companies to begin with; some commentators hold the view that there is a governance gap when it comes to TNCs, whereas others claim that "firms are no longer simply accountable under local law, but to international norms and standards, such as those promulgated by the International Labour Organization (ILO), the Universal Declaration of Human Rights (UDHR), and corporate best practices."[8] The exact scope of regulation relative to transnational companies is thus unclear.

The uncertainty regarding the regulatory setting of TNCs is a consequence of globalization since among the most salient processes of globalization are the proliferation and diversification of actors in international affairs. Alongside states there are now a variety of international actors, leading to a mixture of public and private subjects affecting the daily lives of all of us. Whereas states (perhaps) remain the main actors, their room to maneuver has remarkably declined. By virtue of globalization, especially the role of economic actors has strengthened.[9] In 2008, there were according to the United Nations Conference on Trade and Development (UNCTAD) 82,000 transnational companies.[10] Many of them are as powerful as weaker states, and their activities and decisions have consequences for "national economies, for jobs, for living standards, and for working conditions."[11] Against this background it comes

---

(1955) 22 *Philosophy of Science* 58–62 at 58. In similar terms, Milton Friedman held the view that "only people can have responsibilities." See Milton Friedman, 'The Social Responsibility of Business Is to Increase Its Profits', *New York Times Magazine*, 13 September 1970, available at www.colorado.edu/studentgroups/libertarians/issues/friedman-soc-resp-business.html (accessed 1 April 2011).

[8] World Bank Group, Corporate Social Responsibility Practice, *Company Codes of Conduct and International Standards: An Analytical Comparison*. Part I of II. *Apparel, Footwear and Light Manufacturing, Agribusiness and Tourism*, October 2003, at 1. Those speaking in terms of governance gaps are, for example, Carola Glinski, who states that there has not been direct regulation in public law of different aspects of transnational economic activities. See her 'Corporate Codes of Conduct: Moral or Legal Obligation?' in Doreen McBarnet, Aurora Voiculescu and Tom Campbell (eds.), *The New Corporate Accountability: Corporate Social Responsibility and the Law* (Cambridge University Press, 2007), 119–47 at 119.

[9] Patomäki and Teivainen have elaborated on the many meanings of 'globalization', one of which can be defined in economic terms and the focus on transnational neoliberalism. See Heikki Patomäki and Teivo Teivainen, 'Critical Responses to Neoliberal Globalization in the Mercosur Region: Roads towards Cosmopolitan Democracy?' (2002) 9 *Review of International Political Economy* 37–71 at 40. The economic rationale of globalization can thus explain the rise of especially economic actors.

[10] United Nations Conference on Trade and Development, *World Investment Report: Transnational Corporations, Agricultural Production and Development*, United Nations, New York and Geneva, 2009, at 17.

[11] See General Secretary Neil Kearney, International Textile, Garment, and Leather Workers' Federation, *Privatisation, Globalisation and the Growing Power of Transnational Companies*,

as no surprise that transnational corporations have been called the "main actors of globalization."[12]

The capability of various actors to affect international affairs has generated warranted demands for regulation and accountability. Reports about environmental damage, human rights abuses, and corruption are frequent despite claims from the actors themselves that their powers often are exaggerated.[13] Transnational corporations are the ones most frequently blamed for abuses. Mobile phone companies have been accused of supporting the dictatorship in Turkmenistan or using so-called conflict minerals from the Congo in their phones;[14] garment companies have faced "sweatshop" charges for using child labor or forced labor;[15] private security and military companies have allegedly tortured in Iraq and used indiscriminate weapons in Africa;[16] and companies in the extractive industry have been involved in arbitrary killings in Nigeria, environmental degradation, and even infiltration into national governments and intelligence exchange.[17]

Cairo, 19 March 1997, available at training.itcilo.it/actrav_cdrom1/english/global/clause/nkpriv.htm (accessed 11 January 2011).

[12] See Katarina Weilert, 'Transnational Corporations in United Nations Law and Practice', (2010) 14 *Max Planck Yearbook of United Nations Law* 445–506 at 447.

[13] See René Van Roij, chief legal counsel for Shell in 2000, claiming that "the power of multinational companies is generally widely exaggerated." Cited in Sorcha Macleod and Douglas Lewis, 'Transnational Companies: Power, Influence and Responsibility', (2004) 4 *Global Social Policy* 77–98 at 78.

[14] See Arto Halonen's documentary film *Shadow of the Holy Book* of 2008, claiming that several international companies, including Nokia Siemens, helped the former dictator of Turkmenistan Mr. Saparmurat Niyazov by accepting his propaganda in return for business profits. For more information on the film, see www.ses.fi/en/film.asp?id=798 (accessed 13 January 2011); Frank Poulsen's documentary film *Blood in the Mobile* released in 2010 focused on Nokia Siemens and its use of conflict minerals from the Democratic Republic of Congo. See, e.g., Helsingin Sanomat, 'Dokumentti yhdistää Nokian kännykät Kongon veriseen konfliktiin', 2 November 2010, www.hs.fi/talous/artikkeli/Dokumentti+yhdist%C3%A4%C3%A4+Nokian+k%C3%A4n nyk%C3%A4t+Kongon+veriseen+konfliktiin/1135261360213 (accessed 13 January 2011).

[15] See *Guardian*, 'Indian "slave" Children Found Making Low-Cost Clothes Destined for GAP', 28 October 2007, available at www.guardian.co.uk/world/2007/oct/28/ethicalbusiness.retail (accessed 13 October 2011); *Guardian*, 'Zara Accused in Brazil Sweatshop Inquiry', 18 August 2011, available at www.guardian.co.uk/world/2011/aug/18/zara-brazil-sweatshop-accusation (accessed 13 October 2011).

[16] See Katja Creutz, *Transnational Privatised Security and the International Protection of Human Rights* (Helsinki: Erik Castrén Institute, 2006).

[17] See BBC, 'Shell Settles Nigeria Deaths Case', 9 June 2009, available at news.bbc.co.uk/2/hi/africa/8090493.stm (accessed 13 January 2011); Helene Cooper and Peter Baker, 'U.S. Opens Criminal Inquiry into Oil Spill', 1 June 2010, *New York Times*, available at www.nytimes.com/2010/06/02/us/02spill.html (accessed 13 January 2011); David Smith, 'WikiLeaks Cables: Shell's Grip on Nigerian State Revealed', 8 December 2010, *Guardian*, available at www.guardian.co.uk/business/2010/dec/08/wikileaks-cables-shell-nigeria-spying (accessed 13 January 2011).

When transnational companies or other nonstate actors are accused of child labor, destroying the environment, or even torture, one question presents itself: how are their activities to be regulated? According to UN Special Representative John Ruggie,[18] the lack of regulation or the existence of so-called governance gaps, as he has termed them, generates an environment conducive to wrongful acts. According to Ruggie, the gap is constantly widening: "the scope and impact of economic forces and actors, and the capacity of societies to manage their adverse consequences, [is] unsustainable."[19] The search for rules that bind the actors is thus pressing, but it remains unclear what normative order can manage to set up standards of right and wrong behavior in a given situation, and by which the actor considers itself to be bound.[20] In addition, several regulation processes may be under way, simultaneously leading to a situation of normative pluralism.

The fact is that international law has faced difficulties in addressing the range of nonstate actors empowered by globalization. As Macleod and Lewis have noted, "the traditional Westphalian conception of international law being state-centred is becoming increasingly inappropriate in a global society where non-state actors wield great power."[21] Undoubtedly, international law can develop to encompass the activities of new actors. One example is the formation of rules on the responsibility of international organizations by the International Law Commission (ILC). Progressive development is nevertheless slow, and contemporary international law is able to reach actors such as NGOs and TNCs mainly through the state. Andrew Clapham has pointed to the "strong resistance to including entities such as transnational corporations in a discussion about the subjects of international law."[22] This is witnessed, for example, by the decades of work within the UN framework for laying down legally binding rules on transnational corporations, which to date has failed to materialize. Meanwhile, the search for other options continues. Besides law, which appears the obvious mechanism to regulate

---

[18] John Ruggie is the special representative of the secretary-general on human rights and transnational corporations and other business enterprises, a mandate established in 2005 by the former UN Commission on Human Rights. See Commission on Human Rights, resolution 2005/69.

[19] See UN Doc. A/HRC/14/27, 9 April 2010, Report of the Special Representative of the Secretary-General on the Issue of Human Rights and Transnational Corporations and Other Business Enterprises, John Ruggie, at 3, para. 2.

[20] Alf Ross has described a normative system as something that "comprise[s] a set of rules of conduct which a certain group of persons regularly follow, and which they follow because they feel them to be binding." Alf Ross, *On Guilt, Responsibility, and Punishment* (London: Stevens and Sons, 1975) at 2.

[21] See Macleod and Lewis, 'Transnational Companies', at 78.

[22] See Andrew Clapham, *Human Rights Obligations of Non-State Actors* (Oxford University Press, 2006), at 76.

undesired behavior of various actors, alternative modes of regulation stand out, one of which is self-regulation. Both law and self-regulation are instruments of setting up norms determining what in a given situation qualifies as right and wrong conduct. The process of globalization has, however, shifted focus from governmental regulation to voluntary regulation; companies are now expected to set the standards themselves, especially in the area of labor and environmental standards as well as human rights.[23] As Shell's chief legal counsel noted in 2000: "we have entered the age of self-regulation."[24] This assertion seems plausible against the World Bank's estimations in 2003 that more than one thousand codes of conduct have been developed by individual TNCs.[25] In fact, few transnational companies today lack a code of conduct.[26]

III. CODES OF CONDUCT – CORPORATE TOOLS FOR SELF-REGULATION

Milton Friedman proclaimed in 1970 that the social responsibility of companies is to be more profitable, not to bear responsibility for affairs that apparently belong to the public domain.[27] Today, few companies, however, share Friedman's view.[28] The concept of corporate social responsibility (CSR) has steadily gained prominence and has become a cognizable means of dealing with the highlighted importance of companies in the area of environmental, social, and human rights. A widespread corporate practice of formulating various kinds of declarations, statements, or codes of conduct (CoCs) with regard to social affairs testifies at least partly to the fact that corporations accept the idea of corporate social responsibility,[29] although the reasons behind

[23] See Rhys Jenkins, Ruth Pearson and Gill Seyfang, 'Introduction' in Rhys Jenkins, Ruth Pearson and Gill Seyfang (eds.), *Corporate Responsibility and Labour Rights: Codes of Conduct in the Global Economy* (London: Earthscan, 2002), 1–12 at 1.
[24] See Macleod and Lewis, 'Transnational Companies'.
[25] See World Bank Group, Corporate Social Responsibility Practice, *Company Codes of Conduct and International Standards: An Analytical Comparison. Part I of II. Apparel, Footwear and Light Manufacturing, Agribusiness and Tourism*, October 2003, at 2.
[26] See Lundblad, 'Some Legal Dimensions', at 387.
[27] See Friedman, 'Social Responsibility of Business'.
[28] According to a survey of business executives conducted by McKinsey in December 2005, 16% of 4,238 executives surveyed worldwide agreed with Friedman's claim that the sole purpose of business is to produce high returns for shareholders. McKinsey, 'Global Survey of Business Executives: Business and Society', 2 *McKinsey Quarterly* (2006), available at www.mckinseyquarterly.com/PDFDownload.aspx?ar=1741 (accessed 2 April 2011).
[29] See Ronen Shamir, 'Between Self-Regulation and the Alien Tort Claims Act: On the Contested Concept of Corporate Social Responsibility', (2004) 38 *Law & Society Review* 635–64 at 645.

acceptance may well lie beyond genuine concern for social affairs.[30] Thus, in stark contrast to law, the notion of corporate social responsibility is charged "with a voluntary and altruistic spirit,"[31] because from a regulatory perspective it tends to materialize in self-regulation. Instead of having top-down regulation whereby traditional lawmakers impose legal regulation upon companies, the crux of self-regulation is that the companies themselves regulate their own activities.

Despite the common voluntary nature of such company rules they vary "in terms of their origin, degree of institutionalization, scope, purpose, underlying incentives, and monitoring mechanisms."[32] In general terms, codes of conduct establish standards that aim to "guide the behaviour of the addressee in a particular way."[33] Although no authorized definition of codes of conduct exists,[34] they are often described in terms of their voluntary nature; the distinguishing feature of codes of conduct is their legally nonbinding nature. They are described as morally or politically binding,[35] sometimes as soft law, or as commitments going "beyond law" – whatever that means.[36] Second, precisely because of their nonbinding nature they relate to the regulation of nonstate actors. A third characteristic relates to the fact that codes of conduct often – but not in all instances – are drawn up by the entity that is to be regulated.

---

[30] The McKinsey survey of global executives indicates that only 8% believe companies embrace corporate social responsibility because of genuine concern. McKinsey, Global Survey.

[31] See Shamir, 'Between Self-Regulation and the Alien Tort Claims Act', at 645.

[32] See Helen Keller, 'Codes of Conduct and Their Implementation: The Question of Legitimacy' in Wolfrum and Röben (eds.), Legitimacy, 219–98 at 236.

[33] Ibid. at 220.

[34] Ibid.

[35] Especially codes of conduct with a basis in governments use the expression "politically binding." Examples are, e.g., the EU Code of Conduct for Arms Export and the Hague Code of Conduct against Ballistic Missile Proliferation. Kathleen A. Getz reaches the conclusion that TNCs are "morally responsible" to respect codes of conduct such as the OECD Guidelines: Kathleen A. Getz, 'International Codes of Conduct: An Analysis of Ethical Reasoning', (1990) 9 Journal of Business Ethics 567–77 at 576.

[36] See, e.g., Doreen McBarnet, 'The New Corporate Accountability' in McBarnet, Voiculescu and Campbell (eds.), New Corporate Accountability, 9–56 at 13, who uses the term "beyond law." Another equivalent notion used is "beyond compliance." The meaning of "beyond" remains, however, unclear. Etymologically it could mean two opposite things, either that self-regulation moves away from law or that it covers the same issues as legal obligations but in a broader way. The latter view appears prevalent, as illustrated by Radu Mares, who concludes that "beyond compliance" or "beyond law" means that "legal compliance is the baseline, the minimum expected from all businesses, while CSR represents voluntary attempts on the part of enlightened business to go the extra mile towards sustainable development and social inclusion." See Radu Mares, 'Global Corporate Social Responsibility, Human Rights and Law: An Interactive Regulatory Perspective on the Voluntary-Mandatory Dichotomy', (2010) 1 Transnational Legal Theory 221–85 at 226.

Thus, they frequently are a tool of self-regulation. Indeed, these three features are prevalent in many definitions of codes of conduct. Rhys Jenkins defines codes of conduct as "voluntary initiatives, which have been adopted by the business sector itself."[37] Nils Rosemann defines CoCs as follows: "Codes of Conduct are self-imposed corporate obligations for the adoption of normative, and therefore not necessarily legally enforceable, standards which are not part of the original core business objectives of the company."[38] One frequently referred to definition of the term "code of conduct" is provided by the Organization for Economic Co-operation and Development (OECD), according to which codes of conduct are "commitments voluntarily made by companies, associations or other entities, which put forth standards and principles for the conduct of business activities in the marketplace."[39] The expression is thus used as a generic term to cover all kinds of ethical statements made by companies irrespective of their denomination.[40]

The proliferation of self-regulatory codes of conduct at the expense of legal regulation finds explanation in pragmatic considerations. In contrast to legal standards, the flexibility and cheapness of self-regulation are its main advantages. Whereas the holding of a conference of plenipotentiaries with the purpose of drafting an international convention is considered a "lengthy process, unpredictable in outcome",[41] self-regulatory norms "can often be more easily arrived at and more easily revised" than international agreements concluded among states.[42] Indeed, the preparatory work for an international convention to enter into existence and become binding may well take a decade or even longer.[43] Governmental regulation may in addition to being cumbersome be

---

[37] See Rhys Jenkins, *Corporate Codes of Conduct: Self-Regulation in a Global Economy*, United Nations Research Institute for Social Development, April 2001, at 5. Available at www.unrisd.org/unrisd/website/document.nsf/0/e3b3e78bab9a886f80256b5e00344278/$FILE/jenkins.pdf (accessed 11 April 2011).

[38] See Geneva Centre for the Democratic Control of Armed Forces (DCAF), Occasional Paper no. 15, Nils Rosemann, *Code of Conduct: Tool for Self-Regulation for Private Military and Security Companies*, 2008, at 5.

[39] See OECD, *Corporate Responsibility: Private Initiatives and Public Goals*, 2001, at 48. Available at www.oecd.org/dataoecd/58/54/35315900.pdf (accessed 10 May 2011).

[40] See Lundblad, 'Some Legal Dimensions', at 386.

[41] See International Law Commission, Report of the Fifty-Third Session (2001), A/56/10, chapter IV, at 24, para. 633.

[42] See Jason Morrison and Naomi Roht-Arriaza, 'Private and Quasi-Private Standard Setting' in Daniel Bodansky, Jutta Brunnée and Ellen Hey (eds.), *The Oxford Handbook of International Environmental Law* (Oxford University Press, 2007), 498–527 at 511.

[43] The International Convention on the Rights of Persons with Disabilities may serve as an example. The work to convince states of the necessity of an international convention on the topic while elaborating legal principles applicable to persons with disabilities was conducted by the Department for Economic and Social Affairs (DESA) at the UN Headquarters in New York

costly.[44] Codes of conduct are, however, not free of criticism. The main point of concern with respect to codes of conduct relates to the question of implementation and the voluntary character of the codes. However, the benefits with self-regulatory codes of conducts must clearly outweigh (or at least balance) the uncertainty with regard to their implementation since codes of conduct have become a consolidated practice of business regulation.

The issues addressed in codes of conduct mostly relate to labor rights, health and safety issues, environmental concerns, human rights, security arrangements, community engagement, ethical conduct, good governance, and the rule of law.[45] Lately, the main focus has come to rest on labor rights, environmental norms, and human rights. Undoubtedly corporations nevertheless insert norms that are particularly relevant to their own business into their codes of conducts. Moreover, if companies are implicated in social responsibility scandals this situation tends to reflect their codes of conduct.[46] Codes of conduct emphasizing environmental rights and sustainable development, for example, developed from disastrous corporate activities such as the accident at Bhopal and of the Exxon *Valdez*. The most far-reaching codes of conduct tend to broaden the protection of stakeholders to internationally recognized standards of human rights and freedom from repressive regimes. Such an inclusive approach of social responsibility in codes of conduct is nevertheless limited to a number of "leadership companies," since the further away codes of conduct move from business self-interest the less attractive they become.[47]

In addition to the wide range of issues regulated by corporate codes of conduct, they vary with respect to stakeholders that have been involved in their drafting. The simplest form of a corporate code of conduct is individual in

---

through the 1990s. The convention was finally adopted in December 2006 and entered into force in May 2008 after more than ten years of work.

[44] See John Braithwaite, 'Enforced Self-Regulation: A New Strategy for Corporate Crime Control', (1981–2) 80 *Michigan Law Review* 1466–507 at 1470. Pontus Troberg makes the same point: "by leaving accounting regulation in the hands of the accounting profession, sufficient accounting expertise is secured and a more timely process is also possible." See Pontus Troberg, 'Global Capital Markets and Financial Reporting: International Regulation but National Application?' Chapter 11 in this volume.

[45] See World Bank Group, Corporate Social Responsibility Practice, *Company Codes of Conduct and International Standards: An Analytical Comparison*. Part I of II. *Apparel, Footwear and Light Manufacturing, Agribusiness and Tourism*, October 2003, at 1.

[46] See Errol Mendes and Ozay Mehmet, *Global Governance, Economy and Law: Waiting for Justice* (London: Routledge, 2003), at 132, 133.

[47] See Errol P. Mendes and Jeffrey A. Clark, Human Rights Research and Education Center, University of Ottawa, *The Five Generations of Corporate Codes of Conduct and Their Impact on Corporate Social Responsibility*, available at www.toronto.ca/inquiry/inquiry_site/cd/gg/add_pdf/77/Conflict_of_Interest/Electronic_Documents/Research_orgs/Five_Generations. PDF (accessed 24 January 2011).

the sense that it is created by a single company. Nike's Code of Conduct and Royal Dutch Shell's Code of Conduct are examples of individual corporate codes of conduct. These individual company codes may have been created in anticipation of broader sectoral codes, which "have been negotiated by an industry group, recognizing the need for consistency of policy or practice."[48] Examples of sectoral initiatives are the Apparel Industry Partnership (AIP) or the Code of Conduct for Private Security Services Providers. Country-focused codes again attempt to regulate companies in a certain country. The main example is the Sullivan Principles for South Africa, which targeted U.S. companies operating in South Africa during apartheid. Other examples of national or regional initiatives are the Ethical Trading Initiative (ETI), based in the United Kingdom, and the European Union Code of Conduct on Arms Export. Global initiatives are mostly developed by intergovernmental organizations, but they can also stem from the private sector. An example of the latter is the Caux Round Table Principles for Business, whereas the codes of conduct from the former category are better known. These include the OECD Guidelines for Multinational Enterprises, the 1977 ILO Tripartite Declaration of Principles Concerning Multinational Enterprises and Social Policy, and the UN Global Compact.

For present purposes, the usage of the term "code of conduct" will follow the OECD definition, which is based on voluntariness, normative guidance on business conduct, and the enactment by private actors – foremost individual companies or sectorwide initiatives.[49] This merits the usage of the term "self-regulatory/corporate codes of conduct," which will be used throughout this chapter to indicate that a company itself has authored the code of conduct. Sectorwide initiatives will consequently also be included, as will those multistakeholder initiatives in whose making companies have participated. In line with the OECD definition, codes of conduct that pertain to internal rules of the companies will be excluded. Outside the scope of this chapter is the so-called corporate governance code of conduct, which "primarily deals with the *internal* relations between those directly interested in the company, viz. its shareholders, management, board, and employees."[50] This has consequences also with respect to the substance of the codes of conduct that will be

---

[48] See Ann Cavoukian, Information and Privacy Commissioner/Ontario, *Privacy as a Fundamental Human Right vs. an Economic Right: An Attempt at Conciliation*, September 1999, at 6, available at www.ipc.on.ca/images/Resources/up-1pr_right.pdf (accessed 24 January 2011).

[49] See OECD, *Corporate Responsibility: Private Initiatives and Public Goals*, 2001, at 48. Available at www.oecd.org/dataoecd/58/54/35315900.pdf (accessed 10 May 2011).

[50] See Lundblad, 'Some Legal Dimensions', at 387.

Law versus Codes of Conduct 177

dealt with here; codes of conduct pertaining to human rights, labor rights, and environmental rights will be central to the discussion.

IV. CONVERGENCE RATHER THAN CONFLICT BETWEEN LEGAL STANDARDS AND CODES OF CONDUCT

An exploration into self-regulatory techniques as well as the substance embodied in corporate codes of conduct reveals a pattern of convergence between law and self-regulation. Thus, normative pluralism within this context entails, to begin with, a principled confirmation of existing rules rather than normative dilemmas. The prohibition of child labor, for example, has been accepted by states through legal means but also by companies in their codes of conduct. All repudiate it, although slight disagreement might prevail over what constitutes the age of a child. Corporate codes of conduct strive to protect rights similar to those individuals are afforded through governmental regulation even though the scope of protection varies and usually covers less than a full range of rights. Although international legally guaranteed human rights, labor rights, and environmental rights do not extend to transnational corporations despite numerous efforts to include TNCs within the ambit of international legal standards, I argue that they still constitute one of the sources of inspiration behind the content of self-regulatory initiatives.

First, the subject matters in corporate codes of conduct reflect international and national legal standards. One of the most extensive comparisons between voluntary codes of conducts of various business sectors and international standards with regard to human rights and labor rights, environmental rights, and socioeconomic and community-related issues was conducted by the World Bank in 2003 and 2004.[51] The World Bank study analyzed five sectors: the apparel, footwear, and light manufacturing sector; agribusiness; tourism; the oil and gas industry; and the mining industry. The provisions of codes of conduct on core issues were analyzed against the comparable norms laid down in international standards, which included, inter alia, forced labor and child labor; wages, hours of work, discrimination, freedom of association, and collective bargaining; and materials, emissions, pollution control, and waste management. The results show that the norms laid down in the codes of conduct to a great extent overlap with international standards. In fact, the provisions on

---

[51] See World Bank Group, Corporate Social Responsibility Practice, *Company Codes of Conduct and International Standards: An Analytical Comparison. Part I of II. Apparel, Footwear and Light Manufacturing, Agribusiness and Tourism*, October 2003; and World Bank Group, Corporate Social Responsibility Practice, *Company Codes of Conduct and International Standards: An Analytical Comparison, Part II of II: Oil and Gas, Mining*, March 2004.

human rights and environmental, social, and ethical requirements of codes of conducts take legal standards as their model. They are rarely as a matter of principle in conflict with the law; most codes of conduct, for example, prohibit forced labor precisely as international law does. The potential conflict may rather lie in the contours of the norm than in its nucleus. Although most codes denounce child labor, they might have a different understanding of who is a child than legal standards do. Thus although the ILC Convention on Child labor sets the age limit at fifteen, some codes of conduct adopt a more lenient position by setting the limit at fourteen years. In general terms self-regulatory norms tend to be "less stringent than public ones covering the same subject matter."[52] Although regulation in codes of conduct may be more lenient, clearly motivated by business interests, it still represents an attempt to cover at least partially the same issues as law does rather than holding different values than those embraced in law. The International Code of Conduct for Private Security Services Providers, for example, expressly recognizes in its general provisions, "This Code *complements* and does not replace the control exercised by Competent Authorities, and *does not limit or alter applicable international law or relevant national law.*"[53]

Second, law is relevant to codes of conduct by way of regulatory technique. Two main methods of drawing up codes of conduct can be discerned: either companies set forth their own concrete provisions mirroring the content of legal norms in terms of both subject matter and structure, or they include a direct reference to legal standards.[54] In the latter case, companies may broadly state that they "operate within the framework of existing human rights treaties and agreements" or simply that they adhere to "relevant local legislation." Shell's code of conduct, for example, states that Shell will conduct its activities "in a manner that respects human rights as set out in the UN Universal Declaration of Human Rights and the core conventions of the International Labour Organization."[55] The Code of Conduct for the International Stability Operations Association – an alliance of many private military and security companies – declares that the signatories "will be guided by all pertinent rules of international humanitarian and human rights laws." It further promises commitment to the following international

[52] See Morrison and Roht-Arriaza, 'Private and Quasi-Private Standard Setting', at 523.
[53] See International Code of Conduct for Private Security Service Providers (emphasis added), available at www.icoc-psp.org/ (accessed 5 October 2011).
[54] Rain Liivoja notices this same pattern with respect to law and honor although the situation is the other way around in his study "Law v. Honor: Normative Pluralism in the Regulation of Military Conduct," Chapter 5 in this volume.
[55] Shell, Code of Conduct, available at www-static.shell.com/static/aboutshell/downloads/who_we_are/code_of_conduct/code_of_conduct_english_2010.pdf (accessed 5 October 2011).

conventions: the Universal Declaration of Human Rights, the Geneva Conventions, the Convention against Torture, the Additional Protocols to the Geneva Conventions, and the Chemical Weapons Convention.[56] The appropriateness of this regulatory technique may nonetheless be questioned; the actual legal effect of declaring abidance by international conventions designed to apply to states remains unclear. It is far from obvious under international law that international conventions would assign duties to corporations or individuals.[57]

The other regulatory technique found in codes of conduct would therefore appear more suitable for governing the behavior of the company and its employees. To lay down direct provisions on conduct could potentially prove more effective; the provisions of the code of conduct could add rules to an uncertain legal setting.[58] Puma's code of conduct adheres to the prohibition of child labor by prohibiting employment of minors. It further states, "we consider a minor as one who is below 15 years of age, or the minimum age mandated by the applicable law, or the age for completing compulsory education, whichever of the three is higher."[59] In some instances the provisions of codes of conduct can even go beyond legal obligations. The International Code of Conduct for Private Security Services Providers encompasses a broader prohibition against discrimination than the prevailing standard in international human rights law, which generally does not prohibit discrimination on sexual orientation grounds.[60]

In sum, there is an intrinsic link between law and codes of conduct that justifies the conclusion that there is convergence rather than conflict between legal and self-regulatory norms. It seems even warranted to question the truly voluntary character of self-regulation. Although it cannot be rebutted that TNCs themselves in most cases create and adopt their own codes of conduct,

---

[56] International Stability Operations Association, Code of Conduct, available at ipoaworld.org/eng/codeofconduct/87-codecodeofconductv12enghtml.html (accessed 5 October 2011).

[57] See, e.g., Carsten Hoppe and Ottavio Quirico, 'Codes of Conduct for Private Military and Security Companies: The State of Self-Regulation in the Industry' in Francesco Francioni and Natalino Ronzitti (eds.), *War by Contract: Human Rights, Humanitarian Law, and Private Contractors* (Oxford University Press, 2011), 362–80 at 371–2.

[58] Ibid. at 372.

[59] Puma, Code of Conduct, available at images.puma.com/BLOG_CONTENT/puma_safe/PumaConduct.pdf (accessed 5 October 2011).

[60] No express reference to a prohibition against discrimination based on sexual orientation is found in any of the constitutive international human rights instruments, i.e., the 1948 Universal Declaration of Human Rights, the two International Covenants from 1966, the European Convention on Human Rights, the Inter-American Convention on Human Rights, or the African Charter on the Rights of People. Admittedly the question is nevertheless on the human rights agenda, starting from the decision by the European Court of Human Rights in the *Dudgeon v. United Kingdom* case from 1981.

the decision to embark upon self-regulatory codes of conduct is often made after public pressure or scrutiny of a company's activities or after a scandal. Further pressure to regulate is found in the fact that TNCs often are judged not only by their own behavior, but also by that of associated entities such as "sourcing facilities, licensees, agents, partners and host governments."[61] Businesses are simply held to "higher and broader social and environmental standards than in the past."[62] Thus, companies are forced to deal with allegations somehow, and the least intrusive way to meet regulatory demands may be the creation of a code of conduct.

V. THE PROBLEM OF ENFORCEMENT AS THE DIVIDING LINE BETWEEN LAW AND CODES OF CONDUCT

In principle, one should be satisfied with the realization that self-regulation embodied in codes of conducts lays down rules similar to those in legal instruments. Such a conclusion would ideally support the idea that no conflict between law and codes of conduct exists; both aim to protect the same values and hence they both separately and together generate similar protection via different regulatory means. There must, however, be more to normative pluralism than meets the eye. Whereas the normative substance appears not to be a problem, one must move on to consider whether the norms expressed in codes of conduct actually are enforceable. In other words, do they make a difference: that is, do they deliver what they promise? Is the prohibition against forced labor better protected by self-regulation, or do codes of conduct merely amount to lip service? Focusing on the issue of enforcement is warranted by the fact that many companies that have adopted codes of conduct are still found to violate the very rights they claim to protect. This has caused many scholars to question the effectiveness of codes of conduct; it is claimed that they are considered "ineffective in meeting the goals they seek to attain"[63] or simply that "codes, whether self-imposed or not, are only as meaningful as their enforceability."[64]

---

[61] World Bank Group, Corporate Social Responsibility Practice, *Company Codes of Conduct and International Standards: An Analytical Comparison. Part I of II. Apparel, Footwear and Light Manufacturing, Agribusiness and Tourism*, October 2003, at 1.
[62] Ibid.
[63] See Jane C. Hong, 'Enforcement of Corporate Codes of Conduct: Finding a Private Right of Action for International Laborers against MNCs for Labor Rights Violations', (2000–1) 19 *Wisconsin International Law Journal* 41–70 at 42.
[64] See Veronica Besmer, 'The Legal Character of Private Codes of Conduct: More than Just a Pseudo-Formal Gloss on Corporate Social Responsibility', (2006) 2 *Hastings Business Law Journal* 279–306 at 294.

Law versus Codes of Conduct 181

The aim here is to study what the discourse on the enforcement of codes of conduct looks like in order to determine whether corporate codes of conduct contain norms that truly are effective in terms of protection. If such an examination reveals the unenforceability of codes of conduct, it could be argued that the conflict between law and self-regulatory norms lies not in the normative *content* of the norms but rather in the *result* they generate. An examination into the enforceability of codes of conduct necessarily puts law back into the picture. Since the constituent element of law generally is that it is enforceable,[65] the discussion on possibilities to enforce codes of conduct is based on both implicit and explicit comparison of self-regulatory initiatives to law. In the following an analysis of the relationship between law and self-regulatory codes of conduct will be conducted through the prism of law based on identifiable arguments found in contemporary discourse on the regulation of companies. Three different – but connected – ways of perceiving self-regulatory codes of conduct are identifiable. First, codes of conduct are perceived as constituting a regulatory category completely separate from law; second, claims are set forth concerning the quasi-legal nature of codes of conduct; and third, one can discern arguments that portray codes of conduct as law. Thus, as an articulation of corporate social responsibility, the discourse on codes of conduct shows the same trajectories; at one end of the spectrum are found those emphasizing the voluntary nature of codes of conduct, at the other end those who try to bestow on it a more formal and mandatory character.[66]

A. *Self-Regulatory Codes of Conduct as Nonlaw*

When the American private military company Blackwater shot seventeen civilians to death in Nisoori square in Iraq in September 2007, the International Peace Organizations Associations (IPOA) decided to launch investigations into the incident in accordance with the association's code of conduct – to which Blackwater had signed up.[67] The IPOA Code of Conduct, which all members of the association are obliged to sign, set forth that its members "agree to follow all rules of international humanitarian law and human rights

---

[65] See Anne Peters and Isabella Pagotto for a discussion of various elements of law, 'Soft Law as a New Mode of Governance: A Legal Perspective', available at ius.unibas.ch/uploads/publics/3940/20100219145119_4b7e9757829c2.pdf (accessed 7 May 2011).
[66] See Shamir, 'Between Self-Regulation and the Alien Tort Claims Act', at 644–5.
[67] The organization later changed its name to International Stability Operations Association (ISOA).

law that are applicable as well as all relevant international protocols and conventions."[68] Blackwater nevertheless appeared unwilling to submit to any such investigation but chose to leave the association and its procedures. Although some have claimed the withdrawal to be a testimony to the effectiveness of voluntary regulation,[69] the opposite seems more plausible. The code of conduct with its enforcement mechanism had apparently served its public relations purposes well, but when it came to making reality of the commitments under the code of conduct, Blackwater – entitled to do so – chose to withdraw.

The Blackwater example classically demonstrates the nonlegal nature of self-regulation; corporate codes of conduct are generally not considered as law and cannot therefore be (legally) enforced.[70] This holds especially true for aspirational codes of conduct that merely declare abidance by the law but contain no monitoring or enforcement mechanisms. As Tadeusz Gruchalla-Wesierski has noted, "the more precise the norm, the greater expectations it engenders."[71] Whether the commitments are met or not remains in the open. Thus, corporate codes of conduct lack what has been labeled as the main benefit of legal rules, namely, "the possibility of recourse to legal sanctions."[72] Robert McCorquodale notes that "regulation without law and legal compliance mechanisms is rarely effective as a means of long-term social, economic or public behavioural change."[73] The voluntary nature of codes of conduct is thus seen as the major impediment to their effectiveness. As spelled out by Carsten Hoppe and Ottavio Quirico, "a CoC cannot be effective if both the act of committing to a code *and* the compliance with it are entirely voluntary,

---

[68] The former IPOA Code of Conduct has been replaced by a corresponding ISOA Code of Conduct, which states that "signatories will be guided by all pertinent rules of international humanitarian law and human rights laws"; see stability-operations.org/printableversions/Code_of_Conduct_ISOA_v12.pdf (accessed 11 October 2011).

[69] See Matthew Harwood, 'Let's Leash the Dogs of War', *Guardian*, 14 March 2008, available at www.guardian.co.uk/commentisfree/2008/mar/14/letsleashthedogsofwar (accessed 28 March 2011).

[70] Some codes of conduct even expressly state their nonbinding nature and the lack of legal liability. The Code of Conduct for Private Security Services Providers states in its general provisions that "the Code itself creates no legal obligations or legal liabilities." See the International Code of Conduct for Private Security Service Providers, available at www.icoc-psp.org/ (accessed 5 October 2011).

[71] See Tadeusz Gruchalla-Wesierski, 'A Framework for Understanding Soft Law', (1984) 30 *McGill Law Journal* 37–88 at 47.

[72] Ibid. at 43.

[73] See Robert McCorquodale, 'Corporate Social Responsibility and International Human Rights Law', (2009) 87 *Journal of Business Ethics* 385–400 at 385.

Law versus Codes of Conduct 183

and breaches remain without consequence."[74] Indeed, if obligations are to be useful, they must be enforced.[75]

Accountability exists, however, also outside law. According to Alf Ross, the violation of nonlegal norms may equally be subjected to "accusations, trials and judgments – even though none of these are institutionalized as in law."[76] The idea of moral responsibility, Ross argues, "is an expression of a normative demand for the tying of guilt to the consequences of guilt, the 'punishment,' which here is called 'disapproval.'"[77] Consequently, when a code of conduct is violated by a corporation, the so-called trial consists of having outside actors expressing reproach for the committed act or omission that is contrary to what the corporation has indicated to be bound by. As Ross explains, reproach "has the effect of a punishment, suffering inflicted because of guilt."[78] Ross's explications on moral responsibility bear relevance to holding corporations accountable for acts contrary to their codes of conduct; there are clear connections between the idea of reproach as a judgment or sanction and what Robert Keohane has called market accountability and reputational accountability.[79] Corporations often refer to market accountability, claiming that the only thing that keeps them in business is a good reputation. Should they act in ways that are unacceptable to their clients, investors may reduce stock prices and access to capital in addition to which consumers may opt to buy less of their products or hire fewer services or even boycott the products.[80] As Jason Morrison and Naomi Roht-Arriaza have noted, "industry norms may mandate conformity to a standard as a condition of business, they can become *de facto* requirements for competitiveness in

---

[74] See Hoppe and Quirico, 'Codes of Conduct for Private Military and Security Companies', at 373.
[75] International Council on Human Rights Policy, *Beyond Voluntarism: Human Rights and the Developing International Legal Obligations of Companies*, February 2002, at 3. Available at www.ichrp.org/files/reports/7/107_report_en.pdf (accessed 18 March 2011).
[76] See Ross, *On Guilt, Responsibility, and Punishment*, at 24.
[77] Ibid. at 25.
[78] Ibid. at 26–7.
[79] See Robert O. Keohane, 'Accountability in World Politics', (2006) 29 *Scandinavian Political Studies* 75–87 at 84. Elsewhere, Robert O. Keohane discusses the difference between market accountability and public reputational accountability with regard to which he concludes that although reputational accountability can be considered a part of all other accountability mechanisms, public reputational accountability denotes rather situations in which all other forms of accountability are excluded. See Robert O. Keohane, 'The Concept of Accountability in World Politics and the Use of Force', (2002–3) 24 *Michigan Journal of International Law* 1121–41 at 1133–4. However, as he points out, the different "types of accountability are not mutually exclusive, but overlap" (ibid. at 1134).
[80] See Keohane, 'Concept of Accountability', at 1133.

the international market."⁸¹ Allegedly then, compliance with self-regulatory codes of conduct is not entirely voluntary.

The question that begs to be answered is whether market accountability will suffice. Can the same level of protection – whether it is directed toward environmental, labor, or human rights – be achieved outside legal responsibility? Mathias Koenig-Archibugi has argued that unilateral codes of conduct are unreliable accountability mechanisms because they often exclude key concerns of stakeholders, in addition to which the complaints procedure is left unexplained.⁸² Robert Keohane has paid attention to the existence of sanctions as a main feature of effective accountability:

> Sanctions are central to accountability, and mechanisms for sanctioning available to accountability holders are a key to the operation of accountability in a pluralistic administrative system. Without mechanisms for sanctions, demands on power-wielders for answers are unlikely to be very effective.⁸³

To begin with, the effect of market reputation as a form of sanction cannot be dismissed. The boycott of Nestlé infant formula in the 1980s allegedly cost the company more than U.S.$40 million.⁸⁴ The Brent Spar campaign – which also included a boycott of Shell's petrol – launched by Greenpeace in 1995 against Shell managed to retract the company's decision to dispose of the oil buoy in the Atlantic Ocean. In addition, the boycott was claimed to have decreased Shell's sales 20–50 percent.⁸⁵ Damage to brand reputation is in fact seen by many companies as the biggest risk,⁸⁶ an idea that finds support in surveys on spending patterns that increasingly demonstrate a "rising CSR-oriented consumer practice."⁸⁷ The limits of market accountability must, however, also be acknowledged. The idea that corporate misbehavior results in fewer customers and investments may have some force, but at the end of the day "nice firms do not always finish first."⁸⁸ The research findings in the area are conflicting;

---

⁸¹ See Morrison and Roht-Arriaza, 'Private and Quasi-Private Standard Setting', at 511.
⁸² See Mathias Koenig-Archibugi, 'Transnational Corporations and Public Accountability', (2004) 39 *Government and Opposition* 234–59 at 251.
⁸³ See Keohane, 'Concept of Accountability', at 1130.
⁸⁴ See Emma Boulstridge and Marylyn Carrigan, 'Do Consumers Really Care about Corporate Responsibility? Highlighting the Attitude-Behaviour Gap', (2000) 4 *Journal of Communication Management* 355–86; Marylyn Carrigan and Ahmad Attalla, 'The Myth of the Ethical Consumer – Do Ethics Matter in Purchase Behaviour?' (2001) 18 *Journal of Consumer Marketing* 560–77 at 565.
⁸⁵ Ibid.
⁸⁶ See McBarnet, *New Corporate Accountability*, at 17.
⁸⁷ Ibid.
⁸⁸ See Peter W. Singer, 'Corporate Warriors: The Rise of the Privatized Military Industry and Its Ramifications for International Security', (2001–2) 26 *International Security* 186–220 at 214.

some even claim that the idea of an ethical consumer is to a large extent a myth.[89] Thus, in contrast to what is widely alleged, "good companies" do not straightforwardly attract consumers to a greater extent than do companies with unethical behavior. Emma Boulstridge and Marylyn Carrigan argue that "social responsibility is not the most dominant criteria in their [consumers'] purchase decision."[90] Moreover, studies have shown that consumers are rarely well informed about corporate social responsibility; they simply "lacked information to distinguish whether a company had or had not acted ethically."[91] The availability of information concerning unethical behavior is also not always decisive. Despite knowledge of misdeeds, several companies within the private military and security industry received new substantial contracts shortly after the revelation of the Abu Ghraib abuses in 2004.[92]

Given the uncertainty of leaving noncompliance with codes of conduct to market forces, many advocate enforcement and complaints procedures in conjunction with codes of conduct. Sorting out issues of monitoring and enforcement is, however, more complicated than the creation of a code of conduct. Traditional methods of monitoring are on-site inspections by the company itself or third parties, and the submission of written guarantees by suppliers that they adhere to the code of conduct (contractual monitoring).[93] The availability of such mechanisms in codes of conduct nevertheless varies. Individual company codes of conduct seldom contain clauses regarding enforcement or complaints mechanisms. In the 1990s the ILO found that eight out of ten codes of conduct contained no methods for implementation, and in 1999 an OECD report showed that a little more than 10 percent had provisions on independent and external monitoring.[94] Although enforcement mechanisms are rare in individual company codes, there are examples of intricate complaints systems too. One example is the private military and security company Blue Sky, whose activities are overseen by an Ethical Overview Committee composed of impeccable persons with the power to halt operations that go

---

[89] See Carrigan and Attalla, 'Myth of the Ethical Consumer', at 566.
[90] Ibid. at 564, 565.
[91] Ibid. at 565.
[92] See Creutz, *Transnational Privatised Security*, at 66.
[93] See United States Department of Labour, *The Apparel Industry and Codes of Conducts: A solution to the International Child Labour Problem?* available at actrav.itcilo.org/actrav-english/telearn/global/ilo/code/apparel3.htm (accessed 30 March 2011).
[94] See ILO, Working Party on the Social Dimensions of the Liberalization of International Trade, *Overview of Global Developments and Office Activities Concerning Codes of Conduct, Social Labeling and Other Private Sector Initiatives Addressing Labour Issues*, GB.273/WP/SDL/1, 1998; OECD, Working Party of the Trade Committee, *Codes of Corporate Conduct – an Inventory*, TD/TCWP(98)74/FINAL, 1999, figure 6.

against the company's code of conduct.[95] There is, however, "little empirical research on the implementation of codes of conduct and the operation of monitoring schemes" that would go beyond the letter and adoption of codes of conduct.[96] Consequently, as Rodríguez-Garavito has argued, the real effects of codes of conduct remain unknown.[97]

B. Codes of Conduct as Soft Law

Codes of conduct are not only described as purely voluntary commitments that completely fall outside the legal sphere. Many international legal scholars accept that some codes of conduct can constitute more than voluntary commitments without still amounting to hard or pure law; in other words, they amount to what generally has been labeled "soft law."[98] Soft law established itself as an intermediate category of regulation between nonlaw and law in the 1980s; the traditional binary conception of law had to make room for perceptions of relative normativity of which soft law is an embodiment.[99] The softening of norms has been connected to a new development in governance of international affairs that is characterized by lessened state action in favor of the centrality of private actors.[100] According to Jan Klabbers, it is precisely the blurring of public and private domains coupled with the trend of deformalization in international politics that lies behind the consolidation of soft law.[101]

With regard to codes of conduct and soft law it is important to note that not all codes of conduct amount to soft law. Although "soft law, in many ways,

[95] See Hoppe and Quirico, 'Codes of Conduct for Private Military and Security Companies', at 375; see also 'Ethical Security and Risk Management Consultancy Appoint Newspoint Public Relations', 18 February 2004, available at www.newspoint-pr.co.uk/press_pr5.htm (accessed 11 October 2011).
[96] See Rodríguez-Garavito, 'Global Governance and Labor Rights, at 204.'
[97] Ibid. at 204–5.
[98] The discussion here reflects a pragmatic rather than doctrinal choice by the author to embrace soft law. Since the purpose here is to describe how codes of conduct are perceived through the prism of law the category of soft law could not be left out (even if one were to subscribe to the binary view of law) as it reflects one way of portraying codes of conduct in the doctrinal debate.
[99] See Jan Klabbers, 'Reflections on Soft International Law in a Privatized World', (2005) 16 *Finnish Yearbook of International Law* 313–28 at 315; Anne Peters and Isabella Pagotto define soft law as follows: "the term soft law characterizes texts which are on the one hand not legally binding in an ordinary sense, but are on the other hand not completely devoid of legal effects either" (emphasis omitted). See Peters and Pagotto, 'Soft Law', at 4.
[100] See, e.g., Klabbers, 'Reflections on Soft International Law', at 318–19; Kenneth W. Abbot and Duncan Snidal, 'Strengthening International Regulation through Transnational New Governance: Overcoming the Orchestration Deficit', (2009) 42 *Vanderbilt Journal of Transnational Law* 501–78.
[101] See Klabbers, 'Reflections on Soft International Law', at 327.

Law versus Codes of Conduct

is an appropriate notion in the context of codes of conduct, yet it falls short of encompassing the phenomenon of the codes of conduct in its entirety."[102] Especially corporate codes of conduct discussed previously – meaning those codes of conduct drawn up by the companies themselves – appear at first sight to fall outside the scope of soft law.[103] Instead, multistakeholder initiatives are often categorized as soft law. The underlying reason for categorizing certain codes of conduct as soft law is the involvement of public power in their creation. Jan Klabbers has highlighted the fact that "soft law nonetheless still has to do with the exercise of public power by public authorities."[104] Therefore, codes of conduct authored by governments or international organizations can be called soft law. Oft-mentioned are the UN Global Compact,[105] the OECD Guidelines for Multinational Enterprises,[106] and the ILO Declaration of Principles concerning Multinational Enterprises and Social Policy.[107] These codes of conduct, however, emanate from public power and would thus fall outside the category of self-regulatory codes of conduct that are the focus here.

What should be analyzed here instead is the potential legal effect of so-called private soft law, or hybrid soft law.[108] The focus thus lies on self-regulatory codes of conduct that are authored or coauthored by companies and the question whether they can produce legal effects. Although private soft law at first sight appears a contradictory term – because law emanates from public power rather than from private entities[109] – it has in recent years started to gain

---

[102] See Keller, 'Codes of Conduct and Their Implementation', at 249.
[103] Ibid. at 249.
[104] See Klabbers, 'Reflections on Soft International Law', at 317.
[105] It must be noted that although the UN Global Compact is frequently referred to as a code of conduct, it is stated on its Web pages that "the Global Compact is not a regulatory instrument or code of conduct"; available at www.unglobalcompact.org/issues/conflict_prevention/meetings_and_workshops/privateSector.html (accessed 6 May 2011).
[106] The OECD clearly exposits the OECD Guidelines as a code of conduct: "The Guidelines for Multinational Enterprises represent a non-binding code of conduct of corporate behaviour addressed to the multinational enterprises." See www.oecd.org/document/58/0,2340,en_2649_34889_2349370_1_1_1_1,00.html (accessed 6 May 2011).
[107] The International Labour Organization states that the declaration offers 'guidelines' to various actors on issues on employment, work conditions, etc. See ILO Tripartite Declaration of Principles Concerning Multinational Enterprises and Social Policy, 3rd edn, ILO, Geneva, 2001, at v.
[108] The terminology is borrowed from Anne Peters and Isabella Pagotto. See Peters and Pagotto, 'Soft Law as a New Mode of Governance'.
[109] Many scholars have started to develop theories of transnational law, which ultimately rest on a construct of law different from the traditional dichotomy of domestic and international law. This means according to Craig Scott that "law need not be conceptualized as having to have either a direct or a derivative relationship to the state or to the interstate order.". Hence, for example, internal corporate norms may constitute law, i.e., transnational law. See, e.g., Craig

acceptance. Anne Peters and Isabella Pagotto have noticed that the "privatization" of soft law is "an important recent phenomenon."[110] Dinah Shelton mentions as examples of private soft law the Sullivan Principles and the MacBride Principles.[111]

Having established that codes of conducts can constitute private and hybrid soft law, the question remains what this means in terms of enforcement. What consequences follow from the fact that a code of conduct is considered to be soft law? First, it is important to state expressly that codes of conduct endowed with soft law character generally do not in themselves amount to law.[112] The involvement of private parties in the creation of these documents bestows a nonlegal character on the instruments. As Christopher McCrudden has explained, "any definition of 'law' ... requires governmental or inter-governmental approval or involvement in the creation of norms."[113] Hence, soft law is a means by which nonstate actors come to terms with the fact that they lack formal lawmaking powers.[114] Second, the codes of conduct must nevertheless produce or generate some legal effect; otherwise their classification as soft law would be meaningless. Indeed, the ability of codes of conduct to produce legal effects seems accepted. The International Court of Justice in its advisory opinion in the *Legality of the Threat or Use of Nuclear Weapons* confirmed that nonbinding instruments may "sometimes have normative value."[115] Especially with regard to private soft law, Carola Glinski maintains that "[t]here is no doubt that ... self-regulation – produces a variety

---

Scott, '"Transnational Law" as Proto-Concept: Three Conceptions', (2009) 10 *German Law Journal* 859–76 at 874.

[110] See Peters and Pagotto, 'Soft Law as a New Mode of Governance', at 5.

[111] See Dinah Shelton, 'Editor's Concluding Note: The Role of Non-binding Norms in the International Legal System' in Dinah Shelton (ed.), *Commitment and Compliance: The Role of Non-Binding Norms in the International Legal System* (Oxford University Press, 2000), 554–6 at 555. The aim of the Sullivan Principles was to make American companies comply with a limited set of labor and antidiscrimination standards while conducting business in apartheid South Africa. Analogously the MacBride Principles purported to constrain American business in Northern Ireland to uphold antidiscrimination with respect to the two different religious communities. See Christopher McCrudden, 'Human Rights Codes for Transnational Corporations: The Sullivan and MacBride Principles' in Shelton (ed.), *Commitment and Compliance*, at 421.

[112] Although it is recognized that codes of conduct can amount to law in special cases if so intended by the parties through incorporation, or in court proceedings if invoked or applied (see Section V.c), codes of conduct are prima facie held to be nonlaw.

[113] See McCrudden, 'Human Rights Codes', at 420.

[114] See Peters and Pagotto, 'Soft Law as a New Mode of Governance', at 5.

[115] International Court of Justice, *Legality of the Threat or Use of Nuclear Weapons*, Advisory Opinion, 8 July 1996, ICJ Reports 1996, p. 226 at 254, para. 70.

of legal effects."[116] An important point is further to note that legal "effects may occur irrespective of whether they were intended or not."[117]

The legal effects of soft law in general consist of their ability to affect the application of existing law or the formation of new law. Private soft law features similar legal effects. Anne Peters and Isabella Pagotto have identified "pre-law functions," "law-plus functions," and "para-law functions" of soft law.[118] Prelaw functions entail that soft law is adopted in the absence of law in order to instruct the behavior of the involved actors normatively, potentially with the aim to advance the creation of legal rules. As Peters and Pagotto continue, "soft law thereby contributes to the development of hard law ... and is thus pacemaker of legalization."[119] Indeed, self-regulatory codes of conduct may serve this purpose. The Sullivan Principles deserve mentioning here, as they were used in anticipation of national U.S. law on how to counter apartheid in South Africa. One of the explicit merits of the Sullivan Principles has also been its groundbreaking role in the creation of other broad voluntary initiatives: "by providing an early example of the effectiveness of leveraging voluntary public commitments by private actors, the Sullivan Principles have helped provide the foundation for many recent initiatives, ranging from the US-based Apparel Industry Partnership ... to the UN Global Compact."[120] Another code of conduct that has demonstrated prelaw value is the International Code of Conduct for Private Security Services Providers, which has been accepted in the absence of an international convention on the matter.

The second function of "law-plus" recognized by Peters and Galotto means that soft law instruments allegedly affect already existing legal regimes. Soft law is taken to complement law, either through filling regulatory gaps or through instructing the interpretation of existing law. In a similar vein, Tadeusz Gruchalla-Wesierski has recognized that soft law may have a legitimizing effect on existing law. However, the opposite effect is also possible; there is nothing to preclude the conclusion that soft law can delegitimize existing law too.[121] One would, however, be inclined to perceive the complementary functions of private soft law on government-sponsored regulation as fairly limited. Clas Lundblad has argued that the complementary function

---

[116] See Carola Glinski, 'Corporate Codes of Conduct: Moral or Legal Obligation?' in McBarnet, Voiculescu and Campbell (eds.), *New Corporate Accountability*, 119–47 at 147.
[117] See Lundblad, 'Some Legal Dimensions', at 386–7.
[118] See Peters and Pagotto, 'Soft Law as a New Mode of Governance'.
[119] Ibid. at 23 (emphasis omitted).
[120] See Phillip H. Rudolph, 'The Global Sullivan Principles of Corporate Social Responsibility' in Mullerat (ed.), *Corporate Social Responsibility*, 221–4 at 224.
[121] See Gruchalla-Wesierski, 'Framework for Understanding Soft Law', at 52.

fulfilled by codes of conduct resides in the fact that they draw together various legal obligations stemming from national and international law. A company would therefore benefit from compiling its legal obligations into one code of conduct provided it lives up to it: "to ensure compliance with the law companies are often well advised to create a system of ethical guidelines, which, if transformed into actual behaviour, reduce the risk of violation of the law."[122] As a consequence, "the risk of legal action against the company can thereby be reduced both in the criminal field and in the civil field."[123]

The third "paralaw" function is closely connected to the previous functions described. This entails that the soft law instrument is a substitute for national or international legal regulation – not, however, solely by means of a deliberate choice to regulate something softly, but also as a manifestation of the only regulatory alternative available to the generating entity. Thus, instead of a regulatory vacuum, soft approaches such as codes of conduct are adopted. But whereas a state with its existing lawmaking competence may choose to regulate something softly or not, the same cannot be said about nonstate actors lacking that power. Since a company lacks lawmaking capacity to begin with, it can hardly opt to create soft law instruments. The intention to create instruments with legal effects would – even if it could – hardly be present.[124] Thus, the company creates, for example, a code of conduct that in itself is nonbinding but may later generate legal effects affecting existing law or inducing new law. However, not all codes of conduct display legal effects, and consequently they have no automatic soft law character. Peters's and Galotto's third category of legal effect – the "paralaw" function of soft law – therefore turns out to be difficult to separate in reality from the "prelaw" and "law-plus" functions, at least when it comes to private soft law.

C. Self-regulation as Law

Next to the possible effects that codes of conduct can have on the application of existing law or on the formation of new law, there are mainly two methods through which self-regulatory codes of conduct can per se become law: either they are incorporated into law through contractual agreements or they are held to constitute a source of law in court proceedings.[125] A code

---

[122] See Lundblad, 'Some Legal Dimensions', at 391.
[123] Ibid.
[124] Lundblad states, "It can safely be assumed that the typical corporate originator of a Code of Conduct does not intend to incur legally binding obligations as a result thereof." Ibid., at 390.
[125] The phenomenon of so-called regulated or enforced self-regulation will be left out of the discussion because as an idea it still emanates from a state-centered perception where the

of conduct belonging to the former category is the International Code of Conduct for Private Security Services Providers. When it comes to the latter method of transposing self-regulation into law, the analysis that follows will show that the problems of monitoring and enforcement that are widely held to be the Achilles' heel of corporate codes of conduct – at least those initiated internally by individual companies or different branches – have generated legal action in order to enforce these voluntary initiatives. Doreen McBarnet has noted that especially civil society has chosen to focus on private law mechanisms to turn voluntariness into law instead of solely purporting to enhance national or international regulation of companies.[126] Self-regulation is hence mixed with law, hence departing from the vision that self-regulation and law are two completely separate normative orders. Such an interaction has mainly taken place in national legal proceedings where codes of conduct have been afforded legal status through constituting complementary evidence.[127] But one could go even further and claim that self-regulatory codes of conduct are occasionally viewed even as law. Jan Klabbers has noted with respect to the Court of Justice of the EU that it has appeared willing to apply soft law, including codes of conduct, as hard law.[128] This does not mean that all self-regulatory codes of conduct amount to law; the touching point between codes of conduct and law may be small, but still it exists in some situations.

Codes of Conduct in Litigation

Private litigation constitutes one credible option of ensuring the enforcement of corporate codes of conduct. Especially in the United States several lawsuits have been brought against companies in various business sectors, such as the garment, security, and oil industries. In some of these cases, codes of conduct have been the foundation for the lawsuit, considered as applicable law, or formed part of the defendant's defense. Clas Lundblad has summarized this in the following terms: "The increasing interest in human rights issues has resulted in interest also being directed to Codes of

---

state enacts law requiring corporations to self-regulate within certain outer boundaries or under governmental oversight. Since this chapter has focused primarily on self-regulation as an alternative approach to law, not as an embodiment of it, the reader is referred to, e.g., John Braithwaite, 'Enforced Self-Regulation: A New Strategy for Corporate Criminal Control', (1982) 80 *Michigan Law Review* 1466–507; see also Mares, 'Global Corporate Social Responsibility', at 240.

[126] See McBarnet, *New Corporate Accountability*, at 38.
[127] See Lundblad, 'Some Legal Dimensions', at 390–1.
[128] See Jan Klabbers, 'The Undesirability of Soft Law', (1998) 67 *Nordic Journal of International Law* 381–91 at 388.

Conduct as a possible basis for action against companies."[129] The least common denominator in various cases is that codes of conduct in litigation usually do not constitute the central legal argumentation although they have a certain legal role to play.

In the *Kasky v. Nike case*, a corporate code of conduct – that of the sportswear company Nike – was alleged to constitute part of misleading communications provided to the public by the company. Marc Kasky initiated legal proceedings against Nike and five of its corporate officers in the San Francisco Superior Court in 1998 for false and misleading commercial statements.[130] The case originated in reports by the media in 1996 revealing Nike's sweatshop practices in foreign facilities. Nike responded with a series of public communications aimed at refuting the sweatshop allegations. It was these communications that Kasky based his claim upon, arguing that they represented false statements aimed at maintaining or increasing the company's profits. Among the several communications to the public made by Nike, Kasky included the company's code of conduct. Kasky's complaint set forth, inter alia, that Nike's Code of Conduct prohibited corporal punishment, yet there were several reports of corporal abuse at Nike's foreign factories.[131] His main argument against Nike was that the company's public statements misrepresented the factual working conditions in Nike's foreign factories. Kasky argued that Nike had violated various California laws that prohibited false and misleading statements, thus constituting unlawful business practices.[132] The crux of the case thus came to be the question of whether Nike's statements were to be considered commercial speech, to which free speech restrictions apply.

Several trials ensued from the decision in the San Francisco Superior Court, which dismissed Marc Kasky's demand to have a jury trial decide the issue.[133] Its ruling meant that Nike had the right to issue freely "PR statements without fear of being held to legal account for them."[134] The California Court of Appeals supported the idea that Nike had by its public statements only "engaged in a public dialogue on issues of public concerns" to which full

---

[129] See Lundblad, 'Some Legal Dimensions', at 389.
[130] See *Marc Kasky v. Nike Inc., Philip Knight, Thomas Clarke, Mark Parker, Stephen Gomez, David Taylor*, Superior Court of the State of California, case no. 994446 (complaint filed 2 July 1998).
[131] Ibid.
[132] Ibid.
[133] See *Marc Kasky v. Nike Inc., Philip Knight, Thomas Clarke, Mark Parker, Stephen Gomez, David Taylor*, Superior Court of the State of California, case no. 994446 (Cal. Super. Ct. 5 Feb. 1999) (dismissing complaint).
[134] See Ronald K. L. Collins and David M. Skover, 'The Landmark Free Speech Case That Wasn't: The *Nike v. Kasky* Story', (2004) 54 *Case Western Law Review* 965–1047 at 982.

free speech protection applied.[135] The California Supreme Court, however, reversed the position and found in favor of Marc Kasky, holding Nike's statements to constitute commercial speech enjoying only limited free speech protection and hence under the obligation to be truthful.[136] According to such an interpretation, any company could be held legally accountable for untruthful statements whichever form they might have taken. Consequently, drawing up and maintaining a corporate code of conduct in order to increase business profits were suddenly within the ambit of legal liability. Nike's appeal for review in the United States Supreme Court was later approved; the Supreme Court nevertheless dismissed a writ of certiorari.[137] The parties ultimately settled the case in September 2003, leaving in place the California Supreme Court decision against Nike.

Many transnational companies were concerned with the effects of the *Kasky* case on corporate speech or other comparable policy statements.[138] Still, companies themselves have not shied away from referring to existing codes of conduct as a defense in (potential) litigation they face. The jeans company Levi Strauss in the famous Saipan litigation denied responsibility on the basis, inter alia, of the existing code of conduct. In the 1999 *Saipan* lawsuit, class actions were undertaken in U.S. state and federal courts on behalf of mostly migrant workers in the U.S. territorial island of Saipan alleging widespread violations of the garment workers' rights. According to the lawsuit, the garment workers were subjected to unlawful sweatshop conditions and inhumane living conditions: they were held in indentured servitude, their passports were confiscated, they had to pay recruitment fees, and their salaries were below minimum wage. The workers were allegedly victims of "an appalling scheme which deprives the workers both of wages and working conditions to which they are legally and contractually entitled, and of universally recognized civil and human rights."[139] The subjects of the lawsuits were altogether twenty-six companies and twenty-three Saipan garment factories. The parties ultimately settled the claims in 2004 not only with extensive monetary compensation; the defendant companies further agreed, inter alia, to conclude a code of conduct with independent monitoring in order

---

[135] See *Kasky v. Nike*, 93 Cal Rptr. 2d 854 (Cal. Ct. App. 2000).
[136] See *Kasky v. Nike Inc.*, 45 P.3d 243 (Cal. 2002).
[137] *Nike Inc. v. Marc Kasky*, 123 S. Ct. 2554 (2003).
[138] See *Nike Inc. v. Marc Kasky*, Supreme Court of the United States, no. 02–575, On Petition of a Writ of Certiorari to the Supreme Court of California, Motion of Exxonmobil, Bank of America, Microsoft, Monsanto, and Pfizer for Leave to File Brief *Amici Curiae*, and Brief in Support of the Petitioners, November 2002, at 2.
[139] See Institute for Global Labour and Human Rights, 'Lawsuit against US Corporations Using Sweatshops in Saipan', 1 January 1999, at § 40, www.globallabourrights.org/reports?id=0479 (accessed 10 October 2011).

to guarantee that the workers' labor rights would be respected in the future. Levi Strauss was, however, the only company that refused to settle. Denying any wrongdoing, Levi's claimed that it had undertaken stringent measures of its own through the adoption of a code of conduct to which all its factories had adhered.[140] In a similar but more recent case, the U.S.-based company Kellogg, Brown & Root, Inc. (KBR), sued for human trafficking and forced labor of twelve Nepalese migrant workers in Iraq in the case of *Adhikari et al.*, responded in a statement on the lawsuit that its "employees were expected to adhere to a company code of conduct and complete ethics training that includes information about human trafficking."[141] Whether KBR will include its reference to its company code of conduct in its defense remains to be seen, as the case has not yet proceeded to the merits of the matter.

Although most of the private litigation that targets companies and their responsibilities in the realization of human rights as well as the potential legal enforceability of codes of conduct stems from the United States, Doreen McBarnet has held that "there is plenty of scope in law in other jurisdictions too to transform not just voluntary CSR reports, but also voluntary codes of conduct, into standards to which companies can be held legally accountable."[142] One piece of regulation that might be used similarly to the *Kasky* case is the EU Unfair Commercial Practices Directive, which opens the door for holding noncompliance with a code of conduct "as an instance of misleading commercial practice."[143] The European Union has, however, also dealt with codes of conduct outside the framework of advertisement. The Court of Justice of the EU has in a number of cases applied codes of conduct as law, especially when it comes to a code of conduct adopted by the commission and council in 1993 concerning public access to documents, which was later adopted in the form a decision to which the code of conduct was attached.[144] In *WWF UK v. Commission*, the Court held,

> Although Decision 94/90 is, in effect, a series of obligations which the Commission has voluntarily assumed for itself as a measure of internal

---

[140] Business & Human Rights Resource Center, 'Case Profile: U.S. Apparel Cos. Lawsuit (Re Saipan)', http://www.business-humanrights.org/Categories/Lawlawsuits/Lawsuitsregulatoryaction/LawsuitsSelectedcases/USapparelcoslawsuitreSaipan?sort_on=sortable_title&batch_size=10&batch_start=3 (accessed 13 October 2011).

[141] Business and Human Rights Resource Centre, 'Case Profile: KBR Lawsuit', www.business-humanrights.org/Categories/Lawlawsuits/Lawsuitsregulatoryaction/LawsuitsSelectedcases/KBRlawsuitrehumantraffickinginIraq (accessed 10 October 2011). *Ramchandra Adhikari* et al. *v. Daoud & Partners* et al, 09-cv-1237, 2009, U.S. Dist. LEXIS 126195 (S.D. Tex. 3 Nov. 2009).

[142] See McBarnet, *New Corporate Accountability*, at 41.

[143] Ibid. See EC Unfair Commercial Practices Directive, 2005/29/EC, OJ 2005 no. L149/22.

[144] Commission Decision, 8 February 1994, Public access to commission documents, 94/90/ECSC, EC, Euratom.

organization, it is nevertheless capable of conferring on third parties legal rights which the Commission is obliged to respect.[145]

Codes of Conduct Included in Contractual Agreements

Codes of conduct can be transformed into law by virtue of becoming part of the legal corpus. A company can incorporate codes of conduct in both internal and external contracts, internally through making the code of conduct part of the labor contracts with its employees, and externally via supply chain contracts.[146] In addition, the purchaser may wish to incorporate codes of conduct. Through the method of incorporation, the code of conduct becomes legally binding on the parties and has legal consequences that cannot be circumvented.

Exploring whether a party outside the corporate structures can hold a company legally bound by its code of conduct through incorporation appears the most interesting option for present purposes. Clearly, this method is used. One recent example is provided from the private security and military company industry, which joined signing an International Code of Conduct,[147] which expressly "is meant to be included in service contracts."[148] Furthermore, the United States and the United Kingdom have both expressed their intention to use the provisions of the International Code of Conduct "in their own security service procurements."[149] The International Code of Conduct is, moreover, signed by a respectable number of companies in the business, making it look and feel like law, despite not being law, formally speaking. The hard law aspect of the code of conduct is pointed out also by one of the governmental representatives involved in the drafting of the code, Nils Rosemann, who states:

> Suggesting that these codes of conduct are "soft law" wrongly indicates that they are not binding on those involved and that violations have no consequences. Those who witnessed the negotiations between governments, clients, NGOs and service providers leading up to the ICoC, will attest to the fact that discussions had anything but a soft character.... Once the ICoC is included into a contract, the violation of human rights becomes a reason for contract litigation. Such litigation and the possibility of exclusion from being

---

[145] Case T-105/95, *WWF UK v. Commission*, [1997] ECR II-313, at para. 55.
[146] See Lundblad, 'Some Legal Dimensions', at 392–6.
[147] International Code of Conduct for Private Security Services Providers, available at www.icoc-psp.org/ (accessed 5 October 2011).
[148] See Nils Rosemann, 'International Code of Conduct for Private Security Providers: A Multi-stakeholder Initiative of the 21st Century?' Institute for Human Rights and Business, 24 November 2010, available at www.institutehrb.org/blogs/guest/international_code_of_conduct_for_private_security_providers.html (accessed 12 October 2011).
[149] Ibid.

signatory to the ICoC could go far beyond any consequences of violations of "hard law."[150]

The end result is then that possible human rights abuses committed by private security providers constitute a breach of contract and are thus capable of being litigated.

Including codes of conduct in contracts is not a new phenomenon. Similar arrangements have been in place within the extractive industry since 2000, when a multistakeholder voluntary guideline on security and human rights was adopted. The Voluntary Principles on Security and Human Rights was originally concluded by the governments of the United Kingdom and the United States, nongovernmental organizations, and a number of companies from the energy and extractive industry.[151] One contractual mechanism through which the guidelines in question have been implemented is by way of including them as standard provisions in service contracts.[152] For example, the extractive company Freeport McMoRan Copper & Gold Inc. has inserted the Voluntary Principles both as a reference and as specific requirements in its contracts with private security providers in its operations in Indonesia and the Democratic Republic of Congo.[153] Their contracts stipulate that all security contractors are required to comply with the Voluntary Principles. British Petroleum (BP) has similarly included reference to the Voluntary Principles in its contracts with private security providers.[154] In addition, BP has developed a general model contract that includes a clause on the Voluntary Principles and notably also the recently adopted International Code of Conduct for Private Security Services Providers.[155] Further the spirit and requirements of

---

[150] Ibid.

[151] At the time of writing the participants consist of seven governments, nine NGOs, eighteen major companies, and three organizations with observer status. See www.voluntaryprinciples.org/participants/ (accessed 21 December 2010). For more information on the Voluntary Principles and their crafting, see for example, Bennett Freeman, Maria B. Pica and Christopher N. Camponovo, 'A New Approach to Corporate Responsibility: The Voluntary Principles on Security and Human Rights', (2000–1) 24 *Hastings International and Comparative Law Review* 423–50 with the accompanying symposium articles.

[152] See Voluntary Principles on Security + Human Rights, 'Summary Report of the Voluntary Principles Implementation Efforts 2009', www.voluntaryprinciples.org/files/Vps_Summary_Report_March_10_2010_.pdf (accessed 21 December 2010) at 2.

[153] See Freeport McMoRan Copper & Gold Inc., 'Voluntary Principles on Security and Human Rights 2010 Report to the Plenary', available at www.fcx.com/envir/pdf/policies/FCX_Volun_Princi_Plen_Report_21_Feb_2011_final.pdf (accessed 12 October 2011).

[154] BP-Annual Report on the Voluntary Principles on Security and Human Rights January–December 2010, 21 February 2011, available at www.bp.com/liveassets/bp_internet/globalbp/globalbp_uk_english/sustainability/how_we_operate/STAGING/local_assets/downloads_pdfs/Voluntary_Principles_Plenary_2011_FINAL.pdf (accessed 12 October 2011).

[155] Ibid.

the Voluntary Principles are implemented through a standard set of clauses in contracts with private security providers that relate to conditions on employment, vetting, training, conduct, and monitoring.[156]

VI. CONCLUDING OBSERVATIONS

The excursion into situations of normative pluralism involving codes of conduct and law started with a general repudiation of normative conflicts. The two normative orders display similarities with respect to the substantive content of their norms; both law and codes of conduct strive to protect, for example, human rights or labor rights. The prohibition of torture is, for example, absolute both in international law and most statutory laws, likewise in corporate codes of conduct. The convergence between the content of norms found in law and corporate codes of conduct demonstrates the intrinsic link between self-regulation and law. The question that necessarily arose from this pattern of convergence was whether self-regulatory codes of conduct actually are enforced to such an extent that they provide an effective means of regulation, because legal enforcement is axiomatic to law. If codes of conduct actually proved unenforceable in the sense that there would be no mechanism to guarantee their implementation, a conflict in *result* would arise between law and corporate codes of conduct. The problem of enforcement was potentially what would separate the one normative order from the other; the actual protection of rights would lie at the heart of normative pluralism.

An analysis of the discourse of corporate codes of conduct through the prism of law showed that problems of enforcement may appear. Most corporate codes of conduct are still viewed as nonlaw subjected to enforcement through market rather than legal mechanisms. The question of the effectiveness of such enforcement remains debated. Legal action might be available to enforce corporate codes of conduct, but claiming that it would constitute a realistic way for the ordinary factory worker in remote places to vindicate his or her rights under a corporate code of conduct remains utopian. On the other hand, law is not fully implemented in all states either, making legal enforcement subject to the same criticism, at least to some extent. The problem of enforcement can, however, not be ignored. Every code of conduct has its own procedures of implementation – if such exist to begin with. The uncertainty thus justifies a cautious approach to the enforcement of codes of conduct. Thus, I argue that it is tentatively warranted to draw the conclusion that there

[156] Ibid.

is discrepancy between the way protection in corporate codes of conduct and in law materializes – there is a conflict of result.

So what follows from saying that legal norms are more enforceable than corporate codes of conduct? How does one deal with this conflict? Under the traditional conceptualization of law such potential conflicts do not matter. Law is seen to constitute a viable system of its own, upon which self-regulatory codes of conduct exercise no altering effect. Self-regulation and law remain separate. This is expressly recognized, for example, in the general provisions of the Code of Conduct for International Security Services Providers, which states: "This Code ... *does not limit or alter applicable international law or relevant national law.*"[157] In addition, the code lays down that "nothing in this Code shall be interpreted as limiting or prejudicing in any way existing or developing rules of international law."[158] Thus, the relation to another normative order, law, is clearly established; codes of conduct remain separate and law is to be unaffected by this self-regulatory measure. The relations between law and self-regulatory codes of conduct are, however, asymmetric. The analysis has proven that codes of conduct are open to or even dependent upon law. Allegedly there is always a legal context for voluntary commitments.[159] The proliferation of lawyers advising on corporate social responsibility is a testimony to this. The situation is, however, different the other way around: law shields itself against interference from self-regulation. Codes of conduct become relevant to law only via legal concepts, not as a result of the values embedded in self-regulation. However, the essence of the relationship between law and self-regulatory codes of conduct lies beyond concrete situations instructed by normative pluralism.[160] Three regulatory aspects of the relationship in question merit closer scrutiny: 1) the nature of the regulatory *tool*, 2) the *authority* that regulates, and 3) the *goals* embedded in regulation.

To start with, self-regulatory codes of conduct as tools of regulation are often considered inferior to law; only when law fails can self-regulation become meaningful. This position should, however, be challenged. Self-regulation as

---

[157] See International Code of Conduct for Private Security Services Providers, available at www.icoc-psp.org/ (accessed 5 October 2011) (emphasis added).
[158] Ibid.
[159] See Jonathan Goldsmith, 'Lawyers' Responsibility for Advising on Corporate Social Responsibility', in Mullerat (ed.), *Corporate Social Responsibility*, 417–31 at 424.
[160] See Ulrich Sieber, who has argued with respect to the plurality of the legal system that in order for a pluralistic system to be advantegous as a whole, it must at least in single cases work out the "successful integration of the various orders"; 'Legal Order in a Global World – the Development of a Fragmented System of National, International, and Private Norms', (2010) 14 *Max Planck Yearbook of United Nations Law* 3–49 at 44.

Law versus Codes of Conduct

expressed in codes of conduct is more than merely a "plan B" or a poor cousin of legal regulation. It needs to be recognized that transnational companies have no other regulatory choice than self-regulation. They lack lawmaking powers but still feel the need to regulate matters relating to business activities. Jonathan Goldsmith has argued that "law is the codification of basic human values"; hence mechanisms of corporate social responsibility such as corporate codes of conduct are to be viewed as implementations of these values in the corporate world.[161] Second, self-regulation as a regulatory tool displays benefits law has a hard time dealing with. It has been argued that "law ... is hard put to do justice to the richness and variety of the world around us."[162] The development and consolidation of soft law have constituted recognition of relative normativity. Critics have still fought the idea of perceiving law in nonbinary terms, as something that is more or less binding. The essence of corporate codes of conduct is nevertheless their vague or unclear binding nature. Corporate executives can, for example, issue statements saying that the company is bound by the terms of a code of conduct without specifying the character or degree of bindingness. Thus, self-regulatory codes of conduct possess the characteristic many scholars have tried to bestow upon soft law. They are a versatile tool for nonstate entities such as companies that are not tied down by "the simplifying rigor of law."[163] As such, codes of conduct appear the perfect tool in the age of globalization since it could even be claimed that states have intentionally surrendered their regulatory role with respect to business entities.

Companies have indeed actively seized the opportunity of self-regulation. They appear to have come to terms with the fact that "with their concentration of economic power, wish it or not, they are institutions of global governance."[164] Simultaneously as law has been "denationalized", "the self-regulation of business and society is increasing worldwide".[165] Anne Peters has understood this as a transfer of regulatory capacity from states to global business actors, partly due to the inability of states to "regulate issues which transcend the nation-state."[166] Ulrich Sieber has in a different way argued that "in the global world, the result is a very much stronger dissonance between authority and regulation than

---

[161] See Goldsmith, 'Lawyers' Responsibility', at 424.
[162] See Jan Klabbers, 'The Undesirability of Soft Law', (1998) 67 *Nordic Journal of International Law* 381–91 at 386.
[163] Ibid., at 387.
[164] See Mendes and Mehmet, *Global Governance, Economy and Law*, at 118.
[165] See Sieber, 'Legal Order in a Global World', at 24.
[166] See Anne Peters, 'Membership in the Global Constitutional Community', in Jan Klabbers, Anne Peters and Geir Ulfstein, *The Constitutionalization of International Law* (Oxford University Press, 2009), 153–262 at 255.

in the past."[167] However, private actors may instead be viewed as part of the surfacing of new authorities in a globalized world even though their form of authority may be different from that of states. Thus, transnational companies exercise their participatory rights in the globalized world through the adoption of regulation according to means available to them. Self-regulatory codes of conduct just testify to the fact that norms increasingly stem from various sources reflecting the diversification of international actors.

In practical terms it could be argued that the fact that codes of conduct are created by nonstate actors outside legal parameters is not necessarily decisive as long as they have real life effect.[168] Thus, another important aspect in the analysis of the relationship between law and self-regulatory codes of conduct is indeed the misplaced focus on the tool itself rather than on the goals of regulation. Scholarly debate has tended to focus more on the means of regulation than on the conduct and result these purport to achieve. Phillip Rudolph has stated that

> it must be recognized and remembered that codes of conduct are a means to an end. They are not the end in itself.... But the proliferation of such codes and principles in the past decades has perhaps distracted the participants in the dialogue, who seem at times to focus more attention on the tools for achieving these goals than on the goals themselves.[169]

Thus, the views of the people below the authority issuing the regulation – which traditionally has been the state – are often neglected. Within the legal discipline, William Twining has discerned a predisposition of Western academic legal culture "to adopt the standpoints of sovereigns, rulers, legislators, judges, officials, and elites, without much regard for the points of view of users, consumers, victims, litigants and other subjects."[170] This tendency should not be allowed to dominate also with respect to analyses on other normative orders, or when assessing codes of conduct.

---

[167] See Sieber, 'Legal Order in a Global World', at 23.
[168] This has been argued also within scholarly debate. Jan Klabbers mentions Boaventura de Sousa Santos and Gavin Anderson as examples of scholars willing to discard completely the distinction between law and nonlaw. See Jan Klabbers, 'Law-Making and Constitutionalism' in Klabbers, Peters and Ulfstein, *Constitutionalization of International Law*, 81–125 at 94.
[169] See Phillip H. Rudolph, 'The History, Variations, Impact and Future of Self-Regulation', in Mullerat (ed.), *Corporate Social Responsibility*, 365–84 at 384.
[170] See William Twining, 'Implications of "Globalisation" for Law as a Discipline', (unpublished paper, on file with author) at 14.

7 *Lex Mercatoria* in International Arbitration

Ulla Liukkunen

I. INTRODUCTION

Debates over law and pluralism often refer to *lex mercatoria*. The following seeks a perspective on *lex mercatoria* from the standpoint of normative pluralism by exploring the question of how *lex mercatoria* may be used in international commercial arbitration. Also touched upon is the complex interface between *lex mercatoria* and international law as well as private international law. *Lex mercatoria* is discussed both as an alternative to and as a complement of rules deriving from different legal orders. In addition, *lex mercatoria* is addressed as a method of adjudication in dispute-resolution situations where different sets of rules may coexist. In the international business community, the legitimacy of *lex mercatoria*, be it a set of rules or a method of arbitral decision making, derives from the end users' needs and their acceptance. As a manifestation of pluralism, *lex mercatoria* reaffirms that the question of legitimacy of nonstate law needs to be reformulated in international law.[1]

This chapter approaches *lex mercatoria* from two angles. On the one hand, *lex mercatoria* is considered as a transnational set of rules that is more flexible than state law for contracting parties in international business and that has gained usability in international commercial arbitration. *Lex mercatoria* is optional for parties to international business transactions and can be applied by virtue of their choice in cross-border contractual relations instead of, or in addition to, state law. International commercial arbitration emphasizes the contracting parties' freedom to choose the set of rules that best suits their purposes. By choosing *lex mercatoria* and international arbitration, the parties seek flexible and suitable norms that replace state law and suitable procedure

---

[1] See Jan Klabbers and Touko Piiparinen, "Normative Pluralism: An Exploration," Chapter 1 in this volume.

with the aim of minimizing costs and legal uncertainty related to the application of state law in state courts.

On the other hand, this chapter discusses *lex mercatoria* as a particular method of arbitral adjudication.[2] This understanding emphasizes the way in which arbitrators deal with legal questions and how arbitrators use the latitude provided to them by the applicable substantive rules. Some believe that it also enables rejection of the application of private international law rules in international arbitration.[3] The construction of *lex mercatoria* as a set of transnational rules refers to *lex mercatoria* as a source of normative pluralism. This construction broadens the perspective. However, the distinction between the two approaches is not clear-cut, and they can be seen as more or less intertwined and even mutually supportive.

Essentially, there are two different forms of international arbitration: institutional and ad hoc arbitration. The first is carried out under a particular arbitration institution. The second is designed by the parties and conducted without the framework of such an institution. With "institutional rules" concerning arbitration I refer in this chapter generally to rules on international arbitration provided by international arbitration institutions. By contrast, with "statutory provisions" I refer to provisions on international arbitration in state laws.

This chapter seeks to explore functions that *lex mercatoria* may serve in international commercial arbitration. These functions relate to the process of choice of law required in order to determine the law applicable to the merits of the dispute. In determining the law applicable to the merits of the dispute, the point of departure is party autonomy. The arbitrators have to respect the will of the parties. Generally speaking, if the parties have not chosen the applicable law, the law of the seat of the arbitration, *lex arbitri*, provides rules for determining the applicable law. In the case of institutional arbitration, the arbitrators seek guidance from the institutional rules.

This chapter discusses the question of *lex mercatoria* as applicable law from the standpoint of choice of law based on the applicable conflicts rules. However, it should be emphasized that the role of private international law in determining the law applicable to the merits of the dispute divides opinion. Criticism on private international law is often emphasized in debates on *lex mercatoria*. When *lex mercatoria* is regarded as a set of transnational

---

[2] See Filip De Ly, 'Lex Mercatoria (New Law Merchant): Globalisation and International Self-regulation', in R. P. Appelbaum, W. L. F. Felstiner and Volkmar Gessner (eds.), *Rules and Networks: The Legal Culture of Global Business Transactions* (Oxford, UK: Hart, 2001), 157–88, at 180.
[3] See Emmanuel Gaillard, 'Transnational Law: A Legal System or a Method of Decision Making?' (2001) 17 *Arbitration International*, 59–72, at 62.

rules applicable to a concrete dispute, conflicts law constantly meets criticisms of being an unnecessary intervener, making the outcome of the dispute unpredictable.[4]

The need for choice of law is challenged by many recently adopted institutional rules and statutory provisions on international arbitration that permit the application of substantive law without mediation of choice of law rules. On the other hand, this chapter shows that the growing role of mandatory rules in international arbitration demonstrates an opposite trend emphasizing the need to observe private international law rules.

Whether the applicable law is state or nonstate law, arbitrators are being challenged ever more frequently by the question of the applicability of mandatory rules of various types.[5] In some cases mandatory rules may also limit application of *lex mercatoria*, the role of which will be analyzed in this chapter by looking at the limitations that mandatory rules that affect the applicable law may pose for *lex mercatoria* in arbitration. Collisions between nonstate and state law may arise in certain situations of international arbitration because of the impact of mandatory state rules that reflect state interests in application of *lex mercatoria*. The analysis of mandatory rules pays attention to the two different approaches concerning *lex mercatoria* discussed in this chapter and touches on the interface between private international law and public international law. This chapter also evaluates recent changes in the role of private international law and the impact of those changes on use of *lex mercatoria* in international arbitration. The result-oriented approach, which has gained an increasing foothold in private international law and is manifest in the growing impact of mandatory rules, might mean a new susceptibility to collisions between nonstate and state law in international arbitration.

In the following, the use of *lex mercatoria* in international arbitration will be addressed against the challenges of governance of the pluralism of legal orders and the changing role of private international law as a coordinator of legal diversity. The growing relevance of mandatory rules appears contradictory to the tendency to minimize the role of private international law and to maximize the role of party autonomy in international arbitration. This tendency can be recognized in some recently adopted institutional rules and statutory provisions concerning international arbitration. However, it does not remove the need to observe mandatory rules in certain situations.

---

[4] See Klaus Peter Berger, *The Creeping Codification of the New Lex Mercatoria* (The Hague: Kluwer Law International, 1999), at 10.
[5] See H. A. Grigera Naón, 'Choice-of-Law Problems in International Commercial Arbitration', (2001) 289 *Recueil des Cours*, 9–395, at 185.

Minimizing unnecessary costs and legal uncertainty is a central aim of contracting parties who seek flexible and suitable nonstate rules to replace state law. The applicability of *lex mercatoria* depends to a great extent on the contracting parties' agreeing not only on the law applicable to the merits of the dispute but also on international arbitration being used for resolving contractual disputes. International arbitration has established a position as a channel for resolving disputes that offers parties seeking, in addition to confidentiality, a neutral legal framework and an opportunity to select *lex mercatoria* as the applicable law and thereby avoid the uncertainty created by applying state law. By resorting to *lex mercatoria* and international arbitration, the parties are able to avoid uncertainties that relate not only to the differences between the private international law rules of national states and the substantive laws of different states, but also to their application in national courts.[6]

However, institutional rules and statutory provisions concerning international arbitration may set certain limitations on the application of *lex mercatoria*. When determining the applicability of state laws in cases where the parties have chosen *lex mercatoria* as the applicable law, the relationship between *lex mercatoria* and applicable private international law rules plays a crucial role. By virtue of these rules, the application of substantive state law may sometimes be necessary in order to supplement the applicable nonstate law.

In court proceedings, the law of the forum, *lex fori*, retains a strong role despite the international harmonization of national rules on private international law that has taken place, for example, in the EU. Arbitration does not have a similar connection to the law of the country in which the arbitral tribunal is located. As a result, arbitration is not threatened by *lex forism*, which often affects the decision making of national courts and makes it unpredictable. It is true that the seat of arbitration has an important role to play in international arbitration since the law of the seat, among other things, determines the grounds on which the award may be challenged before a national court. However, *lex forism* is avoided. The neutrality and expertise that are emblematic of international arbitration are also reflected in the way arbitrators approach norms originating from different legal systems in the absence of *lex fori* on a comparative basis.

Hence, the efficiency of *lex mercatoria* does not solely relate to the content of applicable rules tailor-made for the purposes of international commerce.

---

[6] See Maarit Jänterä-Jareborg, 'Foreign Law in National Courts: A Comparative Perspective', (2003) 304 *Recueil des Cours*, 181–385.

It also has to do with the efficiency of the arbitral procedure and the decision-making method used by arbitral tribunals compared to state courts. With this in mind, some authors have argued for determining *lex mercatoria* as a particular method used in international arbitration. According to Emmanuel Gaillard, this means understanding transnational law as a method based not on a traditional choice-of-law process, but on comparative law analysis, whose outcome is the most widely accepted rule.[7] However, even this approach to *lex mercatoria* might be challenged to a certain extent by the need to take into account the effect of mandatory rules.

It is necessary to emphasize right away at this stage that much controversy surrounds the topics in this chapter, starting from the existence and nature of *lex mercatoria*. International arbitration is based on diverse institutional rules and statutory provisions that, together with diverse conflicts rules, in themselves restrict conclusions on the topics in this chapter. The very limited publicity given to arbitral awards is another factor that limits drawing conclusions. Similarly, it should be underlined that the question of the status of mandatory rules in international arbitration is highly complicated and divides opinion.

II. THE NEW *LEX MERCATORIA* – STARTING POINTS

Lex mercatoria made a new appearance around the 1950s and 1960s and started to take its new form first and foremost on the basis of detailed definitions introduced by Clive Schmitthoff and Berthold Goldman. Schmitthoff developed a theory of international business law where international conventions and international usages played an important role. He understood *lex mercatoria* as an independent part of national legal systems.[8] According to Schmitthoff, a central precondition for resolving disputes over international business transactions was that there are rules based on international legislation as well as international commercial custom.[9] Goldman, on the other hand, argued that *lex mercatoria* was an autonomous legal order independent of state law. According to Goldman, *lex mercatoria* can be characterized "at the least" as "a set of general principles, and customary rules spontaneously referred to or elaborated in the framework of international trade, without reference to

---

[7] See Gaillard, 'Transnational Law', at 62.
[8] See Filip De Ly, *International Business Law and Lex Mercatoria* (Amsterdam: North Holland, 1992), at 209–210 and 319–310.
[9] See Clive M. Schmitthoff, 'Nature and Evolution of the Transnational Law of Commercial Transactions', in Norbert Horn and Clive M. Schmitthoff (eds.), *The Transnational Law of International Commercial Transactions* (Deventer: Kluwer, 1982), 19–31, at 23–7.

a particular national system of law."[10] Goldman and some other authors consider *lex mercatoria* separate also from the international legal order.[11]

When *lex mercatoria* is approached as the law applied in international arbitration its content is characterized by heterogeneity. It escapes exhaustive definitions, although it is typically based on norms of private origin, legitimated by use of nongovernmental methods of dispute settlement. The content of *lex mercatoria* is sometimes presented as lists of transnational rules deriving from different sources. This means that their specialty is not seen in their contents but in their sources.[12] Ole Lando has defined the "elements" included in *lex mercatoria* very widely to include public international law, uniform laws, general principles of law, the rules of international organizations, customs and usages, standard form contracts, and reporting of arbitral awards. It is clear that the sources need to be widely accepted by the trading community. Lando does not mean the definition to be exhaustive, and from the viewpoint of arbitration, his emphasis lies on *lex mercatoria* as an invention. He refers to the role of inventor that arbitrators may need to take in situations where they want to find a solution for a legal question to which *lex mercatoria* as the applicable law offers only a partial or a partly unsatisfactory answer.[13] For Lando, applying *lex mercatoria* refers to the judicial process, which is partly an application of rules and partly a selective and creative process.[14] From this viewpoint, the open or partial nature of the substantive content of *lex mercatoria* does not appear as a source of ambiguity endangering decision making since the decision-making process enables arbitrators to construct and complement the applicable substantive rules.

Lando's approach can be combined with that advanced by Filip De Ly according to which *lex mercatoria* is first and foremost "a method of judicial and arbitral adjudication."[15] De Ly stresses that resolving international business law related legal questions is not really about whether the international trading community has common rules or whether it could transform these rules into a formal source of law. Thus, the theories of Goldman and Schmitthoff are

---

[10] See Berthold Goldman, 'The Applicable Law: General Principles of Law – Lex Mercatoria', in Julian D. M. Lew (ed.), *Contemporary Problems in International Arbitration* (Boston: Kluwer Academic, 1987), 113–25, at 116.

[11] See Abul F. M. Manriruzzaman, 'The Lex Mercatoria and International Contracts: A Challenge for International Commercial Arbitration?' (1999) 14 *American University International Law Review*, 657–734, at 670.

[12] See also Gaillard, 'Transnational Law', at 61.

[13] See Ole Lando, 'The Law Applicable to the Merits of the Dispute', (1986) 2 *Arbitration International*, 104–15, at 107.

[14] See Ole Lando, 'The *Lex Mercatoria* in International Commercial Arbitration', (1985) 34 *International and Comparative Law Quarterly*, 747–68, at 747.

[15] See De Ly, 'New Merchant Law', at 180.

insufficient for understanding the role of *lex mercatoria* in international commercial transactions. For De Ly, the key appears to be, without ignoring the international substantive character of *lex mercatoria*, rather the way in which legal questions are dealt with and how arbitrators use the latitude provided to them by international instruments and state laws.[16] Thus, attention is paid to the methodology of legal decision making instead of formal sources of law, and the focus shifts to arbitrators' role as rule makers and developers of international business law.

Lex mercatoria does not exist in a vacuum since it is used in international arbitration, which is under the influence of international law and private international law rules. These rules may in some cases limit the applicability of *lex mercatoria* determined to be the *lex causae*. The impact of mandatory rules may also limit arbitrators' freedom as rule makers in international arbitration. Later in this chapter, more light is shed on the status of *lex mercatoria* by analyzing some aspects of the special characteristics of the relationship between *lex mercatoria* and private international law. In the following, some of the factors affecting the scope of application of *lex mercatoria* are discussed, together with the nuanced impact of the rules originating from state private international law on nonstate dispute resolution. International arbitration will be discussed, particularly from the viewpoint of what kind of impact the principles of private international law that limit choice of law can have on the application of *lex mercatoria*.

Lex mercatoria is sometimes defined so widely that it is considered to encompass private international law rules including procedural rules in addition to applicable substantive law.[17] A related trend that has recently gained momentum is a tendency to formulate institutional rules and statutory provisions concerning international arbitration so that *lex mercatoria* may become directly applicable on their basis. However, this trend does not remove all conflicts of laws questions, and the need remains to take certain conflict questions into consideration in international arbitration. An often underlined advantage of international arbitration is the smooth enforceability of awards. Even though a national court does not have the right to investigate whether an arbitral tribunal has applied a law correctly or may not annul or repeal an arbitration award on the basis of incorrect application of law, the need to ensure enforceability of an award may require arbitrators to consider different types of mandatory rules.

---

[16] See also De Ly, *International Business Law*, at 315.
[17] See Christoph W. O. Stoecker, 'Lex Mercatoria: To What Extent Does It Exist?' (1990) 7 *Journal of International Arbitration*, 101–25, at 109.

III. PRIVATE INTERNATIONAL LAW, PUBLIC INTERNATIONAL LAW, AND *LEX MERCATORIA* – PRELIMINARY OBSERVATIONS

Although party autonomy is highlighted in international arbitration, disregard by the arbitral tribunal of other laws than that chosen by the parties is not always possible.[18] However, private international law, whose rules determine the borders of party autonomy and may also restrict the effect of choice of law, varies in different legal systems. Diversity of private international law rules concerning international arbitration is wide too.

Alex Mills has studied the legal basis of private international law as compared to public international law in general and characterizes the rules of private international law "as a mutually constitutive international system of secondary norms, serving a public constitutional function."[19] According to Mills, federal systems have retained the systemic idea and constitutive function of private international law. Private international law is part of the architecture of such systems. Therefore, from a systemic point of view, private international law must be viewed and evaluated as a form of public international law that provides a structure for the regulatory authority.[20]

Mills's systemic approach sees rules on jurisdiction, choice of law, and enforcement as components of private international law that reinforce and support each other. At the core, private international law rules do not address questions of private justice, but they are implications of justice pluralism, that is, metajustice.[21] For Mills, the international perspective demands that private international law is evaluated according to whether it is international enough to meet its objectives, to coordinate different legal systems in a way that balances the international structure and rights in relation to the diversity of values embodied in different national legal orders. This task is much greater than the traditional and still common view of private international law as merely a way of finding justice in individual private disputes.[22]

Pluralism highlights the task of private international law as a coordinator of applicable rules in international arbitration. According to present trends, conflict rules are increasingly being used to order, and even manage,

---

[18] See also Giuditta Cordero Moss, 'Arbitration and Private International Law', (2008) 11 *International Arbitration Law Review*, 153–64, at 153.
[19] Alex Mills, *The Confluence of Public and Private International Law: Justice, Pluralism and Subsidiarity in the International Constitutional Ordering of Private Law* (Cambridge University Press, 2009), at 308–9.
[20] Ibid., at 300.
[21] Ibid., at 301.
[22] See ibid., at 308.

diversity.[23] It can be argued that arbitration, as a process aiming at justice, and the way of using *lex mercatoria* with different substantive contents based on different transnational sets of rules on different occasions, order diversity in a particular way.

For contracting parties in international business, nonstate law like *lex mercatoria* is a better tool than state law for ensuring the justice they seek. This has to do with a plurality of options: several sets of norms are available to the parties seeking an optimal solution for their individual purposes. In this respect, by offering an alternative to rigid state laws, *lex mercatoria* can be argued to belong to the heart of the debate over normative pluralism. With the understanding of *lex mercatoria* as a method of arbitral adjudication, it could be argued that a connection lies between nurturing justice and the application of *lex mercatoria*.

IV. *LEX MERCATORIA* IN CHOICE OF LAW

It should be emphasized that application of *lex mercatoria* to the merits of the dispute in international commercial arbitration may take different forms. Sometimes *lex mercatoria* is applied to disputes in international arbitration in addition to state law. This application is based not only on the choice of the parties but sometimes also on the supplementary or corrective role of *lex mercatoria* in choice of law.[24] The legal framework of international arbitration for use of *lex mercatoria* is characterized by diversity of institutional rules and statutory provisions concerning arbitration. The diversity also relates to the basic question of whether the institutional rules or statutory provisions concerning international arbitration permit the parties to choose a nonstate law as applicable to the merits of the dispute.[25]

Private international law to be applied in international arbitration is not necessarily private international law of any states. In the absence of party choice, most arbitration systems leave the decision of the applicable law to

---

[23] See Ulla Liukkunen, 'Managing Legal Diversity in the EU: The Case of Subject-Specific Conflicts Rules', (2012) 20 *European Review of Private Law*, 1045–74, at 1068–9.

[24] See also Joanna Jemielniak, 'Legitimization Arguments in the Lex Mercatoria Cases', (2005) 18 *International Journal for the Semiotics of Law*, 175–205, at 193–4.

[25] References to an opportunity to choose a nonstate law take different forms in institutional rules and statutory provisions concerning international arbitration. It is not always clear whether these rules and provisions enable the parties to choose *lex mercatoria* as applicable. See in more detail Linda Silberman and Franco Ferrari, 'Getting to the Law Applicable to the Merits in International Arbitration and the Consequences of Getting It Wrong', in F. Ferrari and S. Kröll (eds.), *Conflict of Laws in International Arbitration* (München: Sellier, 2011), 257–323, at 268–71.

the arbitrators. Many applicable rules or provisions concerning arbitration require use of conflict rules to determine the law applicable to the merits of the dispute. Private international law rules that are applied in the absence of a choice of law clause might give the arbitrators freedom to make a choice of law in the way they consider most appropriate.[26] In some systems, arbitrators are able to apply *lex mercatoria* or another nonstate set of rules instead of state law. However, not every system provides this opportunity. If the institutional rules or statutory provisions concerning international arbitration do not provide a definite answer to the question of the applicable private international law rules, the arbitrators have to solve the question without their support.

Under certain conditions, *lex mercatoria* may become applicable even when the parties have not chosen an applicable law and the arbitrators determine the law. Increasingly in recent years, institutional rules and statutory provisions on international arbitration have been formed so that according to them a choice of law is not needed and arbitrators are entitled to apply the applicable law directly, without mediation of private international rules.[27] This phenomenon of the liberalization of regulation seeks to eliminate the private international aspect of arbitration and better serve the expectations of the parties. However, lack of a reference to private international rules in arbitration regulation may lead to unpredictable results in cases where questions arise whose resolution requires private international law, such as the question of legal capacity.[28]

A. Lex Mercatoria as the Applicable Law

It is sometimes argued that one of the central reasons why the contracting parties choose *lex mercatoria* is to avoid having to apply private international law rules.[29] Thus, the parties select *lex mercatoria* as the applicable law not only because it is the practical choice but also because rules of private international

---

[26] See also De Ly, 'New Law Merchant', at 117, and Lando, 'The Law Applicable', at 111.

[27] See, for example, Jemielniak, 'Legitimation Arguments', at 294. This *voie directe* approach is illustrated by Article 35(1) of the 2010 renewed UNCITRAL Arbitration Rules, under which "the arbitral tribunal shall apply the rules of law designated by the parties as applicable to the substance of the dispute. Failing such designation by the parties, the arbitral tribunal shall apply the law which it determines to be appropriate." On the other hand, for example, Article 28(2) of the UNCITRAL Model Law which has been the basis of the national legislation on international arbitration in several countries, is based on the traditional *voie indirecte* approach and provides that "Failing any designation by the parties, the arbitral tribunal shall apply the law determined by the conflict of laws rules which it considers appropriate."

[28] See also Stoecker, 'Lex Mercatoria', 153, and Silberman and Ferrari, 'Getting It Wrong', at 265.

[29] See, for example, Lando, 'Lex Mercatoria', at 754.

law are considered to represent an unnecessary intervention that should be eliminated. Despite all unification work in the field of private international law, one of the old problems is the *homeward trend* demonstrated by national courts when resolving contractual disputes in international business law.[30] This is not a problem in arbitration, however. When *lex mercatoria* is chosen as the applicable law, neither party can obtain an advantage by applying their own law. Moreover, by choosing *lex mercatoria*, the parties rid themselves of the technicalities of national legal systems and avoid having to apply rules that are unsuitable for international contracts.[31] Typically, in private international law applied to contractual disputes by state courts the option to choose *lex mercatoria* as the applicable law has been rejected.

When *lex mercatoria* has been determined as the applicable law in international arbitration, the fact that the law of a specific state does not have to be applied gives arbitrators a chance to seek the most appropriate solution by making multilayered use of the method of legal comparison. As the arbitrators do not have a *lex fori*, they remove an important risk factor in decision making, that is, an intended or unintended emphasis on one's own law. The nature of *lex mercatoria* supports the fruitfulness of legal comparison as a method of dispute resolution.

As *lex mercatoria* is open by nature, choosing it as the applicable law means that arbitrators operating on a transnational legal basis have to specify the sometimes loose formulations of the principles of international trade, such as *good faith*. Sometimes arbitrators have to cross the boundaries of legal cultures when resolving a case. In some cases it may become impossible to apply *lex mercatoria* determined as the applicable law to every issue at stake.[32] If the contracting parties choose the custom and usages of international commercial law or the rules of law common to all or most of the states involved in international trade to govern their contract and the rules chosen are not ascertainable, the arbitrators apply the rules or choose the solution that appeals to them the most appropriate and equitable.[33] Achieving a solution may involve considering the content of several sets of rules.

Generally speaking, the relationship between arbitration and *lex mercatoria* is less problematic than that between court proceedings and *lex mercatoria*. *Lex mercatoria* is rarely determined as the applicable law by national courts because this is excluded by the private international laws of several states.

---

[30] Ibid., at 748. See also De Ly, 'New Merchant Law', at 160, 170.
[31] Lando, 'Lex Mercatoria', at 748.
[32] See Beda Wortmann, 'Choice of Law by Arbitrators: The Applicable Conflict of Laws System', (1998) 14 *Arbitration International*, 97–114, at 102.
[33] Lando, 'Law Applicable', at 107.

However, many institutional rules and statutory provisions of arbitration enable the application of *lex mercatoria* in international arbitration if the contracting parties so choose.

B. The Growing Role of Codifications

During recent decades, vagueness and uncertainties surrounding the applicability of nonstate law have been reduced by international codifications of principles developed by international organizations.[34] These codifications have provided a new basis for applying *lex mercatoria* and advanced demands for opening an opportunity also to apply *lex mercatoria* in state courts. However, they have also faced criticism according to which the autonomy and adaptability of *lex mercatoria* are significantly enhanced by them.[35]

Since the 1990s, the substantive content of *lex mercatoria* has been specified by these international codifications of contractual principles, which have been prepared, with several objectives in mind, on the basis of extensive comparative efforts.[36] The codifications have been drawn up in order to create norms that cover as many situations as possible and therefore offer the parties to international transactions an opportunity to choose these kinds of norms instead of state law.

Approved in 1994 and renewed in 2004 and 2010, the UNIDROIT Principles of International Commercial Contracts are widely applied in international arbitration.[37] The Principles of European Contract Law (PECL) prepared by the Commission on European Contract Law are meant to be applied as general rules of contract law in the EU.[38] They were primarily drawn with international trade in mind, and they cover the same main issues of substantive law as the UNIDROIT Principles. The aim of their drafters was to create a collection of contract law principles on the basis of national systems of contract law that would meet the needs of business life.[39]

These codifications of contractual principles are also applicable in international arbitration when the parties have chosen *lex mercatoria* for application.

---

[34] De Ly, 'New Law Merchant', at 166, and Wortmann, 'Choice of Law', at 103.
[35] See also Celia Wasserstein Fassberg, 'Lex Mercatoria – Hoist with Its Own Petard?' (2004) 67 *Chicago Journal of International Law*, 67–90, at 78.
[36] See also Berger, *Creeping Codification*, at 29.
[37] See Michael Joachim Bonell, 'Towards a Legislative Codification of the UNIDROIT Principles? Modern Law for Global Commerce.' Congress to celebrate the fortieth annual session of UNCITRAL. Vienna, 9–12 July 2007, available at http://www.uncitral.org/pdf/english/congress/Bonell.pdf. (accessed 30 November 2012).
[38] See Article 1:101(1) of the Principles.
[39] Also legislators and courts may use both codifications.

The Preamble of the UNIDROIT Principles provides that the principles "may be applied when the parties have agreed that their contract be governed by general principles of law, the *lex mercatoria* or the like." Also the PECL can be applied if the merits of the dispute are governed by *lex mercatoria*.[40] The extent to which these principles can override state law in choice of law depends in principle on whether the dispute is resolved in a national court or by arbitration. Institutional rules and statutory provisions on arbitration often allow a choice of a codification of principles as applicable law.

Although state private international law has had a negative attitude toward codified contractual principles, for example, in the EU, and they cannot be chosen as applicable law when the dispute is resolved in a court, substantive incorporation of international contractual principles into contract terms is allowed. For example, the Rome I Regulation, which governs choice of law for contractual relationships in EU Member States except Denmark, does not allow an international codification of principles to be chosen as applicable to a contract even though the European Commission proposed that such a provision be added to the Regulation.[41] The Commission proposed that party autonomy be extended to the effect that the principles and rules of the substantive law of contract recognized internationally or in the European Community could be chosen for application instead of a state law.[42] However, choosing *lex mercatoria* as the applicable law would not have been allowed because *lex mercatoria* was not considered to be specific enough; similarly, private codifications not adequately recognized by the international community would not have been accepted.

C. Supplementing Lex Mercatoria

Typically, party choice of *lex mercatoria* appears as the basis of its application by arbitrators.[43] Contracting parties may choose *lex mercatoria* to be applied wholly or partially to their contract. In situations where the contracting parties have chosen *lex mercatoria* to be applied to the whole contract, a stand often needs to be taken on whether there are gaps in the applicable *lex mercatoria*.[44] The contracting parties may prepare for this in advance by

---

[40] See Article 1:101(3)(a) of the Principles.
[41] See Article 3(1) of the Regulation (EC) no. 593/2008 of the European Parliament and of the Council of 17 June 2008 on the law applicable to contractual obligations (Rome I).
[42] See Proposal for a Regulation of the European Parliament and the Council on the law applicable to contractual obligations (Rome I). COM(2005) 650 final, at 5.
[43] See also Lando, 'The Law Applicable', at 107, and, for example, Naón, 'Choice-of-Law Problems', at 281.
[44] See also Wortmann, 'Choice of Law', at 102–3.

choosing *lex mercatoria* as applicable and the law of a particular state as the supplementary or secondary applicable law. The parties can also choose, for example, a combination of *lex mercatoria* and equity.[45] Also in other cases where *lex mercatoria* does not provide a solution to all disputed issues relating to an international commercial contract, the arbitrators may find it necessary to complement it with other rules. In principle, this does not exclude application of state laws as a supplement to *lex mercatoria*. However, arbitrators have a duty to respect the will of the parties. Gaps in the applicable law are filled taking into account the private international rules applicable.[46]

Partial choices of *lex mercatoria* may take different forms. Sometimes the choice of *lex mercatoria* governs only certain parts of the merits of the dispute and the parties have not chosen a supplementary applicable law. In that case the applicable private international law rules determine whether a state law has to be applied to issues not covered by the chosen applicable law or whether nonstate norms are also to be applied to those issues. Another situation where state laws might need to be considered can be the case where mandatory rules have to be taken into account. In addition to overriding mandatory rules, arbitrators sometimes also need to take the public policy principle into consideration.[47]

D. Lex Mercatoria as a Supplement of the Applicable Law

In cases where the contracting parties have not chosen or the arbitrators have not determined *lex mercatoria* as the applicable law, it may, however, become applicable as a supplementary transnational set of rules in international arbitration.[48] Generally speaking, *lex mercatoria* may become supplementary to the applicable law in two kinds of arbitration situations. First of all, arbitrators may resort to *lex mercatoria* when the applicable clauses of an international contract require supplementary norms. These can be contractual terms that refer to general principles and require a general interpretation. In interpreting these contractual provisions, external norms such as the UNIDROIT

---

[45] See Lando, 'Law Applicable', at 107.
[46] See also Giuditta Cordero Moss, 'Can an Arbitral Tribunal Disregard the Choice of Law Made by the Parties?' (2005) 1 *Stockholm International Arbitration Review*, 1–21, at 7–12.
[47] See also Ole Lando, 'The Principles of European Contract Law and the *Lex Mercatoria*', in Jürgen Basedow, Isaak Meier, Daniel Girsberger, Anton K. Schnyder and Talia Einhorn (eds.), *Private Law in the International Arena – from National Conflict Rules towards Harmonization and Unification: Liber Amicorum Kurt Siehr* (The Hague: T. M. C. Asser Press, 2000), 391–404, at 401–2.
[48] See also, for example, ICC case no. 5314 of 1988, (1992) *Journal du Droit International* and ICC case no. 5835 of 1996, (1999) *The ICC International Court of Arbitration Bulletin*.

Lex Mercatoria in International Arbitration

Principles or *lex mercatoria* might be needed. Sometimes *lex mercatoria* is used in arbitration to interpret the applicable state law. In some cases, contractual provisions have been constructed or interpreted in the light of *lex mercatoria* so that the application of state law has been excluded.[49] In addition, *lex mercatoria* can be used in arbitration to supplement a state or nonstate law that has been chosen as applicable, if that law does not provide answers to all the legal questions at hand or merely a partial choice of law has been made. The supplementary role of *lex mercatoria* in choice of law requires that the contracting parties have not made a specific choice of the applicable law that excludes the application of *lex mercatoria*.

E. Evaluation

Arbitration often solves disputes concerning contracts that are extensive and complex. The core feature of *lex mercatoria* is that it is able to meet the needs of contracting parties in international commerce in a complicated legal operating environment. The underlying idea is that a transnational set of rules like *lex mercatoria* that is open by nature enables arbitrators to identify the rules that, according to Lando, provide greater consistency and harmony in decision making than state laws. By selecting *lex mercatoria* as the basis for resolving a substantive dispute, the parties involved, as well as counsels and arbitrators, are also put in an equal position with regard to the applicable rules. No legal system has precedence over another, and no party can gain the advantage by having better knowledge of the applicable law than the other.[50]

Sometimes arbitrators need to find a new solution and act, in Lando's terms, as "social engineers."[51] From the viewpoint of the parties involved, the justification for the particular decision-making activities by arbitrators involves developing *lex mercatoria* further in order to achieve an appropriate solution. On the one hand, the open nature of *lex mercatoria* is beneficial to international arbitration since it provides arbitrators with tools of construction.[52] On the other hand, arbitrators are then better equipped than courts to adjust the applicable rules to the circumstances of the case at hand. From the viewpoint of international business law, arbitrators have been entrusted with an opportunity to create rules that further the development of the field of law. Arbitrators, authorized by contracting parties to resolve their concrete disputes, may need to develop entirely new rules and apply

---

[49] Naón, 'Choice-of-Law Problems', at 282 and the ICC cases referred there.
[50] Lando, 'Principles', at 402.
[51] Lando, 'Lex Mercatoria', at 752.
[52] See also Lando, 'Law Applicable', at 112.

them together with the existing ones. Their decision-making processes are characterized by a search for solutions that further the dispute-solving process. Even then, however, private international law rules provide a framework for determining the limits of application of *lex mercatoria*. Arbitral practices demonstrate elements affecting choice of law that are peculiar to international commercial arbitration.[53]

Legal comparison may be necessary in different phases of the multilayered arbitration process, which may sometimes require creation of new rules or modification of old ones.[54] The view that the arbitrators' decision-making process will not suffer but may even benefit from the incomplete nature of *lex mercatoria* is quite different from the traditional rejective view of the application of *lex mercatoria* in state private international law. The typical view in the latter sees that lex mercatoria needs to be codified in order to be applied as the law applicable to international contracts in national courts. A related development is, for example, ongoing effort in the EU to codify *lex mercatoria* as the European commercial law, "*lex mercatoria europea*," which consumers and companies could choose as the basis for their contractual relationship instead of a state law. Recently, the European Commission has made a proposal for a Regulation on a Common European Sales Law, which could be a step further. The objective of the proposal is to improve the functioning of the internal market by facilitating the expansion of cross-border trade for business and cross-border purchases for consumers. The Common European Sales law could be used in contracts between traders and in contracts between traders and consumers. The Common European Sales Law would be applicable to cross-border transactions, contracts for the sale of goods, for the supply of digital content, and for the provision of related services.[55] However, the Common European Sales Law would not set aside the applicable choice of law rules. This means that even if a choice of the Common European Sales Law were made in a contract, the conflict rules of the Rome I Regulation would be applied in the national courts of the Member States.[56]

Much of the debate on the European project of codification concentrates on the question of the comprehensiveness of the proposed Common

---

[53] Naón, 'Choice-of-Law Problems', at 373.
[54] See Lando, 'Lex Mercatoria', at 752–3. According to De Ly, "methodologically, arbitrators have had to develop a laboratory of new conflict and substantive methods"; see Filip De Ly, 'Conflicts of Law in International Arbitration – an Overview', in Ferrari and Kröll (eds.), *Conflict of Laws*, at 16.
[55] See Article 3 of the Proposal for a Regulation of the European Parliament and of the Council on a Common European Sales Law. COM(2011) 635 final.
[56] See Proposal for a Regulation of the European Parliament and of the Council on a Common European Sales Law. COM(2011) 635 final.

European Sales Law. This question does not seem to be critical to the usability of *lex mercatoria*. The fact that *lex mercatoria* does not always provide a complete solution to a dispute does not hinder its use as the applicable law in international arbitration. Rather, it advances decision-making processes that are more open to comparative considerations than the decision making taking place in national courts. Rejective views of private international law rules in arbitration gain support from the proponents of understanding of *lex mercatoria* as a method of decision making. However, private international rules are necessary for determining the limits of application of the *lex causae*, even when this law is nonstate law. Private international law rules may also have to be applied, for example, when the question of the validity of a party choice or the arbitrability of a dispute arises. Although they may be needed at different phases of the decision-making process, conflict rules do not disable a creative decision-making process. Conflict rules also enter the picture when a stand needs to be taken on the status of mandatory rules. This has become an increasingly important question in international arbitration.

V. THE IMPACT OF MANDATORY RULES

Mandatory rules of different types have come to play an important role in private international law. Overriding mandatory rules (*lois de police*) are those whose nature requires their application irrespective of the applicable law.[57] In addition to the classic public policy principle (*ordre public*), overriding mandatory rules may limit the effect of the applicable law.

In cases where the contracting parties have sought to select a neutral applicable law by choosing *lex mercatoria*, or the arbitrators have determined *lex mercatoria* as the applicable nonstate law either directly or through choice-of-law rules, mandatory rules may need to be applied. They may in certain situations also limit the application of *lex mercatoria*. The increasing role of mandatory rules in choice of law has increasingly been reflected in the debate over international arbitration, but has met with a mixed response.[58] In the following, the ways in which mandatory rules may intervene in international arbitration are discussed.

---

[57] Ulla Liukkunen, *The Role of Mandatory Rules in International Labour Law – a Comparative Study in the Conflict of Laws* (Helsinki: Talentum, 2004), at 128.
[58] See also, for example, ICC case no. 6294 of 1991, (1991) *Journal du Droit International*; ICC case no. 6320 of 1992, (1995) 20 *Yearbook of Commercial Arbitration*; ICC case no. 6773 of 1992, (1995) *The ICC International Court of Arbitration Bulletin* and ICC case no. 8528 of 1996, (2000) 25 *Yearbook of Commercial Arbitration*.

A. Overriding Mandatory Rules

In private international law, an important distinction is made between "domestically" and overriding mandatory rules. Domestically, or internally, mandatory rules are rules that cannot be deviated from by a contract. Only a limited number of these rules can be considered overriding mandatory. Overriding mandatory rules can be regarded as having a "strengthened" mandatory nature so that they need to be applied by virtue of this. The nature and purpose of the rules provide that they are so important that they have to be applied regardless of the otherwise applicable law.[59] Overriding mandatory rules give effect to important state policies, and the exceptional importance of these rules is often related to the public interest.[60]

Fields where these rules can typically be found are labor law, insurance law, carriage, and agency.[61] In addition, antitrust and securities regulation typically involves overriding mandatory rules. Overriding mandatory rules relate to various interests, such as protection of the national economy or the social order of the society.[62] For example, in a country that is strongly dependent on the import market, the mandatory nature of legislation on the status of retailers could be considered to be "strengthened" so that the legislator may have meant it also to be applied to international contracts that have a strong enough connection to the state in question.

An essential feature of overriding mandatory rules is that they can be applied regardless of a choice of law clause made by the parties. Overriding mandatory rules may thus become applicable in arbitration even when the parties to a commercial transaction have made a choice of *lex mercatoria*. The choice does not exclude the possibility of applying such rules although party autonomy is the main principle in international arbitration. Since *lex fori* is absent from arbitral proceedings, arbitral tribunals may deal only with third country overriding mandatory rules. In terms of the division of overriding mandatory rules into those of the forum and those of third countries, this also means that compared to national courts arbitrators act on a neutral basis, without a need

---

[59] Liukkunen, *Mandatory Rules*, at 128.
[60] See Trevor C. Hartley, 'Mandatory Rules in International Contracts: The Common Law Approach', (1997) 266 *Recueil des Cours*, 345–425, at 348. See also Jens Rinze, 'The Scope of Party Autonomy under the 1980 Rome Convention on the Law Applicable to Contract Obligations', (1994) *Journal of Business Law*, 412–30, at 427.
[61] See Giuditta Cordero Moss, 'International Arbitration and the Quest for the Applicable Law', (2008) 8 *Global Jurist (Advances)*, 1–42, at 21.
[62] See also ibid., at 22.

Lex Mercatoria *in International Arbitration*

for handling the question of differentiating or seeking a balance between the overriding mandatory rules of the *lex fori* and overriding mandatory rules of third countries.[63] It can be thought that the general starting point for arbitrators is to observe overriding mandatory rules of those countries where the award would likely be enforced.

In contrast with overriding mandatory rules of third countries, the role of overriding mandatory rules of the forum has been quite established in European private international law. When the Rome Convention[64] was signed by the EC States in 1980, the application of third country overriding mandatory rules was not established and attitudes toward it were contradictory. Therefore, the signatories were able to make reservations concerning Article 7.1 on third country overriding mandatory rules of the Convention. The explanatory report of the Rome Convention shows that the countries did not want to adopt unified international criteria for overriding mandatory rules of third countries.[65] It was not required that all contracting states consider provisions with equal content as overriding mandatory. This was natural also because the Convention was to be applied universally, so overriding mandatory rules of the countries that had not been parties to the Convention may also have become applicable under it.

In recent decades, the amount of private international law regulation on third country overriding mandatory rules has been increasing.[66] In Europe, the role of overriding mandatory rules has become stronger with the specific EU legislation and the case law of the Court of Justice of the European Union (CJEU). Illustrative of the existing development trend is that the Rome I Regulation, which has replaced the Rome Convention in the EU, contains an

---

[63] See also Bernard Audit, 'How Do Mandatory Rules of Law Function in International Civil Litigation?' in G. A. Bermann and L. A. Mistelis (eds.), *Mandatory Rules in International Arbitration* (Huntington, NY: Juris, 2011), 53–74, at 74.

[64] Convention on the Law Applicable to Contractual Obligations (the Rome Convention) opened for Signature in Rome on 19 June 1980.

[65] See Mario Giuliano and Paul Lagarde, *Report on the Convention on the Law Applicable to Contractual Obligations* (Giuliano – Lagarde Report) [1980], OJ C 282, at 27.

[66] This tendency can be seen, for instance, from the conventions of the Hague Conference on Private International law. For example, Article 16 of the Hague Convention of 14 March 1978 on the Law Applicable to Agency provides that "in the application of this Convention, effect may be given to the mandatory rules of any State with which the situation has a significant connection, if and in so far as, under the law of that State, those rules must be applied whatever the law specified by its choice of law rules." On the other hand, Article 1(4) of the UNIDROIT Principles of International Commercial Contracts provides that "nothing in these Principles shall restrict the application of mandatory rules, whether of national, international or supranational origin, which are applicable in accordance with the relevant rules of private international law."

explicit provision on application of third country overriding mandatory rules and no reservation can be made.[67]

Article 9.3 of the Rome I Regulation contains criteria for the application of third country overriding mandatory rules. The application criteria can also provide guidance for arbitrators dealing with overriding mandatory rules in situations where the Regulation is not directly applied in arbitration. According to the Article, effect may be given to the overriding mandatory rules of the law of the country where the obligations arising out of the contract have to be or have been performed, insofar as those provisions render performance of the contract unlawful. In considering whether to give effect to those provisions, regard should be had to their nature and purpose and to the consequences of their application or nonapplication. Guidance on interpreting the last mentioned criteria can partly be derived from the Rome Convention and its explanatory report. According to the Giuliano – Lagarde Report, the requirement to have regard to the consequences of application or nonapplication of overriding mandatory rules of third countries defines, clarifies, and strengthens the rule. A power of discretion is needed especially when contradictory mandatory rules of different countries would simultaneously purport to be applicable and a choice must be made among them.[68]

It is necessary to underline that arbitrators can only exceptionally end up with application of overriding mandatory rules. It is natural to establish whether the state whose overriding mandatory rules are under consideration has sufficiently close connections to the contract or the case. It can be argued that the connection is strong enough if it is the state where the obligations arising from the contract need to be fulfilled. The provisions have a strong status if ignoring them would make fulfilling the contract illegal according to the law of the state in question.

Even though the Rome I Regulation would not be applied in arbitration, it can be used as a source of inspiration when identifying overriding mandatory rules. According to the nonexhaustive definition in Article 9.1 of the Rome I Regulation, overriding mandatory provisions are provisions respect for which is regarded as crucial by a country for safeguarding its public interests, such as its political, social, or economic organization, to such an extent that they are applicable to any situation falling within their scope, irrespective of the law otherwise applicable to the contract. It is noteworthy

---

[67] The Rome I Regulation (EC) no. 593/2008 of the European Parliament and of the Council of 17 June 2008 on the law applicable to contractual obligations, which took force in 2008, has replaced the Rome Convention in the Member States with the exception of Denmark. The Regulation does not apply to arbitration agreements and agreements on the choice of court.

[68] Giuliano – Lagarde Report, at 27.

that even though it is not explicitly laid down in the Regulation, Member State courts are required to apply the overriding mandatory rules of EU law. Moreover, overriding mandatory rules in state laws of the Member States need to conform to EU law even if this requirement is not explicitly stated in the Article.[69]

The nature of mandatory rules has to be considered from the viewpoint of the legal order in which they originate. It is typical of overriding mandatory rules that their application is discretionary. In arbitration this discretion is guided by respect for the will of the parties and the need to ensure enforceability of the award. The latter might mean taking into account the overriding mandatory rules of the countries where the award is likely to be enforced. Discretion is also affected by what kind of overriding mandatory rules are involved. It could be assumed, for example, that arbitrators need to be especially cautious when taking into account such overriding mandatory rules as those that originate from EU law or that, in part, reflect public policy.[70]

Identification of overriding mandatory rules among mandatory rules is often difficult. National legislators have only rarely explicitly enacted certain substantive provisions as overriding mandatory although they would have meant the provisions to belong to this category. A precise answer to what kind of provisions can be considered overriding mandatory cannot be given. Nor is it possible to provide a precise answer to the question as to when mandatory rules may have to be given effect in arbitration. One of the parties may request application of overriding mandatory rules. It is also possible that the arbitrators need to decide on their own initiative whether certain overriding mandatory rules should be applied. Mandatory rules are sometimes taken into account as "datum" in international arbitration.[71] Since arbitral tribunals lack *lex fori*, it needs to be asked which states' overriding mandatory rules the arbitrators should take into consideration. Article 9.3 of the Rome I Regulation provides some guidance on this question. However, Lando's observation that it is not possible to provide exact rules about when arbitrators should give effect to mandatory rules of a country is still valid.[72]

---

[69] See also Andrea Bonomi, 'Overriding Mandatory Provisions in the Rome I Regulation on the Law Applicable to Contracts', in Andrea Bonomi and Paul Volken (eds.), (2008) 10 *Yearbook of Private International Law*, 285–300, at 290–1.

[70] See also Anne-Sophie Papeil, 'Conflict of Overriding Mandatory Rules in Arbitration', in Ferrari and Kröll (eds.), *Conflict of Laws*, 341–77, at 355 and 360.

[71] The distinction between the application of third country mandatory rules and taking them into account is subtle. See George A. Bermann, 'Introduction: The Origin and Operation of Mandatory Rules', in Bermann and Mistelis (eds.), *Mandatory Rules*, 1–27, at 17.

[72] See Lando, 'Lex Mercatoria', at 767.

The need to take into account mandatory rules in international arbitration does not mean a departure from the contractual basis of international arbitration.[73] However, application of overriding mandatory rules means that these rules override certain rules of the applicable law, whether chosen by the parties or, in the absence of party choice, determined as applicable by the arbitrators. When *lex mercatoria* is the applicable law, the arbitrators may thus need to apply overriding mandatory rules instead of or in addition to some rules of *lex mercatoria*. In a case where the applicable *lex mercatoria* is partial by nature, overriding mandatory rules might not replace some parts of applicable law but be applied in addition to *lex mercatoria*. This requires that overriding mandatory rules govern issues falling outside *lex mercatoria*.

B. Public Policy

Public policy (*ordre public*) is an inviolable part of the legal order of the forum. Violation of public policy is grounds for not recognizing or enforcing an international award by a national court of the country in question. The principle of overriding mandatory rules has to be kept apart from public policy. Overriding mandatory rules relate to the process where the law applicable to the contract is determined, and they may override a certain rule of the applicable law, whereas the public policy principle is a means that the court may use when refusing to apply a certain rule of the applicable law or when refusing to recognize or enforce an award.[74] However, the foundations for overriding mandatory rules may be near to public policy, the basic principles of the entire legal order, whose sphere has to be regarded as very narrow, clearly narrower than that of overriding mandatory rules.[75]

Public policy is divided into material and procedural public policy. The basic principles of a legal order can only prevent the application of a particular legal provision if its application in a concrete case would lead to a solution contrary to public policy. It is thus possible that a foreign law that in abstract terms would be contrary to the legal order in question could nevertheless become applicable if the actual result would not breach the inviolable part of the legal order. There is an established narrow interpretation of public policy in private international law. The principle only protects the inviolability of

---

[73] See George A. Bermann, 'Mandatory Rules of Law in International Arbitration', in Ferrari and Kröll (eds.), *Conflict of Laws*, 325–39, at 335, and Alexander K. A. Greenawalt, 'Does International Arbitration Need a Mandatory Rules Method?' in Bermann and Mistelis (eds.), *Mandatory Rules*, 147–70, at 158.

[74] See also Papeil, 'Overriding Mandatory Rules', at 355.

[75] See also Cordero Moss, 'Quest', at 33.

principles that form the basis of a legal order.[76] Other mandatory provisions do not fall under the principle, even if a breach of them would mean that the legal action would be invalid.

The arbitrators' task to make sure that the public policy principle is respected is not always simple since different states may define the foundations of their legal order in different ways. Arbitrators have to take into consideration the effectiveness of the award, which means that the public policy requirements of the place of the arbitration and the country where the arbitral award is likely to be enforced should be respected.[77] However, in cases where the losing party may follow the award voluntarily, the question of enforceability does not arise.[78] According to Article V(2)(b) of the 1958 New York Convention[79] recognition and enforcement of an arbitral award can be denied if recognition or enforcement of the award would be contrary to the public policy of the enforcing country. The public policy exception in the Convention has been applied very narrowly.[80] However, the significance of the exception has increased with certain EU rules being considered as belonging to the public policy of the Member States by the CJEU.

---

[76] The terminology concerning public policy in the laws of different states varies considerably, from the particular expression of international public policy, in distinction to national public policy, to different kinds of references to national rules, for example, by using the expression "the basic principles of the legal system" or by referring to public policy or public order and good morals. See Audley Sheppard, 'Interim ILA Report on Public Policy as a Bar to Enforcement of International Arbitral Awards', (2003) 19 *Arbitration International*, 217–48, 225, and the examples provided there. See also, for example, ICC case no. 5946 of 1990, (1991) 16 *Yearbook of Commercial Arbitration*, and ICC case no. 5622 of 1988, (1994) 19 *Yearbook of Commercial Arbitration*.

[77] See Yves Derain, 'Public Policy and the Law Applicable to the Dispute in International Arbitration', ICCA Congress Series no. 3, VIIIth International Arbitration Congress New York, 6–9 May 1986, 1987, 227–56, at 256. See also Papeil, 'Overriding Mandatory Rules', at 357, where emphasis is laid on arbitrators' need to find a balance among their different duties, one of which is the duty to ensure that the award is enforceable, and Giuditta Cordero Moss, *International Commercial Arbitration: Party Autonomy and Mandatory Rules* (Oslo: Tano Aschehoug, 1999), at 314.

[78] See also Michael Bogdan, 'Book Review, Giuditta Cordero Moss, International Commercial Arbitration, Party Autonomy and Mandatory Rules', (1999) 68 *Nordic Journal of International Law*, 375–7, at 376.

[79] Convention on the Recognition and Enforcement of Foreign Arbitral Awards, New York, 10 June 1958.

[80] See, for example, Karen E. Minehan, 'The Public Policy Exception to the Enforcement of Foreign Judgments: Necessary or Nemesis', (1996) 18 *Loyola of Los Angeles International and Comparative Law Review*, 795–819, at 817, and Cordero Moss, 'Arbitration and Private International Law', at 156. According to Cordero Moss, with the very limited list of grounds under which an arbitral award may be refused enforcement, the New York Convention contributes to separating international arbitration from the different national systems with which the dispute may have contact. See Cordero Moss, 'Quest', at 3.

C. The Effect of Mandatory EU Law

European integration has strongly shaped the status of mandatory rules in the EU Member States and EU law has made the limits of party autonomy more complex in choice of law. The sphere of mandatory rules of Member States has expanded to cover more and more legislation that originates in EU law. While previously the focus was on legislation adopted at the national level as mandatory, whether originating in a national or an international set of rules, the EU legislator has introduced legislation with an increasing effect on choice of law. EU Member States need to observe mandatory EU rules of public policy or of an overriding mandatory nature. These rules also achieve their impact on international arbitration.

In the case of *ECO Swiss v. Benetton*,[81] the CJEU held that Article 81 of the Treaty establishing the European Community (later Article 101 TFEU) on prohibiting practices that may affect trade between Member States and that restrict or distort competition within the common market is a fundamental provision essential for the accomplishment of community tasks and in particular for the functioning of the internal market. It considered Article 81 as a matter of public policy within the meaning of the 1958 New York Convention. Thus it is part of the public policy of Member State legal orders and protected by the public policy principle. Arbitrators need to consider the public policy nature of Article 101 TFEU in order to render an award that is enforceable in EU Member States. The question of which other EU rules could be considered to belong to public policy is important because arbitration awards that do not conform to these rules are considered invalid by Member State courts. There is no exhaustive answer to this question, but it is clear that EU law has, for example, fundamental rules on human and basic rights that could be similarly considered as public policy.[82]

Arbitrators need also to observe that some of the mandatory provisions of EU law that are binding on EU Member States may be overriding mandatory. In the *Ingmar* case[83] the CJEU adopted the stand that the provisions on indemnity and compensation for damages of the Commercial Agents Directive [84] are

---

[81] CJEU, case C-126/97, *Eco Swiss China Time Ltd v. Benetton International NV* [1999] ECR I-03055.
[82] The Charter of Fundamental Rights of the European Union is noteworthy in this respect.
[83] CJEU, case C-381/98, *Ingmar GB Ltd v. Eaton Leonard Technologies Inc.* [2000] ECR I-09305.
[84] Council Directive 86/653/EEC of 18 December 1986 on the coordination of the laws of the Member States relating to self-employed commercial agents.

overriding mandatory by nature. According to the CJEU, it is essential for the Community legal order that a principal established in a third country cannot avoid application of the mandatory provisions of the Directive by choosing the law of a third state as the applicable law if the commercial agent of the client operates within the Community even though the principal would be established in a non-Member State. The Court ruled that the provisions had to be applied so that the objectives of the Treaty establishing the European Community (later TFEU) would be met. But even though the overriding mandatory nature of these provisions was adopted in the case, their public policy nature was not.[85] Although the regulation on overriding mandatory rules normally provides an opportunity to apply them, the decision in *Ingmar* confirms that in some cases there is no room for discretion.[86]

D. Evaluation

According to the traditional view, overriding mandatory rules are applied directly, without mediation of the choice of law rules.[87] However, some overriding mandatory rules require application of the principle of the most favorable law.[88] This means that these mandatory rules can only be applied if the applicable substantive law does not produce a more favorable substantive result. Arbitrators must therefore carry out a comparison between such overriding mandatory rules and similar provisions of the otherwise applicable law. Arbitrators can be assumed to be already well qualified for such comparisons because when applying *lex mercatoria*, which is incomplete by nature, they often have to make comparisons when seeking guidance from several alternative sets of rules. Thus arbitrators operating on transnational foundations can

---

[85] Cordero Moss has pointed out that the decision in *Eco Swiss* might lead to regarding EU provisions on the protection of commercial agents as public policy. See Cordero Moss, 'Quest', at 37.

[86] Some Member State courts have made similar or even more far-reaching conclusions. See, for example, the analysis of the decision of the Munich Appeals Court (OLG München) in Giesela Rühl, 'Extending *Ingmar* to Jurisdiction and Arbitration Clauses: The End of Party Autonomy in Contracts with Commercial Agents?' (2007) 15 *European Review of Private Law*, 891–903. In this decision, the Court held that jurisdiction and arbitration clauses have to be set aside if they cause a derogation from Articles 17 and 18 of the Commercial Agents Directive and/or if it is "likely" that the designated court or arbitral tribunal will not apply these Articles or compensate the commercial agent on other grounds.

[87] See Liukkunen, *Mandatory Rules*, at 128.

[88] For example, the Directive on Posted Workers contains an open-ended list of issues governed by overriding mandatory provisions that are to be applied insofar as they are more favorable than the otherwise applicable law. See Article 3.1 of the Directive 96/71/EC of the European Parliament and of the Council of 16 December 1996 concerning the posting of workers in the framework of the provision of services.

be assumed to be more open to comparison to start with compared to national courts, which do not have similar capabilities.

The developments of private international law discussed previously demonstrate a result-oriented approach whose role has been growing with the constitutionalization of this field of law in the EU. Their influence on the application of *lex mercatoria* is by no means substantial though. However, in disputes concerning international commercial transactions that are solved in arbitration with *lex mercatoria* as the applicable law, arbitrators may increasingly need to consider overriding mandatory rules. In that case arbitrators need to balance the interests of states and of the parties.[89] Seeking a solution to the question of the applicability of overriding mandatory rules often leads arbitrators to very uncertain judicial ground. Several difficulties and uncertainties mark the decision making concerning the application of such rules. The exceptional nature of overriding mandatory rules supports the view that their effect should remain very limited. However, recent developments in the EU have placed an increasing emphasis on overriding mandatory rules, and the sphere of such rules is likely to grow.[90]

The flexibility sought by the approach that regards *lex mercatoria* as a method of decision making might be narrowed by a need to apply mandatory rules regardless of the otherwise applicable law. With the growth of the significance of mandatory rules, a new tension may arise between state law and *lex mercatoria* as an approach to decision making. Methodological freedom in international arbitration is then likely to be reduced by the intervention of mandatory rules.

Mandatory rules may limit the power of discretion of the arbitrators even in cases where the institutional rules or statutory provisions on arbitration directly allow application of *lex mercatoria*, without the mediation of private international law rules. Lando argues for application of overriding mandatory rules as an expression of international solidarity in which arbitrators should participate.[91] For H. A. Grigera Naón, the reason for arbitrators to take into account overriding mandatory rules when the applicable law is *lex mercatoria* is that *lex mercatoria* originates and develops within the permissive sphere,

---

[89] See Papeil, 'Overriding Mandatory Rules', at 376–7.
[90] See also, for example, Liukkunen, 'Managing Legal Diversity', at 1053–4.
[91] Lando, 'Lex Mercatoria', at 767. In a similar way, Paul Lagarde understood the basic idea of overriding mandatory rules originating in an awareness of the necessary solidarity that exists among the legal policies of the states. See Paul Lagarde, 'The E.E.C. Convention on the Law Applicable to Contractual Obligations', in P. E. Herzog (ed.), *Harmonization of Laws in the European Communities: Products Liability, Conflict of Laws and Corporation Law* (Charlottesville: University Press of Virginia, 1983), 49–62, at 61.

traced by overriding mandatory rules as a conflict methodology and enjoying wide transnational recognition and acceptance.[92] It has been noted that states increasingly rely on arbitrators to apply public policy rules and they also sanction their infringement.[93] The increasing significance of these rules can be seen as a demonstration of a new trend toward strengthening the role of public interest in choice of law. Mandatory rules highlight state interests and they can be argued as being embedded in an increasing interconnection between private and public international law.

VI. CONCLUSIONS

Lex mercatoria plays different roles in international commercial arbitration not only as a manifestation of party autonomy but also when the parties have not used their freedom to select the applicable substantive law. Among other things, the nature of *lex mercatoria* allows it to serve as a supplementary law to the applicable state law. At the same time, the openness of *lex mercatoria* stresses the role of arbitrators as developers of individual solutions based on the comparative method. When understood as a transnational set of rules applicable in international arbitration, *lex mercatoria* provides arbitrators with an opportunity to make an appropriate award that observes the special characteristics of the individual case in question. The application of *lex mercatoria* in international arbitration can be seen as an activity that develops international business law, enabled not only by the openness of *lex mercatoria* but also by the fact that its content is not bound by rigid state laws but built on a transnational foundation. The characteristics of *lex mercatoria* that have been considered detrimental in court proceedings appear to be beneficial in arbitration. The definitions of *lex mercatoria* as a constantly developing set of transnational rules and as an open method of judicial adjudication do indeed support each other.

Even if *lex mercatoria* applied in international arbitration can be formed without national statutory rules, this does not mean that it could be applied to the merits of a dispute independently of private international law. Private international law provides a basis for observing mandatory rules in international arbitration, and even *lex mercatoria* has to be applied in arbitration so that the possible effect of overriding mandatory rules and public policy is taken into account. It could be argued that giving effect to mandatory rules

---

[92] Naón, 'Choice-of-Law Problems', at 333.
[93] Ibid., at 372.

protecting public interests provides a counterweight to a denationalization of the applicable law in international commercial arbitration.[94] However, the ongoing development is not free of problems. The constitutionalized nature of private international law has offered a new legitimacy to result-selective conflict rules whose outcome is a growing susceptibility to collisions between state law and nonstate law in international arbitration.

---

[94] Ibid., at 381.

8 Law versus Tradition: Human Rights and Witchcraft in Sub-Saharan Africa

Timo Kallinen

Development workers, human rights activists, and workers from governmental and non-governmental organizations must acknowledge that "witchcraft is real for those who believe in it" and that "it's no use pretending [witchcraft beliefs] don't exist or seeking some ground of neutrality" in a society where people believe in witches.[1]
— UN Refugee agency research report on witchcraft

Although a strong belief in witchcraft continues in many parts of Ghana, there is no evidence that witches are responsible for inflicting treatment amounting to persecution or which would breach Article 3 [of the European Convention on Human Rights], therefore the availability of adequate state protection is not relevant.[2]
— Operational guidelines for asylum cases

I. INTRODUCTION

Human rights law tends to speak about violence as a theft or removal of the victim's humanity. From this follows an economic logic that measures and compares violence in "actuarial terms" of loss, magnitude, and compensation.[3] In modern times, violence is justified and rationalized by referring to the ends achieved by it, which should be of greater value than the losses inflicted. Accordingly, violence administered on the grounds of "metaphysical

---

[1] Jill Schnoebelen, *Witchcraft Allegations, Refugee Protection and Human Rights: A Review of the Evidence.* New Issues in Refugee Research, Research paper no. 169 (The UN Refugee Service, 2009), at 2.
[2] UK Home Office 2011, *Operational Guidance Note: Ghana* (UK Border Agency, March 2011), available at http://www.ukba.homeoffice.gov.uk/sitecontent/documents/policyandlaw/countryspecificasylumpolicyogns/ghana.pdf?view=Binary (accessed 15 December 2011), at 8.
[3] Allen Feldman, 'Political Terror and the Technologies of Memory: Excuse, Sacrifice, Commodification, and, Actuarial Moralities', (2003) 85 *Radical History Review*, 58–73, at 70.

beliefs" or "superstitions" appears as something particularly irrational and unacceptable.[4] Violence against suspected witches in Africa is often discussed in these terms since the suffering of the victims is perceived as real in contradistinction to its objectives, that is, suppression of malevolent witchcraft, which is considered imaginary. Many African governments have been under considerable pressure to take a firmer stance on witchcraft accusations and violent antiwitchcraft activities by introducing specific legislation. Nowadays, witchcraft activities are seen increasingly as a human rights issue and consequently a global issue, because the human rights situation of African countries is constantly monitored from the outside. Western NGOs and government bodies publish annual reports, where they list physical attacks on witch suspects as human rights violations. This makes African governments even more apprehensive since promotion of human rights is high on the agenda of donor organizations and Western governments that are the major source of foreign development aid to Africa. Yet recent attempts to legislate a solution, like their colonial precedents, have not been successful.

The chapter at hand revolves around a conflict between two normative orders: modern law based on the notion of human rights and witchcraft norms. By "witchcraft norms" I refer to a set of traditional norms that prohibit the practice of malevolent witchcraft and govern the ritual detection and "curing" of witches. I classify witchcraft norms as traditional norms on two grounds. First, I argue that the idea of witchcraft is best understood as a characteristic of an ontology, which we could call for analytical purposes holistic or traditional and antithetical to modern individualism.[5] It is considered to work within social wholes, like clans and lineages, mediated by spiritual substances, and thus it directly denies the separateness of the individual, which is at the heart of the human rights idea. Correspondingly, witchcraft beliefs do not fit the modern blueprint of religion centered on the individual believer's spiritual conviction and experience. In fact, one of the tasks assumed by religious reformers in Africa ever since the colonial period has been to separate witchcraft from so-called indigenous African religions.[6] Second, witchcraft norms are usually not recognized by modern law. On the contrary, they are

[4] Talal Asad, *Formations of the Secular: Christianity, Islam, Modernity* (Stanford, CA: Stanford University Press, 2003), at 109–18.
[5] Bruce Kapferer, *Legends of People, Myths of State: Violence, Intolerance, and Political Culture in Sri Lanka and Australia* (Washington, DC: Smithsonian Institution Press, 1988); cf. Louis Dumont, *Homo Hierarchicus: The Caste System and Its Implications* (Chicago: University of Chicago Press, 1980).
[6] Johannes Fabian, 'Religious and Secular Colonization: Common Ground?' (1990) 4 *History and Anthropology*, 339–55, at 350–1.

Law versus Tradition

actively fought against by modern governments and courts. In this case, witchcraft norms are labeled as traditional, archaic, or obsolete in order to indicate that they do not have a legitimate place in modern society. To be sure, none of the preceding discussion is meant to say that witchcraft would actually be absent from the modern sectors of society and belong to the historical past or rural margins. Quite the opposite, anthropologists have for some time studied witchcraft beliefs and ritual practices in modern settings and suggested that they could be read as critical commentaries on capitalist economy, urbanization, development, and the like.[7]

The chapter approaches the question of normative pluralism mainly from the viewpoint of the objects of global governance. Namely, it stresses that the conflict between the two normative orders can only be solved if it is recognized that witchcraft norms and modern law rest on different ontological foundations. Furthermore, instead of focusing on dichotomies like real/imaginary or rational/irrational, it should be understood that witchcraft norms address existing social concerns. At present, hardly any dialogue or recognition exists between the two orders. From the point of view of the subjects of global governance, that is, the international organizations and the nation states of both Africa and the global north, there should be no pluralism. For them witchcraft beliefs in themselves have no meaning or value, and they are hoped to disappear through "education" or "raising of awareness" of the citizens. Witchcraft accusations and antiwitchcraft activities are considered socially harmful, and therefore they need to be abolished or at least severely restricted by legal means. Since modern law has turned witchcraft into an anomaly, cases involving witchcraft have proved difficult to handle for legislators and courts.

In the following I will discuss witchcraft and its ontological basis in closer detail in one particular African society. This is followed by an examination of modern legal and educational attempts to control the witchcraft phenomenon and the various problems they have involved. The chapter uses ethnographic material, official documents, and news reports from Ghana to illustrate the argument. Comparisons to other African countries are made.

II. WITCHCRAFT NORMS

Peter Geschiere has pointed out that terms like "witchcraft" and "sorcery" are clumsy translations of indigenous African notions with a much broader

---

[7] Jean Comaroff and John L. Comaroff, 'Introduction', in J. Comaroff and J. L. Comaroff (eds.), *Modernity and Its Malcontents: Ritual and Power in Postcolonial Africa* (Chicago: University of Chicago Press, 1993).

meaning.[8] In my opinion, the major problems with such terms are the erroneous and ethnocentric associations made by some members of the Western audience. Especially reports about African witchcraft in the Western mass media pay no attention to local cultural categories and discuss witchcraft as a phenomenon that the audience already knows from movies, fantasy novels, computer games, and other similar sources. The implication is that there are Africans who take such matters seriously, who still believe in their concrete existence, while others have moved on. The disregard for local knowledge has also blurred the differences among regions, countries, ethnic and linguistic groups, and so on. As Terence Ranger argues, the idea of Africa as a single "occult culture" is becoming dominant in the Western media.[9] Then again, the term "witchcraft" is nowadays used by Africans themselves throughout the continent, and therefore it is very difficult to do without it.[10] I do not find supposedly more neutral terms like "occult forces" or "occult practices" any better. For instance, in Ghana the Christian population sometimes use the term "occult" for some traditional ritual practices, which they contrast to their own "church religion." Obviously, people living in rural communities, practicing traditional religion, do not think or speak of their spirituality by using such dichotomies.

In the following the case of Ghana is used to exemplify the normative considerations pertaining to witchcraft beliefs. The focus here is on the dominant Akan culture of central Ghana,[11] with which I am most familiar, but it has to be noted that witchcraft beliefs are shared by the neighboring peoples in all directions.[12] As indicated, this should not be read as a general description of the nature and dynamics of African witchcraft. However, through this example it is possible to demonstrate the deep-rootedness of the problem at hand: one has to go beyond superficial discussions about cultural differences and reach down to the level of ontologies. Here ontology refers to the "fundamental principles of being in the world" that are "beneath the level of conscious reflection."[13]

---

[8] Peter Geschiere, *The Modernity of Witchcraft: Politics and the Occult in Postcolonial Africa* (Charlottesville: University Press of Virginia, 1997), at 225.
[9] Terence Ranger, 'Scotland Yard in the Bush: Medicine Murders, Child Witches and the Construction of the Occult: A Literature Review', (2007) 77 *Africa*, 272–83, at 272–4.
[10] See Geschiere, *Modernity of Witchcraft*, at 225.
[11] The Akan people live in the coastal and forest areas of Ghana and Côte d'Ivoire. In Ghana they are the largest ethnic and language group, constituting roughly 40% of the total population. The Akan language and its dialects are classified under the Tano language family, including Asante Twi, Fante, and Akuapem, which also have their own distinctive written forms.
[12] Jean Allman and John Parker, *Tongnaab: The History of a West African God* (Bloomington: Indiana University Press, 2005), at 258–9; Jack Goody, *Comparative Studies in Kinship* (London: Routledge & Kegan Paul, 1969), at 71–2.
[13] See Kapferer, *Legends of People*, at 79 and 84.

Law versus Tradition 233

A witch is a person who controls a spiritual power known in the Akan language as *bayi* in order to harm other people. Those accused of witchcraft are mostly women, but it is understood that also a man can be a witch. In popular stories about witch attacks witches rip unborn babies out of the wombs of their mothers, eat human flesh, and drink blood, but they are also held responsible for more commonplace, yet very serious, problems like poor harvests, failed business deals, ill health, or unexpected deaths. Suspicions and speculations about the activities and identities of witches are part of everyday life in Ghanaian communities, and most often they do not lead to any dramatic consequences, let alone homicidal violence. *Bayi* itself is understood to be a morally ambivalent force that can be used for either good or evil. Traditional priests use *bayi* for good purposes, for instance, in protective magic.

Nowadays witches are detected and suppressed by using the help of spiritual agents. So-called antiwitchcraft cults are usually developed around a shrine of a god and/or a talisman that has a reputation as an efficient "witch-hunter."[14] The shrines are maintained by traditional priests, who become possessed by the gods and through whom they can speak. Sometimes the deities and talismans have been "imported" to their current location, and it is often said that the most powerful "witch-hunters" have come from northern Ghana or even as far north as Burkina Faso or Mali.[15] Those gods and their priests that are known to perform well may earn a nationwide reputation and people from faraway places consult them. I have heard that some Ghana-based deities are consulted by visitors from the neighboring countries or as far as Nigeria. Sometimes the priests also travel abroad and offer their services to the members of the Ghanaian immigrant communities in Europe and North America.[16]

People consult the gods in times of trouble and confusion. Sudden sicknesses, deaths, missing people or property, rejected visa applications, and all

---

[14] According to the Akan belief system the universe is created by Onyame, the superior being, who has also impregnated it with his own power. Onyame has been described as a typical "withdrawn god, who distanced himself from worldly affairs instantly after he had completed his works of creation (see T. C. McCaskie, *State and Society in Pre-colonial Asante* [Cambridge University Press, 1995], at 105). The local gods are recognized as children and grandchildren of the superior being. They have their origins in nature, but they live with human beings. They are expected to help the human community, for example, by curing illnesses, catching thieves, or telling the future. There are significant differences in their powers as well as their character, and some are known specifically as "witch hunters".

[15] Malcolm McLeod, 'On the Spread of Anti-Witchcraft Cults in Modern Asante', in J. Goody (ed.), *Changing Social Structure in Ghana: Essays in the Comparative Sociology of a New State and an Old Tradition* (London: IAI, 1975), at 113.

[16] Fieldnotes 24 June 2000 and 19 January 2001. Data collected in Ghana 26 April 2000–1 April 2001 and 4 November 2005–10 May 2006.

other hardships imaginable may give reason for seeing a traditional priest. At times people are already under the impression that they have fallen victim to witchcraft and might have a number of suspects in mind. Alternatively, in order to prevent witch attacks in the future, they go to ask for a talisman or a medicine that will protect them from the powers of the witches. On their arrival the visitors are formally welcomed, after which they introduce themselves and their problem to the priest and his/her attendants. From there the case is taken to the god, and at this point a gift, for example, a bottle of strong alcohol and a small sum of money, is presented. The god is consulted when the priest has fallen into a trancelike state called *akom*, marked by shaking and twitching of his/her body, reddish eyes, and changed voice. In *akom* the god speaks through the priest and its messages are communicated to the audience by an attendant of the priest. Instead of entering into *akom*, some priests throw cowries, beads, or bones on a circular area and read the patterns they form as signs from the god. If witchcraft is diagnosed as the cause of the problem in question, the god will give instructions about how the witch can be "caught." Usually, some specific rituals have to be performed in order to unleash the powers that will "catch" the witch. For instance, I once witnessed a case where a list of witch suspects written on a piece of paper was wrapped inside a bundle of poisonous skin-irritating plants according to close instructions of the priest. The actual witch was supposed to feel the sensations caused by the plants and would subsequently need to confess in order to get relief. The deity might also reveal the identity of the witch directly and order him/her to be taken to the shrine house. Nonetheless, it is believed that the spiritual powers of the god are potent enough to force the witch to confess that he/she is behind the misfortunes.[17] The witch is thought to experience physical pain, abnormalities, and mental strain until he/she pleads guilty. One traditional priest described this to me in a following way:

> You have to confess! If you don't confess the spirits will surely kill you. I have seen horrible things happen to those people who wouldn't confess. Right in front of this place [a room where suspects are kept] I have seen a person beaten up by invisible hands. The person was screaming and writhing with pain on the ground, but you couldn't see anybody there doing the beating. And it wouldn't stop before the person promised to confess. (Fieldnotes 19 January 2001)[18]

The confessed witches can be ritually "cured" or "cooled" by the traditional priests, after which they can go on with their lives in their own communities. Those who refuse to confess are sometimes treated cruelly or driven to

---

[17] Fieldnotes, 21 and 24 June 2000.
[18] Fieldnotes, 19 January 2001.

exile from their villages. Customarily, those who had been helped by the god should express their thanks by taking gifts to the shrine. These may include money, drinks, farm animals, or luxury items.[19]

During the precolonial era practicing witchcraft was a "tribal taboo" in Akan society and the officeholders of the community were under obligation to fight against it.[20] Witches were often sentenced to death by chiefly authorities, and the penalty was carried out by burning, drowning, or clubbing those convicted.[21] Even if their lives were spared, they were banished from their natal lineages, which meant a loss of "jural personhood" and degradation to slave status.[22] Witch-finding methods of the precolonial era included poison ordeals and the practice of "carrying the corpse," in which the dead body of a witchcraft victim was believed to be capable of showing the way to the house of his/her killer. These methods were prohibited by the government during the early stages of the colonial rule.[23]

In addition to the cults of the local deities, some Christian churches are thought of as powerful agencies to find witches and exorcise them. These movements are often referred to as "healing churches," and some of them were founded already before World War I.[24] Some of the oldest and smallest of these groups have died out or lost most of their following, while new ones are constantly appearing. For instance, in 2005–6 when I conducted fieldwork in the rural Brong-Ahafo Region I studied a locally founded church that practiced witch finding by using methods that closely resemble those of the traditional priests. Instead of local gods, the pastors of the congregation become possessed by "angels," who are able to identify witches and also to force out confessions. The movement had become more and more popular during the early 2000s and had gained a foothold in urban communities.[25] Moreover, many of the churches belonging to the Pentecostal-Charismatic movement, which has gained a lot of ground in West Africa ever since the 1980s, are dedicated to fighting witchcraft.[26] Although some European missionaries of the

---

[19] Fieldnotes, 24 June 2000.
[20] Robert S. Rattray, *Ashanti Law and Constitution* (Oxford, UK: Clarendon Press, 1929), at 313.
[21] Ibid., at 376.
[22] Ibid, at 19 and 313.
[23] Robert S. Rattray, *Religion and Art in Ashanti* (Oxford University Press, 1959 [1927]), at 31 and 167–70.
[24] Hans W. Debrunner, *Witchcraft in Ghana: A Study on the Belief in Destructive Witches and Its Effect on the Akan Tribes* (Accra: Presbyterian Book Depot, 1961), at 149–62.
[25] Fieldnotes, 10 May 2006.
[26] Sasha Newell, 'Pentecostal Witchcraft: Neoliberal Possessions and Demonic Discourse in Ivorian Pentecostal Churches', (2007) 37 *Journal of Religion in Africa*, 461–90.

colonial era denied the existence of witchcraft,[27] many of them also associated it with the evil powers of the devil and thus in an indirect way confirmed its existence.[28] Consequently, conversion to Christianity in Ghana has not generally brought about "what professional theologians and social scientists tend to expect, namely rationalization and disenchantment."[29]

III. WITCHCRAFT AND HOLISTIC ONTOLOGY

In order to understand the logic of witchcraft, one has to turn to the indigenous Akan notions of human essence, namely, the conception that a person is made of blood, *mogya*, which is inherited from his/her mother, and spirit, *ntoro*, which is transmitted through the paternal line. The former determines a person's political, economic, and legal rights in the community, whereas the latter provides him/her with a cluster of moral rights. Without both acknowledged maternity and paternity, a person is not seen to be complete. In addition to these two, a person has a "soul," *kra*, which affects his/her destiny (*nkrabea*) in life, and a "spiritual backing," *sunsum*, which could be "tall" or "short," that is to say, more or less potent, depending on the experience and knowledge of the person in question. However, *kra* and *sunsum* are not acquired through kinship relations, but directly from spiritual sources, and they did not endow a person with any kind of social status (see, e.g., Fortes 1969, 138–216). In line with more recent anthropological discussions on African conceptions of personhood one could argue that the Akan idea of person is "relational" or "composite."[30]

Of the four "components" of personhood, blood is the most important for the topic at hand. The local lineage group (*abusua*), which could also be described as the basic "wealth holding unit" in Akan society, is based on the notion of shared blood, which can be transmitted by women only. The members of a single lineage trace descent to a common ancestress, and chiefly offices, land, and property rights are vested in it. Amity, solidarity, and mutual support are thought to prevail within the group.[31] In this scheme of things,

---

[27] Debrunner, *Witchcraft in Ghana*, 135–6.
[28] Ibid., at 143–4.
[29] Birgit Meyer, *Translating the Devil: Religion and Modernity among the Ewe in Ghana* (Trenton: Africa World Press, 1999), at 110.
[30] Cf. Harri Englund, 'Witchcraft, Modernity and the Person: The Morality of Accumulation in Central Malawi', (1996) 16 *Critique of Anthropology*, 257–79; Charles Piot, *Remotely Global: Village Modernity in West Africa* (Chicago: University of Chicago Press, 1999).
[31] Meyer Fortes, *Kinship and the Social Order: The Legacy of Lewis Henry Morgan* (Chicago: Aldine, 1969), 154–90.

blood has a prior existence to individuals, which are seen to exist only as "parts" of blood. Consequently, groups of this kind are not seen as collections of individual persons, but as wholes that can be divided into persons: a basic characteristic of so-called holistic societies.[32] The fear and anxiety connected to witchcraft are typical of ideologies based on a holistic ontology.[33] As witches are said to "drink the blood" or "eat the flesh" of their matrilineal relatives, they are thought of individualistically consuming the shared substance on which the very existence of the kin group is dependent. Thus they are perceived as people who have put their own passions before the continuation of the group and are thus guilty of extreme selfishness. In fact, among the Akan witchcraft is believed to operate only among lineage relatives. It is seen to be fueled by jealousy and envy between relatives, which signal disunity and departure from the solidarity demanded by moral and customary law.[34] Consequently, the "clients" of antiwitchcraft shrines are often people who fear that their success in life, especially economic, has attracted the attention of their envious witch relatives.[35] Conversely, in the confessions of witch suspects the victims of their witchcraft are depicted as persons who have exploited the goodwill and helpfulness of their relatives earlier in life but neglected them after becoming successful.[36] Although the subjective points of view differ according to situation, it can be said that the witchcraft discourse as a whole is primarily about morality. This is underpinned by the perception of the unity of the kin group and the inseparability of the individual.

More generally, anthropologists have tended to interpret witchcraft discourses in Africa and elsewhere as ways through which societies express their disapproval of certain kinds of behavior and moral dispositions.[37] Consequently, less attention should be paid to those aspects of witchcraft, which we would interpret as "superstition" or "misperceiving the laws causality," and more to the moral anxieties that it addresses. Witchcraft beliefs should not be viewed as a distinct phenomenon menacing certain societies but rather as a part of societies with a certain type of ontology. One might even suggest a parallel ideology in our own individualist societies, that is, the "therapeutic culture" concerned with the integrity and authenticity of the individual.

[32] Dumont, *Homo Hierarchicus*, at 4–11.
[33] Kapferer, *Legends of People*, at 7–15.
[34] Fortes, *Kinship and the Social Order*, at 179–83.
[35] Jane Parish, 'The Dynamics of Witchcraft and Indigenous Shrines among the Akan', (1999) 69 *Africa*, 426–47, at 431–2.
[36] Barbara E. Ward, 'Some Observations on Religious Cults in Ashanti', (1956) 26 *Africa*, 47–61, at 52–5.
[37] Jarett Zigon, *Morality: An Anthropological Perspective* (Oxford: Berg, 2008), at 49–52.

IV. LEGISLATING WITCHCRAFT

The religious beliefs that legitimated the chiefly rule in Africa posed a problem to the colonial administrators. As the anthropologists of the colonial era had recognized, the European governments were able to replace the chiefs in their secular capacity, but they were never able to assume those credentials of the traditional rulers that were considered "mystical" and "derived from antiquity."[38] The colonizers could never enter these "sacred precincts," and as a result their administration was inevitably perceived as something that was forced on the subject populations. The most efficient way to overcome this problem was the persistent undermining of the value of indigenous systems of religious knowledge. A colonial hierarchy of knowledge was established, in which scientific rationalism was regarded as universal and true and indigenous knowledge as local and superstitious. The administrative machinery was to be operated according to the rules of the former, whereas the latter was to be left for the "natives." Yet, throughout the colonial period and in all colonial empires the "sacred precincts" were constantly intruded on by the European rulers, who, for instance, reformulated customary laws, judged chieftaincy disputes on the basis of origin myths, and created new "traditional" offices. They were dragged in there by more pressing administrative concerns of "upholding peace," "restoring order," and such things, but also by the agency of the colonial subjects.[39] This inconsistency was also the legacy that the administrations of the postcolonial era inherited from the European colonial governments despite their otherwise vast ideological differences. In the name of "modernization" or "development" the rulers of independent African nation-states adopted a European-based concept of how a state should collect and use knowledge and renounced the validity of indigenous forms of knowledge, but they too have faced constant pressures to interfere with local knowledge.[40] Consequently, legislators and administrators have been busy "purifying" local cultures of hazardous elements such as witchcraft.

The colonial bureaucrats' outlook on the world reflected the evolutionist model of human development that was characteristic of early twentieth-century social and political thought, and their decisions derived from and realized that model. The model assumed that the development of each individual and

---

[38] Meyer Fortes and Edward E. Evans-Pritchard, 'Introduction', in M. Fortes and E. E. Evans-Pritchard (eds.), *African Political Systems* (London: KPI (1969 [1940]), at 16.
[39] Stephan Palmié, *Wizards and Scientists: Explorations in Afro-Cuban Modernity and Tradition* (Durham, NC: Duke University Press, 2002), at 71–2.
[40] Frederick Cooper and Ann L. Stoler, 'Tensions of Empire: Colonial Control and Visions of Rule', (1989) 16 *American Ethnologist*, 609–21, at 612.

every society invariably repeated a single linear evolutionary sequence. The "primitive society" of backward African tribesmen would ultimately develop into a "civilized society" governed by rational thinking.[41] The responsibility of the colonizing power was to safeguard and to a certain extent regulate this process. The change had to be gradual, and any sudden, "revolutionary" leaps in progress were considered hazardous. As one of the chief advocates of the British indirect rule, Lord Lugard, put it, in order to "accord with natural evolution" the methods and institutions of the colonial rule had to be deep-rooted in the "traditions and prejudices" of African peoples.[42] Consequently, it was established that the forms of government best suited for Africans were those they had created for themselves. Traditional institutions should be modified by the colonizing power only when it was necessary for the main purpose of colonialism, the exploitation of the colonized country, or when the traditional institutions were repugnant to the European moral ideas.[43] The conventions of African witch finding fell into the latter category, and they were to be suppressed as dangerous superstitions.[44]

This approach developed a new dimension when after the First World War the British colonial policy was reformulated so that it drew its legitimation from international treaties. Namely, the League of Nations had granted a mandate to the victors of the war to take control of the colonies formerly held by the losers, on the condition that they assumed the responsibility over "the wellbeing and development" of the subject populations. According to article 22 of the Covenant of the League of Nations, these territories were inhabited by "peoples not yet able to stand by themselves under the strenuous conditions of the modern world," and hence their administration should be trusted to "advanced nations." The control of material production and markets in the new colonies was viewed as just reward for this tutelage.[45] The architects of indirect rule saw that the mandate system should serve as a model for ruling the colonies throughout the empire.[46] Although the colonial civil servants hardly ever cited any treaty texts in support of their decisions, it is important to note that, at least in principle, the main lines of the new policy were based on an idea about binding obligations between nations and peoples. The colonial administrator saw himself "civilizing" or "developing" the Africans, as his

---

[41] Henrika Kuklick, *The Imperial Bureaucrat: The Colonial Administrative Service in the Gold Coast, 1920–1939* (Stanford, CA: Hoover Institution Press, 1979), at 44–8.
[42] Frederick D. Lugard, *The Dual Mandate in British Tropical Africa* (London: Frank Cass, 1965 [1922]), at 211.
[43] Michael Crowder, *West Africa under Colonial Rule* (London: Hutchinson, 1968), at 168–9.
[44] Lugard, *Dual Mandate*, at 563–4.
[45] Ibid., at 62–3.
[46] Ibid., at 50.

government had vowed to do, and thus he expected "reciprocity" in the form of political submission and economic access.[47]

Right from the beginning of the 1900s the British colonial administration in Ghana investigated and stamped out several witch-finding shrines and "cults" formed around them.[48] These measures were justified on the grounds of extortion and torture that allegedly were part of the witch-finding process and also by the colonizers' conviction that witchcraft did not exist.[49] In the 1930s this policy was taken a step further when an administrative order banning "the practice of witch or wizard finding" was introduced.[50] Nonetheless, the colonial administrators were soon forced to recognize the futility of fighting a truly widespread belief and admit that legal attempts to terminate witchcraft activities would not lead to desired results. On the contrary, such measures created tensions of a different kind. For example, as Natasha Gray has shown in her treatment of antiwitchcraft movements in southern Ghana, the members of the outlawed cults found themselves in a double predicament, where they were forced to risk either being punished by legal fines for taking part in unlawful rituals or suffering the punishment of the gods for not fulfilling their ritual duties.[51] Furthermore, from the point of view of the colonial subjects, witchcraft itself, which had previously been classified as a crime, was now removed from the sphere of law and relegated to the status of superstition, while antiwitchcraft activities, which had been traditional methods of investigating and punishing crimes, were now criminalized.[52] Soon enough, the witch finding specialists found a way to bypass the bans by assuming a new professional identity as "native physicians," who claimed to treat witchcraft suspicions and confessions as symptoms of some sort of psychic disorder. In practice, however, they used their traditional methods. The new "biomedical discourse" eventually met the approval of the colonial administration, which probably considered it as a painless way out of an awkward situation.[53] Later on, in the postcolonial era, "traditional medicine" as a whole became part of what was perceived as Ghana's national culture, and its practitioners founded regional and national professional associations.[54] Despite the talk of therapeutics and

---

[47] Ibid., at 57–62.
[48] Allman and Parker, *Tongnaab*, at 128–48.
[49] McLeod, 'Spread of Anti-Witchcraft Cults', at 109.
[50] Allman and Parker, *Tongnaab*, at 169–70.
[51] Natasha Gray, 'Independent Spirits: The Politics of Policing Anti-Witchcraft Movements in Colonial Ghana, 1908–1927', (2005) 35 *Journal of Religion in Africa*, 139–58.
[52] Karen Fields, 'Political Contingencies of Witchcraft in Colonial Central Africa: Culture and the State in Marxist Theory', (1982) 16 *Canadian Journal of African Studies*, 567–93, at 576–7.
[53] Allman and Parker, *Tongnaab*, at 174–80.
[54] Ibid., at 178–81 and 225–7.

healing, witchcraft-related violence still posed a problem for the postcolonial state, and even though the trend has been to eradicate it through education, legal alternatives are also under consideration.

V. MODERNITY OF WITCHCRAFT?

Those who considered secularization a key feature of modernization labeled witchcraft a traditional and rural phenomenon, which would inevitably disappear as Africa "developed." This never happened. On the contrary, it is interesting to see how the idea of witchcraft has "modernized," responding to the changing circumstances of the postcolonial society.[55] In addition to villages and farms, the witches of today are thought to operate in such intrinsically modern surroundings as international credit institutions and gambling casinos.[56] Furthermore, it has been claimed that the turn of the millennium has been marked by a global proliferation of "occult economies."[57] For example, Jean and John Comaroff maintain that postapartheid South Africa has experienced a dramatic rise in "the deployment, real or imagined, of magical means for material ends," which has in many places led to "violent reactions against people accused of illicit accumulation."[58] According to them, both the magical means and the violence against those who use them are local attempts to cope with the changes and contradictions entrained by global "millennial" capitalism.[59] Also in the case of Ghana similar observations have been made about a new, rising interest in the occult and its connections to global capitalism. For instance, Birgit Meyer has discussed how Ghanaians use the occult imagery to "diabolise negative aspects of the capitalist world economy" such as individualistic accumulation and indifference to the collectivist ethos of the kinship order.[60]

Such views cannot be accepted without certain reservations. First, the modernity of witchcraft seems to be relatively old. Already in the late colonial

---

[55] Geschiere, *The Modernity of Witchcraft*.
[56] Jane Parish, 'From the Body to the Wallet: Conceptualizing Akan Witchcraft at Home and Abroad', (2000) 6 *Journal of Royal Anthropological Institute*, 487–500; Jane Parish, 'Witchcraft, Riches and Roulette: An Ethnography of West African Gambling in the UK', (2005) 6 *Ethnography*, 105–22.
[57] Jean Comaroff and John L. Comaroff, 'Millennial Capitalism: First Thoughts on a Second Coming', (2000) 12 *Public Culture*, 291–343, at 310.
[58] Jean Comaroff and John L. Comaroff, 'Occult Economies and the Violence of Abstraction: Notes from the South African Postcolony', (1999) 26 *American Ethnologist*, at 279.
[59] Ibid., 284–5.
[60] Birgit Meyer, '"Delivered from the Powers of Darkness": Confessions of Satanic Riches in Christian Ghana', (1995) 65 *Africa*, 236–55, at 250.

era (1940s and 1950s) the anthropologists were claiming that the preoccupation with witchcraft in Ghana was essentially a modern phenomenon, which resulted from rising tensions in social relations caused by the ups and downs of the recently introduced cash-based cocoa economy and the individualistic ideology of capitalism and Christianity.[61] So, if indeed such a close connection exists between witchcraft beliefs and capitalist relations and processes, it should be discussed in the context of the developments of the whole twentieth century and not only some recent neoliberal upsurges. Second, as the Comaroffs themselves acknowledge, it is difficult to "quantify the occult" and hence make any definite assertions about its increase.[62] However, it is clear that in Ghana, as in South Africa, witchcraft has now made its way to the public sphere of the modern state.[63] It is now much more visible than it was, for example, fifteen years ago, when I ran into it for the first time in my field research. Partly this has to do with the lifting of state censorship and increasing privatization of media generated by the democratization process of the 1990s. Free and commercial media have truly become a playground of the occult. Nowadays, both tabloid and mainstream newspapers regularly report witchcraft accusations, confessions, and violent attacks on the suspected witches. Witchcraft themes suffuse Ghanaian- and Nigerian-made movies, which are shown by commercial TV stations and distributed on video cassettes and DVDs. Members of the public write letters to daily newspapers and call live radio shows to complain about problems caused by witches.[64] The ubiquity and hugely increased visibility of witchcraft themes must pose a serious problem for the modernist legislators and educators. After all, their core message is that witchcraft is not real. Yet, the pressure to deal with antiwitchcraft activities through official means is probably greater than it has ever been.

VI. WITCHES HAVE HUMAN RIGHTS TOO!

The postcolonial government's position on witchcraft is in a very important way connected to the redefinition of the society that it rules. As the colonial government ruled "natives" who were considered "traditional" in essence (that is to say, for example, members of their "tribe," subjects of their chiefs), the postcolonial society is thought to consist of individual citizens who have systematically defined rights and duties. The idea of fundamental difference between rulers and ruled has been dispelled: while the British colonial

[61] Ward, 'Some Observations on Religious Cults in Ashanti'.
[62] Comaroff and Comaroff, 'Millennial Capitalism', at 310.
[63] Ibid.
[64] Fieldnotes, 20 June 2000.

lawmaker and the African subject were thought to live in completely separate normative realities, the African legislator and the villager share the same status of a citizen. In this construction "traditionalism" appears as an aspect of citizenship in a modern state. The democratic constitution in 1992, after more than two decades of military rule, secured the "fundamental human right and freedoms" to every person in Ghana, including freedom to "to enjoy, practise, profess, maintain and promote any culture, language, tradition or religion subject to the provisions of this Constitution." As a provision, it was added that "all customary practices which dehumanize or are injurious to the physical and mental well-being of a person are prohibited" (CRG, chapter 5 article 26, paras 1–2). This view relies on an ontology in which a social whole, in this case the nation state of Ghana, is constructed of individuals. Here the main concerns are the integrity and autonomy of individuals and their capacity to act freely.[65] Consequently, the public discussion about antiwitchcraft activities revolves around their supposed nature as a "dehumanizing customary practice" that violates the rights of its victims. Hence the problematic aspects of witchcraft beliefs have been reduced to a conflict between individual freedom and public good. As a Ghanaian journalist summarized it, "freedom of conscience is enshrined in the constitution, therefore no one will have any qualms about whether anyone believes in witchcraft," but it is "disgusting to allow someone to suffer because another person thinks he or she is a witch or a wizard."[66] For a person who believes in witchcraft such a statement borders on absurdity: one is free to believe that someone is intending to kill others through spiritual means but strongly prohibited to do anything to stop that.

Since antiwitchcraft activities are now seen mostly as a human rights issue, they are, as a result, also a global issue because the human rights situation of Ghana is constantly monitored from the outside. NGOs like Amnesty International and government bodies like U.S. State Department publish annual "country reports" on Ghana (and other countries) where they list the major human rights violations and evaluate the situation in general. Attacks on suspected witches are frequently mentioned in the reports.[67] Western governments also produce these reports for the use of their officials who are involved with asylum cases. "Traditional practices," a category that includes witchcraft beliefs and witch-finding and suppression activities, are nowadays

---

[65] Kapferer, *Legends of People*, at 15.
[66] Franz Vanderpuye, *Traditional Beliefs Cost Women Their Freedom* (2004), available at http://www.secularhumanism.org/library/aah/vanderpuye_8_3.htm (accessed 15 December 2011).
[67] U.S. Department of State 2005, *Ghana: Country Reports on Human Rights Practices* (Bureau of Democracy, Human Rights, and Labor, February 28 2005), available at http://www.state.gov/g/drl/rls/hrrpt/2004/41606.htm.

also raised in asylum claims.[68] First, there are cases where the asylum seekers "make an asylum and/or human rights claim based on ill-treatment amounting to persecution due to them having been attacked by witches or the subject of a witches' curse or hex." These cases seem to be rejected categorically by the authorities, who state plainly that there is no evidence that "any physical or other type of 'attack' on individuals by alleged witches have any basis in fact" and hence no state protection is needed.[69] The implication here is, of course, that the cases brought forward by the asylum seekers are imaginary. The second type of asylum claims, where the applicants are seeking protection against antiwitchcraft violence in their home countries, have been more complicated for the Western courts. In such cases the issue is whether the African states in question could offer protection for victims of persecution by nonstate actors, and hence they could continue living in their country of origin. What is under scrutiny here is the commitment of African governments to international human rights norms and not so much the "reality" of the beliefs of the people involved. This is problematic for countries like Ghana because it signals a possible inability or, what is worse, unwillingness to protect their citizens from violence and persecution. In the latter case it may even appear that the governments are condoning or sometimes even supporting antiwitchcraft activities.[70]

All this understandably makes the Ghanaian government even more concerned about the country's human rights record since promotion of human rights is high on the agenda of those donor organizations and Western governments that are the major source of Ghana's development aid.[71] In 1993 the Ghanaian parliament established a government agency titled the Commission for Human Rights and Administrative Justice (CHRAJ), which is charged with investigating alleged violations of human rights and taking action to remedy proven violations. The commission also holds workshops to educate the public, traditional leaders, the police, and the military on human rights issues.[72] The commission has also investigated antiwitchcraft activities, and probably the most well-known case has been that of so-called witch camps of northern

---

[68] UK Home Office 2002, *Ghana: Country Assessment*. Country Information and Policy Unit (April 2002), available at http://www.ind.homeoffice.gov.uk/ppage.asp?section=176.

[69] UK Home Office 2006, Operational Guidance Note: Ghana. Home Office: Immigration and Nationality Directorate (December 2006), available at http://www.unhcr.org/refworld/pdfid/46028c862.pdf.

[70] Schnoebelen, *Witchcraft Allegations*, at 35–40.

[71] See World Bank, *Development and Human Rights: The Role of the World Bank* (Washington, DC, 1998).

[72] Commission for Human Rights and Administrative Justice (CHRAJ) 2003, *Annual Report 2002*.

Ghana. The camps are basically asylums for women who have been banished from their home villages by traditional authorities or their relatives for suspected witchcraft. Most of the accused are older women, who fear that they may be beaten or lynched if they try to return to their homes. The camps are led by local headmen or ritual specialists who claim they are able to "cure" the witchcraft.[73] The estimations concerning the population of the camps vary in different sources, suggesting that it might have grown from several hundred to several thousand during the 2000s.[74] The most recent reports indicate that the numbers are currently on a slow decrease.[75] In the past years the camps have received a lot of publicity in Ghana and elsewhere, and they have even made their way to the pages of Western guidebooks for travelers.[76] The commission has sent its field agents to inspect the camps and concluded that closing them down and repatriating the residents would not be a good option. In the CHRAJ Annual Report released after the camp inspections it was stated that

> [the women] share the same view with their caretakers that the camp is not a prison for witches but a safe haven. It is a refuge centre where women whose lives are threatened come for protection after going through a "dewitching" exercise. They see the Tindana or the Tilana [i.e., the ritual specialist] ... as a protector. In fact none of the "witches" interviewed was prepared to return to their communities even if the Commission guaranteed their safety. They do not believe they will be accepted back and are convinced they will be lynched to death.[77]

The main stress has now been laid on eradication of antiwitchcraft activities through education. The commission together with some local NGOs have

---

[73] Ibid.
[74] UK Home Office 2002, *Ghana: Country Assessment*; U.S. Department of State 2006, *Ghana: International Religious Freedom Report 2006* (Bureau of Democracy, Human Rights, and Labor, 2006), available at http://www.state.gov/g/drl/rls/irf/2006/71304.htm.
[75] UK Home Office 2011, *Operational Guidance Note: Ghana*.
[76] Philip Briggs, *Ghana: The Bradt Travel Guide*, 3rd ed. (Bradt Travel Guides, 2004), at 374–5. It seems that some camps might be turning into macabre tourist attractions. One traveler described a well-known camp in Gambaga in her blog: "The witches, as far as I could tell, were just skinny old women who'd outlived their usefulness at home. It was sad and pathetic, like a sort of perverse old age home, where the women live without family in a culture that is built on the idea of respecting elders and carrying[sic] for community leaders and raising everyone in a village. It was just sad to see. These women experienced so much upheaval and by the time we spoke to them, they were so beaten down by it and used to it, it almost seemed like they were reading from a menu when we asked them about how they came to the camp and what they were accused of. (They couldn't talk about. It's a taboo. But Grace got it out of them.)" (Karen Palmer, Gambaga Witches Camp, 2005, available at http://karenpalmerinafrica.blogspot.com/2005/08/gambaga-witches-camp.html).
[77] CHRAJ, Annual Report 2002, at 28.

launched campaigns to educate the Ghanaian public about the destructive consequences of witchcraft accusations and the human rights of the accused. The campaigns are carried out, for example, by handing out leaflets and getting airtime in local radio stations. The focus of the campaigns is on rural people "who find themselves prone to such [anti-witchcraft] practices," as one campaigner put it.[78] The educational content is based on the modernist agenda of the state and in accord with knowledge hierarchies not very different from those of the colonial rule. Witchcraft beliefs are said to be damaging not only because they engender conflicts and violence, but also because they are untrue and traditional in an undesired way. In addition to emphasizing the falsehood and irrationality of witchcraft beliefs by categorizing them as "superstition," it is also emphasized that they have no place in the modern legal system. When speaking to the press in connection with the campaigns, the head of CHRAJ stressed that "witchcraft is not a crime known to our law and no person has the right to take punitive action against anyone suspected of being a witch."[79]

Furthermore, because the majority of the accused are women, antiwitchcraft activities are also nowadays discussed often as a form of gender abuse.[80] For instance, a deputy minister of employment and social welfare described witch suppression as a "discriminatory practice" that is "bad, obnoxious, and a violation of the rights of the women."[81] The redefinition of antiwitchcraft activities as "gender based violence" has also captured the attention of international women's rights organizations. International Women's Rights Action Watch (IWRAW) has insisted that the government of Ghana should "enact legislation that criminalizes banishment of old women from their homes on allegations of witchcraft." These organizations compare antiwitchcraft activities with female genital mutilation and other practices that are perceived as violations of the human rights of girls and women.[82]

---

[78] Isabella Gyau Orhin, *The Witch Menace: Judge Joins Campaign as He Warns Perpetrators* (2003), available at http://www.ghanaweb.com/public_agenda/article.php?ID=1675.

[79] Vanderpuye, *Traditional Beliefs*.

[80] Susanna Osam, *Violence against Women in Ghana: An Analysis of Cases Presented in the Print Media* (Accra: Abantu for Development, 2004).

[81] Vanderpuye, *Traditional Beliefs*.

[82] International Women's Rights Action Watch, *Statement to the Committee on the Elimination of Discrimination against Women on the Combined Third, Fourth and Fifth Reports from the Government of Ghana*, 2006, available at http://www.iwraw-ap.org/resources/ghana.htm. Female genital mutilation was criminalized in Ghana in 1994. In 1998 the parliament passed legislation that amended the 1960 Criminal Code to provide additional protection for women and children. This legislation also banned the practice of "female customary servitude" known as *trokosi* (UK Home Office 2002, Ghana: Country Assessment). Before that the international public learned about *trokosi* in the famous American investigative television newsmagazine *60 Minutes*.

In addition to the CHRAJ and some other government agencies, several Ghanaian NGOs are trying to improve the living conditions of the witch camps. Various organizations have provided food, medical care, and other support to the residents of the camps.[83] The NGOs and their donors seem to share the modernist views of the state officials. A good example is African Women's Development Fund (AWDF), an organization that raises funds for NGOs that promote women's rights in Africa. They collect donations for a local NGO called Timari-Tama Rural Women, who are, among other things, "embarking on sensitization, awareness campaigns through workshops, media publications, traditional rulers, opinion leaders, religious bodies and the health sector."[84] In their campaign letter they describe their strategy to eradicate witchcraft beliefs as follows:

> Research has proven that in communities where poverty is rife and illiteracy is high, people tend to be superstitious. It is, therefore, not surprising that they attribute their misfortunes to witchcraft and sorcery. Superstitious beliefs are so intricate and difficult to eradicate because they are deeply rooted in the people's traditional beliefs. However, when people are educated, rather than attributing their problems to superstitious beliefs, they are armed with the information to explain issues normally regarded with superstitious eyes. Perhaps further research could be undertaken to ascertain that poverty is indeed the driving force, which causes people to accuse old women of witchcraft and their consequence incarceration to witches camps.[85]

The government agencies' and NGOs' way of conceptualizing witchcraft reproduces the knowledge hierarchies established in the colonial era. Witch suppression is defined as a problem of people who are poor, rural, traditional, and uneducated, and consequently their beliefs and worldview are evaluated as lesser knowledge of lesser people. Of course, similar definitions could not be used in explaining the witchcraft beliefs of the wealthy business elite or the higher ranks of academia.[86] Then again, one does not often hear about businessmen or university professors who beat or lynch their "spiritual adversaries," but they are the people who can afford the best protective talismans and medicines money can buy.

---

[83] CHRAJ, Annual Report 2002, at 27–8.
[84] African Women's Development Fund, *Campaign of the Month: The Gambaga Witches' Camp*, 2005, available at http://www.awdf.org/pages/campaign_detail.php?id=3.
[85] Ibid.
[86] Parish, 'From the Body to the Wallet'; Opoky Onyinah, 'Deliverance as a Way of Confronting Witchcraft in Modern Africa: Ghana as a Case History', (2001) 10 *Cyberjournal for Pentecostal-Charismatic Research*, available at http://www.pctii.org/cyberj/cyberj10/onyinah.html.

Since witchcraft beliefs are perceived as an irrational misunderstanding of laws of causality, they do not have to be studied or understood, but abolished. The state machinery sees it as its duty to address the concerns of the citizens, but it lacks competence and legitimacy in certain areas, such as "spiritual beliefs." Yet, phenomena like the witch camps, which are beginning to constitute an internal refugee problem, force the state to become involved.

VII. CONCLUSIONS: LAW AND UNDERSTANDING

Academic literature on witchcraft has often been accused of neglecting the human suffering connected to it.[87] Accordingly, it should be emphasized that the goal of this chapter has not in any way been to trivialize the hardships of those charged and punished of witchcraft or give justification for violence. Then again, this is an accusation that in its own way reproduces the knowledge hierarchies that have been under scrutiny here. In Western culture one is still relatively free to discuss science without making apologetic references to the millions who have suffered and lost their lives as a result of projects relying on science. This is made possible through processes of separation, whereby certain parts of science, like racial theories, have been bracketed off as distortions or contaminations of "real" science.[88] Witchcraft does not enjoy that same privilege. Nothing redeemable is seen in it, and every victim of every "witch hunt" is considered to have suffered in vain. Nevertheless, if we make an attempt to understand witchcraft in its own terms, we will have to accept that witchcraft discourses are not a singular phenomenon but rather an integral part of a different way of being in the world, and they address genuine concerns about morality.[89]

Considering that witchcraft beliefs remain to classified as "dangerous superstitions" in the modernist terminology, the Ghanaian government, like other African governments, is under a lot of pressure to take a firmer stance on it by introducing specific legislation.[90] The colonial precedents and experiences

---

[87] Schnoebelen, *Witchcraft Allegations*, at 2.
[88] Shiv Visvanathan, 'On the Annals of the Laboratory State', in A. Nandy, (ed.), *Science, Hegemony and Violence* (New Delhi: Oxford University Press, 1988).
[89] Cf. Charles Piot, *Nostalgia for the Future: West Africa after the Cold War* (Chicago: University of Chicago Press, 2010), at 127–8.
[90] In the absence of specific laws the courts have in recent years started to set warning examples. For example, in 2003 Tamale High Court in northern Ghana sentenced a 28-year-old man to death after he and his father had clubbed a witch suspect to death in their home village. The harsh sentence was meant to be a message to the public. The judge presiding over the trial said afterward: "The court will not spare anybody caught taking the law into their own hands to mete out instant justice to people especially women perceived as witches" (Orhin, *Witch Menace*).

elsewhere in sub-Saharan Africa are not encouraging. In Tanzania both witchcraft accusations and practicing witchcraft have been illegal since the colonial period. However, in some areas the government officials are reluctant to take cases to the magistrates and try to persuade the accused to undergo the rituals that are needed to "cure" the witch. Moreover, the officials openly support witchcraft suppression institutions and consider them invaluable for maintaining peace. In localities where the officials have adopted a more assertive stance the court cases have dealt mostly with witchcraft accusations and not practicing witchcraft. Although the latter is regarded as equally illegal, evidence fitting the court requirements is virtually impossible to obtain.[91] In parts of Cameroon since the end of the 1970s state courts have convicted witch suspects on the basis of the knowledge of traditional healers. The healers have assumed the role of expert witnesses and have become less concerned about healing the accused, who are sometimes condemned to long prison sentences. Since the proof in these cases depends on the expert opinion of the healers, they have become feared disciplinary figures in their communities – a situation they have been ready to exploit. The state's involvement in these activities has further reinforced the general faith in the power of witchcraft.[92] In postapartheid South Africa, where only witchcraft accusations are illegal, the state has been under growing popular pressure to intervene on the practice of witchcraft; otherwise it is in danger of being perceived as a protector of witches.[93] All in all, it could be said that the contemporary legal solutions have been partial and unable to produce the desired results.

The problems that the subjects of global governance have with witchcraft tell us about the failures of "authoritarian modernism." As James Scott argues the point of "the Enlightenment view of legal codes" was not so much to reflect the distinctive customs and practices of a people but rather to create a new community by refining, amending, and codifying the most "rational" of their customs and suppressing the more "uncivilized" ones.[94] Thus a scientifically planned society was seen as superior to a traditional one.[95] From this point of view, the existence of witchcraft beliefs is in many ways an embarrassment to modernism. They cannot be successfully controlled nor contained through the modern legal apparatus as they rely on differing ontologies. On

---

[91] Maia Green, 'Entrenching Witchcraft: Poverty and Public Bads in Post Adjustment Tanzania', (2005) 30 *Journal of the Finnish Anthropological Society*, 6–21, at 12–15 and 19.
[92] Geschiere, *Modernity of Witchcraft*, at 169–97.
[93] Adam Ashforth, 'Witchcraft, Violence, and Democracy in the New South Africa', (1998) 38 *Cahiers d'études africaines*, 505–32, at 525–31.
[94] James C. Scott, *Seeing like a State. How Certain Schemes to Improve the Human Condition Have Failed* (New Haven, CT: Yale University Press, 1998), at 89.
[95] Ibid., at 93–4.

the other hand, discarding witchcraft beliefs by labeling them as fallacy may have counterproductive consequences for the promotion of human rights in general. If the administrators and human rights activists condemn antiwitchcraft violence but disparage witchcraft as part of local knowledge and, more critically, overlook the underlying moral tensions and conflicts, it is likely that the other ideas they campaign for might be assessed suspiciously. Thus dealing merely with acts of violence and beliefs separated from their social setting confines one to the level of symptoms and inhibits solutions to the conflict. Up until now the solutions offered by states have either strived for eradicating the witchcraft norms or incorporating them in modern legal norms, both of which have proven failures. In effect, pluralism has been denied. Thus the first and necessary step in finding a way out of the present deadlock would be for the governing subjects to recognize the existence normative, or, should we say, ontological, pluralism.

9 Law versus Bureaucratic Culture: The Case of the ICC and the Transcendence of Instrumental Rationality

Touko Piiparinen

I. INTRODUCTION

This chapter will explore the relationship between law and bureaucratic norms. Section II of this chapter will begin with a "positive story," arguing that the normative order of bureaucratic norms and the normative order of international law by definition reinforce one another. Both legal and bureaucratic norms embody "rational-legal authority," as famously coined by Max Weber. They both advance the rule of law (RoL), which implicates impartiality, integrity, and lack of bias in official decision making, set against arbitrary and corrupt power politics. Bureaucratic norms and law thus work toward the same goal, RoL.

The chapter will then examine bureaucratic culture, which seems to overturn the positive story of the mutually amplifying powers of legal and bureaucratic norms. Section III will show that bureaucratic culture is different from, and sometimes counterproductive to, legal norms in that it breeds an inflexible bureaucratic mind-set, which generates unreflective application of international law. In general, bureaucratic culture has an inherent propensity to cause conflicts between normative orders. Hence, the key to understanding the relationship between bureaucratic norms and law is actually the distinction between bureaucratic norms (which open up the "positive story" of that relationship) and bureaucratic culture (which leads to the "negative story").

It is precisely *bureaucratic culture*, rather than *bureaucratic norms*, that needs to be managed and "engineered" in order to prevent clashes between normative orders. This chapter will argue that we would need to tackle two detrimental factors of bureaucratic culture in particular, namely, instrumental

I am indebted to Jan Klabbers, Larry May, Pekka Niemelä, Kirsten Fisher, Rain Liivoja, and Ville Komulainen for helpful comments on an earlier draft. However, the responsibility for the final text and the viewpoints presented in it is mine alone.

rationality and functional differentiation, which can generate norm conflicts and transform the mutually beneficial and symbiotic relationship between bureaucratic and legal norms into a dysfunctional one. Instrumental rationality, termed *Zweckrationalität* by Weber, alludes to a pervasive profit-seeking mind-set of modern and late-modern bureaucracies, in which everything is assessed and valued primarily in terms of its potential benefits and risks for an organization, not in terms of its inherent value.

The underlying force of instrumental rationality is the "flame of pure intentions,"[1] which means a set of strategic and normative objectives of a national or international organization, such as the International Criminal Court (ICC). According to Weber, bureaucracies pursue these intentions single-mindedly, or "blindly." Sometimes they are implemented regardless of, or at the expense of, other bureaucracies, their respective normative orders, and wider ethical reflection on the ultimate consequences of these "pure intentions." In this way, one normative order may undermine or preempt the materialization of another. For example, the issuance of the international indictment against the Sudanese president Omar Al-Bashir by the ICC in 2009 (the pursuit of the normative order of international criminal law) led to a temporary breakdown of humanitarian assistance operations in Darfur (the preemption of the international humanitarian order).

All bureaucracies are, metaphorically, "late modern juggernauts." The metaphor is originally derived from Anthony Giddens, who describes modern organizations as unemotional, computerized, and mechanical machines, the operations of which are difficult or utterly impossible to harness, control, and predict.[2] Martin Albrow further elaborates Giddens's metaphor in the age of globality: "The late modern juggernaut is a complex of computerized systems which threaten to be outside human control."[3] Bureaucracies also include international courts and tribunals that occasionally operate in the absence of (or beyond) human control. The term "human control," in turn, refers to means by which it would be possible to reflect and manage the potential side effects of modern technologies. Such side effects include the detrimental impacts of indictments issued by international courts on humanitarian conditions in conflict and postconflict zones.

Bureaucratic culture, and particularly instrumental rationality programmed in it, can cause norm conflicts on several fronts. This chapter

---

[1] Max Weber, 'Politics as a Vocation', in H. H. Gerth and C. Wright Mills (eds.), *From Max Weber: Essays in Sociology* (London: Routledge, 1970), 77–128, at 121.
[2] Anthony Giddens, *The Consequences of Modernity* (Cambridge, UK: Polity Press, 1990), at 151.
[3] Martin Albrow, *The Global Age: State and Society beyond Modernity* (Cambridge, UK: Polity Press, 1996), at 135.

Law versus Bureaucratic Culture

will focus on the way in which the bureaucratic culture revolving around international criminal law (ICL) can generate clashes between international law and other normative orders, particularly the humanitarian order. Bureaucratic culture generates rigid and unreflective implementation of ICL, which, in turn, may hamper the delivery of humanitarian assistance to conflict zones and even trigger humanitarian emergency (norm conflict of law versus humanitarian order and moral norms), undermine ongoing peace processes (norm conflict of law versus political norms), and incite hatred and allegations of Western imperialism (norm conflict of law versus cultural and religious norms).

Section IV will explore recent empirical cases in which bureaucratic culture has incited norm conflicts between ICL and other normative orders, including the case of Sudan of 2009. Here, the UN Security Council and the ICC pressed charges against Bashir, without initiating sufficient precautionary measures to prevent the looming humanitarian side effects of the issuance of the ICC indictment. The bureaucratic culture instigated – or, to be precise, necessitated – that the ICC pursue the indictment against Bashir *relentlessly* and blindly; that, in turn, *predictably* provoked Bashir to expel more than ten international and national nongovernmental organizations that were providing lifesaving humanitarian assistance in Darfur. As a result, more than a million Sudanese were temporarily subjected to the risk of imminent death by hunger and disease. This reflects a collision between ICL premised on punishment, on the one hand, and international humanitarian order premised on NIHA (Neutral and Independent Humanitarian Action) and IHL (International Humanitarian Law),[4] on the other.

---

[4] This definition of 'humanitarian order' is derived from the ICRC (International Committee of the Red Cross) guidelines. The ICRC states that "the principles of neutrality and independence, as well as a modus operandi which places priority on persuasion and confidentiality, are tools designed to achieve these objectives [of NIHA] and set NIHA apart from political, judicial or military aims." International Committee of the Red Cross, *Professional Standards for Protection Work Carried out by Humanitarian and Human Rights Actors in Armed Conflict and Other Situations of Violence* (Geneva: ICRC, 2009). Michael Barnett's social constructivist account of international relations theory, in turn, defines 'humanitarian order' in wider terms: "International human rights, humanitarian, and refugee law were distant cousins for most of the last century, but over the last two decades they have become intertwined, reinforcing each other and creating an increasingly dense normative structure [international humanitarian order]." See Michael N. Barnett, *The International Humanitarian Order* (London: Routledge, 2010), at 1. This chapter, by contrast, takes a more skeptical stance on the envisaged cohesiveness of international humanitarian order and maintains that there is an urgent need to synchronize and mediate between its subsets, which are set on a collision course as a result of the instrumental rationality of international bureaucracies.

Bashir naturally bore the direct legal responsibility for the deterioration of the humanitarian situation in Darfur. Nevertheless, the UN Security Council and the ICC were causally and indirectly, albeit not legally, responsible for aggravating the dire humanitarian situation and for undermining the international humanitarian order in the region. *The question, then, arises as to whether the de facto humanitarian risks ensuing as a side effect of the accountability measures by international courts and tribunals could be avoided, without undermining the effective implementation of international criminal law.* The answer presented here is affirmative: the risks could and should be avoided, for example, by initiating a new category of norms that could be called "bureaucratic metanorms." These include the principle of responsibility to protect (RtoP).

Sections V–VII will proceed to examine the bureaucratic metanorms, focusing on RtoP. The prefix "meta-" applied here refers to the fact that bureaucratic metanorms are designed to administer and regulate global problems that cross-cut geopolitical boundaries and various policy sectors. Hence, bureaucratic metanorms apply to a greater number and diversity of organizations than ordinary bureaucratic norms. RtoP, for example, regulates the protection of civilians (a global cause) beyond sectoral and organizational boundaries: it aims to synchronize and combine peacekeeping, diplomacy, development aid and humanitarian aid, as well as ICL, in a global effort to protect civilians. For individual organizations such as the Security Council and the ICC this requirement of RtoP means that they need to synchronize their operations, for instance, accountability measures, with the actions of other organizations such as the ICRC (the International Committee of the Red Cross) with a view to the protection of civilians.

International organizations, including international courts, have tended to apply *traditional instrumental rationality* (Weberian *Zweckrationalität*) according to which the synchronization of their operations with other organizations beyond sectoral boundaries is undesirable. For example, in the traditional form of *Zweckrationalität* the accountability measures of the ICC, including indictments, need to be pursued in an incessant and blind manner. A bureaucratic metanorm such as RtoP has the potential to *transcend* that type of instrumental rationality by harnessing it to serve a global cause and by synchronizing the workings of individual normative orders with one another.

Bureaucratic metanorms thus promote a *new, transcended form of instrumental rationality*. In this post-Weberian *Zweckrationalität*, the accountability measures of the Security Council and the ICC could be more flexible and reflective, allowing, for example, the temporary suspension or deferral of the issuance of an indictment, if it were expected to generate a supreme humanitarian emergency⁵ and thus delegitimize ICL in the long run. In both traditional and transcended forms of instrumental rationality, the ICC would engage in the fight against impunity as effectively as possible, but only in the latter, post-Weberian, scenario would that fight be fought in a sustainable way without undermining the long-term legitimacy of ICL. The justifiability of ICL would surely be undermined, if its unreflective application led to thousands of deaths – whether intentionally or unintentionally.

Concretely the transcended instrumental rationality of RtoP recommends a two-track approach for the Rome Statute system. On the one hand, RtoP strongly supports the effective working of the Rome Statute system in normal circumstances. The UN secretary-general's report on RtoP, for example, calls for all UN member states to join the Rome Statute system.⁶ Yet, in exceptional circumstances RtoP requires the Security Council and the ICC to defer or suspend the issuance of an indictment, in cases when that is expected to put thousands of lives at risk, clearly contravening the ultimate purpose of RtoP – the protection of civilians. It is beyond any doubt that the Security Council and the ICC had the legal competence and legitimate reasons to pursue ICL in the case of Bashir. But the way in which they acted undermined and burdened the efforts of the ICRC and other humanitarian agencies in protecting civilians on the ground and in filling the humanitarian gap, as the indictment effectively and predictably led to the expulsion of major international humanitarian agencies from Darfur. These detrimental side effects of accountability measures could have been overcome by the application of the bureaucratic metanorm of RtoP, calling for self-limitation and temporary deferral or suspension of the issuance of the indictment.

II. PROMOTING THE RULE OF LAW: A POSITIVE STORY OF THE NEXUS BETWEEN BUREAUCRATIC AND LEGAL NORMS

> Bureaucracy can ... also be seen as an institution with a raison d'être and organizational and normative principles of its own.⁷

The norms of international organizations (bureaucratic norms) are independent of, but corollary to, international law, and they typically coexist in

---

⁵ The term "supreme humanitarian emergency" applied in this chapter is derived from Nicholas J. Wheeler, *Saving Strangers: Humanitarian Intervention in International Society* (Oxford University Press, 2000), at 41.
⁶ *Implementing the Responsibility to Protect: Report of the Secretary-General*, UN doc. A/63/677, 12 January 2009, pp. 10–14.
⁷ Johan P. Olsen, 'Maybe It Is Time to Rediscover Bureaucracy', (2005) 16 *Journal of Public Administration Research and Theory*, 1–24, at 3.

a mutually beneficial symbiosis. Both legal and bureaucratic norms embody the rule of law (RoL), which implicates rule-bound, unbiased, and apolitical decision making based on the principles of objectivity and equality. Decisions are made on the basis of depersonified rules, due process, codes of appropriate behavior, and a system of rationally debatable reasons, set against political favoritism. The impersonal procedures of both bureaucratic and legal norms are often considered as particularly legitimate by virtue of their efficiency, predictability, lack of bias, and universality.[8]

Martti Koskenniemi, who represents critical theory in legal scholarship, points out that RoL provides counterweight to realpolitik, which engenders power politics, international anarchy, and violent pursuit of national interests of the most powerful states over the weakest members of international society.[9] Johan Olsen, an organizational scholar, makes a strikingly similar point on bureaucracies, arguing that they serve as the "guardians of constitutional principles, the law, and professional standards" and as the "institutional custodian of democratic-constitutive principles and procedural rationality."[10] As Olsen summarizes his viewpoint, bureaucracies are expected to "speak truth to power."[11]

In practice, bureaucracies and their norms are necessary for the implementation of law: without them, law would remain inefficient and crippled – an empty letter. The bureaucratic norms of various institutions – international organizations, courts, tribunals, states, and other agencies – enable the *most effective* implementation of law and its rapid expansion on the globe. Bureaucracy is the optimal form of administration to implement law because of its capacity to optimize precision, speed, discretion, unity, strict subordination, reduction of friction, and material and personal costs.[12] Second, bureaucracies enable the continuity and consistency of the implementation of law on account of one of their greatest assets, namely, knowledge of the files and archives. Bureaucracies allow the methodical documenting of legal precedents and their continuous use and reuse in the application of international law.

The synergy between the normative order of law and the normative order of bureaucratic norms is also necessary for various tasks of global governance,

---

[8] See, e.g., Michael Barnett and Martha Finnemore, 'The Politics, Power, and Pathologies of International Organizations', (1999) 53 *International Organization*, 699–732, at 708.
[9] Martti Koskenniemi, 'The Politics of International Law', (1990) 1 *European Journal of International Law*, 4–32, at 5.
[10] Olsen, 'Maybe It Is Time to Rediscover Bureaucracy', at 18. This metaphor, however, overlooks the possibility of bureaucratic politics and the fact that international organizations themselves can, and will, use political powers, as explained in Barnett's accounts.
[11] Ibid., at 3.
[12] Ibid., at 5.

including the prevention of genocide. On the one side, the Convention on the Prevention and Punishment of the Crime of Genocide adopted by the UN General Assembly on 9 December 1948 constitutes part of a *legal normative order*, which, like any other set of legal norms, is universally applicable to all subjects within a given legal remit. The Genocide Convention specifically establishes a universal duty to prevent genocide. RtoP constitutes part of another, bureaucratic normative order, which supports and complements the legal normative order of the Genocide Convention by *normatively ordering* (mobilizing) agents to implement the aforementioned legal norms. RtoP is designed to raise awareness of impending mass atrocity crimes, to lobby for popular support and international action to protect civilians affected by those crimes, and to synchronize the activities of international bureaucracies with the aim of protecting civilians.

In sum, bureaucratic norms can "organize" agents "around" legal norms in global governance. On the one side, the normative order of international law provides the clout of universality and permanency to the implementation of a global function (e.g., genocide prevention), while the normative order of bureaucratic norms serves to concretize and contextualize the materialization of that global function. Hence, the Genocide Convention (as part of a legal normative order) and RtoP (as part of a bureaucratic normative order) are two sides of the same coin – the prevention of genocide. Without the internationally recognized legal norms prohibiting the most heinous crime against fundamental human rights, an international action to prevent and manage a genocide threat would be interpreted as nothing but an attempt to interfere in the internal affairs of a foreign country and to infringe its sovereignty. In fact, there would not be any crime of "genocide" to begin with, as the crime itself is defined and codified in the Genocide Convention.[13] And without bureaucratic (meta)norms such as RtoP there would not be any concrete operational guidelines for bureaucratic machineries to take action to prevent and manage genocide.

III. PATHOLOGIES OF BUREAUCRATIC CULTURE: INSTRUMENTAL RATIONALITY AND FUNCTIONAL DIFFERENTIATION

The previous section drew a positive picture of normative pluralism by examining the principal advantages of the synergy between international law

---

[13] The Genocide Convention, which was signed by UN Member States on 9 December 1948, defines genocide as a criminal act with intent to destroy a national, ethnic, racial, or religious group in whole or in part. Convention on the Prevention and Punishment of the Crime of Genocide, 78 UNTS 277, 12 January 1951, article 2.

and bureaucratic norms. The argumentation of this chapter will now shift gears to a more pessimistic story. This section will focus on the drawbacks, or "pathologies," of bureaucratic rationalization inhering in the application of ICL. Social constructivist theories of political science, notably Michael Barnett and Martha Finnemore's account of international relations (IR), have already (re)invoked Weber's classic texts to demonstrate how bureaucratic rationalization affects decision making. Barnett draws upon his insider experiences of UN conflict management to describe the way in which the bureaucratic culture of the UN shapes the behavior of its officials and diplomats by alienating them from their original ethical positions and socializing them to a different, organizationally situated, morality. According to Barnett, bureaucratic culture breeds inflexible decision making, in which assessments and judgments on any given situation are determined more by preexisting and universal categories set by the organization than by the unique characteristics and particular requirements of that situation.[14]

The theory of bureaucratization is premised on the hypothesis that bureaucratic culture permeates practically all sectors of society and all fields of social life. According to Weber, only a narrow sector of society, including representative and parliamentary bodies, can remain immune from bureaucratization. Weber maintains that these exceptions also include *lay* judges,[15] but not *professional* judges, who are subjected to bureaucratization and instrumental rationality as any other professional group is. Weber's insight crucially implies that international tribunals and courts, including prosecutors and judges, must be affected by bureaucratic politics, and their conduct can therefore be analyzed by reference to the theory of bureaucratization.

Koskenniemi, however, explains that international law was never intended to function as bureaucratic machinery. Law was originally designed to embody situational ethics rather than technical-instrumental rationality. And situational ethics encompasses not only rules but also a fairness of process, an attitude of openness, and a spirit of responsibility. These attributes implicate the openness of ICL to a dialogue with other normative orders about the community's principles and purposes.[16] The openness of law described by Koskenniemi stands in striking contrast to the closeness of law portrayed

---

[14] Michael Barnett, 'Bureaucratizing the Duty to Aid: The United Nations and Rwandan Genocide', in Anthony F. Lang (ed.), *Just Intervention* (Washington, DC: Georgetown University Press, 2003), 174–91; Michael Barnett, *Eyewitness to a Genocide: The United Nations and Rwanda* (Ithaca, NY: Cornell University Press, 2002).

[15] Max Weber, *The Theory of Social and Economic Organization* (New York: Free Press, 1964), at 337.

[16] Martti Koskenniemi, *The Politics of International Law* (Oxford, UK: Hart, 2011), at 100–1.

in Niklas Luhmann's theory of self-referential, that is, autopoietic, systems.[17] Luhmann's theory has been gaining ground particularly in social science theory and sociology.

The two disparate conceptions of law described earlier can be merged by arguing that law by default mirrors situational ethics, as suggested by Koskenniemi, but bureaucratic culture has the potential to turn the meaning of law upside down and to transform any of its subsets, including ICL, into a travesty of law, as explained by Luhmann. The fact that the application of ICL is increasingly distancing from the ideal of situational ethics toward organizationally situated morality based on functional differentiation and specialization can be explained not by law per se but by bureaucratic culture, which has the propensity to transform international law from its original design of open systems to an autopoietic one: it breeds a rigid and inflexible bureaucratic mind-set in which accountability measures are conducted stubbornly and unreflectively.

Instrumental rationality constitutes an integral part of bureaucratic culture. It is also the driving force of international bureaucracies – the motor of the "late modern juggernaut," to paraphrase Giddens here. The prevalence of instrumental rationality in global society can be partly explained by the fact that efficiency, accuracy, and precision of decision making, which all stem from instrumental rationality, are highly regarded values per se in global society – in spite of the fact that from the viewpoint of value rationality (*Wertrationalität*) these characteristics should be conceived of as means, rather than ends, of social action. In instrumental rationality (*Zweckrationalität*), everything and everybody, including bureaucrats themselves, is instrumentalized to maximize profit for bureaucracies and to enhance their rational-legal authority. For present-day international bureaucracies the yardstick for measuring the "profit" might be a global cause, such as humanitarian aid (e.g., the number of aid packages delivered) or accountability measures (the number of *génocidaires* convicted).

In instrumental rationality, situational ethics must gradually subside and give way to the pursuit of the predetermined "global cause." That cause is pursued energetically despite – and sometimes at the expense of – ethical requirements arising from particular situations. Means thereby overcome ends by becoming ends in themselves.[18] Barnett and Finnemore's definition of the "irrationality of rationalization" seems apposite here: "the 'rationalization'

---

[17] Niklas Luhmann, *Social Systems* (Stanford, CA: Stanford University Press, 1995).
[18] Heikki Patomäki, 'Maailmanpoliittisen mielikuvituksen rajat', in E. Lagerspetz, H. Patomäki and J. Räikkä, *Maailmanpolitiikan moraali* (Helsinki: Edita, 1996), 75–109, at 83–4.

processes at which bureaucracies excelled could be taken to extremes and ultimately become irrational if the rules and procedures that enabled bureaucracies to do their jobs became ends in themselves."[19]

To apply Weber's theory (and Barnett and Finnemore's more contemporary insights) concerning *Zweckrationalität* here, international courts and tribunals such as the ICC function primarily on the basis of an instrumental understanding of responsibility. These organizations, like any other international bureaucracy, feel responsible only in that their "flame of pure intentions"[20] or "global cause" is not quelched. As Weber further elaborates this mind-set, "if an action of good intent leads to bad results, then, in the actor's eyes, not he but the world, or the stupidity of other men ... is responsible for the evil."[21] This bureaucratic mind-set of *Zweckrationalität* explains why the ICC's primary concern is to see that indictments are issued and enforced as effectively as possible. Only the secondary concern is to take care of the potentially harmful humanitarian side effects of these accountability measures, and even then it is not the duty of the ICC but of humanitarian agencies, which are mandated to perform humanitarian functions. For example, the responsibility to deal with the side effects ensuing from ICC indictments on humanitarian situations in conflict zones falls to organizations such as the ICRC, not the ICC. The ICC Policy Paper on the Interests of Justice states that "the broader matter of international peace and security is not the responsibility of the [ICC] Prosecutor; it falls within the mandate of other institutions."[22] As the policy document was drafted by the ICC Office of the Prosecutor, it is a product of the bureaucratic culture of the ICC. It perfectly captures the way in which the Court *itself* sees its role as limited to the (blind) pursuit of international criminal law.

Hence, in traditional *Zweckrationalität* the conception of social and political responsibility – what counts as "responsible" behavior – differs crucially among international bureaucracies, depending on the particular functional sector in which each bureaucracy is operating, its respective global cause, and its underlying normative order. For humanitarian agencies such as the ICRC, responsibility principally alludes to *short-term humanitarianism*, that is, the effective delivery of humanitarian relief to suffering victims, rather than bringing the perpetrators of human rights crimes to justice. For the ICC, by contrast, responsibility means the *realization of retributive and restorative justice*, which necessitates the punishment of criminals and accurate and objective

---

[19] See Barnett and Finnemore, 'The Politics, Power, and Pathologies', at 720.
[20] See Weber, 'Politics as a Vocation', at 121.
[21] Ibid.
[22] International Criminal Court, Office of the Prosecutor, 'The Interests of Justice', Policy Paper on the Interests of Justice, ICC-OTP-2007, September 2007, at 9.

recording of past atrocities. The bureaucratic metanorm of RtoP attempts to transcend the aforementioned disparate ideas of responsibility among individual organizations to a holistic understanding thereof by *unifying*, homogenizing, and mainstreaming the notion of responsibility, as will be examined in more detail in the last three sections of this chapter. According to RtoP, responsibility first and foremost refers to *long-term humanitarianism*, that is, the sustainable protection of civilians from mass atrocity crimes, to which *all* organizations, including the ICC and the ICRC, should subscribe.

In bureaucratic culture, instrumental rationality combines with functional differentiation. According to Luhmann's theory, functional differentiation in global society is maintained by "autopoietic systems."[23] These are closed and self-referential systems that reproduce themselves through their own operations.[24] As Luhmann describes the way in which autopoietic systems conceptualize their surrounding environment, "meaning always refers to meaning and never reaches out of itself for something else."[25] Luhmann's thesis explains the pathological tendency of international bureaucracies to remain unreflective on their surrounding environment and society, other organizations, and their underlying normative orders. International bureaucracies, like autopoietic systems in general, never fully "understand" each other, let alone genuinely "speak to" one another, simply because that is not their modus operandi. Autopoietic systems produce meanings of global causes in their own terms and communicate these meanings to other systems only *strategically*, without a genuine interaction, mutual response, or common understanding. They also do not easily adapt their operations in synchronization with other systems.

As Olsen points out, the functionally best solution is not always politically or culturally feasible, and vice versa.[26] This self-contradiction of functional differentiation presents a particular challenge for global governance. That is because functional differentiation among various sectors and segments of global society is rapidly increasing, or worsening, as a result of the rising complexity of global problems and the consequent need for elaborate division of labor and specialization. As new autopoietic systems and functionally differentiated regimes spring up to tackle these global problems, each pursuing its respective global cause, the usual outcome of their strategic maneuvers and competition is not their cooperation or amalgamation, let alone coordinated global governance, but a growing number and intensity of regime collisions.

[23] Luhmann derives his definition of "autopoiesis" from Humberto Maturana's and Francisco J. Varela's original account.
[24] Luhmann, *Social Systems*, at 34.
[25] Ibid., at 62.
[26] Olsen, 'Maybe It Is Time to Rediscover Bureaucracy', at 5.

The next section will examine one autopoietic system, namely, the Rome Statute system, which is composed of a political organ (the UN Security Council), international bureaucracy (the ICC), and its underlying normative order (ICL). Perhaps the greatest impediment of the Rome Statute system, as of any other autopoietic system, is the lack of reflectivity. As for *external (un) reflectivity*, the operations of the Rome Statute system remain uncoordinated with the humanitarian order, for instance. Neither the state parties of the Rome Statute system nor the UN Security Council has established guidelines to synchronize legal interventions, for example, ICC proceedings launched by the Security Council, with the overall wheelwork of international interventions aimed at conflict management, including peace processes and mediation, so that these various forms of intervention would not undermine one another. The council has not, for example, established a set of general criteria under which the deferral of ICC proceedings should be applied under article 16 of the Rome Statute,[27] in cases where such legal interventions are expected to undermine humanitarian interventions, such as the delivery of humanitarian aid. This is peculiar particularly in light of the fact that all of these interventions, which may be contradictory to one another, may be launched by the same organ – the Security Council – at the same time.[28]

From the autopoietic viewpoint, the ICC indictment against President Bashir issued in March 2009 was indisputably the most viable solution in *functional and legal* terms. At the same time, however, the Rome Statute system failed to relate its operations to the requirements of humanitarian and diplomatic actors and their respective normative orders. As a result, the issuance of the indictment became counterproductive in political and humanitarian terms. Perhaps the worst self-defeating side effect of this particular legal intervention was the expulsion of more than ten international and national nongovernmental organizations working in the humanitarian sector in Darfur and the consequent risk of the complete breakdown in the provision of lifesaving assistance to more than a million people.

As for *internal reflectivity*, even the constitutive parts of the Rome Statute system remain unreflective and unresponsive in relation to one another. For example, the Security Council and the ICC have not set up any mechanism to determine the division of labor between them in initiating accountability measures. As a result, it remains unclear as to when the ICC prosecutor – in

[27] Such guidelines and criteria could also be established by the Friends of the ICC group composed of like-minded member states of the UN.
[28] See, for example, Touko Piiparinen, *Law Enforcer or Mediator? The Libya Crisis Reveals Paradoxes in UN Conflict Management*, FIIA Comment 4/2011 (Helsinki: Finnish Institute of International Affairs, 2011).

place of the Security Council – should initiate proceedings independently under article 15 of the Rome Statute,[29] and whether it should adopt cases that are under the council's purview. Even worse, the fragmentation between the constitutive parts of the Rome Statute system has enabled the Security Council to "dump" situations under its purview to the ICC, in an attempt to distract, "outsource," avoid, or bypass its own responsibility to resolve these conflicts on its agenda by political means.

Here, the referral of cases to the ICC by the Security Council serves as an "automation of justice" and as a (false) panacea of global conflict management. In fact, such referral serves as a distraction, by which the Security Council can portray itself to outsiders as an active and engaged player in the field of global conflict management, but simultaneously outsource the responsibility of conflict management to the ICC. In this context, Martti Koskenniemi's argument appears highly relevant: "Our inherited ideal of a World Order based on the Rule of Law thinly hides from sight the fact that social conflict must still be solved by political means."[30] In conclusion, the bureaucratic culture revolving around the Rome Statute system prioritizes universal, mechanic, automated, and fixed – in a word, bureaucratic – responses to crises over contingent, case-specific, political, and tailor-made solutions, thus hiding the fact that the Security Council itself, not the ICC, is in the driver's seat in global conflict management.

IV. THE ROME STATUTE SYSTEM AS AN AUTOPOIETIC SYSTEM

> I hope to convey a realistic view of the operation of international law as a *practice* of decision-making that interferes in peoples' lives instead of a theoretical exercise in deduction-subsumption from abstract rule-formulations, principles of "justice" or the "policies" of international institutions.[31]

This section will analyze lessons learned of various cases in which the autopoietic operations of the Rome Statute system have led to norm conflicts, focusing on the ICC interventions in Libya, Uganda, and Sudan. In line with Koskenniemi's preceding formulation, the purpose here is not to examine the precedents of the ICC as a universal yardstick to determine what constitutes "right" and "wrong." Instead, they are viewed as constitutive of one, legal form of global interventions among many other interventions launched by

---

[29] The legal term *proprio motu* derived from Latin, meaning "acting on his or her own initiative," refers to the authority of the ICC prosecutor to initiate indictments on his/her own discretion.
[30] See Koskenniemi, *Politics of International Law*, at 38.
[31] Ibid., at vi.

international bureaucracies, including political, diplomatic, and humanitarian ones. The primary aim here is to discover how these legal interventions interfere in people's lives and in other ongoing global interventions, such as peace processes.

In many ways, the subject matter of this section touches upon the classic "justice versus peace" debate in legal and political science. As Alex Bellamy notes, "the court [the ICC] will add a new layer of complexity to international society's engagement with genocide and mass atrocities because it involves balancing the pursuit of justice and the pursuit of peace."[32] It is agreed here with Bellamy that the proceedings of the ICC can generate not only positive effects but also negative ones, hampering peace processes, for instance. However, the problem pertaining to the operations of the ICC is actually much wider, when it is considered in the framework of normative pluralism: it concerns norm conflicts between normative orders, as explained later.

As for the conflict between law and the humanitarian order, the issuance of indictments and other accountability measures by the ICC may antagonize parties of interstate conflicts and civil wars and in some circumstances intensify violence and deepen humanitarian suffering, prevent the creation of humanitarian spaces to protect endangered civilians, disrupt humanitarian access to vulnerable groups that are in need of lifesaving assistance in areas controlled by belligerent parties, lead to the expulsion of humanitarian organizations from areas where humanitarian relief and emergency aid provided by them are desperately needed, and incite violence against humanitarian workers, peacekeepers, and other international agencies on the ground. From the moral point of view based on value rationality (*Wertrationalität*), the practice of the ICC premised on instrumental rationality (*Zwecktrationalität*) can paradoxically and unintentionally transform the guardian of law into a renegade sheriff: the ICC serves the global cause of ICL by investigating, prosecuting, and punishing criminals, but it also tends to ignore the humanitarian consequences of its own accountability measures. In the latter aspect, ICL stands in an uneasy and anarchical relation to the international humanitarian order.

William A. Schabas views *penalty* as the centerpiece of ICL, which guides the work of international courts and tribunals, including the ICC, and distinguishes it from other normative orders: "Criminal law, in all domestic systems, culminates in a penalty phase. This is what principally distinguishes

---

[32] Alex J. Bellamy, *Responsibility to Protect: The Global Effort to End Mass Atrocities* (Cambridge, UK: Polity, 2009), at 123.

Law versus Bureaucratic Culture

it from other forms of judicial and quasi-judicial accountability.... And the International Criminal Court is no different."[33] Occasionally the legal rationality of international courts and tribunals fixated on punishment stands in diametrical opposition to the rationalities and organizational mind-sets associated with other normative orders. Because of instrumental rationality and functional differentiation affecting the Rome Statute system, the objectives of the normative order of ICL and the international humanitarian order may become mutually contradictory and colliding. The former may hamper the fulfillment of the legal and moral values enshrined in the humanitarian order, notably NIHA (Neutral and Independent Humanitarian Action) and IHL (International Humanitarian Law).

Examples of the norm conflict described are manifold: The issuance of ICC indictments and other accountability measures may undermine peace settlements and hamper ongoing peace processes. For example, research conducted by the Department of Peace and Conflict Research of Uppsala University points out that criminal charges issued by the ICC against political leaders who are involved in peace negotiations may function as "external violent shocks" on mediation processes and may even derail these processes altogether.[34] The issuance of indictments may diminish the willingness of the parties of a conflict to conclude a peace settlement and may actually motivate them to continue fighting. A case in point here is the legal intervention of the ICC in the Libyan conflict in 2011.

The civil war in Libya erupted in mid-February 2011 when Colonel Muammar Gaddafi's regime set out to quell the popular uprisings and demonstrations by resorting to conventional war against rebels, which also involved indiscriminate violence against civilian populated areas. On 6 March 2011 UN Secretary-General Ban Ki-moon appointed the former Jordanian foreign minister Abdelilah Al-Khatib as his special envoy to Libya, mandated to mediate between the belligerent parties, that is, Colonel Gaddafi's government and its opposing National Transitional Council. Khatib's task was particularly to ensure the delivery of humanitarian assistance to the conflict zones and to end the violence. However, a week earlier on 26 February 2011 the UN Security Council had adopted Resolution 1970, which authorized criminal inquiries by the ICC against the Libyan leadership. Consequently, the UN found itself

---

[33] William A. Schabas, *An Introduction to the International Criminal Court*, 2nd ed. (Cambridge University Press, 2004), at 162.

[34] Mathilda Lindgren, Peter Wallensteen and Helena Grusell, *Meeting the New Challenges to International Mediation*. Report from an International Symposium at the Department of Peace and Conflict Research of Uppsala University, organized in Uppsala on 14–16 June 2010, at 20 (on file with the author).

in an awkward position, attempting to play the double role of "mediator" and "law-enforcer" in the conflict.[35]

The referral of the Libya case to the ICC by the Security Council predictably triggered the issuance of indictments, but the rapidity of the whole process came as a surprise to many. On 16 May 2011, the ICC prosecutor, Luis Moreno-Ocampo, requested ICC judges to issue indictments against the Libyan president, Colonel Gaddafi, and other members of the Libyan government for crimes committed in Libya since February 2011. Consequently, on 27 June 2011 the ICC issued the warrants of arrest for Gaddafi and two other members of the Libyan regime for crimes against humanity. The case of Libya, however, raised concerns as to whether these indictments closed the door for peace mediation, or at least diminished its prospects.

The ICC indictments logically motivated, or forced, the leadership of Colonel Gaddafi's regime to continue a fatalistic war of regime survival against the opposition and the coalition forces led by NATO, which had intervened militarily in Libya. Given the ICC indictments and the jurisdiction conferred by the Security Council, Colonel Gaddafi and his supporters had no *rational* option other than to continue fighting: even if they had reached a negotiated settlement allowing them to leave the country, they could have been captured abroad under the ICC's warrants of arrest and transferred to The Hague to face criminal charges. Moreover, the indictments logically diminished the prospects for the closest members of the Gaddafi regime to switch sides to the opposition forces. That concern was explicitly raised by some members of the Security Council during its deliberations leading to the adoption of Resolution 1970.

The majority of political and legal scientists emphasize that Resolution 1970 marks the first time the Security Council has referred a case to the ICC with a unanimous vote. On the other hand, these mainstream accounts ignore the fact that there were actually quite deep political divisions in the Security Council prior to its crucial vote. Russia, China, India, African members, and even Portugal held a skeptical view on the referral of the case to the ICC (for various political reasons), while France and the United Kingdom viewed the referral as necessary not only for tackling the Libyan conflict but also for the ICC's credibility. As a compromise solution put forward by France, the resolution includes a clause that confirms the council's readiness to review the appropriateness of the measures contained in the resolution,[36] including the referral to the ICC. This clause was intended to reflect the council's readiness

---

[35] See Piiparinen, *Law Enforcer or Mediator?*
[36] UN Doc. S/RES/1970 (2011), 26 February 2011, p. 7.

to defer the ICC investigations (as outlined in article 16 of the Rome Statute), if the situation in Libya so required. Such deferral was never applied.

It is beyond any doubt that the Security Council's referral of the Libya case to the ICC was commendable per se, but the *way* in which it was conducted was unusually fast. As a point of comparison, it took two years for the Security Council to refer the conflict in Darfur to the ICC. In that case, it is obvious that the referral, which was made in spring 2005, occurred too late, since the crisis had already erupted in spring 2003. In the case of Libya, the gap between the beginning of the conflict (mid-February 2011) and the referral to the ICC (26 February 2011) was only a couple of weeks. The sheer rapidity of the process bore serious disadvantages. For example, it preempted the possibility to use the activation of ICC accountability measures as a political deterrent against Gaddafi's regime. Permanent members of the Security Council could, for example, have applied the *prospect* of the ICC referral as leverage in diplomatic negotiations with the Gaddafi regime to persuade it to stop massacres of the civilian population.

These measures were unused because of the prevailing autopoietic logic of global governance: they would have required some kind of link between the Rome Statute system and the wider conflict management system, particularly between ICC accountability measures and peace processes. Such a link is simply missing in the current autopoietic world order. Indeed, the whole idea of "subjecting" the accountability measures of the ICC to political objectives, such as mediation, would be blasphemous for those who stress the integrity of the Rome Statute system. Yet, they also ignore that these accountability measures were launched by a *political* actor – the Security Council – in the first place.

In the most extreme form, the autopoietic operations of the Rome Statute system can put the lives of thousands at risk, as evidenced by the case of Darfur. The referral of that case to the ICC was delayed, as already mentioned. Yet, when the decision on it was finally made, it opened up new problems. The issuance of the ICC indictment against President Bashir prompted him to expel thirteen international NGOs and three national NGOs from Darfur on 4 March 2009, leaving approximately one and a half million people without humanitarian assistance and relief, and approximately half of humanitarian aid delivery temporarily compromised. The expelled organizations had been conducting a wide range of humanitarian tasks and protection of civilians, including food distribution and food security, health care and emergency medical care, water and sanitation, and gender-based violence response. The UN reported a near-collapse of protection activities in the field of gender-based violence in the region, as ten of the thirteen expelled organizations had been undertaking programs with that focus. The case in point here is one of the most striking examples of the drawbacks of the current autopoietic system of global governance: it reveals a gaping hole in mechanisms that could synchronize the operations of the Rome Statute system with the humanitarian regime.

Perhaps the most disconcerting detail of the Darfur case is that some international experts of conflict management, including the ICG (International Crisis Group), had issued *prior* early warning signals on the potentially detrimental effects ensuing from the issuance of the indictment, but these warnings were unheeded. This reflects the closure and unreflectivity of the Rome Statute system at its starkest. Nick Grono, the deputy president of the ICG, made the following prediction before the release of the indictment, which proved chillingly accurate a few weeks later: "[The government of Sudan] could lash out at the UN missions in Sudan and international humanitarian operations, and could go so far as to unleash attacks on peacekeepers and Darfuri civilians in camps to ram home the message."[37] Such early warnings were ignored. When the indictment was issued, it put more than a million lives at risk.

The case of Uganda, in turn, provides an example of the way in which legal interventions undertaken by the ICC can hamper national reconciliation processes in countries emerging from conflict. The issuance of the ICC indictments against Joseph Kony, the leader of the main insurgency group in Uganda; the Lord's Resistance Army (LRA); and four other high-ranking members of the LRA in October 2005 reportedly contributed to the stalling of the Juba peace process, which attempted to end the Ugandan conflict. Many other adverse effects ensued from the ICC's criminal proceedings. According to some analysts, the international warrants of arrest against the LRA leaders actually empowered and incited the Ugandan government to suppress not only the LRA but also the popular democratic opposition. The LRA, on its part, has continued to commit crimes regardless of the international indictments against its members.[38] Kony, on his part, has made precisely the same "rational" decision as Gaddafi: to continue to fight and flee in the face of the ICC indictment.

---

[37] Nick Grono, 'Sudan: "After the Indictment"', *International Herald Tribune*, 3 March 2009.
[38] Some researchers also point to positive effects of the ICC indictments on the peace process in Uganda. According to some estimates, the ICC warrants initially induced the LRA to go to the negotiating table and to stop fighting. See David Tolbert and Marieke Wierda, *Stocktaking: Peace and Justice: A Case Study Presented at the Rome Statute Review Conference in Kampala on June 2010*, May 2010 (International Center for Transitional Justice, 2010), available at http://www.ictj.org/static/Publications/ICTJ_RSRC-PeaceandJustice_bp2010.pdf. (accessed 20 August 2010).

What is perhaps most disconcerting in the case of Uganda is that the parliament, the legitimate representative body of the Ugandan people, had passed a bill offering amnesty to the entire leadership of the LRA, but the ICC intervened in favor of the president by launching criminal proceedings against the LRA. The ICC thus symbolically contravened the parliament's will. For this reason, the ICC has been criticized for demonstrating a progovernment bias and for running against the country's main constitutional body, the parliament.[39] These empirical findings again demonstrate the need to devise new mechanisms and means to manage the potentially adverse side effects generated by the accountability measures of the Rome Statute system.

The vigorous pursuit of ICL by the ICC in northern Uganda ultimately contributed to the faltering of the peace negotiations and thus hampered the whole international peace building and reconstruction effort in the fragile state, when the murderous rebel group LRA insisted that the charges against its leader should be dropped as part of any peace agreement. The LRA specifically asked the ICC to suspend its indictment against Kony; the ICC, however, was unwilling (and unable) to do so. The bureaucratic procedures and the bureaucratic ethos of the ICC, like any other autopoietic system, always tie the hands of its officials.

To summarize the main conclusions of the empirical cases presented here thus far, it could be argued that the instrumental rationality integral to bureaucratic culture bears negative side effects on ICL and normative pluralism in two ways. First, it can generate *actual and causal conflicts between normative orders* even where there are no juridical or moral grounds for such fragmentation. Second, the instrumental rationality of bureaucratic culture can *undermine the legitimacy of international law*. The value rationality of the ICC, which would entail ethical reflection on humanitarian conditions, is always constrained by its instrumental rationality, which requires the unfaltering and unconstrained pursuit of ICL – even at the expense of moral and humanitarian considerations. This, in turn, undermines the legitimacy of the ICC, ICL, and international law as a whole in the long run: the ICC acts as a mechanistic automation that is seemingly insensitive to the attainment of peace and stability in conflict zones and in countries emerging from conflict such as Uganda.

It should be emphasized here that the drawbacks of bureaucratic rationalization, including instrumental rationality and functional differentiation, do not stem from bureaucrats but from bureaucratic culture. ICC officials, like

---

[39] Mahmood Mamdani, 'Responsibility to Protect or Right to Punish?' in Philip Cunliffe (ed.), *Critical Perspectives on the Responsibility to Protect: Interrogating Theory and Practice* (London: Routledge, 2011), 125–39, at 134.

any other group of bureaucrats, find themselves in the vicious circle of bureaucratic culture – the "iron cage," as Weber famously described it. Bureaucratic culture obliges individual bureaucrats and international tribunals and courts as a whole to pursue international law *incessantly*; that, however, simultaneously undermines the legitimacy of international law in the long run. On the one hand, bureaucrats themselves know that their action will prove self-defeating in the long term. On the other hand, they also know that the credibility, neutrality, independence, and rational-legal authority of the ICC – and any other international court, for that matter – would be questioned if they did not apply the unreflective, maximum, and rapid implementation of ICL. Justice is blind, and individual officials do not want to break that image.

Ronald Takaki characterizes "rationalized" settings as places in which the "self was placed in confinement, its emotions controlled, and its spirit subdued."[40] For the Rome Statute system, the dehumanizing effects of bureaucratization relate to the dissociation of ICC officials and UN diplomats working in The Hague and New York from side effects inflicted by ICC accountability measures on humanitarian conditions in local settings. In fact, the rationalized "iron cage" of the Rome Statute system wields dehumanizing effects both on the subjects (ICC officials) and on the objects of its operations (individuals suffering from the deterioration of humanitarian conditions as a result of ICC indictments). The bureaucratic logic requires that the ICC does not slow down its investigations and proceedings on account of moral or humanitarian considerations. Moreover, morality appears too vague, abstract, hypothetical, and speculative to form any "rational" basis for decision making from the viewpoint of instrumental rationality, which emphasizes the calculability of the envisaged outcomes of social action and public goods. After all, no one can *accurately or numerically* predict the *potentially* detrimental effects of ICC indictments on any particular peace process or on the future development of the humanitarian situation in a conflict zone. This is the recipe of the "irrationality of bureaucratic rationality" in the Rome Statute system.

V. CAN INSTRUMENTAL RATIONALITY BE TAMED? THE PROSPECTS OF BUREAUCRATIC METANORMS

This section will argue that the bureaucratic culture and its side-effects could be managed by devising bureaucratic metanorms such as RtoP, which have the

---

[40] Quoted in George Ritzer, 'Precursors: Bureaucracy and Max Weber's Theory of Rationality, Irrationality, and the Iron Cage', in George Ritzer (ed.), *McDonaldization: The Reader*, 2nd. ed. (Thousand Oaks, CA: Pine Forge Press, 2006), 26–31, at 29.

potential to function as "normative traffic lights," coordinating and orchestrating the working of different normative orders. The different – and occasionally clashing – global causes and rationalities of divergent normative orders could be related, regulated, and embedded under the wider normative umbrella of global governance, which is provided by bureaucratic metanorms. For example, the rationale of RtoP could be used to synchronize the working of the Rome Statute system (the normative order of ICL) in relation to humanitarian agencies (the humanitarian order). In the framework of RtoP, both of these normative orders should preserve a fundamental human value – the protection of civilians from mass atrocities.

How, then, do "bureaucratic metanorms" actually work, and how do they differ from ordinary bureaucratic norms? Bureaucratic norms are typically "earmarked" to national and international organizations, constituting their institutional competences, regulating their operations, defining rigid divisions of labor and hierarchies among different offices within bureaucracies, and allocating specific duties to bureaucrats. Bureaucratic metanorms, by contrast, are not assigned to any specific organizations but to functionally defined sectors of global society, and they are applicable to all organizations operating in those sectors. RtoP, for example, is applicable to the protection of civilians as a whole (a specific functional sector of global governance) and to all organizations working in that sector – whether explicitly or implicitly.

The official definition of RtoP is detailed in paragraphs 138 and 139 of the UN World Summit Outcome, agreed on by more than 150 heads of state and government in 2005. It captures the dual responsibility of all states individually and the international community as a whole to protect populations from four types of mass deaths: genocide, crimes against humanity, war crimes, and ethnic cleansing.[41] What is often overlooked in the existing literature[42] is that RtoP also applies to international agencies. That is because international organizations also form part of the international community and thus fall under the remit of RtoP: the literal interpretation of the official definition of RtoP demonstrates that not only potential *génocidaires* but also ostensible "rescuers" – all individuals and organizations, including the UN Security Council and the ICC – should refrain from activities and interventions that may lead to devastating humanitarian outcomes, whether intentionally or unintentionally.

The ultimate raison d'être of RtoP is not indict or punish *génocidaires*, but its primary objective is to protect populations from mass atrocities. RtoP requires international courts to refrain from taking those accountability measures that

---

[41] 2005 *World Summit Outcome*, UN doc. A/RES/60/1, 24 October 2005, 60/1, p. 30.
[42] See, e.g., Bellamy, *Responsibility to Protect*, at 4.

are expected to instigate crimes against humanity or other atrocity crimes and *actively to seek alternative accountability measures* that do not trigger such crimes. In the case in point here, RtoP would at minimum have required international bureaucracies to prepare contingency plans to prevent the expulsion of humanitarian agencies from Sudan, which was a foreseeable and predicted side effect of the issuance of the ICC indictment against Bashir. Such plans were never made.

The purpose of this chapter is not to challenge Larry May's interpretation in his chapter, according to which RtoP can be conceived of as a moral norm.[43] In its present form, however, RtoP constitutes more than a moral norm: the official definition of RtoP in paragraphs 138 and 139 of the UN World Summit Outcome document entails precise and operational regulations for global actors, including international organizations such as the UN, individual states, regional organizations, and indeed the ICC, with a view to the protection of civilians and on the actualization of peaceful means in the implementation of RtoP under chapter VI of the UN Charter prior to coercive measures outlined in chapter VII. Ordinary moral norms like "Thou shalt not kill" lack such precise operational guidelines for national, international, and regional actors that litter paragraphs 138 and 139 and other official documents on RtoP. Therefore RtoP could be understood as a bureaucratic rather than a moral norm or doctrine.

While May is correct to argue that the concept or principle of "responsibility to protect" enshrined in the report of the International Commission on Intervention and State Sovereignty[44] has the character of a moral norm, in the parlance of multilateral diplomacy and global security policy "Responsibility to Protect" has already evolved into an operationalized doctrine of international conflict management. Indeed, since the publication of the Report of the UN Secretary-General[45] on the implementation of RtoP in 2009, the discussion on RtoP at the UN has been centered on how to operationalize RtoP.[46] Perhaps the best illustration of this shift is the expression "RtoP" per se: such acronyms

[43] See Chapter 12 in this volume.
[44] See International Commission on Intervention and State Sovereignty, *The Responsibility to Protect: Report of the International Commission on Intervention and State Sovereignty* (December 2001), available at http://www.responsibilitytoprotect.org/ICISS%20Report.pdf (accessed 8 August 2010).
[45] *Implementing the Responsibility to Protect: Report of the Secretary-General*, UN doc. A/63/677, 12 January 2009.
[46] Thakur and Weiss take this viewpoint even further, arguing that the current research should go beyond the analysis of the normative conception of RtoP altogether and examine the ways in which RtoP could be transformed "from a norm to a template for policy and action." Ramesh Thakur and Thomas G. Weiss, 'R2P: From Idea to Norm – and Action?' (2009) 1 *Global Responsibility to Protect*, 22–53, at 26.

(and an even more futuristic term "R2P," which is commonly applied in the existing literature) are typically used in relation to operational and bureaucratic norms in order to emphasize their precise applicability or mechanistic automation in professional spheres.

To paraphrase Michael Walzer's description of humanitarian intervention, a bureaucratic metanorm such as RtoP is a "duty that doesn't belong to any particular agent."[47] RtoP, like any other bureaucratic metanorm, reflects a multicontextual logic: RtoP entails a universal and legitimate obligation, namely, the protection of civilians, for *every individual, group, and organization*, including those operating outside the UN system, although RtoP was officially approved and formulated at the UN World Summit of 2005. In this sense, RtoP goes far beyond the UN bureaucracy. According to RtoP, all actors should be alert to potential early warning signals of impending mass atrocities in all aspects of their daily work and bureaucratic routines, and they should also act on the basis of that information. Hence, the ultimate purpose of RtoP is to *mainstream* the protection of civilians.

It is argued here – perhaps somewhat counterintuitively at first sight – that the instrumental rationality of bureaucratic culture should not be suspended, but transcended. Moreover, bureaucratic norms (regulating individual institutions) should not be cast off per se, but they should be coupled with the bureaucratic metanorms at the holistic level (regulating whole sectors of global governance). This means that, *instead of eliminating instrumental rationality, instrumental rationality itself should be instrumentalized* for the purposes of global governance via bureaucratic metanorms. Such norms prescribe measures to impose order on the disorderly constellation of competing international bureaucracies and their respective normative orders that instrumental rationality produced in the first place. But they would not eliminate instrumental rationality as such, which boosts the performance of international organizations, including international tribunals and courts, and thus enables effective global governance.

Bureaucratic metanorms would thus preserve the instrumental rationality of bureaucratic culture but also function as a safety valve that prevents the instrumental rationality from overheating into what Anthony Giddens terms the "runaway world" of "late modern juggernauts." Hence, bureaucratic metanorms could tackle the side effects of instrumental rationality "from within" the uncontrolled and chaotic battle field of competing international bureaucracies that pursue different normative orders. On the one hand, this

---

[47] Quoted in Philip Cunliffe, 'A Dangerous Duty: Power, Paternalism and the Global "Duty of Care"', in Cunliffe (ed.), *Critical Perspectives*, 51–70, at 52.

vision of human emancipation based on the idea of transcendence complies with Max Weber's thesis on bureaucratization, according to which bureaucratization – with all its disadvantages and flaws, notably instrumental rationality – is so pervasive that the escape from it is virtually impossible. Weber describes such a dilemma:

> When those subject to bureaucratic control seek to escape the influence of the existing bureaucratic apparatus, this is normally possible only by creating an organization of their own which is equally subject to the process of bureaucratization.... Even in case of revolution by force or of occupation by an enemy, the bureaucratic machinery will normally continue to function just as it has for the previous legal government.[48]

Hence, the vision of human emancipation based on the idea of "transcended instrumental rationality" would be realistic in that it accepts Weber's hypothesis regarding the inevitability and unavoidability of certain elements of modernity, including the instrumental rationality of bureaucratic culture. On the other hand, transcended instrumental rationality is simultaneously "post-Weberian" in that it involves an emancipatory impulse: it aims to harness instrumental rationality to *empower* humanitarian action. RtoP, for example, explicitly calls for the maximum implementation of ICL and effective working of the Rome Statute system as a whole in normal circumstances,[49] thus retaining instrumental rationality. But in exceptional circumstances, including those in which the issuance of indictments is expected to contribute to the emergence of *supreme* humanitarian emergencies such as genocide, RtoP allows ethical and political discretion to defer or delay indictments. In this scenario, the element of "human emancipation" is materialized in the fact that both ICC officials and vulnerable groups in conflict zones are free of the mechanistic (and fatalistic) application of ICL based on traditional (nontranscended) instrumental rationalization.

There are also alternative suggestions for human emancipation, which reject the modernity discourse altogether. For example, Martin Albrow's theory of globalization states that "modernity holds its adherents in a double bind: it promises new futures and at the same time denies any possibility of an alternative to itself. As we know from interpersonal relations, double binds are designed to lock people in by involving them in irresolvable argument. Escape comes by refusing to accept the terms of discussion."[50] However, Albrow's thesis

---

[48] See Weber, *Theory of Social and Economic Organization*, at 338.
[49] *Implementing the Responsibility to Protect: Report of the Secretary-General*, UN doc. A/63/677, 12 January 2009, p. 11.
[50] Albrow, *Global Age*, at 1.

could be criticized by the fact that the replacement or reconceptualization of the modernity discourse would be an epistemological, but not ontological, move: it would provide merely a linguistic, and thus insufficient and superficial, quick fix to a problem that is fundamentally ontological – a problem that resides in the deep structures of late modern culture and society. As Weber points out, instrumental rationality is deeply embedded in the structures of modernization and globalization and cannot therefore be "undone" or banished by language games. Instead, instrumental rationality could be "worked on" – accommodated, transformed, adjusted, and transcended to new levels of analysis, for example, the holistic level of metanorms proposed here.

VI. BUREAUCRATIC METANORMS AS COLLISION NORMS AND TOOLS OF REFLEXIVE JURISPRUDENCE

The conception of "bureaucratic metanorms" developed here is similar to so-called collision rules in contemporary legal scholarship. Bureaucratic metanorms such as RtoP and collision norms share the same objective: to control and intervene in the clashes between normative orders, for example, between ICL and the humanitarian order, in those exceptional circumstances in which their mediation is absolutely necessary. Aidan Hehir aptly notes that "R2P constitutes no more than a restatement of existing international law."[51] RtoP is, indeed, premised on already well-established strands of international law, namely, human rights law, IHL, ICL, and refugee law. The real added value of RtoP cannot therefore be attributed to its capacity to create new norms but to its potential to mediate the relations among already existing normative orders.

Drawing upon Philippe Nonet and Philip Selznick's account, Stefan Oeter notes that collision rules should guarantee the minimum degree of mutual responsiveness among normative orders, sets, and units.[52] In concrete terms, such minimum responsiveness has both substantive and procedural implications: "In a *substantial* perspective, the new system of collision rules should provide for norms which force the various legalized policy sectors to a 'self-limitation' of its legal claim of applicability.... In a *procedural* perspective the new system of collision rules should create duties of cooperation."[53] To

---

[51] Aidan Hehir, 'The Responsibility to Protect and International Law', in Cunliffe (ed.), *Critical Perspectives*, 84–100, at 84.

[52] Stefan Oeter, *The Fragmented World of International Courts and Tribunals: Are There Chances to Form a Global Network of Courts?* paper presented at the 7th Pan-European Conference on IR organized by SGIR in Stockholm on 9–11 September 2010 (on file with the author).

[53] Ibid.

elaborate and apply Oeter's suggestions in relation to bureaucratic metanorms examined here, the use of RtoP as a collision norm would mean that autopoietic systems, including the Rome Statute system based on ICL, should exercise a degree of "self-limitation" to ensure the basic protection of civilians from mass atrocities, even by temporarily suspending the issuance of ICC indictments, if necessary.

However, bureaucratic metanorms differ from the collision rules envisaged in Oeter's account in that their applicability extends far beyond legal systems: they are not limited to international law and its subdisciplines but cover the plurality of all normative orders in global governance, including humanitarian, diplomatic, and military ones. All of these systems should exercise self-limitation under the overall normative umbrella of RtoP. For the ICC, the self-limitation required by RtoP means that the Court can continue business as usual in normal circumstances, maximizing the number of issued indictments and other accountability measures,[54] but in those *exceptional* circumstances in which ICC officials or experts of crisis management can foresee supreme humanitarian emergencies unfold as a result of the accountability measures to be initiated by the ICC, the Court should, on its own initiative, defer or delay them until other mechanisms of global crisis management have been put into use to minimize the risks involved in the implementation of the accountability measures. In the cases of Darfur and Uganda, the use of RtoP would have meant the deferral or "rescheduling" of the issuance of the ICC indictments, or the application of other precautionary measures such as sealed indictments, until the safety of civilians would have been ensured.

Bureaucratic metanorms, like collision norms, are designed to ensure the mutual reflectivity and responsiveness of normative orders. The expression "reflexive jurisprudence" has already been applied in the previous literature of legal studies, in which the concept refers to the management of the plurality of functionally differentiated regimes and normative orders. According to Olav Schram Stokke, "reflexive judicialization" means "regime interplay management," which aims to "prevent, encourage, or shape the way one regime affects problem solving under another."[55] The term also intimates Giddens's notion regarding the need for "reflexive self-identity"[56] in modernity. In terms of the Rome Statute system, the idea of reflexive jurisprudence encourages officials working for international courts and tribunals to reflect

---

[54] *Implementing the Responsibility to Protect: Report of the Secretary-General*, UN doc. A/63/677, 12 January 2009, pp. 11–12.
[55] Olav Schram Stokke, *The Interplay of International Regimes: Putting Effectiveness Theory to Work* (Oslo: Fridtjof Nansen Institute, 2001), at 11.
[56] Giddens, *Consequences of Modernity*, at 150.

on their actions in relation to a plurality of normative orders, including the humanitarian, diplomatic, and military ones – not international law alone. Legal experts and practitioners should even reflect on the requirements of RtoP in their daily work.

David Tolbert and Marieke Wierda's stock-taking account of the ICC's work appears a viable starting point for the analysis of reflexive jurisdiction in the ICC's conduct. Tolbert and Wierda observe that in the past eight years since the entering into effect of the Rome Statute system the primary focus of the ICC has not been on whether to enforce justice, but how.[57] Tolbert and Wierda's notion implies that the adoption of reflexive jurisdiction in the ICC's conduct, including the reflection on RtoP in its legal proceedings and other accountability measures, would not lead to distorted adjudications or to the undermining of the ICC's legal rationality, which is to indict and punish the perpetrators of mass atrocity crimes. Quite the opposite, reflexive jurisdiction and the referral to RtoP would help the ICC to manage the side effects of its accountability mechanisms, which, in turn, would enhance its legitimacy in the long run.

Tolbert and Wierda outline some concrete recommendations for the exercise of reflexive jurisdiction in the ICC's conduct:

> In exercising this responsibility [for seeking an arrest warrant], the Prosecutor does have discretion and leeway, particularly regarding timing. Some of these decisions are strategic, such as the timing of a request, so as to make an arrest more likely, perhaps through the use of a sealed indictment. *Another appropriate matter that legitimately can affect a prosecutor's timing of such a request is the safety and security of civilians, particularly victims.* While the latter is not reflected in the Rome Statute, it is an appropriate consideration of the Prosecutor to take into account in the exercise of his or her discretion.[58]

Tolbert and Wierda's suggestions concern the discretion of the ICC on the most appropriate *way* in which the ICC can exercise its mandate, for example, how best to implement accountability measures, not *whether* to do so. Tolbert and Wierda argue that the protection of civilians is a legitimate concern for the ICC, and the timing and method of the issuance of indictments should be determined in a way that would not harm civilians in conflict zones. In precisely the same way, the adoption of the bureaucratic metanorm of RtoP by the ICC would not be incommensurable with the legal duties assigned to the Court by the Rome Statute, and RtoP would necessitate that the Court reflect on the legitimate objective of the protection of civilians and modify its

---

[57] Tolbert and Wierda, *Stocktaking: Peace and Justice*, at 1.
[58] Ibid., at 4. Emphasis added by author.

actions accordingly. The ICC can, if necessary, defer or delay the initiation of its investigations or prosecutions in order to protect civilians from mass atrocity. The "deferral" could mean the ICC's own decision to consider the most appropriate time for launching its proceedings, or the deferral under article 16 of the Rome Statute. In the latter scenario, the UN Security Council decides to defer the referral of any particular situation on its agenda to the ICC, for example, for humanitarian reasons.

VII. NORMATIVE PRECONDITIONS FOR THE DOMESTICATION OF RTOP IN THE ICC'S PROCEDURES

The idea developed here is that the ICC could implement RtoP concerns first and foremost in the office of the prosecutor of the ICC. That is because the prosecutor is situated on the critical dividing line between the internal realm of the ICC, which is most heavily affected by autopoietic logic and instrumental rationality, and the external realm of global politics in which the ICC itself is situated. The Pre-Trial, Trial and Appeals Chambers of the ICC are "locked" in the internal realm of the Court and its bureaucratic culture – the Weberian "iron cage." These organs are bound to adopt the purely judicial logic, which is – for good reasons – unreflective on the outside realm of global security politics. Indeed, it would be unfair and counterintuitive to require the ICC trial chambers to consider all potential social ills pertaining to global politics and to predict all possible eventualities arising from the legal decisions it issues. These include the *possible* detrimental impacts of the ICC's warrant of arrest against Bashir on the humanitarian situation in Darfur. Figure 9.1 below demonstrates that the UN Security Council has by far the best chances of implementing RtoP, which would limit and manage the accountability measures of the Rome Statute system with a view to their potential side-effects on the humanitarian situation in target states, while the hands of the ICC Prosecutor – let alone judges – are more tied by the Weberian iron cage of the ICC.

It is most beneficial not only for the ICC but for global society as a whole that the judges of the ICC Trial Chambers close their eyes to the surrounding political and moral environment and blindly pursue their legal rationality. Erkki Kourula, who worked as the presiding judge of the ICC Pre-Trial Chamber at the time of the Bashir case, aptly noted to the author that the ICC would, in fact, have committed the fallacy of "hyperrationality" if it had intentionally chosen not to press charges against Bashir and other suspected criminals on the basis of *speculation* on the hypothetical effects of its decisions on humanitarian situations, ignoring the *legally valid evidence and reasoning* that

Law versus Bureaucratic Culture

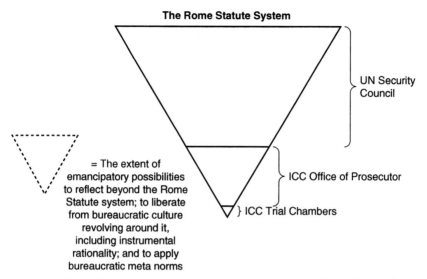

Figure 9.1. Possibilities of emancipation from the bureaucratic culture of the Rome Statute system.

necessitated that the ICC press charges.[59] If the officials of the ICC allowed emotions and speculations on future contingencies to affect their decisions, they would simultaneously compromise their rational-legal authority and possibly even make legally erroneous adjudications, which, in turn, would further undermine the fairness, equality, and legitimacy of ICL.

In sum, it is the office of the prosecutor of the ICC, not the Pre-Trial, Trial, or Appeals Chamber, that has a fair (or at least theoretical) chance of applying RtoP, for it is the only organ in the ICC that can legitimately reflect on wider moral issues pertaining to the potential consequences of the Court's decisions on other sectors of global governance. Once a decision by the prosecutor has been made to adopt a case, it will automatically be followed by mechanistic legal processes based on the autopoietic juridical logic, which cannot – and should not – be halted or interfered with. The following concluding analysis will explain in more detail how the office of the prosecutor could domesticate RtoP.

When asked by the author whether RtoP could be referred to in any official document of the ICC, such as legal decisions or at least the ICC's explanations of its decisions given to the public, Kourula replied to the author that possibilities for such incorporations are limited in terms of the substance of

---

[59] Personal communication with Erkki Kourula on 19 August 2010.

ICC decisions.[60] Kourula's argument was premised on the fact that article 21 of the Rome Statute regarding the applicable law of the ICC restricts the basis of ICC deliberations to the established norms and principles of international law. Article 21 thus excludes from the ICC's remit those normative arrangements that have no direct legally binding force, and RtoP seems to constitute precisely that kind of arrangement. RtoP was approved by more than 150 heads of state and government at the UN World Summit in 2005 and has therefore substantial procedural legitimacy, but it is not incorporated in any legally binding international convention as such. The relevance of RtoP is related more to its legitimacy than to legality.

On the other hand, Kourula also pointed out that according to article 21(3) of the Rome Statute the application and interpretation of law must be consistent with internationally recognized human rights. On the basis of this legal provision, RtoP might theoretically be taken into consideration in the ICC's deliberations and application of law on account of its status as a widely accepted standard of human rights promotion. Nevertheless, RtoP as such does not explicitly constitute "internationally recognized human rights" as referred to in the article.

Another provision of the Rome Statute that potentially provides legal grounds for the inclusion of RtoP in the ICC's deliberations is article 53(1) concerning the initiation of investigation, which states that the ICC prosecutor can drop a case if there are substantial reasons to believe that an investigation would not serve the interests of justice, considering the gravity of the crime and the interests of victims. The expression "interests of justice" reveals the autopoietic logic of the Rome Statute system: moral considerations and norm conflicts between legal and moral norms per se do not warrant the limitation of accountability measures by the ICC. Instead, such self-limitation is permitted only when accountability measures are expected to be counterproductive to the Rome Statute system in the long run. The Policy Paper on the Interests of Justice drafted by the ICC Office of the Prosecutor confirms this assessment:

> The concept of the interests of justice established in the Statute, while necessarily broader than criminal justice in a narrow sense, must be interpreted in accordance with the objects and purposes of the Statute. Hence, it should not be conceived of so broadly as to embrace all issues related to peace and security.[61]

[60] Ibid.
[61] International Criminal Court, Office of the Prosecutor, 'The Interests of Justice', Policy Paper on the Interests of Justice, ICC-OTP-2007, September 2007, at 8. I am indebted to Ville Komulainen for drawing my attention to this policy document.

The previous sections of this chapter have demonstrated that the interests of ICL or the Rome Statute System would not be served if they generated extreme humanitarian emergencies as a side effect of their accountability measures. These would in fact severely undermine the legitimacy of the Rome Statute system and ICL in the long run. Thus, RtoP – which aims to prevent supreme humanitarian emergencies – actually constitutes a continuum and extension to ICL. Since RtoP serves the interests of the Rome Statute system and ICL, it could be adopted by the ICC. In sum, the legal framework of the ICC, including the Rome Statute, neither prescribes that RtoP *should* be applied in the ICC's deliberations nor *precludes* its use in the ICC's deliberations. In fact, article 53(1) provides some legal basis for the incorporation of RtoP in the ICC's deliberations and accountability measures.

However, the working of the ICC has thus far been strongly affected by bureaucratic culture, which entails instrumental rationality and functional differentiation. This is reflected by the fact that the ICC Office of the Prosecutor has never actually applied the "interests of justice" clause of the Rome Statute: it has not yet made a decision not to investigate or not to proceed with a prosecution on the grounds that doing so would not serve the interests of justice – not once.[62] Although the relevant *legal norms*, particularly article 53(1) of the Rome Statute, would allow the ICC to limit its proceedings on the basis of the expected side effects of ICC accountability measures on humanitarian conditions in target states, the *bureaucratic culture* of the ICC has nevertheless driven the Court to maximize the extent to which it pursues those accountability measures – unreflectively. The ICC's own policy paper cited earlier, which is essentially a product of the bureaucratic culture of the ICC, clearly reflects its attempt to maximize its accountability measures.

There is, however, some basis upon which the ICC could build a more reflective approach. The ICC's policy paper, for example, states that the ICC investigations in the Democratic Republic of the Congo, Uganda, and Darfur required the Court to reflect on whether the interests of justice were served before the warrants of arrest and summonses were initiated.[63] As the policy document concludes, "considerations about potential adverse impact on security and crime prevention may be addressed by managing the profile of investigative activities and working with partners to ensure all possible security measures are in place, as was the case in Uganda."[64]

---

[62] Ibid., at 4.
[63] Ibid.
[64] Ibid., at 9.

VIII. CONCLUSIONS

This chapter has argued that the first step in analyzing the nexus between bureaucratic and legal norms is the analytical distinction between bureaucratic culture and bureaucratic norms. On the positive side, both legal and bureaucratic norms embody the Weberian rational-legal authority and can thus potentially complement, empower, and enforce one another, guarding RoL against realpolitik. On the negative side, bureaucratic culture has the ubiquitous tendency to undermine international law by generating uncontrolled, and often unnecessary, competition among bureaucracies and their respective normative orders. As a result, the legitimacy of international law can be diminished in the long run.

The effects of bureaucratic culture are not solely negative. Bureaucratic culture in the global age opens up the dynamics of normative pluralism by putting different normative orders – including legal ones – in dynamic interaction. The picture of normative pluralism would certainly remain static without taking into consideration the crucial role played by bureaucratic culture. Nevertheless, the two main drivers of bureaucratic culture, namely, instrumental rationality and functional differentiation, tend to transform international bureaucracies into "late modern juggernauts," to paraphrase Anthony Giddens's definition here. As for the Rome Statute system, the "juggernaut" rolls on legal and bureaucratic norms (the Rome Statute and the ICC's own bureaucratic standards). To elaborate the metaphor further, instrumental rationality represents the motor of that juggernaut, while functional differentiation constitutes its steering wheel.

The Rome Statute system, like any other autopoietic system, is "steamed" by instrumental rationality and functional differentiation. The former generates energetic, but unreflective, pursuit of criminal law, while the latter refers to closed and self-contained systems of legal rationality. Consequently, the ICC is sometimes pathologically unreflective on information emanating from other normative orders, fails to react to that information, and does not adjust its operations accordingly. The ICC can even unintentionally create humanitarian emergencies, as demonstrated by the looming humanitarian emergency in Darfur in the aftermath of the issuance of the ICC indictment against Bashir in March 2009. These humanitarian crises and other norm conflicts ensuing from the operations of the Rome Statute system tend to undermine its legitimacy and reveal tensions between law and morality.

As a solution, this chapter has proposed the application of *bureaucratic metanorms*. In concrete terms, that "emancipatory vision" envisages the domestication of RtoP in the Rome Statute system. As for the first policy recommendation, the ICC could increasingly apply preliminary inquiries as a means of conflict prevention. The primary objective of RtoP is precisely conflict prevention, which presents a much more cost-effective way of conflict management than reaction, particularly military intervention.[65] Second, RtoP could *in exceptional circumstances* exercise self-limitation and restrain the activation of ICL, for example, by deferring the issuance of international warrants of arrest. This emancipatory vision is different from Mahmood Mamdani's more radical suggestion, according to which the punitive measures of international courts and tribunals should be replaced with alternative means of justice altogether: "The search for survivor's justice needs to be two-pronged: prioritize peace over punishment; and explore forms of justice – not criminal but political and social – which will make reconciliation durable."[66] Contra Mamdani, it is viewed here that the solution resides in reflective *self-limitation*, not reduction or complete elimination, of the ICC's accountability measures. For example, the deferral of accountability measures of ICL for pressing humanitarian causes would minimize, but not completely eliminate, the detrimental side effects of the practice of ICL such as those seen in Darfur, Uganda, and Libya.

---

[65] Bellamy, *Responsibility to Protect*, at 4.
[66] Mamdani, 'Responsibility to Protect or Right to Punish?' at 135.

10 Law versus Religion: State Law and Religious Norms

Rubya Mehdi

I. INTRODUCTION

This chapter deals with the parallel existence of Muslim religious norms and state laws, with special reference to Denmark. The relationship between the normative order of Muslim religious norms, on the one hand, and secular state law, on the other, involves a number of different situations of normative pluralism. This chapter, however, will concentrate on one particular aspect in that relationship, namely, the tensions in family laws and specifically laws of marriage and divorce. The chapter will present five models through which the pattern of that relationship can be understood and analyzed.

In the struggle between religion and law the influence of religion was never totally abolished. This is more or less true of all societies, even in the global age. All religions entail normative orders, especially those relating to family matters. These have been reformed in all religions, but the orthodox or conservative "nucleus" of the norms has not disappeared. During the colonial period Islamic law was changed radically. Typically only Muslim family law was incorporated in legislation. All other branches of law were secularized and transmuted into modern state laws. However, in the postcolonial period some of the Muslim countries reincorporated Islamic laws in the criminal law.

The sources of religious normative orders include religious books, customs, and traditions. There is a lot of debate on whether state law and other normative orders are distinguishable and where the line should be drawn. In the case of Muslim religious laws, particularly family laws, it becomes more complicated to distinguish these norms as a normative order or law. That is because Islam does not strictly distinguish law from morality or from religious rituals and norms. Moreover, religious norms stem from the religion, which is supposed to be immutable, but at the same time it is changeable, as can be seen in religious reforms and changes throughout human history.

During the colonial period, Muslim religious normative orders came under the influence of the Western pattern of laws. Contrary to legal positivism and normative pluralism, *shariah* is a religious law and can be classified as natural law. It is considered by Muslims to be binding simply because it is divine. Muslim schools of law are supposed to reflect the will of God. However, its flexibility is a controversial issue among Muslims. It brings about two extreme reactions: those closer to the pluralism claim that challenges to the religious normative order can be met through the concept of *ijtihad* (interpretations in the light of changing circumstances), while the other group argues for the adoption of *taqlid*, that is, resistance to change.

II. MUSLIM MARRIAGES IN DENMARK IN THE OFFICIAL AND UNOFFICIAL SPHERES

This section will first analyze those situations and critical points in which religious normative sets and normative orders collide with state law. Second, it will analyze various consequences and problems these norm collisions and situations of normative pluralism generate. Muslim marriages and divorce practices in Denmark have been selected as a set of case studies to analyze the two questions.

In examining the law and religious normative orders we will look at the marriage as well as divorce patterns. Under Islamic law marriage is a civil contract. Therefore, it has the two essential elements of a contract, that is, offer and acceptance.[1] It requires that there should be two adult witnesses of good character (sane, adult, and reliable). In practice these are usually male witnesses, but theoretically this requirement is gender-neutral and faith-neutral.

In 2008 the Muslim Institute of London developed a model of a Muslim marriage contract, which has proved to be very useful. It would be beneficial to analyze and adopt it to encourage similar models through which gender equality in family matters can be ensured through a marriage contract. A great many problems in Denmark arise because a variety of individually designed marriage contracts are issued by different local imams.[2]

In most of the divorce cases, the vague nature of marriage contracts complicates the issues relating to a wife's right of divorce and economic dealings, for example, payment of *mahr*. The problem of limping marriages, which will

---

[1] Jamal J. Nasir, *The Islamic Law of Personal Status*, 2nd ed. (London: Graham and Trotman, 1990); Asaf A. A. Fyzee, *Outlines of Muhammadan Law* (Delhi: Oxford University Press, 1974).
[2] See the appendix in Rubya Mehdi (ed.), *Integration og retsudvikling* (Copenhagen: Jurist- og Økonomforbundets Forlag, 2007).

be discussed in the section on divorce to a greater extent, can also be resolved through inducing *talaq-i-tafwid*, that is, a woman's equal right of divorce delegated to her by her husband in the marriage contract.[3] This is the reason that in Muslim countries there are standard marriage contracts and now and then reforms are made in them.[4] Attention may be drawn to the fact that the practice of Muslim family laws in Europe generally involves a mixture of classical marriage laws in Islam, modern laws of the Muslim countries, and traditions and customs.[5]

Just as a marriage is considered in the traditional communities to constitute an arrangement not only between two people but also between the families, in the same way divorce is between the two families, and the whole of the family is involved in such processes. In Islam divorce is allowed but despised.[6] In spite of the fact that the younger generation is more open and liberal toward divorce, socially divorce is still a stigma. Sometimes a woman also has to face harassment from a husband who does not want to be divorced. If a woman asks for divorce it is taken as a threat to masculinity and honor.[7] Moreover, a woman may have to face all types of accusations of having loose character or being in love with another man or involved in adultery. Therefore, it may be difficult on the personal and psychological levels to divorce, because of emotional blackmail or social pressure.

Especially when the families have children divorce becomes more difficult in the normative sense.[8] However, this cannot be generalized because in many

[3] Rubya Mehdi, 'Facing the Enigma: *Talaq-e-tafweez* – a Need of Muslim Women in a Nordic Perspective', in Mehdi (ed.), *Integration*, 131–50.
[4] Abdullahi A. An-Na'im (ed.), *Islamic Family Law in the Changing World: A Global Resource Book* (London: Zed Books, 2002).
[5] Mehrdad Darvishpour, 'Intensified Gender Conflicts within Iranian Families in Sweden', (1999) 7 *Nora: Nordic Journal of Women's Studies*, 20–33; Eli Ferrari de Carli, *Religion, juss og rettigheter: Om skilsmisse, polygami og shari'a-råd* (Oslo: Institutt for samfunnsforskning, 2008), at 5; Marie-Claire Foblets, 'Marriage and Divorce in the New Moroccan Family Code: Implications for Moroccans Residing in Europe', in R. Mehdi, H. Petersen, E. R. Sand and G. R. Woodman (eds.), *Law and Religion in Multicultural Societies* (Copenhagen: DJØF Publishing Copenhagen, 2008), 145–76; Pascale Fournier, *Muslim Marriage in Western Courts – Lost in Transplantation* (Farnham, UK: Ashgate, 2010); Georges Fouron and Nina Glick Schiller, 'All in the Family: Gender, Transnational Migration, and the Nation State' (2001) 7, 4 *Identities*, 539–82.
[6] Mads Koudal, *Of All the Lawful Acts the Most Detestable to Allah Is Divorce – en kvalitativ analyse af muslimske kvinders ret til skilsmisse i krydsfeltet imellem islamisk ret og den danske familieret* (Copenhagen: University of Copenhagen, 2008).
[7] Lotte Kragh, *Kampen om anerkendelse, spillet om ære* (Copenhagen: Academic Books, 2010).
[8] T. M. Jesuloganathan, *Hellere gift 30 gange end at leve i et ulykkeligt ægteskab – Et kvalitativt studie af en skilsmisses betydning for førstegeneration somaliske kvinder i Danmark*. (Aalborg: Aalborg Universitet, 2010); Anika Liversage, 'Divorce among Turkish Immigrants in Denmark', in K. Charsley (ed.), *Transnational Marriage: New Perspectives from Europe and Beyond*

examples women also have the support of their parents when going through a divorce process. Moreover, with the development of education the situation is changing and young Muslim women are becoming more open to divorce in comparison to the earlier generations.[9] One set of factors that make it difficult for a woman to end an unwanted relationship are the consequences of divorce under the Danish law of migration. Those Muslim women who have entered Denmark under the law of family reunion have to stay in bad relationships because of the fear of being deported from Denmark.[10]

According to the Islamic law a marital bond that does not function anymore should be terminated to prevent further problems.[11] However, before the breakup, Islam also prescribes mediation between the husband and wife.[12] Under the classical Muslim law *talaq* is a power available exclusively to a husband; however, he can delegate the power to pronounce *talaq* to his wife, who then can use this right if she wants to free herself from the marriage bond.[13] Moreover, a wife can also initiate divorce but only with the help of a *qadi* (Muslim judge) or through court procedures. *Khul* is a popular procedure. If a husband agrees, *khul* can be effected without the intervention of a court, but if he does not agree, a court can pass a decree of *khul*. In any case the wife has to forgo her *mahr*. *Khul* is an agreement to allow the dissolution of marriage if the wife seeks it by paying an amount of money in compensation or as consideration to her husband.

However, the family law reforms in the Muslim countries have changed the extrajudicial regulations of Muslim divorce to judicial intervention. The

---

(London: Routledge, 2011); Anika Liversage, 'Gender, Conflict and Subordination within the Household – Turkish Migrant Marriage and Divorce in Denmark', *Journal of Ethnic and Migration Studies* (forthcoming).

[9] Rubya Mehdi and Jørgen S. Nielsen, 'Islam and Law in the Nordic Countries in the 21st Century Challenges and New Perspectives', in L. Christoffersen, K. å Modeer and S. Andersen (eds.), *Law and Religion in the 21st Century – Nordic Perspectives* (Copenhagen: DJØF Publishing, 2010).

[10] Garbi Schmidt, Brian Krogh Graversen, Vibeke Jakobsen, Tina Gudrun Jensen and Anika Liversage, *Ændrede familiesammenføringsregler – hvad har de nye regler betydet for pardannelsesmønstret blandt etniske minoriteter?* (Copenhagen: SFI – Danish National Centre for Social Research, 2009); Amnesty International, *Valget mellem vold og udvisning – dilemmaet for voldsramte familiesammenførte kvinder i Danmark* (Copenhagen: Amnesty International, 2006).

[11] Abdur Rahman I. Doi, *Sharia: The Islamic Law* (London: Ta Ha, 1984); Berit S. Thorbjørnsrud, *Evig din? Ekteskaps- og samlivstradisjoner i det flerreligiøse Norge* (Oslo: Abstrakt Forlag AS, 2005).

[12] Amr Abdalla, 'Principles of Islamic Interpersonal Conflict Intervention: A Search within Islam and Western Literature', (2002) 15 *Journal of Law and Religion*.

[13] Doi, *Sharia: The Islamic Law*, at 169, 173; Sonia Nurin Sha-Kazemi, *Untying the Knot – Muslim Women, Divorce and Shariah* (London: Signal Press, 2011).

reforms generally include a reconciliation procedure, restrictions on men's free right of divorce, and recognition of more grounds of divorce for women. But still an element of discrimination between men and women in terms of their right of divorce is not completely eliminated.[14] Recently in Pakistan a discussion has been initiated on the issue of complete gender equality in matters of divorce, documented from the original sources in the Quran, which is very much opposed by the conservative parties and groups.[15]

III. MODELS OF RELATIONSHIP BETWEEN STATE LAWS AND MUSLIM LAWS OF MARRIAGES AND DIVORCES IN EUROPE: EXAMPLES FROM DENMARK

Following are empirical examples set out for analytical purposes to show the relationship of the state law with Muslim norms of marriages and divorces.[16] The classification of models was worked out and presented at conferences and was first published in an anthology in 2010.[17] The idea was developed by Gordon Woodman. These models consider ways in which the relationship of state law and religious normative order can be seen, namely, assimilation, continuing conflict, agglomeration, noninstitutionalization, and integration.[18]

A. Assimilation

One possible outcome of cultural diversity is called "unification"[19]: "This outcome means the end of legal pluralism: the condition of coexistence of two or more laws is replaced by a single law. Taking again the simple instance in which there are just two laws, Unification may come about through the demise

---

[14] Javaid Rehman, 'The Sharia, Islamic Family Laws and International Human Rights Law: Examining the Theory and Practice of Polygami and Talaq', (2007) 21 *International Journal of Law, Policy and the Family*, 108–27.

[15] Bilal Qureshi, 'Council of Islamic Ideology's Historic Recommendations on Talaq', in *Muslim Family Law Ordinance 1961: Review and Recommendations* (Council of Islamic Ideology, Government of Pakistan, 2009). Rubya Mehdi, Werner Menski and Jørgen S. Nielsen (eds.) *Interpreting Divorce Laws in Islam* (Copenhagen: DJØF Publishing, forthcoming).

[16] The relationship of law and religious normative orders in Denmark follows more or less the same pattern of problems as in other Western countries. See, for example, Samia Bano, 'Muslim Family Justice and Human Rights: The Experience of British Muslim Women', (2007) 2 *Journal of Comparative Law*, 38–67.

[17] Mehdi and Nielsen, 'Islam and Law', at 516–20.

[18] Gordon R. Woodman, 'The Possibilities of Co-existence of Religious Laws with Other Laws', in R. Mehdi, H. Petersen, E. R. Sand and G. R. Woodman (eds.), *Law and Religion in Multicultural Societies* (Copenhagen: DJØF Publishing, 2008).

[19] Ibid.

of one law and triumph of the other Law."[20] This model also entails a legal centralist standpoint. Applying this model in practice means that "Muslims should accept the existing secular laws as they are on the secular terms."[21] The "unification" or "assimilation" model of marriage and divorce is not very prevalent among the Muslims in Nordic countries and in Europe. It is therefore not a realistic model. It also entails problems, as explained later.

Danish Civil Marriage Only
The application of this model concretely means that Muslims may have only Danish civil marriage. If Danish civil marriage is not combined with Muslim *nikah*, this can give rise to both social and legal problems. The problem of control and strong social pressure among the Muslim community is obvious in both the country of migration and the country of origin. Besides social pressure for a *nikah* marriage one could also face legal problems in Muslim countries. With rising waves of extreme Islamist trends, at times there have been incidents in Pakistan in which young people have been stopped to show their *nikah nama* (marriage contract). If such a contract is not produced, dangerous legal complications can ensue: the couple might be arrested under the rules of *zina*.[22]

Another religious obligation worth noting here related to *nikah* marriages is that if a Muslim man or woman wants to marry a non-Muslim, there is an issue of conversion to Islam. It is not much of a problem for a Muslim man, as he can marry a non-Muslim woman who is one of the "people of the book," that is, Jews and Christians.[23] On the other hand, if a Muslim woman wants to marry a non-Muslim man, according to *shariah* interpretations he has to convert to Islam.[24] This also has consequences in the assimilation model as is shown with the help of an example that reveals how socially important it is for Muslims to have a Muslim marriage. A young woman from the Middle East had a civil marriage with an ethnic Danish man. She said:

> We have often thought about going through a Muslim marriage so that we are not caught up in any problem while visiting my home country.

---

[20] Ibid., at 38.
[21] Mehdi and Nielsen, 'Islam and Law', at 517–18.
[22] *Zina* is the offense of illicit sexual relations, i.e., sexual intercourse between persons who are not married to each other. This term also includes adultery, fornication, and prostitution. See Asma Jahangir, 'What the Protection of Women Act Does and What Is Left Undone', in *State of Human Rights in 2006 in Pakistan* (Lahore: Human Rights Commission of Pakistan, 2006); Mehdi and Nielsen, 'Islam and Law'.
[23] Doi, *Sharia: The Islamic Law*.
[24] Nasir, *Islamic Law of Personal Status*, at 27 and 69.

Besides I think my family – though they know that I am civil married in Denmark – want a Muslim ceremony which give them more satisfaction. What's wrong if for their satisfaction we just go through it? I feel that the blessings of my parents will come from heart if I also have a Muslim-marriage.

In another example a young Pakistani woman was married under the civil law to a young Danish Catholic man. She describes her situation:

When I decided to civil-marry my husband we were in love. But because he comes from a Catholic family there was no question of conversion to Islam. My parents were very upset they would not speak to me. They did not come to my civil marriage wedding ceremony – they did a kind of social boycott of me. They said that I was living in a *haram* (illegitimate or forbidden) relationship which means I was living in sin. I experienced the pain of their attitude with intensity when our first son was born. In fact my parents were more scared of the Pakistani community as they said "what face can we show them?" Usually when norms are broken people face social isolation within their own community.

Danish Civil Divorce Only

In context of the assimilation model, Danish civil law divorce alone should be sufficient, but on the condition that there should be a Danish civil marriage or a *nikah* marriage registered with civil administrations. Not all Muslim women think that after civil divorce Muslim divorce is necessary. There are various ways of arguing this stand. Moreover, according to one interpretation of Islam Muslims are advised to live according to the law of the land.[25] A young Pakistani woman who had both a civil and a *nikah* marriage, argued: "I am very much satisfied with my civil divorce. There is no mention in religion to register divorce with any institution. In Islam marriage is a contract and when it is ended and signed by the parties it is finished."

However, again only a limited number of Muslims are satisfied with this model. As demonstrated later, divorces – like marriages – are considered to be valid only when conducted in accordance with the Muslim customs and religious laws. The problem of "limping marriages" is well known: Muslim women after civil divorce still feel themselves married unless they also go through a Muslim divorce.[26]

---

[25] Tariq Ramadan, *Western Muslims and the Future of Islam* (Oxford University Press, 2007); Tariq Ramadan, *To Be a European Muslim* (Islamic Foundation, 1999).
[26] See Anika Liversage and Tina Gudrun Jensen, *Parallelle retsopfattelser i Danmark* (Copenhagen: SFI – Det Nationale Forskningscenter for Velfærd, 2011).

B. Continuing Conflict

Muslim *Nikah* Marriage Only

This section considers situations in which Muslim men and women choose to live in a *nikah* marriage in an unofficial sphere and do not consider it important that a civil marriage should be registered. *Nikah* marriage is performed to legalize sexual cohabitation. So this is the exact opposite of the previous model. First, the young Muslims who want to have only *nikah* marriages are those who want to live together in a boyfriend/girlfriend relationship. They are in the process of finding out whether they are compatible to live as a husband and wife in the long run. *Nikah* is performed to legitimize their sexual relationship and thus to satisfy their religious conscience.

The second group who have only the *nikah* marriages are those who do not think it necessary to register civil marriage. They have more confidence in the traditional bond of family relations. These are usually arranged marriages and may also entail an element of force. Men may react differently than women to this type of marriage. A man may think civil marriage is not important and nonregistration with the civil authorities keeps the possibility of a polygamous marriage open for him. Therefore, *nikah* marriages must be considered in relation to situational power and the positioning of women in family and marriage relationships. Saima Bano found out in her empirical investigation in the United Kingdom that "after the completion of the marriage ceremony once the consummation of the marriage had taken place some husbands had simply refused to register the marriage according to civil law."[27] From the perspective of the law of Denmark this is seen as living together, that is, not legal marriage.

Let us look at some concrete examples to illustrate this model in real life. A young couple explained:

> Both of us were students and came to Copenhagen to study. We loved each other and decided to move together in a rented room of my boyfriend. One of our Muslim friends said that we were living in sin. We wanted to legitimize our sexual relationship. We came across a Palestinian Imam who agreed to perform our *nikah*. We did not bother to register it with civil administration as we only wanted to legitimize our sexual relationship. We were not thinking about a long term relationship, therefore we did not inform our families about it.

---

[27] Samia Bano, 'Muslim Marriage and Mahr: The Experience of British Muslim Women', in Rubya Mehdi and Jorgen Nielsen (eds.), *Embedding Mahr in the European Legal System* (Copenhagen: DJØF Publishing, 2011), 263–88, at 268–9.

In another example a young Afghan woman who married unofficially in a traditional Afghan way in Denmark sought out counseling, accompanied by her father. She described her situation like this:

> My family arranged my marriage to a young Afghan man. I also liked him at that time. We had a big traditional wedding party where all our family members and friends and their families were invited. We belong to a Shia sect of Islam. In our family traditions are more important for us. My father employed a Shia Iranian Imam from Iran to perform a telephonic *nikah*. Later when my father was travelling to Iran he got hold of a copy of the marriage contract (*nikah nama*). There was a big marriage party held in a school hall, booked in Copenhagen, and all Afghan families we knew were invited and everybody knew that there was our wedding. Video film and photographs were made. A *mahr* of hundred thousand kroner was fixed.

> We are Palestinian and found each other and shortly after we got engaged by the family. After six months we wanted to get married and the family arranged a traditional wedding party. We were married only in *nikah* marriage and had two daughters. When the daughters were four and two years, after five years of our marriage, we wanted to regularize our marriage and then we registered our marriage at the town hall in Copenhagen.

Muslim *Talaq* Only

In the cases in which only *nikah* marriage is performed to legalize sexual cohabitation young people may face problems related to *talaq*. They cannot have a divorce by the public administration (*statsforvaltningen*) because they are not considered married under Danish law. There is a possibility for a Muslim woman to have the right of *talaq* equal to that of the man inscribed in the marriage contract, but in the cases under discussion usually these are young people who are not aware of their rights, and marriage contracts formulated by the imams differ from one imam to another. Most of these do not mention the possibility of woman's equal right to divorce or *mubarat*, whereby dissolution of marriage occurs by mutual agreement with mutual waiving of financial obligations.

Some young people who want to have a boyfriend/girlfriend relationship enter into a marriage contract to legalize their relationship in accordance with the teachings of Islamic law. There seems to be an unspoken understanding between them that their relationship is just a boyfriend/girlfriend relationship to find out whether they are suitable for each other and want to live with each other on a permanent basis. But the lives of young Muslim women in this type of arrangement who have a bad relationship can become difficult. For example, if a young woman wants to have a divorce for one reason or another and the young Muslim husband refuses to divorce, misusing his traditionally assigned power to divorce, he can make the life of his wife miserable. He can also use violence and other methods to make her withdraw her initiation of *talaq*.

The following are examples of problems a woman may face when she wants to have Muslim *talaq* because she does not have the option of civil divorce as her marriage is not registered. The following example of an Afghan woman proceeds from the first example of marriage models, *nikah* marriage only.

> Later on our relationship did not work. He was also violent sometimes. I was very miserable and could not concentrate on my studies. I could not talk to anybody about my situation. I decided to move from the room he had rented and where we were living together. He did not want me to move. One of my friends helped me find another place for myself. Afterwards I asked him to give me a *talaq* which he refused. He was revengeful. Now I really do not know what to do.

The following example is of Muslim *nikah* marriage only.

> Our marriage lasted for four years during this time we were living together in a flat. A son was born (who was two years at the time of *talaq*). After Muslim *nikah* and especially after the birth of our son I persuaded my husband to register the marriage with Danish authorities which he evaded (kept putting off), saying that it was not important as "we have already fulfilled our religious duty which needs no registration." However, my differences with my husband became sharper. My father invited resourceful and influential people of the Afghan community in Copenhagen so that with the help of the community a reasonable settlement could be reached. A few times this worked very effectively as my husband asked for forgiveness and after that we continued married life again. There was a little change in his behavior though. After some time, my husband shifted to another flat not far from the place where I lived. And then I was surprised to discover that he was living in the flat with a new wife, whom he had brought from Afghanistan. When I learnt that my husband had married another woman from Afghanistan, I was in great shock and wanted to get divorce. The resourceful and influential people of the Afghan community in Copenhagen were called for a meeting again, this time to put pressure on my husband to divorce me and also pay *mahr*. It was not easy to get him around to come to the meeting but at last he came to the meeting and an Imam was there and before everybody my husband gave me *talaq* and also promised to pay *mahr* to me. My son continued to live with me, to which his father did not object and he has visitation right.[28] The support of my family and the community made this possible.

---

[28] This situation is in accordance with the Muslim law, in which a minor child stays in the custody of the mother.

They put their best efforts consistently in arranging meetings contacting relevant people of community for reaching this far. Without this support I would have been in much trouble as my marriage was not registered with the Danish authorities.

My parents arranged my marriage to my cousin who was living in UK. He was not willing to get married but after pressure from the parents he married me. A wedding party was arranged in Copenhagen. All marriage rituals were carried out. In a traditional way bride was taken away with the bridegroom to UK. The marriage was not registered in Denmark nor was it registered in UK. Not many days had passed before it was revealed that my husband was also married to another woman and this was the reason that he was refusing to register his marriage with me. As soon as I discovered this I was shocked and wanted to come back to Denmark and demand for *talaq*. Since my husband was also my first cousin there he was condemned for his act and pressurized by his parents as well as the family to divorce me. This is how I got a *talaq* now. I have been through very difficult time emotionally thinking that my husband told a lie and also economically I was fully dependent on my husband and in-laws. My parents were very much annoyed and therefore refused to demand dower or dowry from him. I am remarried to a young Pakistani man in Denmark now.

C. Agglomeration

This is the third model illustrating the relationship between state laws and religious normative orders. The pattern of Muslim marriages and divorces that can be classified under this model is the one in which people have both Danish civil marriage and Muslim *nikah* marriage. Agglomeration means "that conflict may be avoided, and there may be measures of recognition, but still the relationship between the laws is not fully ordered. ... This outcome may result in the peaceful coexistence of diverse cultures, although this is not fully stable because it contains no obstacles to changes in laws which bring it into conflict with the other."[29]

Danish Civil Marriage and Muslim *Nikah* Marriage

This is the most popular model of marriage among the Muslims in Europe, whereby double marriage registration occurs, both civil and *nikah* marriage. Usually in this type of double marriage ceremony, *nikah* marriage is considered real and civil marriage as an official obligation. Consequently, sexual relations only occur after *nikah* marriage. A young Pakistani woman who had

---

[29] Woodman, *Law and Religion in Multicultural Societies*, at 39.

consummated the marriage after *nikah* and before civil registration said: "we could not wait for the civil marriage. We waited for the *nikah* marriage and that was enough. Anyway who waits for the civil marriage?"

D. Danish Civil Divorce and Muslim Talaq

In the type of marriages in which husband and wife have had both Danish civil marriage and Muslim *nikah*, if they later want to have a divorce on the same pattern, that is, both Danish civil divorce and Muslim *talaq*, a woman could easily end up in a typical limping situation. In this type of situation the couple is divorced under one legal system (Danish civil divorce), but under another system (Muslim *talaq*) she is still married if the husband refuses to pronounce *talaq*.

As mentioned, not all Muslim women think that they need a Muslim *talaq* after a civil divorce. But I have met a number of women who were divorced under civil law and wanted to have Muslim *talaq* because they felt that the community had not recognized the civil divorce as proper enough to remarry. Some of these young women who are waiting to remarry become desperate to have Muslim *talaq*. They do not remarry without *talaq* as their status as properly divorced from their first husbands can be challenged. A commonly mentioned incident is a situation in which a young Pakistani woman was about to remarry, but during the wedding ceremony somebody reported that the bride was not properly divorced from her previous husband, and the wedding ceremony was stopped.

The following examples reveal the problem with more clarity.
Example 1:

> I was civil divorced and wanted to have a Muslim *talaq*. I contacted various Imams in Copenhagen but nobody was ready to give me a *talaq* paper. Some of them even offered to mediate between me and my ex-husband. I was very annoyed as I found them very male chauvinist. However after several months of constant struggle a *shia* Imam promised to give me *talaq* papers on the face of the Danish civil divorce.

Example 2:

> I got divorced from my husband through the Danish court because my ex-husband was not willing to be divorced. I asked him to divorce me in a Muslim way but he refused. My parents did not approve of having divorce from my husband. It should be underlined that a woman with children has more difficulty to initiate divorce because of the pressure to compromise for the sake of children. My life was all shattered, I was not able to take adequate

care of my children. Although a Danish court had issued a divorce decree I felt myself forced to continue living with my ex-husband with whom I felt divorced and I had to struggle to obtain a Muslim divorce. Therefore I contacted an Imam who refused to cooperate as he heard from my husband that I was a woman of bad character. This situation affected my repute adversely among family and my social network resulting that I was isolated and they avoided contacts with me and my children.

E. Noninstitutionalization

In Danish society nonmarried cohabitation is a social institution and usually not considered socially deviant. Therefore, Danish law provides family law rights to such partners while Islamic law has no such category. In Denmark nonmarried family arrangements became popular in the 1960s, as marriage patterns were said to assign women to a subordinate position to men. The welfare state has also played a part in taking up the supportive and protective function of the family.

Nonmarried Cohabiting Families or Living Together without Marriage: Neither Danish Civil Marriage nor Muslim *Nikah* Marriage

Among Muslim families in Denmark there is moral and social pressure to be married formally. Nevertheless, there are Muslims who live in a nonmarried cohabiting form of family. However, living together without marriage may not have similar consequences for Muslim young men and women. Young Muslim men live more frequently with ethnic Danish women without much of a problem. There could be social pressure on them but not as much as a Muslim woman would face. The reasons for this vary. In the case of a young man the family might not consider the relationship serious or long-lasting, while in the case of a woman it could be considered more serious because virginity is considered significant. A sense of honor also exists and later the woman may experience difficulty when marrying into a traditional relationship.

One can observe various types of situations in which young people with a Muslim background do decide to live together without marriage. One example is a situation in which young couples are in a relationship and wait for their parents' approval. They start living together, waiting for an appropriate moment to satisfy or convince their parents. They may also want to see whether they are compatible with each other before they marry. They are different from those young couples, described later, who contract *nikah* marriage before entering into sexual relations to satisfy their religious conscience.

A relatively extreme example is young Muslims who do not consider themselves as practicing Muslims or consider themselves as atheists and refuse to live in the institution of marriage because of existential reasons. There are also examples of young people who start living together but later, as a result of social or emotional pressures, make compromises to enter into a traditional marriage and thus also form part of a third type of model of Muslim marriages in this section.

Consider the following examples:

> I met a Danish guy and we were in love. We just wanted to live together. We did not want to be part of a marriage institution. There was lot of pressure from my parents. They were very annoyed. They were anxious what people of their community would say. Then our first child was born. My brother and sister convinced my parents that they should meet me, Peter and their first grandchild. When they met Peter and our first child they were very pleased. They started telling lies in the community that we were in fact married. Now we have got two children and my parents are very happy to have grandchildren and us. We usually do not discuss the issue of marriage at all.

A Pakistani young couple explained:

> We were living together in a smooth relationship without any institution of marriage. We believed we were in fact spiritually married to each other. We wanted to have a child. We thought we may regularize our marriage as living together may be acceptable but a child born outside of the wedlock may be completely unacceptable for a traditional community. This was the biggest worry for us about our parents and also about the coming child whose status may also be discriminated (child born outside of the wedlock may face social discrimination and denied inheritance right according to Muslim law). We also had this emotional consideration. We went through *nikah*-marriage and photos were sent to the relatives in Pakistan. They were really very happy. And then we had our first daughter, after she was one year old we wanted to regularize our marriage even more, this time because of economic considerations. So we went to the town hall, our six months old daughter was with us, to register ourselves with the Danish civil administration.

F. Integration

Integration has been defined as a process that "creates a law which brings together, without totally obliterating, laws of different origin."[30] It differs from unification in that it entails the continuance of legal pluralism, but here, unlike in the cases of continuing conflict and agglomeration, it is an ordered

---

[30] Anthony N. Allot, 'What Is to Be Done with African Customary Law?' (1984) 28 *Journal of African Law*, 56–71.

pluralism, regulated by reasonably clear choice of law norms.[31] Obviously the only instance in a Western country where an attempt has been made officially to implement anything on these lines has been the controversial Arbitration Act 1991 of the province of Ontario, Canada. It regularized the processes of arbitration in commercial and family law. Implicit in this act was that family arbitration could be conducted on the basis of Islamic law, Jewish law, canon law, or aboriginal spirituality.[32] However, a number of associations, including Muslim women, human rights groups, and legal groups, have campaigned against the application of the act to personal status matters, and this dimension of the act is currently in suspension.[33]

IV. PROCESS OF CHANGE

Islamic law took its basic form in a society that was tribal in nature. During the period of colonization of the Muslim countries, family law was the sphere least affected by the colonial influence. Therefore, the Islamic laws of most Muslim countries today still reflect a patriarchal and hierarchical family structure.

However, attention should also be drawn to the reforms arising in the family laws of the Muslim countries. Those aspects of Muslim family laws that were always protected by conservatives and were difficult to affect, for example, issues of inheritance and divorce, are becoming controversial now. Globalization is presenting new challenges and Muslim countries are prone to make reforms in their family laws.[34]

In the period between 2003 and 2006 there was a clear trend of reforms in the Muslim family laws. There are noticeable trends that reflect a growing recognition of women's rights, including major reforms in Algeria, Egypt, Fiji, Malaysia, and Morocco, which for the first time adopted a codified law of personal status, the Moudauwana. The marriage institution is the key agent of socialization and cultural transmission from generation to generation. It has been cherished as a value in itself. In the traditional family structure, marriage is valued as a source of honor and prestige for the family. Divorce should occur only in very adverse situations, and therefore a stigma is attached to

---

[31] Woodman, 'The Possibilities of Co-existence'.
[32] Mehdi and Nielsen, 'Islam and Law', at 521.
[33] Natasha Bakht, 'Family Arbitration Using Sharia Law: Examining Ontario's Arbitration Act and Its Impact on Women', (2004) 1 *Muslim World Journal of Human Rights*, 1–24.
[34] Lawrence Rosen, *The Culture of Islam: Changing Aspects of Contemporary Muslim Life* (Chicago: University of Chicago Press, 2002). See also Mehdi, Menski and Nielsen (eds.) *Interpreting Divorce Laws*.

Law versus Religion

divorce. However, after a long period of migration and settlement the traditional concept of family is also affected.

The changed circumstances confront immigrants with many questions regarding their customs, traditions, and Islamic law. Customs and traditions are commonly mixed in with Islamic law. When young people find themselves stuck between two legal cultures there is a dire need to do something about it. Young people find themselves under constant stress to find their own identity between two cultures.[35]

Within their own culture young people obviously would look for those dimensions and patterns most suitable for them. One dimension is Sufism, which is more liberal and gives a universal message and corresponds with the social reality. Another dimension is that of *ijtihad*, which means to reach an understanding of Islamic law related to the new situations with the changing world, for example, in the Danish setting. This requires a new understanding of Islamic law. A third dimension could be militant Islam, which may not be very positive. A fourth dimension could be a total negation of Islamic law and persistence to achieve a completely secularized form of a Muslim person.[36]

The way religious education is carried out also plays an important part in the changing process of development for young people in Denmark. The formal education of Islam traditionally consists of reading the Quran in Arabic without understanding the meaning of it. This usually does not satisfy young Muslims who are raised in the Danish institutions and schools. They have many questions concerning Islam and Islamic law that their parents are not acquainted with, and they are not in a position to satisfy all the curiosity of their children about religion and law. It is important to understand the dynamic of change in family matters and relationships.[37] This will help policy makers not only to understand how to make reforms but also to solve problems and to do future planning. However, the process of change in the customary sphere can dawdle, and it can take generations to replace a custom. This prolonged and painstaking process at times makes people suffer under those customs that are not compatible with new situations. One factor that slows the pace of change could be that already established ideas are not easy to change.

---

[35] Prakash Shah and Werner F. Menski, *Migration Diasporas and Legal Systems in Europe* (Oxford, UK: Cavendish, 2006).
[36] Mehdi and Nielsen, 'Islam and Law', at 516–20.
[37] Mogens Nygaard Christoffersen, *Familiens udvikling i det 20.århundrede – demografiske strukturer og processer* (Copenhagen: Socialforskningsinstituttet, 2004); Sofie Danneskiold-Samøe, Yvonne Mørck and Bo Wagner Sørensen, *"Familien betyder alt". Vold mod kvinder i etniske minoritetsfamilier* (Copenhagen: Forlaget Frydenlund, 2011).

On the other hand, change is strongly demanded in response to new situations facing young people. Young people suffer from customary laws that do not correspond to their situation and their upbringing in Danish society. They may be pulled in opposite directions by different normative orders and become victims of dilemmas and crises not easily resolvable in the existing legal systems. The response to the process of change may also differ from one group to another. Young people are often more open to and flexible about change, while older people find it harder. A person's attitude toward change also partly depends on whether migration has taken place from an urban or rural setting.

V. RECOMMENDATIONS

Young people should be educated to understand Islam and Muslim family laws in a more liberal and open way. New interpretations should seek gender equality and other universal human rights. A standard Muslim marriage contract should also be made in accordance with human rights standards and gender equality. It is important that the legal profession take the responsibility of acquiring expertise in Islamic law so that it can help young people to resolve problems in which they are entangled between the two systems.

Therefore, it would not be recommended that imams become engaged in family law matters. Traditionally the function of imams in Muslim countries is to perform religious rituals; they are not trained to resolve legal problems. Rather, legal professionals should be equipped with tools by which they can solve already existing problems, and policies should be developed in the official sphere to prevent potential problems.

11 Global Capital Markets and Financial Reporting: International Regulation but National Application?

Pontus Troberg

I. INTRODUCTION

International barriers to trade have been considerably lowered during the last twenty years. The same holds for barriers to capital flows across national boundaries. Currency restrictions have largely been lifted, thus making it possible for capital to flow freely from one country to another. Consequently, investors are not nationally bound anymore but can freely invest anywhere they like using the whole world as their playing field. Thus they try to maximize their return on investment on a global basis, not on a national basis. A prerequisite for being able to use these enlarged global opportunities is that the investors are able to read the financial information provided by the investment objects (enterprises) to the market. In order to make global capital allocation effective and enhance international prosperity, common standards for financial reporting are needed. Such harmonization tools are provided through the International Financial Reporting Standards (IFRS), which have the objective to provide relevant and reliable financial information to readers of financial reports. Because the IFRS standards are argued largely to be principles-based (judgment-based), the question remains how similar the actual applications of the reporting standards between countries and enterprises are and to what extent these applications are affected by local practice and culture. Is normative pluralism present, and, if so, to what extent? How far can the actual application of an accounting standard be from the letter of the standard and who decides on what constitutes an acceptable deviation?

This chapter aims to discuss the relationship between financial reporting standards and legal rules but does so with a twist. It transpires that the main tension is not so much between international law and international nonlaw, if only because there is little or no international law properly so-called on the topic. Rather, the main tension that exists is a tension between international standards and national laws. Therewith, financial reporting engages with normative pluralism in a different way than most of the other chapters in this volume, adding depth to the very notion of normative pluralism.

II. HISTORICAL BACKGROUND

The presumption is that effective global capital markets will facilitate doing business across national boundaries, which in turn will promote growth of national economies, thus creating international wealth. In order to achieve global capital markets we need a common financial language in the same way as English is the business language of the world. During the last twenty years major efforts have been made to find this common financial language. Various factors of varying strength have affected national financial reporting practices and thus have formed obstacles to international harmonization. Significant institutional factors that have influenced financial reporting practices are[1]

- Providers of finance
- Tax system
- Role of accountancy profession
- Legal system

The Industrial Revolution in Britain laid the foundation of "modern" business. Prior to the Industrial Revolution, trade was primarily conducted nationally in the form of small family companies without any significant external financing. The Industrial Revolution led to growth and the question for the enterprises was how to finance their growth. In Britain, both (shareholders') equity capital and loan capital markets were developed. The development of equity capital markets meant the introduction of owners outside the traditional family sphere. In addition, business enterprises started to be managed more and more by professional managers and less and less by family members. A prerequisite for obtaining external financing was to inform potential new owners about the performance of the business. The portrayed development laid the foundation for modern financial reporting, the objective of which is to give a true and fair view (present fairly) of the financial position and results (performance) of operations of the business enterprise. If investors perceive that they are not receiving reliable information about the enterprise, they are not going to invest in it.

---

[1] Christopher Nobes and Robert Parker, *Comparative International Accounting*, 11th ed. (London: Financial Times Prentice Hall, 2010), at 28–41.

Continental Europe and Japan experienced an evolution different from that of the Anglo-Saxon countries in that the increased financing needs were not satisfied in the form of equity capital but primarily by borrowing from banks or banking houses. Predecessors to modern banks were banking houses like Rothschildt. As a consequence the debt-to-equity ratio was very high (unfavorable) in Germany and many other Continental European countries in comparison to the United States and Great Britain. The last two countries are still in their own league with respect to the sizes of capital markets as measured in the form of market capitalization of listed companies.

When banks constituted the primary sources of financing for most Continental European enterprises, they usually had their own representation on the board of the enterprises. Consequently, the banks possessed insider information regarding the financial development of the enterprise and thus had no real incentive to develop external financial reporting because such reporting would have benefited competitor banks and other interest groups rather than the banks themselves. The power of the banks extended even to limiting dividend payments (stipulated in law) so as to ensure that sufficient funds were retained in the enterprise in order to protect creditors.

The government influence on accounting reporting has in many countries been extensive through taxation. The objective of financial reporting in Japan and Continental Europe has traditionally been to minimize taxes rather than to give a true and fair view of the financial position and results of company operations. The strong link between financial reporting and taxation is typically found in countries that do not have an explicit investor approach in their financial reporting orientation. Enterprises have been using depreciation charges and provisions for the specific purpose of tax minimization. In the United States and Great Britain (also the Netherlands) the link between taxable income and accounting income is much weaker than in the Continental European countries and Japan. Separate accounts are filed for tax purposes.

The Industrial Revolution also laid the basis for the auditing (accounting) profession of today. Owners, separated from the daily operations of the enterprise, can neither follow on site the development of the enterprise nor necessarily judge for themselves the reliability of the financial information provided. By using their knowledge and expertise auditors add (but do not guarantee) credibility to the financial reports. The auditors' firsthand responsibility is to the owners, who have formally employed them. Of course, the audit report is also valuable to other interest groups. The relationships among owners, management, and the auditor are illustrated in Figure 11.1.[2]

---

[2] See Pontus Troberg, *IFRS and US GAAP: A Finnish Perspective* (Helsinki: Talentum, 2007), at 21.

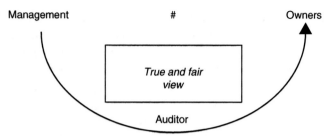

Figure 11.1. The relationships among owners, management, and the auditor.

The auditing profession has had a strong impact on financial reporting in all Anglo-Saxon countries. The influence of the profession was so strong that, in practice, it set the accounting and reporting standards in the United States (until the 1970s) and Great Britain for a long time (until the 1980s).

The advantage of the described system is that financial reporting is in the hands of highly qualified professionals. This implies, however, that the rest of society has a limited possibility of affecting accounting rules. Today, other interest groups such as preparers of financial statements, financial analysts, and accounting professors are also involved in the accounting standard-setting process in the Anglo-Saxon countries. The representatives of the interest groups mentioned are financial reporting experts; thus standard setting still is primarily retained in the hands of professionals. The traditional process in Continental Europe had a more political (and democratic) orientation in that financial reporting took the form of (accounting) laws prepared by the relevant Ministry (of Economy/Finance/Trade) in question, after hearing different interest groups, many of which were not financial reporting experts, and finally approved by parliament.

The Anglo-Saxon legal system is a common law system, while the Continental European legal system is a code law system. The common law system originated in England and is developed from case law. Such a legal system is developed case by case and does not prescribe general rules that can be applied to several cases. Accounting rules in the Anglo-Saxon countries are not a part of law, but accounting regulation is in the hands of professional organizations of the private sector that set the accounting standards. Company law in these countries is kept to a minimum. The code law system originated in Roman law and is characterized by a wide set of rules that try to give guidance in all situations. In code law countries, the company law is typically very detailed, and accounting rules are often embodied in the company law, or accounting law. Accounting regulation is in the hands of the government. In a common law system, the threshold for suing is generally lower than in code law countries and will often lead to a large number of cases, each of which is to be decided separately. In a code law system, a potential violation of a specific law paragraph is normally assumed for a plaintiff to sue an enterprise. An enterprise runs a much higher risk for being sued for misleading financial reporting in the United States than in Continental Europe.

With the liberalization of the capital markets in the mid-1980s, the European and Japanese business cultures and financial reporting practices collided with the American business culture and reporting practices. International trade, picking up its pace in the 1990s, enforced the collision, and consequently the need to find harmonized financial reporting practices started to become most pertinent. The Continental European and Japanese business cultures and especially financial reporting practices have clearly moved in the direction of those of the United States. The most important international accounting standard setters are the International Accounting Standards Board (IASB) and the American Financial Accounting Standards Board (FASB). Although significant differences can still be found between the International Financial Reporting Standards (IFRS) of the IASB and the corresponding American standards (Statement of Financial Accounting Standards, SFAS) issued by FASB, the two sets of standards are largely developing in a similar direction because IASB and FASB are currently working closely together in order to enhance international harmonization.

III. ACCOUNTING LAWS VERSUS ACCOUNTING STANDARDS

A fundamental question is why international accounting regulation today is carried out in the form of accounting standards and not accounting (or company) laws. The explanation for this can be derived from the development of the Anglo-Saxon capital markets and the following factors related thereto:

- The size of the stock market and its importance for the economy
- the pace of stock market development and need for timely regulation
- the reliance on accounting expertise in financial reporting regulation

As has already been described, shareholders' equity financing has been of much greater importance in the Anglo-Saxon countries than in Continental European countries or Japan, where bank financing has played the major role. For growing enterprises and economies loan capital is not necessarily sufficiently available or even always desirable, and thus the creation of equity markets provides complementary or alternative sources of financing. The New York Stock Exchange, NASDAQ, and London Stock Exchange are the largest stock exchanges in the world, and their importance for the development of their respective countries' economies has been fundamental.³ However, in order to have functioning equity markets, timely financial reporting as well as trading rules have to be in place to instill confidence in the markets – or the markets will not work. In the twentieth century the pace of development of the Anglo-Saxon stock markets as well as the countries' economies (specifically the American) was high, but traditional lawmaking was necessarily not speedy enough for producing up-to-date accounting rules. In a European setting a typical way of making new accounting laws is that a Ministry (Economy/Finance/Trade) appoints a working party (committee) consisting of civil servants and some accounting experts with the mission to make a draft of new accounting legislation. Once the draft is finalized it is sent to so-called interest groups (employer organizations, employee organizations, tax authorities, stock exchange authorities, among others) for commenting. After the commenting round(s) adjustments to the draft are made and subsequently the draft is taken to parliament for deliberation and finally, if there is sufficient political backing, for final approval (by the parliament). This kind of process may take a long time (several years) and is not necessarily speedy enough to satisfy the needs of dynamic stock markets. In addition, representatives of different interest groups in society are involved in the lawmaking process and are thus affecting the final outcome of the accounting law although they do not generally possess in-depth accounting expertise.

By leaving accounting regulation in the hands of the accounting profession, sufficient accounting expertise is secured and a more speedy process is also possible. Prior to the creation of the FASB in the United States in 1973, the American Institute of Certified Public Accountants (AICPA) set the accounting rules through its body the Accounting Principles Board in form of so-called official Opinions. Similarly in Britain, the accounting profession through the Institute of Chartered Accountants in England and Wales (ICAEW) set the British rules in the form of so-called Statements of Standard Accounting Practice (SSAPs). The accounting profession has traditionally been and is playing a major role in securing the credibility of financial information in the economies of the Anglo-Saxon countries, as is evidenced by the huge number of qualified accountants in these countries as compared to other countries.⁴ However, both the American and British governments and securities market regulators wanted to have a more independent (from the accounting profession) accounting standard setting body, and thus the American FASB and

---

³ New York Stock Exchange, *Fact Book for 2000* (New York: April 2001).
⁴ John Flower with Gabi Ebbers, *Global Financial Reporting* (New York: Palgrave, 2002). Qualified accountants per million inhabitants: the United States 1,496, Great Britain and Ireland 3,540, Australia 6,243, Canada 6,229, France 235, Japan 98, and Germany 93.

British Accounting Standards Board (ASB) were set up. Still, the accounting expertise requirement is retained in these bodies because their members represent the preparers of financial statements (previous chief financial officers of listed companies), investors (senior financial analysts), auditors (previous partners of audit firms), and the accounting academia. Thus, government or political representation was kept out because from a capital market and especially stock market perspective it was deemed more desirable and more credible to have candidates selected to the accounting standard-setting bodies purely on the basis of their accounting competence and experience. IASB was formed in the same spirit backed up by the American securities market regulator the Securities and Exchange Commission (SEC), and thus country representation is not a relevant selection criterion for this body either.

IV. GLOBAL FINANCIAL REPORTING INFRASTRUCTURE

The American capital market oversight body (securities market regulator) the SEC has historically had a major influence on world capital market regulation and development because of the economic power of the United States and its early stock market creation. SEC has issued two major press releases addressing the premises for a functioning effective global financial reporting infrastructure. In 1996 SEC emphasized that a prerequisite for approving international accounting standards in the United States (in addition to American standards) is that these standards fulfill the following quality requirements:[5]

- The standards must include a core set of accounting pronouncements that constitute a comprehensive generally accepted basis of accounting;
- The standards should be of high quality – they must result in comparability and transparency, and they must provide for full disclosure; and
- The standards should be rigorously interpreted and applied.

In 2000 the SEC further elaborated on the acceptance of international accounting standards for U.S. markets as well as on the challenges facing the auditing profession and regulatory oversight bodies in creating global capital markets. SEC raised several questions. Can possible inconsistencies in the interpretations and applications of the standards be sufficiently reduced? What are the specific practice guidelines and quality controls accounting firms use to ensure full compliance with the accounting standards? Are the auditors subject to sufficient quality control requirements? Is there significant variation

---

[5] United States Securities and Exchange Commission, 'Three Key Elements for Acceptance of the IASC's Core Standards', SEC Press Release, 11 April 1996.

in the interpretation and application of international accounting standards permitted or required by different regulators? Is effective enforcement action taken against financial reporting violations and fraud?[6]

To summarize, a functioning global financial reporting infrastructure should have the following elements:

1. High-quality international accounting standards
2. Audit committees in each listed enterprise with major responsibility for the content of financial statements
3. High-quality international auditing standards
4. Quality control of auditing entailing both within audit firm quality inspection and quality control of auditors and audit firms by outside oversight body
5. Regulatory oversight of financial reporting as well as auditing

a. International Accounting Standards

As already discussed, high-quality international accounting standards are today represented by the IFRSs and US Generally Accepted Accounting Principles (GAAP), of which the former seems to gain more and more acceptance as the international financial reporting standards. Consequently, the International Accounting Standards Board and the American Financial Accounting Standards Board are the most important international accounting standard setters. The European Union has, on the other hand, lost its momentum in standard setting because no new accounting directive has emerged (only revisions) since the issuance of the fourth and seventh council directives.[7] The credibility of the fourth and seventh directives suffered from delays in incorporating the directives into the member countries' legislation. Another problem was caused by the fact that the directives were rather loose in nature, leaving a lot of room for variances in interpretation and allowing a member country rather free hands in the way the directives were incorporated into national law. The efforts to harmonize financial reporting within the EU have thus been insufficient. The EU has, however, retained its decision-making power over financial reporting within the EU, and thus the European Parliament and Council of Ministers approved the regulation in 2002 that IFRS (IAS) standards would become mandatory for EU listed companies by

---

[6] United States Securities and Exchange Commission, 'SEC Approves Concept Release on International Accounting Standards', SEC Concept Release, 16 February 2000.
[7] Council Directive 78/660/EEC of 25 July 1978 on the annual accounts of certain types of companies; Council Directive 83/349/EEC of 13 June 1983 on consolidated accounts.

2005.[8] An alternative approach would have been to allow or require the application of US GAAP, but this was politically impossible. Simultaneously with the IFRS introduction, the EU eliminated the inconsistencies between the fourth and seventh directives and the IFRS standards. It has also revised the eighth directive, which regulates auditing. The EU is trying to regain even more initiative in accounting standard setting through the European Financial Reporting Advisory Group (EFRAG), which was set up in 2001 and has Standards Advisory Council status in IASB. EFRAG provides endorsement advice to the European Commission prior to its approval of IFRS standards.

The objectives of the International Accounting Standards Board are

1. to develop in the public interest, a single set of high-quality, understandable and enforceable global accounting standards that require high quality, transparent, and comparable information in financial statements and other financial reporting to help participants in the various capital markets of the world and other users of the information to make economic decisions;
2. to promote the use and rigorous application of those standards; and
3. to work actively with national standards setters to bring about convergence of national accounting standards and IFRSs to high-quality solutions.

Financial statements shall present fairly the financial position, financial performance, and cash flows of an entity. An enterprise whose financial statements comply with IFRSs shall make an explicit and unreserved statement of such compliance. Financial statements are not complying with IFRSs unless they comply with all the requirements of IFRSs. IFRSs are standards and interpretations adopted by IASB. The acceptance of IFRSs as the worldwide financial reporting standards is gaining more and more ground. Outside Europe, Australia and Canada have adopted the IFRSs. Japan allows certain Japanese companies to use IFRSs as of the beginning of 2010 and was considering making adoption of IFRSs mandatory by 2016. China is considering adopting IFRSs and is moving away from a US GAAP orientation. In 2007 the Securities and Exchange Commission made the decision that foreign registrants in the United States are allowed to use IFRSs as approved by the IASB without the requirement of reconciliation of the financial statements to US GAAP. In addition, according to current plans American companies may be

---

[8] European Parliament and Council of Ministers, Regulation no. 1606/2002: Application of International Accounting Standards.

given the opportunity to use IFRSs in the American capital markets from 2015 onward (the original plan was for 2014) if they so desire.[9]

The stated objective of financial reporting in IAS 1 to "present fairly" raises the question as to how literally the accounting standards have to be interpreted and applied within the given framework, now and in the future. Is there room for deviation from the letter of the standard under certain circumstances: that is, does normative pluralism exist in international financial reporting? "Substance over form" is a traditional accounting principle meaning that transactions must be accounted for "in accordance with their substance and economic reality and not merely their legal form." "Present fairly," or the British concept "to give a true and fair view," can be interpreted to be intimately related to the principle of "substance over form." Flint regards "true and fair view" as having a conceptual quality of great merit because it recognizes the cultural dependence of accounting and financial reporting and the fact of its evolving continuously to meet the expectations of the changing social and economic environment. What is perceived to be "a true and fair view," he argues, is ultimately a matter of ethics or morality.[10] This seems implicitly to assume that preparers, auditors, and users of financial statements all share a common understanding of the purposes of financial reporting, and that, in some indefinable way, choices among alternative accounting procedures are made by managers, verified by auditors, and accepted by shareholders on the basis of consensus as to what is fair. Walton tends toward the view that "true and fair" is defined by current accounting practice.[11] Such an interpretation seems to be supported by the legal opinion of Arden in 1993 in that she states that the task of interpreting the "true and fair view" requirement cannot be performed by the courts without evidence as to the practices and views of accountants.[12]

The European Union (or its predecessor European (Economic) Community) laid down the normative order for adhering to financial reporting rules in the

---

[9] United States Securities and Exchange Commission, 'SEC Approves Statement on Global Accounting Standards', SEC Press Release (27), 24 February 2010.

[10] See David Flint, *True and Fair View in Company Accounts* (London: Institute of Chartered Accountants of Scotland/Gee & Co. Limited, 1982), at 1 and 30.

[11] Christopher Nobes, and Robert Parker, 'True and Fair: A Survey of UK Financial Directors', (1991) *Journal of Business Finance & Accounting*, 359–75, at 360. Peter Walton, 'Introduction: The True and Fair View in British Accounting', (1993) 2 *European Accounting Review*, 49–58, at 50–1.

[12] Mary Arden, *Opinion: Appendix, Accounting Standards Board – the True and Fair Requirement: Accounting Standards 1996/97* (London: Accounting Standards Board, Accountancy Books, 1993).

Fourth Council Directive of 1978, that is, prior to the existence of any international financial reporting standards. In adopting the IFRSs as the mandatory reporting framework for listed companies from 2005 onward, EU retained the original normative order of 1978 for financial reporting application. In the Fourth Council Directive (1978) it is stated as follows (section 1, art. 2, paragraphs 3–5)[13]:

1. The annual accounts shall give a true and fair view of the company's assets, liabilities, financial position and profit or loss.(§3)
2. Where the application of the provision of this Directive would not be sufficient to give a true and fair view within the meaning of the paragraph 3, additional information must be given.(§4)
3. Where in exceptional cases the application of a provision of this Directive is incompatible with the obligation laid down in paragraph 3, that provision must be departed from in order to give a true and fair view within the meaning of paragraph 3. Any such departure must be disclosed in notes on the accounts with explanation of the reasons for it and a statement of its effect on the assets, liabilities, financial position and profit or loss. The Member States may define the exceptional cases in question and lay down the relevant special rules.(§5)

The last paragraph (§5) is evidence that the financial reporting objective "to give a true and fair view" has an overriding (overruling) status within the EU. Nobes stated that the distinguished features of "a true and fair view" is the implication of an underlying reality, the portrayal of which is more important than any particular rule of practice, and therefore the requirement of rules to be broken if this is necessary in order to portray reality.[14] Thus, accounting practices may be legal but misleading. The perception that the legality of accounts did not provide an adequate defense against the presentation of a misleading view was reinforced by the case of the *Royal Mail Steam Packet Co.* in Britain.[15] This case involved the use of secret reserves to boost profits over a number of years, which, although deemed not to be illegal, was generally regarded as deceitful. As a result, the need to present "a true and fair view"

---

[13] Council Directive 78/660/EEC of 25 July 1978 on the annual accounts of certain types of companies.
[14] Christopher Nobes, 'The True and Fair View: Impact on and of the Fourth Directive', (1993) 24 *Accounting and Business Research*, 35–48, at 37.
[15] *Rex v. Kylsant and Morland* 1931, quoted in John Forker and Margaret Greenwood, 'European Harmonization and the True and Fair View: The Case of Long-term Contracts in the UK', (1995) 4 *The European Accounting Review*, 1–31.

despite written rules became increasingly apparent and accounting practices that were legal but misleading were to be departed from and overridden.[16]

The main problem, however, is to judge when departure from the rules is justifiable and to determine the extent of permissible departure. Different EU countries have different social and economic environments, which are likely to affect the actual applications of the override possibility and thus the consistency of application between countries. Furthermore, the override option also leaves room for opportunistic behavior in financial reporting. Forker and Greenwood and van Hulle are of the opinion that the override alternative should be applied in the exceptional circumstances of individual firms.[17] In other words, a restricted application of the overriding feature is more appropriate than a broad-based application. The overriding clause in the Fourth Directive can be contrasted with American accounting practice that, in spite of the existence of the "substance over form" principle, has been regarded as following a very rule-oriented approach, thus generally not (or extremely rarely) permitting any override of the rules. What has to be kept in mind is the stated quality requirement proclaimed by the SEC in 1996, that is, that accounting standards should be rigorously interpreted and applied. With the Americans possibly accepting IFRS reporting as an option also for American companies in 2015, the possible differences in interpretations of IFRSs between EU and American regulatory authorities regarding permissible deviations from the rules may cause friction between these regulatory authorities (and other jurisdictions accepting IFRSs) and confusion among reporting enterprises. Extensive differences in interpretations and applications are likely to have detrimental effects on capital markets.

b. Audit Committees and International Auditing Standards

The purpose of an audit committee in an enterprise is to secure that in preparing financial statements international accounting standards are rigorously interpreted and applied. To meet that end, the enterprise preparing the financial statements should safeguard that the committee consists of at least three independent board members who are financially literate, one of whom should be an accounting expert. "Independent" means independent of the executive team of the enterprise so that the audit committee's and executive team's interests are not fully aligned. The assumption is that independence

---

[16] Ibid., at 5.
[17] Ibid., at 25 and Karel van Hulle, 'Truth and Untruth about True and Fair View', (1993) 2 *European Accounting Review*, 99–104.

would secure a more unbiased preparation of the financial statements of the enterprise. This is supported by research evidence.[18] Audit committees are mandatory in U.S. markets and strongly recommended in most other stock exchanges.

High-quality international auditing standards are represented by the International Standards on Auditing (ISAs) published by the International Federation of Accountants (IFAC). These auditing standards are widely accepted around the world and are included in national laws or recommendations. However, international auditing standards per se do not guarantee that auditing is carried out in the same way everywhere in the world and that the international auditing standards are rigorously followed. The big accounting (auditing) firms (Big 4)[19] have established their own internal control procedures to secure that their auditing meets the same (minimum) quality level irrespective of where in the world the audit is carried out. However, government authorities cannot purely rely on audit firms' internal control procedures but have to conduct their own quality inspection of auditors and audit firms in order to secure unbiased quality control. In the United States, the Public Company Accounting Oversight Board (PCAOB) was created by the Sarbanes-Oxley Act of 2002 to oversee auditors of enterprises in order to protect the interests of investors and further the public interest in the preparation of informative, fair, and independent audit reports. The EU has adopted a model similar to the Americans' in founding the European Group of Auditors' Oversight Bodies consisting of nonpractitioners to ensure independence from the audit profession. In practice the EGAOB is a European coordination body and the actual quality inspection is carried out by local (national) auditing oversight bodies.

c. Regulatory Oversight

The ultimate responsibility for effective, responsible, and fair operation of capital markets rests with the authorities of the respective countries. The Securities and Exchange Commission assumed the responsibility in the United States with the adoption of the Securities Act of 1933 and Securities and Exchange Act of 1934, which were consequences of the Great Depression in 1929 and the 1930s. Because of its early establishment the SEC has in practice exerted

---

[18] Joseph V. Carcello and Terry L. Neal, 'Audit Committee Composition and Audit Reporting', (2000) 75 *The Accounting Review*, 453–67, and Joseph V. Carcello and Terry L. Neal, 'Audit Committee Characteristics and Auditor Dismissals Following "New" Going-Concern Reports', (2003) 78 *Accounting Review*, 95–117.

[19] These are Deloitte, Ernst & Young, KPMG, and PricewaterhouseCoopers.

market regulatory influence not only in the United States but also outside the American national borders. One of the key responsibilities of an oversight body is to secure fair and reliable financial reporting. Most European countries, except Britain, have been rather late in establishing an oversight body of financial reporting. When the EU introduced the mandatory adoption of the IFRSs for listed companies in 2005, oversight bodies were established in each EU country. On the EU level, the Committee of European Securities Regulators is the coordination body of the different national oversight bodies within the member states.

The key question, however, is whether the European national oversight bodies and CESR have the regulatory and financial means as well as willingness to secure that the IFRSs are rigorously interpreted and applied. To add complexity to the issue, rigorous interpretation and application concern not only Europe but also Canada, Australia, and other countries, such as Japan, China, and the United States, that have adopted or are considering adopting or allowing the use of IFRSs in their markets. We cannot afford development in which European interpretations and applications are very different from those of the others because that condition would be detrimental to the ultimate goal of global harmonization of international financial reporting. To the extent that standards are principles-based and guidelines or more specific interpretations are not provided, there exists a real danger that applications will be (too) heterogeneous in practice, and this in turn would undermine the trustworthiness of global capital markets.

V. IFRS – INTERNATIONAL "LEGISLATION" BUT NATIONAL APPLICATION?

A. *Culture*

Cultural differences play a significant role in international business. From a financial reporting and investor perspective, the key issue is whether differences in cultures significantly affect the interpretation and application of IFRSs so that the financial statements prepared by enterprises of different national origins materially differ from one another. As a result of the so-called principles-based nature of IFRSs, there is a danger of significant reporting differences among enterprises as well as among countries in general. Thus legal requirements such as the EU's requirement for listed EU companies to use IFRSs may fail in providing sufficient reporting harmonization and homogeneity. It is evident that differences in thinking and social actions exist among the citizens of different nations. Cross-cultural research has been long-standing in anthropology, political science, psychology, and sociology. In the late 1960s and early 1970s Hofstede carried out a cross-cultural study in a large multinational business organization with employees in forty countries.[20] A significant part of the study explored people's values. Hofstede defined value as "a broad tendency to prefer certain state of affairs over others" and culture as "the collective programming of the mind which distinguishes the members of one human group from another."[21] Four main dimensions on which cultures differ were revealed. These four dimensions affect financial reporting; thus they will be briefly introduced, along with their implications for financial reporting. The four dimensions were labeled power distance, uncertainty avoidance, individualism, and masculinity.

The basic issue involved in power distance is human inequality. On an organizational level this translates into the extent to which hierarchy and unequal distribution of power in institutions and organizations are accepted. Hofstede measured power distance in the business organization as the interpersonal power of influence between the superior (manager) and his subordinate as perceived by the less powerful of the two, the subordinate. The issue in Hofstede's survey that most clearly expressed power distance was the extent to which employees were afraid to express disagreement with their managers. According to Hofstede's survey, countries having a tendency to exhibit high power distance are the Philippines, Mexico, Venezuela, India, Singapore, and Brazil. Low power distance is shown in Austria, Israel, the Nordic countries, New Zealand, Switzerland, Great Britain, Germany, and the United States (medium low).[22]

Uncertainty about the future is a basic fact of human life with which we try to cope through the domains of technology, law, and religion. Extreme uncertainty creates intolerable anxiety. Coping with the inevitable uncertainties in life is partly a nonrational process that different individuals, organizations, and societies resolve in different ways. The main dimension in uncertainty avoidance is the tolerance for uncertainty (ambiguity), which can be found in individuals and which leads some individuals in the same situation to perceive a greater need for action for overcoming the uncertainty than others. Tolerance for uncertainty is partly a matter of personality, partly a matter of culture. On a societal level, uncertainty avoidance is the degree to which society is uncomfortable with ambiguity and an uncertain future. Countries exhibiting high uncertainty avoidance are Greece, Portugal, Belgium, and Japan

---

[20] Geert Hofstede, *Culture's Consequences* (Beverly Hills, CA: Sage Publications, 1984).
[21] Ibid., 18–21.
[22] Ibid., 70–7.

while countries showing low uncertainty avoidance are Singapore, Denmark, Sweden, Ireland, Great Britain, India, and the United States.[23]

Individualism can be described as the relationship between the individual and collectivity that prevails in a given society. Is there a preference for a loosely knit social fabric over an interdependent, tightly knit fabric? The norm prevalent in a given society as to the degree of individualism/collectivism expected from its members will strongly affect the nature of the relationship between the person and the organization to which he/she belongs. More collectivist societies call for greater emotional dependence of members of their organization. The level of individualism in society also affects the type of persons who will be admitted into positions of special influence in the organization. Countries exhibiting high individualism are the United States, Australia, and Great Britain while countries scoring low on individualism are Venezuela, Colombia, and Pakistan. European countries scoring low are Portugal and Greece. These two countries scored high on uncertainty avoidance.[24]

The duality of sexes is a fundamental fact with which different societies cope in different ways. According to Hofstede, the issue is whether the biological differences between sexes should or should not have implications for their roles in social activities.[25] The sex role distribution common in a particular society is transferred by socialization in families, schools, and peer groups and through the media. The predominant socialization pattern is for men to be more assertive and for women to be more relationship oriented and caring (traditional feminine values). These traits have implications for business organizations in that there are "masculine" goals and "feminine" goals. The results of Hofstede's survey showed high consistency with the masculine/feminine division in that men scored high on thinking that advancement and earnings are important goals while women emphasized interpersonal aspects, rendering service, and the physical environment. Application of the masculinity versus femininity dimension, also called achievement orientation, to the countries included in Hofstede's survey showed that Japan, Austria, Venezuela, Italy, Switzerland, Mexico, Ireland, and Great Britain scored high on masculinity (also the United States rather high) – Japan very high. Low scoring was exhibited by the Nordic countries, the Netherlands, Chile, and Portugal.[26]

---

[23] Ibid., 118–22.
[24] Ibid., 148–58.
[25] Ibid., at 176.
[26] Ibid., 176–89.

B. Culture and Accounting

On the basis of Hofstede's culture analysis, Gray proposed a framework linking culture and accounting. He suggested four accounting value dimensions that affect a nation's financial reporting practices[27]:

1. Professionalism versus statutory control
2. Uniformity versus flexibility
3. Conservatism versus optimism
4. Secrecy versus transparency

According to the first value dimension, a preference for the exercise of individual professional judgment and professional self-regulation is contrasted with compliance with prescriptive legal requirements. According to Gray, a preference for independent professional judgment is consistent with a preference for a loosely knit social framework where there are more emphasis on independence, a belief in fair play, and as few rules as possible, and where a variety of professional judgments will tend to be more readily tolerated. Professionalism is also more likely to be accepted in a small power distance society where there are more concern for equal rights, where people at various power levels feel less threatened and more prepared to trust people, and where there is a belief in the need to justify the imposition of laws and codes.[28]

According to the second value dimension, preference for uniformity and consistency is contrasted with flexibility in reacting to circumstances. Having a preference for uniformity is consistent with having a preference for strong uncertainty avoidance leading to a concern for law and order and rigid codes of behavior, a need for written rules and regulations, a respect for conformity, and the search for ultimate, absolute truth and values. Uniformity is also in line with a preference for collectivism with its tightly knit social framework, a belief in organization and order, and respect for group norms. Uniformity is more easily facilitated in large power distance societies in that imposition of laws and codes of a uniform character is more likely to be accepted.[29]

A key issue in financial reporting is measurement. The measurement principle applied to assets and liabilities in the balance sheet and revenues and expenses in the income statement has a bearing on the perceived usefulness of the information being disseminated to the users of the financial statements.

---

[27] Sidney J. Gray, 'Towards a Theory of Cultural Influence on the Development of Accounting Systems Internationally', (1988) 24 *Abacus*, 1–15.
[28] Ibid., at 9.
[29] Ibid., 9–10.

A preference for a cautious approach to measurement to cope with the uncertainty of future events is to be contrasted with a more optimistic, risk-taking approach. More conservative measurements of profits are consistent with strong uncertainty avoidance following from a concern with security and a perceived need to adopt a cautious approach to cope with uncertainty of future events. In contrast, an emphasis on individual achievement and performance is likely to foster a less conservative approach to measurement.[30]

The secrecy-versus-transparency value dimension deals with having a preference for confidentiality and the restriction of business information to a need-to-know basis versus being willing to disclose information to the public. Having a preference for secrecy is consistent with strong uncertainty avoidance following from a need to restrict information disclosures so as to avoid conflict and competition and to preserve security. Societies with high power distance are likely to be characterized by the restriction of information in order to preserve power inequalities. Secrecy is also consistent with a preference for collectivism with its concern for those closely involved with the business firm rather than external parties. On the other hand, societies where more emphasis is given to the quality of life, people, and the environment will tend to be more open, especially regarding socially related information.[31]

In Table 11.1 the relationships between Gray's accounting values and Hofstede's cultural dimensions are displayed. Individualism is expected to promote professionalism but to be negatively related to the other three dimensions, that is, uniformity, conservatism, and secrecy. Power distance does not fit with professionalism but is expected to be positively related to uniformity and secrecy. Its relationship to conservatism is unclear. Uncertainty avoidance correlates negatively with professionalism but is expected to have positive relationships with uniformity, conservatism, and secrecy. As a contrast, masculinity is expected to be negatively related to conservatism and secrecy while its relation to professionalism and uniformity is unclear.

On the basis of the framework described and Hofstede's research results, one can conclude that countries likely to exercise professionalism in financial reporting are Great Britain and the United States. Both score high on individualism, low on power distance (the United States, however, is less low than Great Britain), and low on uncertainty avoidance. These countries have had a tradition in which the accounting profession has set the accounting rules. Today accounting rules in these countries are set by independent professionals representing not only the accounting/auditing profession but also

---

[30] Ibid., at 10.
[31] Ibid., at 11.

TABLE 11.1. *Relationships between Gray's accounting values and Hofstede's cultural dimensions*

Accounting values (Gray)				
Cultural dimension	Professionalism	Uniformity	Conservatism	Secrecy
Individualism	+	−	−	−
Power distance	−	+	?	+
Uncertainty avoidance	−	+	+	+
Masculinity	?	?	−	−

"+" *indicates a direct relationship between the variables.*
"−" *indicates an inverse relationship between the variables.*
"?" *indicates that the nature of the relationship is indeterminate.*

the preparers (previous chief financial officers of listed companies), investors (represented by senior financial analysts), and the accounting academia. Thus professionalism has been retained. Great Britain has clearly remained in the principles-based domain, leaving a lot of room for professional judgment (individualism), while the United States has become rather rule-oriented because of its litigious environment. However, the difference between the American and British practices is in reality a question of degree rather than an absolute difference. The question is not only that of having only rigid rules nor full freedom to exercise judgment but of how the balance is struck between the two poles. Thus the extent of normative pluralism in international financial reporting is currently unknown and will be evolving in the coming years.

The European Union requires listed companies to apply IFRS standards that represent a more principles-based system leaving room for professional judgment. The EU consists of many different countries that score differently on the cultural dimensions, and these dimensions are likely to have an influence on the actual interpretations and applications of IFRSs. The Netherlands exhibits cultural characteristics similar to Britain's and has had a similar accounting tradition to some extent. Thus, they are likely to give more weight to professional judgment. France and the southern European countries like Italy, Greece, Portugal, and Spain score high on power distance, especially France and Portugal. These countries also score high on uncertainty avoidance, especially Greece and Portugal, and generally low on individualism, except France and Italy. Except for the noise caused by France and Italy on individualism, one could conclude that the aforementioned countries are likely to favor more exact regulation over professional judgment. The implication of this is that where IFRS is lacking exact rules or guidance, the countries mentioned are likely to draw on their national rules (regulation) and tradition in their interpretations and applications. This is a contrast to the British professional judgment tradition. Germany's score on power distance is low (but not very low), on individualism medium high although clearly lower than Britain and the United States, and medium high on uncertainty avoidance. Thus Germany exhibits a mixed combination on the cultural dimensions and its impact on financial reporting is unclear. To conclude, the mandatory IFRS application for listed companies within the EU will not necessarily mean homogeneous interpretation and application. The question to be raised is whether the actual reporting differences are going to be sufficiently large to have a detrimental effect on the comparability of financial reporting among EU countries and consequently on the confidence instilled in the capital markets. In addition, when differences in opinions and conflicts emerge as to what constitutes "correct reporting," what instance is going to be the "judge" thereof? We will return to this issue later.

Among the emerging economies Brazil, not surprisingly, shows features similar to Portugal's, that is, low individualism, high power distance, and high uncertainty avoidance. Also China is likely to exhibit similar features (it was not included in Hofstede's 1984 survey). India has mixed features in that it scores high on power distance and rather low on individualism (not as low as, e.g., Portugal) but scores low on uncertainty avoidance (a contrast to southern European countries). On the other hand, India has had a rather deeply rooted British reporting culture as a consequence of the British rule until 1947. Japan scores high on uncertainty avoidance, like India on the lower end of the scale on individualism, and medium high on power distance. In the 1990s the American influence on Japanese financial reporting was strong, but in the beginning of the 2000s Japan began to orient itself toward IFRS.[32]

VI. UNACCEPTABLE APPLICATION OF IFRS – WHO DECIDES?

According to one of the Big Four accounting firms in the world, Ernst & Young, it is necessary to recognize that complete comparability is never possible in financial reporting. Instead, more emphasis needs to be placed on explaining the key judgments made by preparers of financial statements, including the sensitivities around those judgments.[33] However, the biggest challenge facing regulators is to ensure that unacceptable national variations in the interpretation and application of IFRSs do not emerge. The International Financial

---

[32] See Nobes and Parker, *Comparative International Accounting*, at 305.
[33] Ernst & Young, *International GAAP 2007* (London: LexisNexis, 2006), at 69.

Reporting Interpretations Committee (IFRIC) is the interpretation body of IASB. It is not possible for IFRIC to deal with issues of interpretation that arise on a day-to-day basis. According to Ernst & Young the role of IFRIC and IASB will principally be to monitor the practical application of standards and, if deemed necessary, issue an interpretation or amend a standard in a response to what they consider to be the development of unacceptable treatment or inacceptable practices.[34] There exists, however, evidence that IFRIC does not necessarily respond sufficiently often and extensively to requests for guidance in applying standards, partly as a policy, partly as a result of limited resources. For example, IFRIC did not think that guidance on accounting for internally generated intangible assets (IAS 38) was necessary, but Ernst & Young had a different opinion.[35]

When differences in opinions and conflicts emerge as to what constitutes "correct reporting," who is going to be the "judge" and final decision maker on "correct reporting"? CESR has the oversight responsibility in EU to monitor whether listed EU enterprises adequately adhere to IFRS standards. The actual daily oversight is delegated to each national oversight body, but a common database of decided cases has been formed at the CESR level for the purpose of enhancing similar decisions around Europe in similar cases. Because the SEC allows foreign registrants to apply IFRS in U.S. markets and is likely to allow American companies to use IFRS starting in 2015, the SEC will have its say on what is "correct" IFRS reporting. Consequently, if IFRIC does not provide the necessary interpretations, CESR and SEC are likely to make their own IFRS interpretations, necessitating a closer dialogue between the two bodies, thus undermining the position of IFRIC and IASB. If SEC and CESR find sufficient common grounds, their interpretations are likely also to have a greater bearing on IFRS interpretations and applications around the world.

VII. CONCLUSION

Globally financial reporting is in a transition stage in that more and more countries are moving away from their national accounting laws toward accepting or requiring the application of International Financial Reporting Standards, at least for listed companies. In order to have functioning capital markets on a global basis, such a development is necessary because it is impossible for international investors, and thus for the global flow of capital, to know the peculiarities of financial reporting in each country. There are

---

[34] Ernst & Young, International GAAP 2007, at 70.
[35] Ernst & Young, International GAAP 2007, at 827.

still, however, many obstacles left for achieving sufficient harmonization of international financial reporting rules. The characteristic that IFRS is largely principles-based in many instances leaves a lot of room for interpretation. Cultural traditions of each country will no doubt influence the actual interpretation and application of the IFRS reporting standards. When is an application unacceptable? Nowadays the United States and each EU member state have their own oversight body, but differences in cultural traditions within the EU will affect the decisions taken by these bodies and may endanger sufficient harmonization despite that the common coordinative EU body CESR exists. Because of the reluctance of IASB and its interpretation body IFRIC to provide interpretations on many issues, the danger exists that SEC and CESR will provide their own interpretations, thus threatening the authority of IASB. In addition, as China is developing into a major economic power it will certainly have its say about the interpretations and applications of IFRS reporting standards in the future.

Because of the existing cultural and economic differences among countries, the extent of normative pluralism currently present in the application of IFRSs is unknown. It is clear that a rigid interpretation and application of IFRSs in accordance with the stated objectives of the American SEC in 1996 do not exist on a global basis. Thus, it is likely that the Americans have to give in to some extent, even regarding the possible application of IFRSs by American companies from 2015 onward. However, the other side of the coin is that if flexibility in interpreting and applying IFRSs and specifically in overriding accounting standards results in extensive inconsistencies in financial reporting among countries as well as enterprises, the effects on capital markets will be detrimental. We would have American IFRSs, Australian IFRSs, Brazilian IFRSs, Chinese IFRSs, and EU IFRSs, and even within the EU German IFRSs, French IFRSs, and so on. Consequently, such a development would endanger the whole objective of having international financial reporting standards, which is to create a common "financial language" that is understood by all investors and other interest groups around the world. It is of great importance to find the "correct" balance between flexibility and rigidity in the future. Will this challenge be successfully met?

12 Responsibility to Rebuild and Collective Responsibility: Legal and Moral Considerations

Larry May

I. INTRODUCTION

At the beginning of the twenty-first century, a movement developed that conceptualized global justice in terms of the "Responsibility to Protect." Most of the discussion about this idea has focused on intervention to thwart or prevent atrocities, fueled in large part by the failure of the international community to do anything to stop the genocides in Rwanda and the former Yugoslavia in the 1990s. But part of the UN mandate is also to help

> states build capacity to protect their populations from genocide, war crimes, ethnic cleansing, and crimes against humanity and to assisting those which are under stress before crises and conflicts break out.[1]

It is this underexplored part of the responsibility to protect that will be the focus of this chapter. But I will also say quite a bit about the general idea of responsibility to protect, especially concerning its relationship to collective responsibility.[2]

I will begin by looking to the just war tradition for assistance in beginning to think about this complex idea.[3] In particular, I will look to the work of Grotius and Vattel. Vattel is the best known advocate of a responsibility to intervene,

---

[1] UN General Assembly World Outcome Document (2005), para. 139.
[2] See my books on the nature of collective responsibility: Larry May, *The Morality of Groups* (Notre Dame, IN: University of Notre Dame Press, 1987); Larry May, *Sharing Responsibility* (Chicago: University of Chicago Press, 1992); and Larry May, *The Socially Responsive Self* (Chicago: University of Chicago Press, 1996).
[3] My recent books in international law all proceed from a consideration of the just war tradition: Larry May, *Crimes against Humanity: A Normative Account* (Cambridge University Press, 2005); *War Crimes and Just War* (Cambridge University Press, 2007); *Aggression and Crimes against Peace* (Cambridge University Press, 2008); and *Genocide: A Normative Account* (Cambridge University Press, 2010). My *Global Justice and Due Process* (Cambridge University Press, 2011) looks back at the theoretical debates about Magna Carta.

but his work can also, I believe, easily support a responsibility to build, or rebuild, capacity to protect as well, as a general part of *jus post bellum*. I will then sketch several conceptual problems that Vattel's approach elicits but does not clearly solve. In the end I will attempt to solve some of these problems, but two problems remain a major sticking point to the idea of a responsibility to build or rebuild the capacity to protect. As a result, we will find that some *jus post bellum* principles sit uncomfortably with other principles in the just war tradition. And we see the difficulty of figuring out a clear dividing line between the moral and the legal as we proceed.

In contemporary debates in philosophy of law, one of the central questions concerns whether, and to what extent, law and morality overlap or intersect. Justice, it is often said, is the site of the overlap between law and morality, especially that aspect of justice that calls for like cases to be treated alike and different cases to be treated differently. This is to treat justice procedurally, and it is hard to deny that law and morality overlap at least insofar as law must achieve minimal procedural fairness. What is harder is the question of the overlap between law and more substantive conceptions of morality.

In this chapter I consider the way that morality, understood as a set of minimal substantive norms, might overlap with legality in the international domain. I choose the case of the responsibility to protect because the language used in the debates about this recent normative regime seems to be poised between moral and legal. I also choose this example because there have been similar debates in the just war tradition that blurred some of the borders between morality and legality; indeed the very idea of natural law is a self-conscious blurring of this border.

II. HISTORICAL AND PHILOSOPHICAL ROOTS OF THE RESPONSIBILITY TO PROTECT

Grotius was probably the first thinker in the modern era to explore the idea that there was a society of states that had moral obligations toward each other. In his book, *On the Law of War and Peace* (1625), Grotius said that "there is a common law among nations, which is valid alike for war and in war."[4] Grotius posited that there is "an association which binds together the human race"[5] and that the law of such an association is the law of nature, just as is true for associations among individual human persons. And, importantly, he

---

[4] Hugo Grotius, *On the Law of War and Peace* (F. Kelsey trans.) (Oxford, UK: Clarendon Press, 1925 [1625]), at 20.
[5] Ibid., at 17.

maintained that "the state which transgresses the laws of nature and of nations cuts away also the bulwarks which safeguard its own future peace."[6] But while Grotius famously discussed the rules or laws of the conduct of soldiers that bind in war, especially, what came to be called *jus in bello* rules, as well as the rules governing when it is just to go to war, *jus ad bellum* rules, he said very little about *jus post bellum*, other than to maintain that if states transgress the laws of nature especially against their own people, these states lose their prerogative and hence cannot complain about intervention from other states. But Grotius had a strong influence on Pufendorf, who did discuss these issues of *jus post bellum* rules explicitly, as well as Vattel, who argued, a century later, that Grotius had gone too far in thinking that sovereigns could go to war to punish any violations of the laws of nature, rather than merely those that jeopardized their own safety or by extension the safety of another state.[7]

Vattel is a model for those who wish to defend the contemporary doctrine of the responsibility to protect. In book I, ch. V of his treatise, *The Law of Nations or the Principles of Natural Law* (1758), he says:

> If a Nation were to make open profession of treading justice under foot by despising and violating the rights of another whenever it had the opportunity of doing so, the safety of the human society at large would warrant all the other Nations in uniting together to subdue and punish such a Nation.[8]

Vattel discusses this issue under the heading of the "right to use force to obtain justice,"[9] and this right is said to follow from "the offices of humanity," which are "common duties." "Nations mutually owe one another" to do all they can "to promote the welfare and happiness of others."[10]

Much later in the text, he makes the most direct reference to the part of the responsibility to protect I wish to address when he says:

> If a sovereign is dealing with a perfidious enemy, it would be imprudent to trust his word of his oath. In such a case the sovereign may with perfect justice act as prudence requires, and take advantage of a successful war and follow up his victory until he has broken the excessive and dangerous power of the enemy, or forced him to give adequate security of proper conduct in the future.[11]

---

[6] Ibid., at 16.
[7] Emer de Vattel, *The Law of Nations or the Principles of Natural Law* (C. Fenwick trans.) (Washington, DC: Carnegie Institution, 1916 [1758]), at 116.
[8] Ibid., at 135.
[9] Ibid.
[10] Ibid., at 114.
[11] Ibid., at 345.

Vattel then also seemingly commits himself to total submission in some cases, what he calls "a complete and final victory,"[12] certainly contrary to what most authors would argue for today.

Included in Vattel's offices of humanity is that a state "should not limit its good offices to the preservation of other States, but in addition should contribute to their advancement according to its ability and their need of its help."[13] Here the "need for help" captures the insight behind the provision of the responsibility to protect that I wish to investigate, namely, the aid that helps states build or rebuild a capacity to protect the state's own people from massive human rights violations. Vattel's view is consistent with the kind of capacity building that seems to many theorists today to be a distinctly contemporary requirement of all states, but that Vattel clearly implies in these remarks from the mid-eighteenth century.

Grotius's "common law among nations" and Vattel's "common duties" or "offices of humanity" envision a collective responsibility of states for the maintenance of peace across the globe. In many ways these duties or responsibilities are collective in a distributive sense, where each state has a duty to go to the aid of other states and perhaps to populations within states that are in need of assistance. In addition, there is a sense that both Grotius and Vattel seem also to countenance a nondistributive collective responsibility of states. Insofar as states are associated in a society of states bound by a common law, *jus gentium*, of the sort envisioned by Cicero,[14] there may be a nondistributive collective responsibility of the states of the world to go to the aid of states or populations that are in need. But in the just war tradition there was not much discussion of this nondistributive sense of collective responsibility of states or nations, with the exception of scattered references such as Grotius's idea of an association or society of states.[15]

III. THE DISTRIBUTIVE AND NONDISTRIBUTIVE COLLECTIVE RESPONSIBILITY OF STATES

For there to be nondistributive collective responsibilities of states, there must indeed be a sense in which there is an association or society of these states in the first place. I have elsewhere tried to make out a case for such an idea in terms of a common solidarity among states that goes beyond mere self-interest.[16] But

[12] Ibid.
[13] Ibid., at 115.
[14] See Cicero, *De Officiis* (On Duties) (c. 45 B.C.).
[15] See Grotius, *War and Peace*, at 17.
[16] See May, *Aggression and Crimes against Peace*, ch. 3.

the doctrine of the responsibility to protect does not need a robust solidarity among states; nor does it need a nondistributive sense of collective responsibility. A shared responsibility of the distributive sort is sufficient for thinking that states have a responsibility to protect other states that are the victims of such gross harms as aggression, famine, or genocide, just as it is not necessary that there be an association of persons for each of us nonetheless to feel that fellow humans are our brothers and sisters who are owed our help, as Vattel recognized more than two hundred and fifty years ago.[17]

Collective responsibilities can attach to very loosely formed groups, such as a collection of states that are not bound by an association. To speak of collective responsibility here is, again in the words of Vattel, to speak of what each state must do for each other state:

> if a Nation is suffering from famine, all those who have provisions to spare should assist it in its need, without however exposing themselves to scarcity.... Whatever be the calamity afflicting a Nation, the same help is due it.[18]

The sharing of responsibility as a form of collective distributive responsibility seems to be all that is called for in the UN General Assembly World Outcome Report that announced the doctrine of the Responsibility to Protect, and I shall proceed in this spirit throughout the chapter.

The rest of this section will be explaining what even this somewhat weaker version of the collective responsibility of states could be based in. Vattel thought that it was the brotherhood of all humans that was the main premise in the argument for thinking that individuals and states should go to the rescue of those who are in need of help. Today it is sometimes said that it is the shared humanity of all people that is the central premise in that argument. Even if it is accepted that all individual humans are morally obligated to go to one another's aid by their common bonds of humanity, it remains to be seen why states would have an obligation to go to the aid of individual humans, and more difficult yet, why states would have an obligation to go to the aid of other states.

The first of these problems is perhaps not so difficult to solve. If we think of states as simple collections of individual human persons, the states can be the repository of the moral obligations of individuals. When we speak of states there is a sense that we are speaking primarily of the members of states, the individual human persons. As I have argued in several other places, we are also speaking of the way these individual human persons are related

---

[17] See Vattel, *Law of Nations*, at 120.
[18] Ibid., at 115.

to each other as well, where these relations have ontological significance.[19] Morally, states can certainly have obligations insofar as their members have acted in appropriate ways to bind their states. Insofar as this is true, states may have an obligation to go to the aid of specific individuals based on the state's vicarious obligations arising out of the obligations of the members of states.

Or, alternatively, it seems to make sense at least that states can meet the moral obligations of their individual members when they act. As I have just explained, speaking of the actions of states is in a sense shorthand for speaking of the actions of individual members of states. So, there should be no conceptual problems at all in states' meeting the obligations of their members, even if it is still thought to be problematic to say that the states themselves take on the obligations that began life as the obligations of members. The satisfying of obligations by states really would only be a way for the state to act on the shared obligations of its members. And the acting of states would also be just a way to speak of a mechanism by which individual humans acted to meet their obligations. States play an obvious role in the way that individual humans meet their shared, that is, distributive and collective, responsibilities.

In this vein, it might also make sense to allow states to bind themselves, by the making of treaties, for instance, where the state takes on obligations that did not arise first as obligations of the members of states, as long as the obligations are still attributable to individual humans. These obligations could still be thought of in distributive terms, but where the state is somehow authorized to create obligations that are then shared by the members of these states. And it is not unreasonable to think that the state is obligated to meet these obligations as the repository of the shared obligations of its members. In this way, the state is a placeholder in two senses: as a repository of obligations of individual humans, even if those individuals did not originate those obligations, and as a way to meet the obligations of individual humans.

All of the preceding considerations now allow for one possible way to understand the responsibilities or obligations that states might have to one another, such as supposedly occur in the responsibility to protect doctrine. We can think of such obligations or responsibilities as elaborate placeholder arrangements. One state, thought of as a placeholder for that state's human members, has an obligation to another state, also thought of as a placeholder for its human members. Or to put it differently, an organized group of individual humans has a distributed collective responsibility toward another organized group of humans. Of course, it is not just any organized group of persons

[19] See May, *Morality of Groups*, ch. 1.

but ones that are related to each other by characteristic relationships of state membership.

For there to be nondistributed collective responsibilities of states, it would have to be true that something other than the human members of the state was involved in the creation of the responsibility. And one way to think of this is that the relationships among the members played an instrumental role in the creation of the state's responsibility. Vattel thinks that states have relations among themselves just as individual humans have relations as brothers or sisters. Or only slightly less controversially, it could be that members of states, qua members, not qua individuals, have relationships with the members of other states, qua members, that give rise to state responsibilities of mutual aid.

In my view, states are ontologically infirm. We can speak of them as acting and as taking on obligations, but this is best seen as shorthand. Even the making of treaties, the paradigmatic way that states bind themselves, is best thought of in a much more complex way that involves reference to what the individual members of states do at each crucial juncture. So, states are not easily conceptualized as persons or entities that can act in their own right, in a nondistributive way. And it is also hard to characterize states as having nondistributive responsibilities. But one can think of states as embodying the distributive responsibilities of their members and hence, in this sense, to think of states as having collective responsibilities nonetheless.

If states are ontologically infirm, so too are the obligations of states when seen in their own right rather than as placeholders for the members of states. Yet, as I said, this is the lynchpin of thinking that states have responsibilities to go to the aid of other states. Ontology matters for the way we understand the responsibility to protect doctrine. If states are infirm, then the society or association of states is infirm as well, and especially if such a society is seen in terms of nondistributive responsibilities. But this only means that the responsibility to protect should be understood in terms of shared responsibility of people rather than nondistributive responsibility of states. Whether this helps or hurts the doctrine of the Responsibility to Protect will remain to be seen as we proceed to look at the specific responsibility to build or rebuild the capacity to protect a state's people. This much is already clear: the members of states, at least the high-ranking members, will have to take their own responsibilities seriously when it is claimed in the international domain that their states have responsibilities to other states.

One last point worth mentioning is that state capacity to respond or to build capacity is also primarily a matter of how individual members of states are enabled to engage in joint action. When state responsibility is understood as distributive responsibility of the members of states it will be easier to avoid the problem of no one's taking responsibility when collectivities are said to be responsible. This is similar to the problem of accountability of states. Concerning this matter, at Nuremberg Justice Jackson famously said that leaders of States should be held accountable for the wrongdoing of states since states do not commit wrongs without individuals doing so.

IV. RESPONSIBILITY TO BUILD OR REBUILD CAPACITY

The responsibility to protect embraces three specific responsibilities:

1. *The responsibility to prevent*: to address both the root causes and direct causes of internal conflict and other man-made crises putting populations at risk
2. *The responsibility to react*: to respond to situations of compelling need with appropriate measures, which may include coercive measures like sanctions and international prosecution, and in extreme cases military intervention
3. *The responsibility to rebuild*: to provide, particularly after a military intervention, full assistance with recovery, reconstruction, and reconciliation, addressing the causes of the harm the intervention was designed to halt or avert.[20]

The responsibility to protect is thought to be a responsibility not only of a given state but also of the society of states. And this means that the responsibility falls especially hard on the leaders of states, whether we are talking of responsibility to protect a population from within (the first prong) or to intervene to protect from without (the second prong) the state where the mass atrocities are occurring, or are likely to occur. This also helps explain the unpopularity of the responsibility to protect among state leaders at the moment. But I would point out that this reaction is in part misdirected since part of the responsibility to protect involves only the responsibility to build capacity (the third prong) not necessarily to intervene militarily or put a state's citizens at grave risk due to invasion. So, some of the problems can be ameliorated if one focuses only on this third prong. I would readily admit that there are still serious problems that remain for the first two prongs of the responsibility to protect.

In both the first and second prongs of the responsibility to protect it is assumed that a state where a mass atrocity is occurring has the capacity either to stop the atrocity on its own or to do so as a response to pressure from outside

---

[20] Gareth Evans, *The Responsibility to Protect* (Washington, DC: Brookings Institution Press, 2008), at 41. Also see UN General Assembly World Outcome Document (2005), para. 139.

forces, such as the United Nations or NATO acting in behalf of the society of states. But such an assumption is rebuttable and has indeed been proven wrong in a number of recent cases such as contemporary Rwanda in the 1990s. As it turned out, Rwanda did not have this capacity, or was actively choosing not to exercise it. In so-called failed states, it is even clearer that the state does not have the capacity to protect members of its own society. Rebutting the presumption that a state can protect its own population is not always easy to do, but there are some clear cases, especially concerning states decimated by war. When the assumption that a state can protect its own citizens is rebutted, then we move to a third prong of the responsibility to protect, the responsibility to build or rebuild the capacity to protect.

In one sense the responsibility to build or rebuild the capacity of a state to protect its citizens is like the responsibility we have to help people regain autonomy after they have been the victim of especially horrible abuse. The responsibility is grounded in the idea that we are all better off if we do not have to care directly for each other but if we can enable these others to care for themselves. And for others to care for themselves they sometimes need help to develop, or redevelop, capacities of self-help. This is like the old saying that if you give a fish to a person he or she can eat for a day, but if you teach a person to fish, he or she can eat for a lifetime. The capacity to fish rather than the provision of food in the form of a single fish is what is needed to make a person independent and no longer someone who needs to rely on the rest of us to provide food in the future. Similarly, states sometimes need to be helped to develop the equivalent capacities of the ability to fish. I will explore this idea in more detail here and provide some examples before turning to a set of problems with this idea.

As I suggested previously, the responsibility of states is largely to be understood on the model of the aggregated or shared responsibilities of the persons who constitute those states. The capacity to protect is thus to be analyzed in terms of the ability of individual persons in a given state to band together sufficiently to engage in joint actions necessary to protect fellow members of that state from atrocities. Of course, in those cases when the atrocity in question is not committed by the state itself, building or rebuilding the capacity to protect will mean aiding in reconstituting the institutions of the state. Rebuilding capacity to protect is not merely about inspiring the state to act; instead, it is primarily about organized joint action. In this sense, the responsibility to protect is primarily a matter of collective responsibility.[21]

---

[21] On this issue see Larry May and Stacey Hoffman (eds.), *Collective Responsibility: Five Decades of Debates in Theoretical and Applied Ethics* (Lanham, MD: Rowman and Littlefield, 1991).

Being capable of something is not the same as actually doing it. So, the capacity to protect is not the same as actually protecting. What needs to happen is that individuals are given the organizational skills or other means so that they could confront an emerging or ongoing mass atrocity. And what this involves will at least somewhat vary on the basis of the kind of atrocity and the situation on the ground. A persecution or genocide that is fomenting as a result of media incitement is very different from one that is being orchestrated by a segment of the government itself. And in the context of war or armed conflict, often a state loses its capacity to protect its own citizens, which of course is very different from merely choosing not to protect or actively engaging in abuse of the rights of its citizens. In all of these cases, what is involved in the responsibility to build or rebuild capacity may vary quite a bit, but the form of the responsibility is quite similar.

There is another phenomenon that is curious in this respect, namely, that in some cases when a state first moves from authoritarian to democratic government, the state finds it more difficult to prevent mass atrocity. This may be a temporary problem of states that move too quickly to democracy without having first established the proper infrastructure for such a change. But whatever the cause, new democratic states have recently seen an increase in ethnic violence and other forms of mass atrocity. Outside help is needed to curtail the violence, where it had not been needed before the turn to democracy.[22] Here is an example of where capacity building is needed, even in cases where a state seems on the road to a more progressive form of government than it had before.

Some authors have worried about the two prongs of intervention to stop an atrocity or to put pressure on a state that has previously been jeopardizing its population.[23] In this chapter I have been focusing on what could be called the third prong of the responsibility to protect, intervention or pressure to build or rebuild capacity to resist mass atrocities and other major human rights abuses. The third prong is perhaps best seen as a *jus post bellum* principle, or more broadly as a principle of "aiding" rather than a principle of direct military or even civilian intervention. Indeed, it is unclear why the responsibility to rebuild or build the capacity to protect would involve military intervention of any sort. And the kind of civilian intervention can seemingly be more easily

---

[22] See Michael Ignatieff, 'State Failure and Nation Building', in J. L. Holtzgrefe and Robert O. Keohane (eds.), *Humanitarian Intervention: Ethical, Legal, and Political Dilemmas* (Cambridge University Press, 2003), 299–321, especially at 300.

[23] See Jennifer M. Welsh and Maria Banda, "International Law and the Responsibility to Protect: Clarifying or Expanding States' Responsibilities?" (unpublished manuscript, on file with the author).

Responsibility to Rebuild and Collective Responsibility 333

controlled by the target state, where capacity is to be enhanced, than would be true of normal military interventions.

The kind of intervention of the third prong of the responsibility to protect, concerning building or rebuilding capacity, may still be something that recipient States are suspicious of, especially given the long history of supposed helping hands in velvet gloves turning into imperialists with iron fists. In the next section of the chapter I address these worries and attempt to respond to them. Similar worries have been expressed about so-called humanitarian intervention, and I have voiced some of these criticisms myself.[24] But I shall try to show that concerning the third prong of the responsibility to protect such worries can be shown to be less serious than worries that I and others have voiced about the two other prongs of the responsibility to protect. I will address these worries under the label of worries about infringement of sovereignty.

V. CONFLICTING NORMS OF SOVEREIGNTY AND PROTECTION OF RIGHTS

All of international law faces the problem that as it increases in scope state sovereignty is seemingly diminished. Personal autonomy is seemingly diminished whenever one person interferes with what another person has chosen to do. Since sovereignty is a kind of autonomy for states, the same kind of problem exists at the level of states that exists at the level of individuals. The infringement on state autonomy or prerogative by international law represents a conflict of norms: statist versus cosmopolitan. Or at least so it seems. In this section I will argue that this conflict is not as great as it is often portrayed to be. My position is that autonomy can be enhanced by various forms of intervention, and that in any event autonomy is not mere license, as John Stuart Mill argued.[25] It can be in a state's interest to be interfered with, at least when the interference is benevolent, so that the worst abuse of rights of its citizens can be prevented now as well as in the future.

The component of sovereignty that is most like personal autonomy can be enhanced, rather than diminished, by certain temporary forms of interference in what a state is trying but failing to do. And here we can return to the third prong of the responsibility to protect, the responsibility to rebuild capacity for agency. Agency is the ability to carry out what one has chosen to do. Autonomy is the capacity to do what one has chosen where one's choices are in some significant sense choices of the self. If a person completely lacks agency, that

---

[24] See the final chapter of May, *Aggression and Crimes against Peace*.
[25] John Stuart Mill, *On Liberty* (London: Penguin, 1985 [1859]).

person also does not have autonomy, since the capacity to act on choices that are one's own turns on the capacity to act on choices of any sort. In this sense, the weaker one's agency is, the weaker one's autonomy is. The same seems to be true of states as of selves. So, any improvement in a person's, or a state's, agency is highly likely to have a positive impact on that person's or state's autonomy, not to be a restriction on autonomy, at least in the long run.

Indeed, it makes little sense to talk of sovereignty, or its abridgment, for so-called failed states, since these states (if they can be called such) are so weak that they lack the capacity to take actions, and hence to be autonomous. So, there is a strong sense that when one state intervenes in the affairs of a failed state to build or rebuild capacity to act, this is not a straightforward violation of the sovereignty of the failed state. Of course, it will matter how strongly coercive the intervention has to be, and how strongly the recipient state objects to the intervention. There is also the autonomous choice about whether one wants to be helped. But if one is very weak indeed, then it would be odd to say that aid that strengthens the capacity to act is in some sense a violation of autonomy or sovereignty, unless there were so many strings attached to the aid that future autonomous action would indeed be curtailed.

If there is a conflict here, it is a conflict between narrowly focused legal norms and broader norms of morality. The narrow legal norm of sovereignty says that a state's sovereignty is to be respected at all times. Here is article 2, paragraph 4 of the United Nations Charter: "All members shall refrain in their international relations from the threat or use of force against the territorial integrity or political independence of any state." On the narrow, legal, construal of the UN Charter, acts of humanitarian intervention that employed or risked the use of force are seemingly proscribed. The only exception concerns article 51's stipulation of "the individual or collective self-defense" "against an armed attack" and only until the United Nations itself is prepared to act. And this exception does not concern humanitarian crises unless we are thinking of those that are caused by armed attacks.

But there is a moral norm that is well articulated in the nonbinding Preamble of the United Nation's Charter, namely, "to employ international machinery for the promotion of the economic and social advancement of all peoples." This very broad provision certainly could be read to include humanitarian intervention of the sort that would fall under the responsibility to protect's third prong. Notice that like the Preamble of the UN Charter, the responsibility to protect has not yet earned the status of a legal norm in international law. It is thus much more like a moral norm, and one that seemingly conflicts with the legal norms of articles 2, paragraph 4, and 51 of the UN Charter. And yet even here, there is no necessity that these legal and moral provisions are read as being in conflict with each other, since the responsibility to protect is a last resort provision that comes into effect only when a state's capacity to protect its citizens is gravely undermined.

How last resort is understood in *jus post bellum* terms is itself not an easy matter to understand. At least one plausible way to understand *jus post bellum* last resort is as a situation where a state is incapable of doing something that it chooses concerning postwar reconstruction, and there is no other way for the state to regain this capacity on its own. If the state really does lack this capacity and cannot help itself to regain the capacity, then outside help for the state to gain or regain this capacity is a last resort. When there is no other way for the state to become an autonomous agent except through another state's intervention to help build its capacity, morally such aid should be given, even though we are left with the paradoxical situation of heteronomous aid's being necessary for autonomous action.

There is another matter to consider as well. There is a paradox in that helping one state achieve self-determination may embolden factions of other states to demand the same, thereby destabilizing regions of the world. Such self-determination movements may jeopardize the sovereignty of states that are not currently failed states and may even be moving toward democracy, although at a slower pace perhaps than is desired by factions within the state. Of course, the demand for a faster pace may cause a reaction that would not be for the best. And this is especially true if the self-determination movement is used as a pawn by global actors to extend their own influence in a given region. Such considerations should not be ignored and may complicate the ability of a state to attain true autonomy.[26]

The point of this section of the chapter can be put this way: humanitarian intervention is at least morally acceptable when it makes benevolent or at least nonmalevolent sovereignty possible. In such situations, humanitarian intervention, especially of the third prong, should not be straightforwardly seen as an abridgment of sovereignty. As long as the last resort condition is satisfied, an act of humanitarian intervention that rebuilds the capacity for agency is an aid rather than an abridgment of sovereignty. And if the state could recapture its lost capacity to act to secure the rights of its citizens, without the intervention of another state, then the responsibility to protect provision of responsibility to rebuild would not authorize intervention. In this way, it is possible to bridge the gap between the narrow legal norm of sovereignty and the broader moral norms concerning aiding states in social and economic development. The solution is in seeing the value of a normative pluralism that allows for

---

[26] On this point see Ignatieff, 'State Failure and Nation Building', at 301.

reaching across seemingly unbridgeable gaps of legal and moral norms in the international arena.

VI. FOUR PROBLEMS

There are several seemingly intractable problems to address before closing this discussion of the responsibility to protect. The first is that when one state intervenes in the affairs of another, even with the best of intentions and spurred on by a collective responsibility to protect, matters are likely to backfire in that the target state and the majority of its citizens may feel threatened and respond by making it even harder to stop the human rights abuses. Second, if the intervention is by one group of a state's citizens against another, the likelihood of civil war or even secession is increased, and at the very least the animosity caused is likely to make future intervention efforts less effective. Third, well entrenched minority governments will often resist efforts of capacity building because they fear that their hold on power will be undermined. And fourth, using the law to motivate states to do what is largely a moral duty runs the risk of many unintended practical consequences of the sort that results from mixing legal and moral norms.

Concerning this first point, aiding a state to build or rebuild the capacity to protect its citizens from mass atrocity should be seen as a relatively uncontroversial collective responsibility of the society of states. Aiding to build capacity of a state can not normally be conceptualized as a violation of that state's sovereignty. In most cases, the aid is requested and hence not a violation of sovereignty at all. In other cases, a state may initially resist any form of foreign intervention, but it is hard to see a state as wanting less capacity to act than more. As I noted previously, this third prong of the responsibility to protect is not like forcing someone to accept a gift of food, but rather like helping a person to see how he or she can produce food on his or her own. Such aid ties into the natural need of persons to be self-sufficient and can hardly be something that is resisted for long.

In addition, the state required to go to the aid of another state will normally not see the forms of aid as a major burden, especially since it will not normally involve putting troops on the ground, or even placing civilians of that state in harm's way. I suppose it could be said that a serious economic burden could be substantial, depending on what specifically is needed to raise a state to the point where it can protect its population from mass atrocity. But this is where the society of states enters the picture. The responsibility to build or rebuild capacity as with other prongs of the responsibility to protect is a distributed collective responsibility of the society of states. Because of this, the burden on any one state can be minimized. And when the responsibility to help is spread throughout the international community, there will be less of a likelihood that one of these states will try to take advantage of the situation and oppress the state and its citizens.

The possibility of abuse is always present, and it is important that the society of states monitor any situation when one of its member states intervenes to aid another state. Whichever prong of the responsibility to protect is under discussion, it is crucial that the aiding state not use the responsibility to protect as a pretext to "colonize" or otherwise significantly interfere with the sovereign affairs of a state. Sometimes this is benevolent and sometimes malevolent. It is benevolent concerning the one exception to this rule where a state is persecuting a portion of its population. In that case, last resort may dictate that the offending state be temporarily taken over until the human rights abuses are stopped. But in our discussion of the responsibility to build or rebuild capacity to protect this is generally not what is at stake.

Concerning the second point, that increasing the capacity of one segment of a population may increase the likelihood of civil war or secession, I must admit that this is always a serious worry with any attempt to aid one part of a citizenry that has historically been persecuted or deprived of the ability to become self-sufficient. Indeed, when a people becomes self-sufficient, or sees itself as not dependent on another population, there is always the risk that this will increase the likelihood that the newly self-sufficient population will sue for greater levels of self-determination, including breaking away from the rest of the population, through either violent or diplomatic means.[27] Such a possibility cannot be denied. But it must also be recognized that the risk of its happening is offset by the good that is accomplished when a people is no longer oppressed and becomes able to fend for itself.

Of course, movements of self-determination are not necessarily a bad thing in the international arena, even if it takes a civil war to resolve the difference between those who want to secede and those who want this population group to remain connected to a historical state. Not all marriages last forever and not all states remain with the same population groups forever either. In an abusive marriage, sometimes it is for the best that a breakup occur. Similarly, when there has been a history of one part of a population oppressing another part, perhaps the best solution is for the two parts to be separated. In any event, it is not always an unmitigated bad thing that a segment of a state secedes, even

---

[27] See Christopher Heath Wellman, *A Theory of Secession* (Cambridge University Press, 2005); and Allen Buchanan, *Justice, Legitimacy, and Self-Determination: Moral Foundations for International Law* (Oxford University Press, 2004).

violently, once it has seen its capacity to protect itself enhanced or rebuilt by the efforts of other states, or by the society of states acting jointly.

Concerning the third point, there are indeed practical difficulties to be overcome, just as is sometimes true when intervention is resisted by a person who does not wish to be more in control of his or her life, fearing that this will usher in a new person altogether. These practical difficulties should not be underestimated. And we should not underestimate the worries that a given state that achieves more capacity will be seen as a very different state than it was before. If the previous incarnation of the state was one where security and other related matters were easily taken care of, any change in the character of the state may indeed be feared since openness often makes security matters more difficult within a state.

There are indeed risks when a state engages in change. But if the change involves increased empowerment, it is not very likely that the state will have less rather than more ability to confront its security threats. For this reason most states will not complain about this type of interference. And we should not forget that internal threats are often more significant than external threats. The responsibility to protect's third prong is aimed at providing states greater capacity to thwart or prevent one of the most significant of these threats, namely, the mass atrocities that arise from ethnic or religious tension within the society.

The fourth point returns to the issue of how moral and legal norms intersect and also how they diverge. The moral norms that undergird the responsibility to protect, especially its third prong, seemingly call for strong intervention to make states more autonomous. But the legal norms that are suggested by the responsibility to protect do not necessarily call for strong intervention. Indeed, given the possible problems with intervention, even of the third prong variety, I believe that it would be a mistake to have strong legal norms of intervention of the sort some have called for. Legal norms that set duties with attendant penalties for nonfulfillment of the duty are not grounded in moral considerations alone. Attention must also be paid to the practical issues of the effects of implementing a coercive norm. Morality is not generally dependent on coercive norms, although of course moral norms are assumed to have motivational force. This is one of the salient differences between legal and moral norms – law is backed by coercive sanctions that often impose liberty limiting demands on those who violate the law, whereas morality is backed by much more amorphous sanctions, if "sanctions" is the correct term.

The sanctions of morality are largely those of the operations of custom and conscience. Custom is itself backed by social pressure of various forms, such as guilt and shame instilled by one's fellow community members when one violates a moral norm. But when social pressure takes these forms it really is operating through the medium of a given person's conscience. Conscience is a form of self-sanction.[28] There is a sense that states can be influenced by conscience. Of course, I am here thinking of the conscience of the people who compose a state, especially its leaders. It may well be a good thing to try to motivate a state by appealing to the conscience of the state's leaders, but the law is not normally a good mechanism for such motivation.

I am supportive of the idea that there should be a plurality of norms at the international level. But I am also leery of the often assumed linking of moral and legal norms at the international level. In particular, it is sometimes asserted that the strength of the immorality of an act is such that it should trigger a legal response, such as in the case of crimes against humanity or genocide. While morality and legality obviously overlap in some respects, each is best suited to a particular range of cases and of remedies. There are practical, conceptual, and normative reasons to keep morality and legality separate even as we acknowledge the domain of their overlap.

The responsibility to build or rebuild capacity to protect is the least controversial and in many ways the most likely to be successful aspect of the general Responsibility to Protect doctrine. I have argued in this chapter that it is best seen as a relatively benign responsibility to provide aid that should be seen as a form of collective responsibility that falls in a distributed way on the society of states and most directly affects the leaders of states. Capacity to protect is a form of enhancing agency, especially joint agency, which can be accomplished in a variety of ways. I have suggested that the forms of this aid should not pose a burden on the state that provides the aid nor on the recipient state. And while there will be possibilities for abuse, as there almost always are in cases of intervention, abuse can be minimized by international oversight. In this way, the third prong of the Responsibility to Protect doctrine should be embraced by the international community (the society of states) as a positive way to produce an international rule of law where states are able to act in a timely manner to prevent mass atrocities within their borders.

---

[28] See Larry May, 'On Conscience,' (1983) 20 *American Philosophical Quarterly*, 57–67.

Conclusions

Touko Piiparinen and Jan Klabbers

I. FINDINGS

The purpose of this book has been to reveal the broad diversity of sectors and fields of global society in which individuals and collectives encounter normative pluralism. Its aim has also been to identify different ways in which these actors modify their behavior to overcome norm conflicts ensuing from normative pluralism. The theoretical and conceptual analysis of normative pluralism in the first part of the book was followed by the analysis of pluralism within the law in the second part. André Nollkaemper and Jan Klabbers and Silke Trommer analyzed interactions between national and international legal orders and within the international legal order, as well as various ways to organize their connections in global society. In the third part, researchers in several disciplines, including legal science, political philosophy and political science, anthropology, and theology, set out to explore the many and various normative orders that are effective in global society, including self-regulation in global trade, military codes of conduct, *lex mercatoria*, bureaucratic culture, customary norms, and religious norms.

As it happens, the chapters of this book share three common characteristics. First, they all reject any "grand theory" of normative pluralism, and appreciate a *via media* approach in which the starting point in explaining and understanding normative pluralism is that each case must be seen in its particularity, rather than according to a prefixed theoretical model of normative pluralism. Second, all authors are skeptical about the possibilities for solving normative conflicts in a hierarchical manner. Concretely this means that one should rely more on context-specific and tailor-made means in tackling each situation of normative pluralism or norm conflict, rather than invoke universal and hierarchical models of normative orders. Third, they all recognize (albeit some more implicitly so than others) that normative conflicts in global governance involve not only ontological pluralism pertaining to the research object, but also epistemological pluralism: the different ways in which we look at the world inevitably color our understanding of normative conflicts and largely determine the descriptive and evaluative assessment of the object. These three characteristics will be further tackled later.

As for the first factor outlined, relating to the "middle position" on normative pluralism, this book suggests not only that there is a wide diversity of sectors and normative fields in which one encounters normative pluralism, but also that each encounter in itself may reveal such wide diversity. A common denominator of all chapters is the rejection of a grand theory of normative pluralism. Such a theory would hold that all situations of normative pluralism in global society are characterized by either actual or potential harmony between normative orders, enabled by a hierarchical and all-encompassing framework of global governance, or the perpetual rivalry and disaggregation between normative orders.

All chapters navigate between these two extreme poles by advocating a middle position, sometimes labeled as a *"via media* approach," according to which every encounter of normative pluralism entails aspects pertaining to both harmonizing and rivaling positions. In most cases, there is a space left, so it seems, for pragmatic problem solving, and even where there is not, nonetheless the "poly-paradigmatic wealth"[1] of solutions on offer often results in facilitating a political or diplomatic solution. The argument for a *via media* approach immediately takes us to the second point: given that each situation of normative pluralism entails possibilities for both harmony and disharmony, it is always possible to identify and devise context-specific means to resolve actual or potential conflicts among normative orders. Even if some might contend that positing a hierarchy might be desirable, it does not seem to be, strictly speaking, necessary, at least not for solving actual conflicts. The risk nonetheless exists that in the absence of any formalized mechanism (hierarchical or otherwise), the political space that is left open becomes the playground of the rich and powerful. Put differently, it is no doubt easier for the United States to suggest, when intervening, that the law should be cast aside and that what matters is the morality of action, than it would be for, say, Kenya or Costa Rica. Hence, there is no universal formula for an emancipatory vision of normative pluralism. Instead, each situation of normative pluralism requires tailor-made and contingent solutions.

It would be apposite here to summarize briefly how the chapters of this book reflect the aforementioned *via media* approach, with its insistence.

---

[1] We owe this term to Richard Wouters.

Katja Creutz provided an alternative viewpoint of the normative order of "self-regulation" that is usually considered as an autopoietic system functioning independently of international law. Creutz demonstrated the way in which self-regulation is closely interconnected with and intrinsically dependent on international law. Creutz pointed out that self-regulation is occasionally mixed with law, while sometimes it can actually turn into law, and law can actually function as a basis or inspiration for the codification of self-regulation. According to Creutz, it even seems warranted to question the truly voluntary character of self-regulation. In sum, the question of whether self-regulation and law exist in harmony or disharmony is misplaced: self-regulation nods to both harmonious and disharmonious positions at the same time.

Timo Kallinen similarly challenged the sweeping generalization according to which witchcraft norms are either commendable or deplorable from the viewpoint of basic human rights. While the individualist standpoint adopted by a modern lawgiver normally conceives witchcraft norms as irrational, Kallinen demonstrated that a more contextual understanding of witchcraft norms can reveal their rational function as a customary norm reinforcing and reproducing the customary structures of a society and collective culture. Kallinen adopted the anthropological model of holistic and individualistic societies to demonstrate that the ultimate judgment of witchcraft norms depends on one's methodological viewpoint. From the standpoint of holistic societies, witchcraft norms present themselves as structures that confirm and reinforce relationships of social wholes such as clans and lineages, while the individualistic understanding of witchcraft norms characterizes them as fundamentally irrational. Both Kallinen and Touko Piiparinen (in his contribution involving the norms of bureaucracy) challenged the modernist attempts at capturing the world within a grand theory, which typically lead to a lack of understanding of and perspective on local norms and conditions (whether cultural or humanitarian) and may even engender practices that subjugate local collectives.

Ulla Liukkunen also maintains that the understanding of *lex mercatoria* in relation to law cannot be captured in a universal model but depends on one's methodological approach: *lex mercatoria* can be understood either as a set of transnational norms or as a method of arbitration. More generally, both Liukkunen's and Kallinen's accounts imply that normative pluralism defies any attempt to capture it in a grand theory because of epistemological pluralism, that is, the possibility of different approaches and viewpoints of the perceived subject. Larry May similarly pointed out that one's assessment of normative pluralism in any particular situation largely depends on which aspects of the perceived object one emphasizes. The moral norm of responsibility to protect calls on international society to launch "timely and decisive" action, including military intervention, if necessary, to protect civilians from mass atrocities, a policy that occasionally requires the infringement of the territorial sovereignty of states. In this sense, the mainstream viewpoint correctly implies that the moral norm (responsibility to protect) clashes with international law, notably with article 2, paragraphs 4 and 7 of the UN Charter requiring all actors, including the UN, to respect the political independence and territorial integrity of states.[2] May, however, pointed out that this provides only a partial picture of responsibility to protect: the moral norm of responsibility to protect also, more crucially, calls for international assistance and capacity building provided to failed, weak, and fragile states. This moral norm entailing collective responsibility to build is not in breach of international law containing sovereignty norms and, as others have argued, may well be on its way to becoming the template for a new justification for the exercise of international authority.[3]

Rain Liivoja, in turn, points predominantly to the possibilities for interplay among various normative orders, with law allowing for the importation of nonlegal norms through open-ended clauses. Much the same transpires, *mutatis mutandis*, from the two "intralaw" chapters, those by Klabbers and Trommer on normative conflicts within international law, and Nollkaemper's chapter addressing the relationship between international law and domestic law. Here, the absence of any particular "one-size-fits-all" rule allows for the fruitful interplay among normative orders and, importantly, therewith allows for considerations of justice and fairness to enter the picture.

The preceding considerations suggest that normative pluralism is not a "fixed" property existing "out there," independently of one's methodological and epistemological viewpoint. This book thus appears to confirm the central thesis of the "politics of framing," which was introduced and briefly elaborated in the introductory chapter written by Klabbers and Piiparinen. According to this thesis, the picture of normative pluralism is determined not only by the objective reality of normative orders operating on the global stage but also, and perhaps more crucially, by the subjective standpoint of the researcher or practitioner himself or herself, including a particular methodological approach adopted by a researcher to study normative pluralism (see, e.g., Kallinen's and Liukkunen's chapters) and on the scope and focus of one's viewpoint (May's and Creutz's chapters).

[2] Note, though, that the Security Council can set aside article 2, paragraph 7 UN Charter if it acts under chapter VII of the charter.
[3] For such an argument, see Anne Orford, *International Authority and the Responsibility to Protect* (Cambridge University Press, 2011).

In this context, it would be appropriate to speak of "epistemological pluralism," that is, the plurality of different worldviews. In epistemological pluralism, the perceived normative object may be viewed from different angles simultaneously. Creutz, for example, pointed out that self-regulation can be portrayed as nonlaw, as soft law, and even as law, depending on the particular situation at hand. Similarly, Piiparinen argued that responsibility to protect can be seen as a bureaucratic norm when one focuses on its implementation by international organizations, while May regards responsibility to protect, from his perspective, first and foremost as a moral norm. It might even be possible (although many have remained skeptical of the idea) to view responsibility to protect as an emerging norm of international law: its endorsement by the UN General Assembly and the emphasis on a responsibility to protect civilians in the Security Council's main resolution on Libya might provide building bricks for such an argument.[4]

While the preceding conclusions call for a greater attention to the plurality of epistemologies in studying normative pluralism, this book also has important ontological implications: it contravenes the portrayal of the international normative order as a monolithic entity. As for the descriptive dimension, individuals and collectives are always and routinely subjected to the plurality of normative orders – whether they want to be or not. The increase of transnational relations in the global age, including migration and global economic and trade relations, correlates with an increase in normative pluralism, as evidenced in Rubya Mehdi's and Pontus Troberg's chapters. Both these chapters, moreover, suggest a tension between domestic legal norms and nonlegal norms (be it of religious origin or more expertise-based) that transcend national boundaries.

II. FUTURE DIRECTIONS

It is by definition somewhat hubristic to stipulate possible directions for future research, but nonetheless, since this volume was explicitly conceived and elaborated as an exploration of a relatively novel topic, it might be appropriate to do so. What, in other words, are further research questions that have presented themselves, in one way or another, when conceiving of and writing this volume?

The first of these is, to some extent, a classic and involves the relations between the various normative orders. Normative orders, it transpires, do not always conflict with one another; nor do they always point in the same

---

[4] See Security Council Resolution 1973 (2011).

direction. Instead, in some cases, they refer to each other. For lawyers, this is not a novel insight. It applies, for instance, to many treaty norms: the Rights of the Child Convention, for example, in article 3 refers to the "best interests of the child" as a general, overarching norm, guiding the way the concrete rights of the convention must be applied. Hence, the legal rights are to be read, and are in part dependent, on a norm that is itself highly contextual and that cannot, in all likelihood, be further fleshed out. Whether the "best interests of the child" is itself a norm of morality, a social norm, or perhaps even (one shudders to think) the residue of economic analysis is less relevant for present purposes: the interesting circumstance is that a legal instrument refers to an extralegal norm and does so not merely in subsidiary fashion, but posits it as an overarching requirement.

International lawyers are familiar with other examples as well, although here the role of the extralegal standard is more subsidiary in nature. In the field of humanitarian law, a prominent place has been reserved, since the late nineteenth century, for the so-called De Martens clause: whenever the law reveals a gap, the gap should be filled by recourse to "the usages established among civilized nations, ... the laws of humanity, and the dictates of the public conscience," in the formula of the Fourth Hague Convention of 1907.[5] And by the same token, the International Court of Justice held Albania responsible for the presence of mines in the Corfu Channel and did so, in part, on the basis of "elementary considerations of humanity."[6] Hence, here too the law contained a reference to extralegal considerations, although it seems fair to say that the references were less prominent than in the case of the Right of the Child Convention. In short, then, as both Liivoja and Creutz suggest in their respective chapters, one way of conceptualizing normative pluralism is by incorporation, and while this is not, as such, a novel idea, what is innovative is that doing so might be a way of coming to terms with normative pluralism.

A second question to look into is, again, an old one, but possibly given new shape by the recognition of normative pluralism. For centuries, religious and secular authorities did battle over the domination of the hearts and souls of individuals, culminating in the papal division of the globe between Spain and Portugal at the turn of the fifteenth century and, a century and a half later, the Peace of Westphalia. These battles could be construed as normative pluralism but were, no doubt, to a large extent also battles between institutions (church, state) with their own will to power. This raises questions about today's normative pluralism: to what extent can today's debates be seen as conflicts between

[5] The clause makes an appearance in many instruments on armed conflict, often with minor variations.
[6] See *Corfu Channel* case, [1949] ICJ Reports 4, at 22.

institutions? If the battle between law and religion nowadays, as many would suggest, predominantly involves Islam, does the circumstance that Islam is not hierarchically organized (at least not in the same way as the Catholic Church) affect the debate, and how does it do so? Is the increasingly visible presence of the Organisation of Islamic Cooperation (OIC) as an international organization itself a manifestation of the desire to safeguard normative pluralism or to provide an alternative to secular power (i.e., liberal Western power) in the global arena?

A third possible avenue for further research hooks up to the traditional agency-structure debate, so beloved among international relations scholars.[7] The current volume has adopted, if you will, an agent-centered perspective: what is the agent to do when confronted with normative pluralism, and how can agents themselves influence which normative order should be used to evaluate and possibly justify their actions? That is not, however, the only feasible perspective: one might also legitimately wonder to what extent normative pluralism is directed by, or helps direct, structural settings. To what extent, for instance, does global capitalism dictate the choice of the use of self-regulation and provide it with overarching normative force? Or, more radical perhaps, it has been suggested that even the humanitarian intervention in Kosovo was not, actually, conducted for moral reasons, but served foremost to draw a reluctant Serbia into the global market economy.[8] On such a reading, the idea that the Kosovo intervention was morally justified even if illegal merely serves as a veneer to hide the underlying market-based logic, which raises the question to what extent normative pluralism is ever anything else but window-dressing. Indeed, is normative pluralism itself then a manifestation of late-modern capitalism, allowing capital to go where it needs to go while providing the normatively most suitable justification?

A fourth possible item of future research resides in the picture of governance that emerges from the study of normative pluralism. While this volume has refrained from looking into the causes of normative pluralism (we have treated the existence of normative pluralism as a given), it would seem that a strong argument can be made that it is a consequence of the relative withering away of traditional modes of political decision making. These, in a nutshell, typically involve hierarchical authority along established lines and following

---

[7] See, for example, Walter Carlsnaes, 'The Agency-Structure Problem in Foreign Policy Analysis', (1992) 3 *International Studies Quarterly*, 245–70; J. D. Singer, 'The Level-of-Analysis Problem in International Relations', in Klaus Knorr and Sydney Verba (eds.), *The International System: Theoretical Essays* (Princeton, NJ: Princeton University Press, 1961), 77–92.

[8] See Naomi Klein, *The Shock Doctrine: The Rise of Disaster Capitalism* (London: Penguin, 2008).

established procedures. This now is increasingly replaced, or complemented, by what is sometimes referred to as "network governance": political decision making involves the participation of all sorts of actors, not just states and, within states, governments, parliaments, and advisory or consultative bodies given a formal role in the decision-making process, but also industries, interest groups, and civil society representatives, whether or not they have been assigned a formal role.[9] In other words, much relevant decision making takes place in an "institutional void" by actors vying for authority, and the presence of such an institutional void itself suggests that there is no longer any way to tell in advance which decisions should be followed, and which exercise less authority.[10] And from there, it is but a small step to reach the kind of normative pluralism that has been central to this volume.

In one sense, then, normative pluralism owes much to changed models of decision making and changed patterns of authority, in short, to the changing nature of global politics, a change often captured in the phrase "global governance." In another sense, normative pluralism may help to strengthen global governance: not only does it feed upon the changing nature of politics, it also helps to feed and sustain this change. How to assess this is a matter of taste and inclination, no doubt: some might point to the possible emancipatory potential of involving all sorts of actors in the norm-setting process; others might suggest that, if nothing else, at least this will contribute to the efficiency and effectiveness of governance,[11] whereas yet others might warn that this opens up new possibilities for domination.

This then leads almost automatically into a fifth direction, and this concerns the politics of framing. If it is indeed true that there is an institutional void waiting to be occupied and instilled with meaning, then the obvious next question is who is to occupy the void and impose its meaning (its rendition, its version of events, its preferred normative control system) on global governance, and how can this be justified? The politics of framing thus does not merely, as Fraser[12] has it, influence the question of who is entitled to justice, but goes much, much deeper. It does not merely involve a battle about participation and recognition (although it does that too), but more fundamentally

---

[9] For a plea that the role of such actors be recognized as relevant to international lawmaking, see Alan Boyle and Christine Chinkin, *The Making of International Law* (Oxford University Press, 2007).

[10] For an illuminating discussion, see Maarten A. Hajer, *Authoritative Governance: Policy-making in the Age of Mediatization* (Oxford University Press, 2009).

[11] See, e.g., Anne-Marie Slaughter, *A New World Order* (Princeton, NJ: Princeton University Press, 2004).

[12] See Nancy Fraser, *Scales of Justice: Reimagining Public Space in a Globalizing World* (Cambridge, UK: Polity, 2008).

involves the battle to give meaning to events. The Kosovo intervention may once more serve to illustrate matters, in that many have viewed it as a morally justified (if possibly illegal) humanitarian intervention. Others may have regarded it, more straightforwardly, as a violation of Serbia's territorial integrity, for whatever reason, and yet others have contended that it had nothing to do with humanitarian impulses, but everything with moving Serbia into the global market economy. Those are rather dramatically different framings of the same event, and there seems to be no way to tell which one is correct – indeed, it cannot even be excluded that several framings are equally acceptable and accurate. All that remains, then, is to see ex post facto which version seems to meet with the greatest acceptance, therewith turning dramatic political events into a kind of Eurovision song contest.

In turn, this leads to a sixth and final point to ponder: would there be any merit in considering the creation (or re-creation) of a more stable and fixed framework for framing and governance? Traditionally, that role was played by law, and perhaps for good reason, as law is the only normative order that can boast democratic credentials: public law specified how state authorities should behave domestically when setting standards, whereas international law specified how states should relate to one another.[13] Without lapsing into nostalgia or legalism, it seems that something of value has been lost with the rise of network governance: there is no way to tell where governance begins (this, after all, is the hallmark of a network: it has no natural starting point),[14] there is no way to tell who is allowed to participate or at least to be heard, and there is no way to tell whether the resulting proscriptions ought to be taken seriously, and by whom. It is probably no coincidence that the last two or three decades have seen an increased focus on accountability, auditing, and the like, focusing on ex post facto control of the exercise of public power: this is typically what happens if *ex ante* control (i.e., control over the creation of norms) has gone out of the window, therewith is abandoned for those in positions of power. Hence, the identification of normative pluralism should naturally lead to a rethinking of the role of normative control systems, all the more so as there is little point in curtailing public power by means of accountability mechanisms if private power can act unhindered.

---

[13] See also Jan Klabbers, 'Law-making and Constitutionalism', in Jan Klabbers, Anne Peters and Geir Ulfstein, *The Constitutionalization of International Law* (Oxford University Press, 2009), 81–125.

[14] On networks generally, see Annelise Riles, *The Network Inside Out* (Ann Arbor: University of Michigan Press, 2000).

Index

Aaltola, Mika, 2
Abraham, 5
Abu Ghraib, 185
Abusua, 236
Accountability, 170, 184, 254, 283, 348
Accountancy standards, 3, 18, 29, 301–22
Accounting Standards Board, 307
Additional Protocol I. *See* Geneva Conventions
Adhikari case, 194
Afghanistan, 292, 293
Africa, 8, 49, 101, 170, 229–50, 266
African Women's Development Fund, 247
Agency, 333–4
Aggression, 26
Ahmed and others case, 121
Akan society, 229–50
Akom, 234
Al-Bashir, Omar Hassan, 43, 62–3, 252, 253, 255, 262, 272, 278, 282
Albrow, Martin, 60, 252, 274–5
Algeria, 298
American Institute of Certified Public Accountants, 306
Amnesty International, 243
Andersen, Betsy, 2
Antigone, 5
Apparel Industry Partnership, 176, 189
Aquinas, 23
Arbitration, 201–28
Archbishop Leo, 166
Arden, Mary, 310
Aristotle, 4, 22, 23, 24
Asia, 99, 102, 103, 107, 125
Asylum, 166, 243–4
Atlantic Charter, 69

Auditing, 312–3
Augustine, St., 23
Austin, John, 39–40
Australia, 145, 309, 314, 316
    Defence Force, 151
    Defence Force Discipline Act, 151
    Defence Force Discipline Appeals Tribunal, 151–2
    Federal Court, 151
    Navy, 164
Austria, 315, 316
Auto-interpretation, 113
Autonomy, 333–6
Autopoiesis, 53, 61–2, 259, 261, 262, 263–70
Avena case, 111

Balancing, 72, 79
Bangladesh, 125–6
Ban Ki-moon, 265
Bano, Saima, 291
Barber, Benjamin, 20
Barnett, Michael, 49–50, 258, 259–60
Bashir. *See* Al-Bashir
Baxter, Richard R., 87
Bayi, 233
Behrami and Saramati cases, 78
Belgium, 102, 315
Bellamy, Alex, 264
Bentham, Jeremy, 22
Berger, John, 2
Berman, Paul Schiff, 109
Beyond Constitutionalism, 96
Bhopal, 175
Biomedical discourse, 240
Bismarck, Otto von, 36
Blackwater, 181–2

Blue Sky, 185-6
Boulstridge, Emma, 185
Bowen, John, 2
Brazil, 45, 57, 315, 320
Brent Spar, 184
British Petroleum, 196
Brong-Ahafo region, 235
Buchanan, Allen, 33
Buddhism, 22
Bureaucratic culture, 4, 9, 40, 62, 251-83, 340
Bureaucratic metanorms. See Metanorms
Bureaucratic norms, 251-83, 342
Bureaucratic standards. See Bureaucratic norms
Burkina Faso, 233
Bush administration, 147-8
Bush, George H.W., 143
Bushido, 145
Business ethics, 3
Butterfly effect, 60

California Court of Appeals, 192-3
California Supreme Court, 193
Calvin, John, 23
Cameroon, 249
Canada, 150, 298, 309, 314
    Capacity-building, 323-39
    National Defence Act, 150
    Ontario Arbitration Act, 298
Capitalism, 39, 346
Caroline doctrine, 82
Carrefour, 59
Carrigan, Marilyn, 185
Cassese, Antonio, 14
Catholicism, 23, 36, 290, 346
Caux Round Table Principles for Business, 176
Centre of Excellence in Global Governance Research, 1, 2
Charisma, 48-9
Charney, Jonathan I., 168
Chemical Weapons Convention, 179
Chevrolet, 59
Chile, 316
Child labor, 3, 177, 178, 179
China, 9, 45, 57, 266, 309, 314, 320, 322
Chivalry, 3, 18, 143-65
Choice of law, 201-28
Christian churches, 235
Christianity, 236
Cicero, 326

Civil society organizations, 89, 171, 196, 230, 243, 245-7, 267, 298
Civil war, 264
Clapham, Andrew, 171
Climate change, 37, 60
Codes of conduct, 166-200
Cohabitation, 296
Collective responsibility, 323, 336
Colombia, 316
Colonialism, 230, 238-9, 242-3, 337
Comaroff, Jean, 241, 242
Comaroff, John, 241, 242
Commission on Global Governance, 44
Committee of European Securities Regulators, 314, 321, 322
Companies, 166-200, 301, 312, 322
Compliance pull, 31
Conflict minerals, 170
Conflicts between international and national law, 70, 94-139
Conflicts between national law and accountancy standards, 301-22
Confucianism, 22
Congo, Democratic Republic of, 170, 196, 281
Consequentialism, 22
Consent, 104
Constitutional pluralism, 19, 95
Constitutionalization of international law, 15-17
Convention against Torture, 179
Conventional pluralism, 98-103
Copenhagen, 291, 293, 294, 295
Corfu Channel case, 345
Corporate social responsibility, 3, 166-200
Costa Rica, 341
Council of Europe, 78
    Committee of Ministers, 133
Creutz, Katja, 2, 8, 342, 343, 344, 345
Crimes against Humanity, 271
Criminal law, 5
Critical legal studies, 55, 256
Critical methodology, 55
Critical theory, 55, 58
Cultural differences, 314-20
Customary international law, 68, 71, 81-90
Customary norms, 229-50, 340, 342
Cyprus Supreme Court, 132
Czech Republic, 120

Darfur, 253, 254, 267, 276, 278, 281, 282, 283
Death row, 67
Deformalization, 116, 186

De Jure Belli ac Pacis, 51, 324
Democracy, 105, 118, 135, 335
Democratization, 56, 243
Denmark, 9, 53, 213, 284–300, 316
Deontology, 22
Development aid, 244
Devlin, Lord, 20
Disaggregation, 60
Disconnection clause, 78
Dualism, 98, 99, 103, 104
Duality of sexes, 316
Duel, 5, 148
Dungeon case, 132
Duvall, Raymond, 49–50
Dworkin, Ronald, 20

ECO Swiss case, 24
Economic logic, 229
Egypt, 126, 166, 298
  Administrative Court, 126, 130
Enforcement, 197, 207
English school, 45, 51
Enlightenment, 249
Environmental rights, 177
Erga omnes obligations, 16
Eriksen, Thomas Hylland, 5
Ernst & Young, 320–1
Ershad case, 125–6
Ethical Trading Initiative, 176
Ethnic cleansing, 271
Europe, 100, 101, 102, 125, 233, 286, 289, 301–22
European Community. *See* European Union
European Convention on Human Rights, 67, 72–3
European Court of Human Rights, 78, 106, 112, 113, 119, 132, 133, 137
European Financial Reporting Advisory Group, 309
European Group of Auditors' Oversight Bodies, 313
European Union, 9, 57, 67, 70, 76, 78–9, 105, 107, 115, 124, 131, 133, 212, 219, 224–5, 301–22
  Code of Conduct on Arms Export, 176
  Commercial Agents Directive, 224–5
  Commission, 213, 216
  Common European Sales Law draft regulation, 216
  Court of Justice, 76–7, 80, 90, 96, 106–7, 191, 194–5, 219, 223, 224–5
  Fourth Council Directive, 310–2
  Rome I Regulation, 213, 216, 219–21
  Treaty, 79–80, 224–5
  Unfair Commercial Practices Directive, 194
Expertise, 27
Experts, 8
External pluralism, 94–139
Exxon Valdez, 175
Eysinga, Judge van, 74

Fadayel, Eveline, 166
Family law, 284–300
Fatwa, 46–7, 50, 53
Fiji, 298
Financial Accounting Standards Board, 305, 306–7
Financial reporting, 9, 301–22
Finland, 166
Finnemore, Martha, 258, 259–60
Fisher, Kirsten, 2
Fischer-Lescano, Andreas, 2
Fishing vessels, 71
Fitzmaurice, Sir Gerald, 108
Flint, David, 310
Forced labor, 180, 194
Forker, John, 312
Fragmentation, 6, 42, 77–8, 261, 281, 282
Framing, politics of, 25, 347–8
France, 266, 319
Frankenstein, 61–3
Frankfurt School, 55
Fraser, Nancy, 347–8
Freeport McMoran Copper & Gold Inc, 196
French, Shannon, 146
Friedman, Milton, 172
Fukuyama, Francis, 56–8, 59
Fuller, Lon, 20
Functional differentiation. *See* Fragmentation
Fundamental rights. *See* Human rights
Fürst, Christiane, 2

Gaddafi, Muammar, 265–7, 268
Gaillard, Emmanuel, 205
General principles of law, 71–2
Generally Accepted Accounting Principles, 308–9
Geneva Conventions, 161–4, 179
  Additional Protocols, 161–4, 179
Genocide, 271, 332
Genocide Convention, 257
Germany, 303, 315, 320
  Bundesverfassungsgericht, 119, 133
Geschiere, Peter, 231

Ghana, 229–50
  Commission for Human Rights and
    Administrative Justice, 244, 245–6
Giddens, Anthony, 6, 44, 47, 252, 259, 273,
    276, 282
Giuliano-Lagarde Report, 220
Glinski, Carola, 188–9
Global citizens, 53
Global Compact, 29, 176, 187, 189
Global Complexity, 41
Global governance, 1, 7, 15, 28, 42, 43, 44, 45,
    199, 273, 347
Global government, 45
Global justice, 31, 323
Global village, 6, 36, 37, 60
Globalization, 5, 35–63, 169, 172, 298
Good faith, 211
Good governance, 175
Goldman, Berthold, 205–6, 207
Goldsmith, Jonathan, 199
Görgülü case, 119
Grand theory, 340, 341, 342
Gray, Natasha, 240
Gray, Sidney J., 317–9
Greece, 315, 316, 319
Greenpeace, 184
Greenspan, Morris, 162
Greenwood, Margaret, 312
Grenada, 26
Grigera Naón, H.A., 226–7
Grono, Nick, 268
Grotian tradition, 40
Grotius, 40, 51–2, 323, 324–5, 326
Gruchalla-Wesierski, Tadeusz, 182, 189
Grundnorm, 128
Gulf War, 144
Gustavus Adolphus, 148, 150

Hague Convention IV, 345
Hague Regulations, 159–64
Hague, The, 266, 270
Halberstam, Daniel, 115, 128
Halliday, Fred, 45
Harper's Magazine, 6
Hart, H.L.A., 20, 21
Hehir, Aidan, 275
Held, David, 44, 45
Helsinki Final Act, 69
Highway of death, 143, 144
Hirst, Paul, 60
HIV/Aids, 25
Hobbes, Thomas, 33, 39

Hofstede, Geert, 315–20
Hohfeld, Wesley N., 70
Honor, 3, 5, 7, 143–65, 298
Honor killings, 17
Hoppe, Carsten, 182–3
Horncastle case, 137
Hulle, Karel van, 312
Human rights, 16, 25, 79, 103, 105, 110–11, 118,
    123, 177, 229, 230, 243, 244, 250, 260,
    275
Human trafficking, 194
Humanitarian intervention, 13–14, 17, 26, 335,
    348
Hurrell, Andrew, 45, 56
Hussein, Saddam, 143

Identity politics, 6
Ignatieff, Michael, 145
Ijtihad, 285, 299
Immigration, 18
India, 45, 57, 266, 315, 316, 320
Individualism, 316–20
Indonesia, 196
Industrial revolution, 302
Informal instruments, 90–2
Informal law, 117
Ingmar case, 224–5
Institute of Chartered Accountants in
    England and Wales, 306
Institutional conflicts, 345
Institutional pluralism, 44, 46
Instrumentalization of law, 28
Instrumental rationality. *See Zweckrationalität*
Inter-American Court of Human Rights, 106
Internal pluralism, 36–7, 94–139
International Accounting Standards, 301–22
International Accounting Standards Board,
    305, 307, 309, 321
International Code of Conduct for Private
    Security Services Providers, 176, 178,
    179, 189, 191, 195, 196, 198
International commercial arbitration, 201–28
International Commission on Intervention
    and State Sovereignty, 272
International Committee of the Red Cross,
    254, 255, 260, 261
International Covenant on Civil and Political
    Rights, 126, 130
International Court of Justice, 72, 83, 86,
    87–9, 106, 188, 345
International Criminal Court, 9, 43, 62–3,
    251–83

Elements of Crime, 159, 163–4
Office of the Prosecutor, 260, 262–3, 277, 279, 280
Statute. See Rome Statute ICC
International criminal law, 37, 251–80
International Crisis Group, 268
International Federation of Accountants, 313
International Financial Reporting Interpretations Committee, 320–1
International Financial Reporting Standards, 301–22
International humanitarian law. See Law of armed conflict
International Labour Organization, 169, 178, 185
  Convention on Child Labor, 178
  Tripartite Declaration of Principles, 176, 187
International Law Commission, 73, 171
International Peace Organizations Association, 181
International Stability Operations Association, 178
International Standards on Auditing, 313
International Women's Rights Action Watch, 246
Internet, 47, 58
Iran, 57, 292
Iraq, 143, 181, 185, 194
Ireland, 316
Iron cage, 278
Islamic law, 9, 43, 54, 284–300
Israel, 315
  Supreme Court, 163
Italy, 316, 319

Jackson, Justice, 330
Jackson, Robert H., 51
Jaspers, Karl, 60
Japan, 57, 145, 303, 305, 309, 314, 315, 316, 320
Jenkins, Rhys, 174
Jones, Andrew, 46
Jus ad bellum, 325
Jus cogens, 16, 72, 76, 81, 82
Jus gentium, 326
Jus in bello, 325
Jus post bellum, 323–39
Just war tradition, 323

Kadi case, 76, 96, 106–7, 111, 119, 121–2, 126, 127, 133
Kagan, Robert, 56–8

Kallinen, Timo, 2, 8, 49, 342, 343
Kant, Immanuel, 22, 24, 56, 59
Kasky case, 192–3, 194
Kasky, Marc, 192, 193
Kellogg, Brown & Root Inc, 194
Kelsen, Hans, 38, 39–40
Kenya, 341
Keohane, Robert O., 33, 56, 183, 184
Khul, 287
Kickbacks, 3
Klabbers, Jan, 2, 7, 166, 186, 187, 191, 340, 343
Koenig-Archibugi, Mathias, 184
Kony, Joseph, 268–9
Koskenniemi, Martti, 2, 128–9, 256, 258, 259, 263
Kosovo, 4, 13–14, 17, 78, 166, 346, 348
Kourula, Erkki, 278, 279–80
Kra, 236
Krisch, Nico, 96, 122, 129, 136
Kumm, Mattias, 135, 136
Kuwait, 143

Labor rights, 177
LaGrand case, 111
Lando, Ole, 206, 215, 216, 221, 226
Latin America, 101, 125
Latvia, 102
Lauterpacht, Hersch, 160
Law of armed conflict, 18, 37, 143–65, 253, 265, 275, 345
Law of coexistence, 16
Law of cooperation, 16
Law of Nations or the Principles of Natural Law, 325
Law-plus, 188–90
League of Nations, 79, 239
  Covenant, article, 22, 239
Legal pluralism, 19–20
Legal rule, concept of, 69
Legitimacy, 1, 7, 8, 16, 29–33, 40, 97, 100, 103, 228, 269–70, 280
Legrain, Philippe, 58
Leino, Anssi, 2
Levi Strauss, 193–4
Lewis, Douglas, 171
Lex arbitri, 202
Lex causae, 217
Lex fori, 204, 211, 218
Lex mercatoria, 4, 8, 34, 36, 201–28, 340, 342
Lex mercatoria europea, 216
Lex posterior rule, 73–5
Lex prior rule, 74

Lex specialis rule, 75–6, 81
Libya, 263, 265–7, 283, 344
  National Transitional Council, 265–6
Lieber Code, 160
Lieber, Francis, 148
Liivoja, Rain, 8, 343, 345
Limping marriage, 290
Lincoln, Abraham, 149
Liukkunen, Ulla, 8, 342, 343
Lockhart, Justice, 151
London Stock Exchange, 305
Lord's Resistance Army, 268–9
Lohr, Michael, 147
Lois de police. See Mandatory rules
Lugard, Lord, 239
Luhmann, Niklas, 52, 61–2, 259, 261
Lundblad, Clas, 189–90, 191–2
Luther, Martin, 23
Ly, Filip de, 206, 207

MacBride Principles, 188
MacCormick, Neil, 117
Macleod, Sorcha, 171
Mahr, 285, 287, 293
Maimonides, 23
Malaysia, 298
Mali, 233
Mamdani, Mahmood, 283
Mandate system, 239–40
Mandatory rules, 207, 214, 217–22, 224–5, 226–7
Margin of appreciation, 113
Market accountability, 184
Martens Clause, 345
Martineau, Anne-Charlotte, 2
Marx, Karl, 41
May, Larry, 2, 5, 9, 272, 342–3, 344
McBarnet, Doreen, 191, 194
McCorquodale, Robert, 182
McCrudden, Christopher, 188
McDonaldization, 6
McDonalds, 6
McGrew, Anthony, 44, 45
McLuhan, Marshall, 6, 36, 60
Medellin case, 120, 126
Mehdi, Rubya, 9, 344
Memoranda of understanding, 69, 90–2
Merrills, John G., 89
Metajustice, 208
Metanorms, 9, 251–83
Methodological pluralism, 37
Mexico, 315, 316

Meyer, Birgit, 241
Middle Ages, 145
Middle East, 289
Militant Islam, 299
Military codes, 8, 340
Military commands, 18
Military discipline, 148–56
Military ethics, 143–65
Mill, John Stuart, 333
Mills, Alex, 208
Modern pluralism, 104–7
Mogya, 236
Mohammed, 23, 53
Monism, 107
Moral responsibility, 183
Morality, 1, 3, 5, 7, 20, 21–4, 25, 29, 33, 323–39
Moreno-Ocampo, Luis, 266
Morgan, Jamie, 2
Morocco, 298
Morrison, Jason, 183–4
Moudauwana, 298
Mubarat, 292
Multilevel governance, 19
Multipolar world, 45
Muslim Institute of London, 285
Muslim marriage contract, 285

NASDAQ, 305
National courts, 8
National law, 70
NATO, 13–4, 29, 266, 331
Natural Law, 3, 24, 51
Neo-medievalism, 36, 51
Nepal, 194
Nestlé, 184
Netherlands, 107, 120, 303, 316, 319
Network governance, 347, 348
Networks, 60–1
Neutral and Independent Humanitarian Action, 253, 265
Newsweek, 143, 144
New York, 270
New York Convention, 223, 224
New York Stock Exchange, 305
New Zealand, 315
NGOs. *See* Civil society organizations
Nicaragua case, 83, 87–9
Nigeria, 170, 233, 242
Nikah, 289, 290, 291–2, 293, 294–5, 296–7
Nikah nama, 289
Nike, 176, 192–3
Nisoori Square, 181

Index

Nkrabea, 236
Nollkaemper, André, 2, 7–8, 36–7, 340, 343
Nonet, Philippe, 275
Noninterference, 57
Nonintervention, 57
Non-law, 90–2, 167, 197, 344
Non-legally binding agreements, 90–2, 166–200
Non-state law, 201–28
Nordic countries, 289, 315, 316
Normative control system. *See* Normative order
Normative encounters, 3
Normative order, 7, 14, 21, 39, 340–8
Norm-creating rules, 86
Norms and sanctions, 38–9, 50
North America, 101, 233
North Sea Continental Shelf cases, 86
Nuclear Weapons opinion, 188
Nuremberg, 330

O'Connor, James, 2
Oeter, Stefan, 275–6
Olsen, Johan, 256, 261
On the Law of War and Peace. *See De Jure Belli ac Pacis*
Ontological pluralism, 250
Operation Desert Storm, 144
Opinio juris, 83–4, 87
Oppenheim's International Law, 159–60
Ordre public. *See* Public policy
Organization for Economic Co-operation and Development, 174, 176, 185
  Guidelines for Multinational Enterprises, 176, 187
Organization of the Islamic Cooperation, 19, 54, 57, 346
Oscar Chinn case, 74
Osiel, Mark J., 147
Oxford Dictionary of Philosophy, 38, 55
Oxford Manual on the Laws of War on Land, 159

Pacta sunt servanda, 74, 84, 117
Pagotto, Isabella, 188, 189–90
Pakistan, 288, 290, 294, 316
Para-law, 188–90
Parlamentaires, 158
Party autonomy, 208
Passenger Name Records agreement, 105
Patomäki, Heikki, 2
Pentecostal-charismatic movement, 235

Perfidy, 159–64
Perpetual peace, 56
Persistent objector doctrine, 71
Peters, Anne, 188, 189–90, 199
Philippines, 315
Phillips, Lord, 137
Piiparinen, Touko, 2, 7, 9, 55, 166, 342, 343, 344
Pluralism, 19, 43, 55, 57
Plurality of pluralisms, 42
Political decision, principle of, 80–1
Political pluralism, 57
Polk, William, 143
Portugal, 266, 315, 316, 319, 320, 345
Positivism, 3
Powell, Colin, 143–4, 147
Power distance, 315–20
Precautionary principle, 67
Pre-law, 188–90
Principles of European Contract Law, 212, 213
Prisoners of war, 158
Private international law, 8, 207, 208–9, 211, 217, 227
Private organizations, 89
Private persons, 101
Private security companies, 170, 178, 195–6
Professional ethics, 146, 152
Professional standards, 1, 7, 27
Proliferation of international courts, 106
Proportionality, 72
Protestantism, 23
Public Company Accounting Oversight Board, 313
Public policy, 214, 217, 221, 222–3
Pufendorf, Samuel von, 325
Puma, 179
Punishment, 183, 264–5

Qadi, 287
Quirico, Ottavio, 182–3
Quran, 288, 299

Racial theories, 248
Radicalized modernity, 6
Ranger, Terence, 232
Rational-legal authority, 251–83
Raz, Joseph, 164–5
Reflexive jurisprudence, 276
Refugee law, 275
Religion, 3, 4, 9, 18, 21, 25, 33, 230, 284–300
Religious norms, 284–300, 340

Res inter alios acta, 80
Rescuing nationals abroad, 26
Resolutions, 90–2
Responsibility to Protect, 9, 251–83, 323–39, 342–3
Return of History and the End of Dreams, the, 56–8
Rieff, David, 49
Rights of the Child Convention, 345
Risse, Thomas, 42
Riyadh, 59
Robins, Kevin, 60
Rodríguez-Garavito, César, 186
Roht-Arriaza, Naomi, 183–4
Roman military law, 150
Rome Convention on the Law Applicable to Contractual Obligations, 219
Rome Statute ICC, 43, 62, 159, 163, 255, 262, 263–70
  Article 53, 280, 281
Rosemann, Nils, 174, 195
Rosenau, James N., 46
Rosenfeld, Michel, 127, 128
Ross, Alf, 183
Rousseau, Jean-Jacques, 22
Roy, Olivier, 47
Royal Australian Navy, 145
Royal Dutch Shell. *See* Shell
Royal Mail Steam Packet case, 311
Rudolph, Phillip, 200
Ruggie, John G., 171
Rule of law, 118, 135, 175, 251, 256, 263
Russia, 45, 57, 266
Rwanda, 323, 331

Saipan case, 193–4
Samurai, 145
San Francisco Superior Court, 192
Saudi Arabia, 58–9
Schabas, William, 264–5
Schachter, Oscar, 89
Schmitt, Carl, 32, 33
Schmitthoff, Clive, 205, 206–7
Schücking, Judge, 74
Schwarzkopf, Norman, 144
Science, 248
Scott, James, 249
Securities and Exchange Commission, 307–8, 312, 313, 321, 322
Self-contradictions of law, 53
Self-defense, 81–2, 334
Self-determination, 335, 337

Self-regulation, 1, 3, 8, 25, 29, 36, 166–200, 340, 342, 346
Sellers, Tim, 2
Selznick, Philip, 275
Sen, Amartya, 43
Serbia, 346, 348
Shari'a, 39, 59, 120, 126–7, 130, 285, 289
Shell, 172, 176, 178, 184
Shelton, Dinah, 188
Shia, 292
Sieber, Ulrich, 199–200
Siikala, Jukka, 2
Simma, Bruno, 13–4
Singapore, 315, 316
Situational ethics, 258
Slaughter, Anne-Marie, 60–1, 62
Slotte, Pamela, 2
Social engineers, 215
Social norms, 1, 7, 17, 33
Sociological perspective on law-making, 90
Soering case, 67
Soft law, 8, 55, 69, 90–2, 116, 117, 166–200, 344
Soft power, 39
Solange case, 133
Sorcery, 231–2
South Africa, 57, 176, 189, 241, 242, 249
South Korea, 3
Sovereign equality, 69
Sovereignty, 15, 44, 57, 86, 103, 333–6
Spaight, James, 162
Spain, 319, 345
Spatial pluralism, 42–3
Spheres of Authority, 46
Spontaneous norms, 4
Sports, 18
Statements of Standard Accounting Practice, 306
States, 67–93, 97, 100, 323–39
Stoke, Olav Schram, 276–7
Sudan, 43, 62–3, 252, 253, 263, 267, 272
Sufism, 299
Sullivan Principles, 176, 188, 189
Sunsum, 236
Superstition, 248
Supremacy clause, 79
Sweatshops, 170, 192, 193
Sweden, 316
Switzerland, 315
Systems theory, 61–2

Takaki, Ronald, 270
Talaq, 287, 292–4, 295

Talaq-i-tafwid, 286
Tamanaha, Brian Z., 99
Tanzania, 26, 249
Taqlid, 285
Taxation, 303
Technocracy, 49
Teivainen, Teivo, 2
Ten Commandments, 3
Thakur, Ramesh, 36
Third World Approaches to International Law, 100
Timara-Tama Rural Women, 247
Toivanen, Reetta, 2
Tolbert, David, 277
Torture, 70
Traditional authority, 48–9
Transnational corporations, 166–200
Treachery, 8, 158–64
Treaties and customary international law, 81–90
Treaty conflict, 7, 67–93
Treaty interpretation, 78, 88
Treaty on the Functioning of the EU. *See* European Union Treaty
Treaty reservations, 111–2
Troberg, Pontus, 2, 9, 344
Trommer, Silke, 2, 7, 340, 343
Tuori, Kaius, 2
Turkmenistan, 170
Twining, William, 2, 200

Uganda, 26, 263, 268–9, 276, 281, 283
Ummah, 39, 47
Uncertainty avoidance, 315–20
UNIDROIT Principles of International Commercial Contracts, 212, 213, 214–5
Unilateral declarations, 72
United Kingdom, 67, 100, 124, 176, 195, 196, 266, 291, 294, 301–22
  Administration in Ghana, 240, 242–3
  Armed Forces Act, 150, 154
  Articles of War, 152
  House of Commons, 153
  Manual of Military Law, 153, 160, 162–3
  Supreme Court, 121
United Nations, 54, 76, 78, 96, 171, 331
  Charter, 29, 87–8, 272
    Article, 51, 81–2, 334
    Article, 79, 103
  Conference on Trade and Development (UNCTAD), 169
  diplomats, 270
  General Assembly, 54, 57, 90, 257, 327, 344
  Global Compact. *See* Global Compact
  Human Rights Council, 57
  missions, 268
  sanctions, 67, 72–3, 119–20
  Secretary-General, 255, 265, 272
  Security Council, 29, 30, 31, 106–7, 133, 143, 253, 254, 255, 262, 265–7, 278, 344
  World Summit Outcome, 271, 272, 273, 280, 327
United States of America, 9, 26, 67, 87, 105, 111, 115, 143–4, 191, 195, 196, 243, 301–22, 341
  Articles of War, 152, 154–6
  Court of Claims, 156
  Field Manual on the Law of Land Warfare, 157, 160, 162
  Joint Doctrine Manual, 158
  Manual of Courts Martial, 155
  Navy, 147
  Navy Board of Review, 156
  Navy-Marine Corps Court of Military Review, 156, 165
  Sarbanes-Oxley Act, 313
  Securities Act, 313
  Securities and Exchange Act, 313
  Supreme Court, 156, 165, 193
  Uniform Code of Military Justice, 150, 154
Universal Declaration of Human Rights, 169, 178, 179
Uppsala University, 265
Urry, John, 41

Validity rule, 86
Value pluralism, 19–20
Vattel, Emeric de, 93, 323–4, 325–6, 327, 329
Väyrynen, Raimo, 49
Venezuela, 315, 316
Via media, 340, 341
Vienna Convention on Consular Relations, 111, 114
  Article, 36, 114
Vienna Convention on the Law of Treaties, 73, 80, 88, 112
  Article, 30, 73–5, 79
Vigil Nolasco, Damarys, 2
Virtue ethics, 22, 23
Vogt, Henri, 2
Vogüé, Monsieur de, 6
Voionmaa, Hannele, 2

Voluntary Principles on Security and Human Rights, 196–7

Walker, Neil, 128
Wallendahl, Åsa, 2
Walzer, Michael, 273
War crimes, 271
Weber, Max, 5, 30, 36, 48–9, 251, 252, 258, 260, 270, 274, 275, 278, 282
Wertrationalität, 259, 264
Westphalia, 44, 46, 171, 345
Wierda, Marieke, 277
Winthrop, William, 154–5
Witchcraft, 4, 7, 8, 49, 229–50, 342
Women's rights, 247

Woodman, Gordon, 288
World Bank, 172, 177
World Court. *See* International Court of Justice
World Health Organization, 25
World Trade Organization, 25, 58, 76, 77
    Dispute Settlement Understanding, 106
World War II, 60
Wrongful act, 71
WWF case, 194–5

Yugoslavia, 166, 323

Zina, 289
Zweckrationalität, 252, 254, 258, 260, 264, 269, 273, 281, 282